Structural Change, Competitiveness and Industrial Policy

The onset of the global crisis has emphasised the persistence of substantial differences in development and social progress within the euro area. The specific case of countries located in the southern periphery region has come to the centre stage, due to the harsh economic conditions that all these countries have experienced in the recent past.

In the aftermath of the American subprime credit bubble, these countries' high indebtedness raised doubts as to their ability to sustain public finances, with the financial crisis developing and gaining momentum due to the fragilities presented in the economy. To varying degrees of severity, all of these economies have since been forced to introduce strong fiscal tightening programmes in order to achieve fiscal consolidation, which have translated into recession and rising unemployment.

This book undertakes a comprehensive analysis of the causes of the crisis in southern European countries, showing that the 'Achilles heel' of these economies is rooted in the dismal evolution of productivity and in a specialisation pattern excessively based on the so-called 'traditional', low and low-medium tech industries, which yield low margins, declining export shares and, ultimately, withering international competitiveness. Such evidence suggests that the southern European periphery industrial growth model has reached its limits, demanding a multidimensional policy approach capable of overcoming the magnitude and complexity of the present crisis.

Without denying the need to adjust public and private balance sheets, it is argued that finding a sustainable path out of the present problems requires addressing the challenges of productivity growth and competitiveness in the long term.

Aurora A.C. Teixeira is Associate Professor with Habilitation at Faculdade de Economia, Universidade do Porto, Portugal.

Ester G. Silva is Assistant Professor at Faculdade de Letras, Universidade do Porto, Portugal.

Ricardo Paes Mamede is Assistant Professor at ISCTE – IUL, Lisbon, Portugal.

Routledge advances in regional economics, science and policy

1 **Territorial Patterns of Innovation**
An inquiry on the knowledge economy in European regions
Edited by Roberta Capello and Camilla Lenzi

2 **The Political Economy of City Branding**
Ari-Veikko Anttiroiko

3 **Structural Change, Competitiveness and Industrial Policy**
Painful lessons from the European periphery
Edited by Aurora A.C. Teixeira, Ester Silva and Ricardo Paes Mamede

Structural Change, Competitiveness and Industrial Policy

Painful lessons from the European periphery

Edited by Aurora A.C. Teixeira,
Ester Silva and Ricardo Paes Mamede

Routledge
Taylor & Francis Group
LONDON AND NEW YORK

First published 2014 by Routledge

2 Park Square, Milton Park, Abingdon, Oxfordshire OX14 4RN
52 Vanderbilt Avenue, New York, NY 10017

Routledge is an imprint of the Taylor & Francis Group, an informa business

First issued in paperback 2019

British Library Cataloguing in Publication Data
A catalogue record for this book is available from the British Library.

Library of Congress Cataloging in Publication Data

A catalog record for this book has been requested.

ISBN: 978-0-415-71382-5 (hbk)
ISBN: 978-0-367-86875-8 (pbk)

Typeset in SabanLTStd
by: diacriTech, Chennai, India

Contents

Figures

Tables

Boxes

Contributors

Robert Boyer, Professor at EHESS – *École des Hautes Études en Sciences Sociales* (France), co-organizer of the PhD program 'Institutional Economics'. Senior researcher at National Center for Scientific Research (CNRS) and Head of the Research Unit. President of the Association Research and Regulation.

Carlos Carreira, Assistant Professor of Economics, Faculty of Economics, University of Coimbra (Portugal). Researcher at GEMF-Group for Monetary and Financial Studies.

Adelaide Duarte, Associate Professor, Faculdade de Economia, Universidade de Coimbra; and Researcher, GEMF (Group for Monetary and Financial Studies), Universidade de Coimbra, Portugal.

Miguel Lebre de Freitas, Assistant Professor, Universidade de Aveiro, Portugal.

Tassos Giannitsis, Emeritus Professor of Economics, Department of Economic Sciences, National Kapodistrian University of Athens (Greece).

Manuel Mira Godinho, Professor of Economics at ISEG (Lisbon School of Economics & Management), University of Lisbon (Portugal).

Inés Granda, Ph.D. in Economics. Researcher at GRINEI Research Group, Universidad Complutense de Madrid, and INNOPRO Research Group, Universidad Politécnica de Madrid.

Ioanna Kastelli, Researcher at the Laboratory of Industrial and Energy Economics, National Technical University of Athens (Greece).

Edward Lorenz, Professor of Economics, University of Nice-Sophia Antipolis (France); and Adjoint Professor, Aalborg University (Denmark).

Bengt-Åke Lundvall, Professor, Secretary General for Globelics (www.globelics.org), expert on the Economics and Management of Knowledge and Innovation, Department of Business and Management, Aalborg University (Denmark).

Michele Di Maio, Assistant Professor of Economics, Department of Business and Economic Studies, University of Naples Parthenope (Italy).

Ricardo Paes Mamede, Assistant Professor at the Department of Political Economy of ISCTE – University Institute of Lisbon. Researcher at Dinâmia'CET (Center for Research on Socioeconomic Change and Territory).

Sandro Mendonça, Assistant Professor at ISCTE Business School. Researcher at BRU (ISCTE-IUL), Dinâmia (ISCTE-IUL) and UECE (ISEG). Visiting Fellow at SPRU, University of Sussex.

José Molero, Professor of Applied Economics. Complutense Institute for International Studies. Universidad Complutense de Madrid.

Rui Costa Neves, MSc Economics, Nova School of Business and Economics.

Luis C. Nunes, Associate Professor, Nova School of Business and Economics.

Argentino Pessoa, Assistant Professor, Faculdade de Economia, Universidade do Porto. Associate Researcher at CEF.UP (Center in Economics and Finance) and NIFIP (Núcleo de Investigação em Finanças Públicas e Política Monetária).

Fernando Teixeira dos Santos, Associate Professor, Faculdade de Economia, Universidade do Porto. Associate Research at CEF.UP (Center in Economics and Finance). MBA Programmes' Director, Porto Business School.

Ester Gomes da Silva, Assistant Professor, Faculdade de Letras, Universidade do Porto. Associate Researcher at ISFLUP (Institute of Sociology) and Researcher at CEF.UP (Center in Economics and Finance).

Marta Simões, Assistant Professor, Faculdade de Economia, Universidade de Coimbra; and Researcher, GEMF (Group for Monetary and Financial Studies), Universidade de Coimbra, Portugal.

Vítor Corado Simões, Professor of Innovation Management and International Management, Instituto Superior de Economia e Gestão (ISEG), University of Lisbon. Former President of the European International Business Academy (EIBA). EIBA Fellow since 2005.

Miguel St. Aubyn, Professor of Economics at ISEG (Lisbon School of Economics & Management), University of Lisbon (Portugal).

Aurora A.C. Teixeira, Associate Professor with Habilitation, Faculdade de Economia, Universidade do Porto. Associate Research at CEF.UP (Center in Economics and Finance), INESC Porto, OBEGEF, and UTEN (University Technology Enterprise Network, Portugal-Texas Austin University).

Part I

The context

EMU, convergence, austerity

1 Introduction

Structural change, competitiveness and industrial policy

Ester Gomes da Silva and Aurora A.C. Teixeira

Industrial policy, understood as the set of policy instruments that stimulate specific economic activities and promote structural change, has long been absent from the forefront of the policy agenda in Europe, and particularly in the countries of the southern periphery (Greece, Portugal, Spain and Italy). Still, the profound crisis affecting these countries cannot be understood without acknowledging that growth dynamics in the real economy have been exhausted, leading subsequently to credit bubbles and the deviation of capital into high-risk financial assets to pump the growth engine, and the inability of broad macroeconomic instruments to deal with it. Apart from economic and financial disruptions, competitiveness problems of the southern European periphery, strongly related to their structural deficiencies, are also a major cause for concern. A new set of policy measures seems thus to be in order to stimulate structural change towards the accumulation of knowledge and the creation of conditions for sustainable growth, under the challenges imposed by economic globalisation, financial market distress, and technological, institutional and societal challenges.

The onset of the global crisis has emphasised the persistence of substantial differences in development and social progress within the euro area. The specific case of countries located in the southern periphery region has come to the centre stage, due to the harsh economic conditions that, although to varying degrees, all these countries have experienced in the recent past.

After a few decades of convergence to the European core, southern European economies have faced increasing growth difficulties since the turn of the century. In the aftermath of the American subprime credit bubble, these countries' high indebtedness raised doubts as to their ability to sustain public finances, with the financial crisis developing and gaining momentum due to the fragilities presented in the economy. To varying degrees of severity, all of these countries have since been forced to introduce strong fiscal tightening programmes in order to achieve fiscal consolidation, which have translated into recession and rising unemployment. Despite the widespread contours of the crisis, involving the economic, financial and institutional spheres, the adjustment of public and private balance sheets has been at the forefront of political strategy in the periphery of the Eurozone. Excessive public deficits were taken as the culprit, and from this view, fiscal consolidation has been seen as the major priority, acting both as a means to correct macroeconomic imbalances and to ensure the return to the growth path (e.g., European Commission 2011; Forni et al. 2010). Reality has shown otherwise. The excessive focus on a single dimension of the overall problem has made it impossible for indebted countries to escape from their debt trap and has been accompanied by mass unemployment, weakening of knowledge and production capabilities, and rising inequality.

In this volume, we undertake a comprehensive analysis of the causes of the crisis in southern European countries, showing that the 'Achilles heel' of these economies is rooted in the dismal evolution of productivity and in a specialisation pattern excessively based on the so-called 'traditional', low, and low-medium tech industries, which yield low margins, declining export shares and, ultimately, withering international competitiveness. Such evidence suggests that the southern European periphery industrial growth model has reached its limits, demanding a multidimensional policy approach capable of overcoming the magnitude and complexity of the present crisis.

Without denying the need to adjust public and private balance sheets, it is argued that finding a sustainable path out of the present problems requires addressing the challenges of productivity growth and competitiveness in the long term.

In the context of the (nationally driven or externally determined) austerity adjustment programmes that are being put in place in southern euro area countries, the answer to such long-run challenges has been focused on changes in the regulation of labour and product markets, which aim to increase the flexibility and cost-competitiveness of the overall economy. It is the purpose of the present volume to discuss to what extent the above-mentioned changes, which constitute the prevailing strategies to overcome the crisis, can or should benefit from a greater focus on policies designed to foster structural changes in these economies. More precisely, attention is given to a number of factors that lie at the basis of economic backwardness and the erosion of international competitiveness: the limited capability for change in the southern periphery, visible in the maintenance of a low-skill and low-tech bias in the productive structure and, more recently, in an overall tendency for adverse structural change—premature deindustrialisation, with manufacturing being replaced by non-tradable activities; a noticeable mismatch between labour market needs and the supply of skills conveyed by the education system; the strong relevance of small and micro-sized firms, which face greater difficulties in financing their growth opportunities; low innovation records and low investment shares in GDP, with a strong relevance of 'infrastructure', rather than 'soft', productive investment.

The structure of the book reflects these concerns, providing an assessment of the multidimensionality of the current crisis and discussing the ways to overcome it, based on a more active strategy to successfully restart growth in the southern European periphery. We argue that there is a role for more governmental and European support to build up strategic intelligence for structural change processes in these countries, with a focus on the real economy and international positioning.

Part I is dedicated to the challenges posed by the co-participation in the Eurozone of countries with very different productive, social, and institutional structures. The coordination problems stemming from increasing integration in monetary and financial terms, while economic union lagged behind, are approached, taking into account the experiences of southern European countries after joining the European and Monetary Union (EMU).

In Chapter 2, "The unsustainable divergence of national productive systems: Seven lessons from the Eurozone crisis", Robert Boyer argues for an eclectic approach in order to achieve a full understanding of the crisis and the ways it affected south-western European economies. The author emphasises differences in productive systems within the EU, and particularly the North/South divide, as the main root cause underlying the present crisis, in a context marked by a strict adherence to mainstream economics on the part of central banks, ministries of finance and financiers. Due to a poor institutional design and a general lack of concern for financial regulation, these differences were aggravated by the inception and development of the EMU, making southern economies particularly vulnerable to the effects of the subprime world crisis. Boyer draws attention to the need for improved governance of the EMU, and to the importance of the implementation of innovation, industrial and income policies in order to counterbalance the loss of autonomy in terms of national economic policy, determined by the adoption of a common currency.

The poor institutional design of the EMU is also underlined as a major factor accounting for the spread and severity of the crisis in Chapters 3 and 4, by Fernando Teixeira dos Santos and Miguel St Aubyn, respectively. Being developed at the macro level of analysis, these contributions explicitly recognise the multidimensionality of the crisis and the need for a multidimensional (policy) response. According to Teixeira dos Santos, former Portuguese Minister of Finance (2005–2011), the lack of common fiscal instruments for crisis resolution, combined with excessive optimism about the functioning of the Eurozone and an increasing deregulation and globalisation of finance, were fundamental sources of distress. The unbalanced policy mix between, on the one hand, strict rules regarding national fiscal policies in order to meet fiscal targets and, on the other, soft coordination schemes with regard to real convergence among member states, led to the neglect of real economy issues and to the persistence over time of significant disparities in competitiveness, potential growth and living standards. When the euro area was hit by the sovereign debt crisis, the institutional frailties became clear and less competitive economies, which benefited from easy money after the introduction of the euro and thus delayed the implementation of reforms to correct macroeconomic imbalances, were subject to an abrupt change in markets' assessment and pricing of risk. The overarching impact of the crisis and the inadequacy of European fiscal instruments and policies to deal with it are illustrated with the Portuguese case.

Teixeira dos Santos concludes his chapter arguing for the need for a coordinated adjustment policy involving all members of the euro area. In the absence of such policy, it is argued, individual member states will be left in an austerity-trap situation that will ultimately affect the performance of the euro area as a whole and the credibility of its institutions. Miguel St Aubyn develops this argument a bit further, assuming that the transformation of the institutional design of the Eurozone towards the creation of a political union would provide a sounder political response to the problems currently faced by countries in the southern periphery. According to the author, the deep external imbalances of these countries were ultimately caused by the architectural flaws of the EMU and their neglect of the profound structural differences across member countries. In these terms, the introduction of a meaningful European Union budget, with fiscal receipts, transfers and spending and a shared common budgetary policy would not only be desirable, but would also give new meaning and more positive expectations to the adjustment programmes already in place.

The neglect of growth and convergence issues by the EMU is the major focus of Bengt-Åke Lundvall and Edward Lorenz's essay on the European crisis and the failure of the Lisbon Strategy. In their chapter, it is argued that the gap between the ways people work and learn among different countries constitutes a fundamental weakness of the euro area. Such weakness could be narrowed if a European policy targeted at the development of the quality of jobs and at the strengthening of social cohesion were undertaken, in line with the major goals of the Lisbon Strategy. EU governance, however, set a different path, based on the adoption of measures conducive to the lowering of wages and to the deterioration of the quality of jobs (the so-called 'structural reforms'). In the context of the 'globalising learning economy', the authors emphasise the need for a more ambitious and coordinated response to the crisis focused on the strengthening of knowledge creation and learning in the south, offering in this way an alternative vision for the development of competitiveness in these countries.

The **second part** of the book addresses the root causes of the competitiveness problems faced by south-western European economies, analysing the role played by economic structure, technology, innovation and skills. It starts with a broad view of trends in growth, productivity, and structural change in these countries in the last few decades. Argentino Pessoa shows that the dismal evolution of competitiveness is related to a number of structural weaknesses, most notably the persistence over time of a significant technology deficit, and a disproportionate share of micro-sized firms and self-employed professionals in the economy.[1] According to the author, these problems are not addressed by current policy strategies, which rely on a rather limited notion of (cost) competitiveness, based on the lowering of wages. Moreover, the exclusive focus of national policies on financial equilibrium and deregulation of labour markets may not only increase current difficulties in paying debt, due to the contraction of economic activity, but may also have enduring negative effects on growth, by eroding countries' technology and production capabilities.

Chapter 7 explores a complementary feature of competitiveness, related to the development of non-technological innovation capabilities: the successful exploitation of trademarks. Using European Union data on Community Trade Marks for the period between 1996 and 2012, Sandro Mendonça finds that, along with science and technology, southern periphery countries persistently lagged behind in terms of softer innovation capabilities. Evidence is also shown regarding the reversion of the path of cumulative strengthening of the knowledge base in these countries after the crisis, in line with the fears expressed by other authors in this volume. Based on this view, it is argued that structural policies have to acknowledge the plural set of factors behind competitiveness, in order to address the challenges of improving economic performance.

Chapter 8, by Marta Simões and Adelaide Duarte, investigates a side effect of the decline in competitiveness in south-west Europe—the increasing relevance in the economy of non-tradable sectors, and most particularly, services—and its effect on aggregate growth. In recent years, there has been a change in the ways services are supposed to influence growth, with many studies indicating a positive influence that contrasts with the well-known Baumol 'stagnation' hypothesis. However, such arguments apply mostly to modern, skill-intensive services, which benefit intensively from advances in technology. This does not seem to apply in the southern periphery case, in which a bias towards traditional personal services is still present (e.g., Silva and Teixeira 2011; Zambarloukou 2007). The results, based on the Portuguese case, reveal that the most influential services category seems to be community, social and personal services. Such evidence is interpreted by the authors as reflecting the links between the consumption of 'household services' and human capital formation, although the apparent incapacity of business services to influence growth may also be indicative of the insufficient development of this sector in Portugal.

Part II ends on a more optimistic note, providing an assessment of the potential opportunities available to south-west European countries from economic globalisation and the increasing integration of markets (Chapters 9 and 10). Chapter 9 estimates the potential impact on productivity growth from an increase in exports, based on the experience of Portuguese firms. The evidence put forward by Carlos Carreira shows that exporting firms are more productive than non-exporting ones (at least in the manufacturing sector), and constitute the dominant source of aggregate productivity growth. The results are thus in broad agreement with theoretical arguments according to which increasing exports are conducive to growth, due to both efficiency improvements within individual firms and to inter-firm market share reallocation towards more productive firms. Chapter 10 provides a comparison of the specialisation patterns of Portugal, Italy, Spain, and Greece, based on current sectoral diversification, the income content of exports, and the consistency of the specialisation patterns, taking Germany as the benchmark. Miguel Lebre de Freitas, Luis C. Nunes and Rui C. Neves also assess the extent to which the current productive experiences are more or less favourable to the development of comparative advantages in 'upscale products', that is, products with higher income content than the country average. The main conclusion is that the productive experience achieved by south European countries appears to be quite favourable in this process of structural transformation, since the number of upscale opportunities is more than double that of Germany.

The finding that there are a significant number of opportunities for growth and structural transformation from increased economic integration does not mean, however, that those opportunities will be effectively materialised. As a matter of fact, this seems to be strictly dependent on the countries' productive systems and their relationship with the requirements imposed by the 'knowledge economy', namely, their capabilities to create and absorb knowledge, through innovation and diffusion processes. The chapters included in **Part III** approach the role played by public policy in the creation of such an economic environment, providing a discussion on the scope of possibilities, opportunity, and (potential) relevance of industrial policies to address the challenges faced by the countries in the periphery of the Eurozone.

The scope and relevance of industrial policy has changed considerably over time. In the early post-war decades, it was practiced widely as a strategy for economic development, but its connotation with protectionism, bureaucracy and the favouring of specific interests determined its bad reputation and almost total neglect in the latter part of the twentieth century. Chapter 11, by Tassos Giannitsis and Ioanna Kastelli, and Chapter 14, by Michele di Maio, document the failures of such policies in Greece and Italy, respectively, and their subsequent political de-legitimisation.

Recently, there seem to be some signs of a change in attitude towards industrial policy, although one which is understood and practiced very differently than before. The views expressed in Chapters 11 to 14 are admittedly in favour of a more active government intervention directed at the transformation of the productive basis of south European countries, in order to improve their competitive position towards more complex and high value-added activities and products. Interest in providing support to particular industries, especially in new sectors, and in promoting an upward movement along the value chain in existing activities, takes into account the need to preserve competition and to accommodate to the constraints imposed by the international rules from the WTO and the EU. Also, a major concern relates to the need to frame policies within the specific background of each country, using industrial policy in the definition of the countries' development strategies and articulating it with other instruments of the policy mix. Such an understanding is particularly evident in Chapter 13, by Ricardo Paes Mamede, Vitor Corado Simões and Manuel Mira Godinho, which argues in favour of a (selective) adoption of policies contributing to the development of innovation capacities, illustrating with the outcomes of previous policy interventions in the Portuguese economy.

Under a constrictive macroeconomic environment, marked by liquidity constraints and reluctance of banks to lend, it is argued that policy action plays a fundamental role in stimulating other funding mechanisms and directing the available EU resources from Structural Funds to the modernisation of the productive basis. The menu of possible policies envisaged by the contributions in this volume, listed more clearly in Chapter 12, by José Molero and Inés Granda, includes a selective promotion of science and technology activities, in particular by subsidising private and public R&D to support the development of new activities and products, the deployment of strategies favoring education and training and narrowing the mismatch between the supply and demand of skills in the labour market, and the attraction of potentially growth-enabling FDI.

All contributions emphasise that a critical condition for the success of these policies is related to the quality of governance and institutions in general, which links to the discussion of the institutional framework at both national and European levels developed in the first part of the volume. It is argued that the complexity and multidimensionality of the crisis, related to both macroeconomic and structural factors demands a policy action defined in terms of a compatible mix of stabilisation and pro-active policies regarding industrial structures. In other words, without policies aimed at addressing and solving the longer term, structural growth weaknesses, fiscal consolidation plans are doomed to fail.

Note

1 It is important to bear in mind, however, that the evidence on the influence of size on innovative capabilities is mixed, at best (see in this respect, Dosi et al. 2013).

2 The unsustainable divergence of national productive systems

Seven lessons from the Eurozone crisis

Robert Boyer

1. Introduction

The Euro crisis has raised and continues to raise heated debate among economists and the number of interpretations is impressive and growing as time elapses. The diffusion of austerity plans assumes that excessive public deficits are the culprit and this is the mainstream explanation within contemporary neo-classical macroeconomics that postulates that pure market economies are self-regulating. The view of ordoliberalism adds that the violation of European treaties is the underlying reason for the Euro crisis, thus rules should be strictly enforced again, which is at odds with free marketers' recommendations. Other analysts blame the European Central Bank for setting such low interest rates that real estate bubbles and easy public deficit financing have destabilised the Eurozone. Still others reiterate that the European Union was not an optimal currency zone and thus the euro is not viable and will collapse anyway. This list could easily be extended with an impressive number of mono-causal interpretations. At one end of the spectrum, the crisis is typically political and specific to Europe: no common currency without fiscal federalism; no federalism without democratic control. At the other end, external and quite abstract forces are dominant: the Euro crisis is the unintended consequence of the collapse of Lehman Brothers; the speculative nature of financial capital is the real obstacle to euro viability; the shift in the global economy towards Asia is a more fundamental origin of slow growth in Europe, a major obstacle to the euro's viability.

This chapter proposes a different approach. First, the monetary and financial sources of instability should be related to the combined trends in the real economy, against the neutrality of money embedded in modern macroeconomics. Second, the heterogeneity of national economies has to be taken into account to understand the structural macroeconomic imbalances that turn a speculative attack on Greek public debts into a systemic crisis of the euro, and even the European Union as a whole. Third, such a dramatic turmoil does not have a unique cause, but derives from the interplay of a complex web of cognitive, economic and political factors. This chapter deals with the following themes.

Within leading macroeconomic thinking and the models used by central banks, ministries of finance and financiers to assess the viability of the euro, the key variable was the relative frequency of symmetric shocks easily dealt with by a common monetary policy and asymmetric ones that would justify maintaining national monetary policies. It is an invitation to survey the debates that took place in the preparatory phase of the euro in the 1990s. Dissenting analyses had been developed that were able to anticipate some, if not all, of the possible imbalances generated by the shift from the European Monetary System to an irreversible euro: they were disregarded in the public debate. In fact, the elites and politicians have dramatically underestimated the loss of autonomy in national economic policy: the interest rate, exchange rate and the banning of monetisation of domestic public debt should have been replaced by other instruments, such as innovation, industrialisation, income policies, and selling treasury bonds on the world market. In their absence, the shrinking of the domestic productive system is the logical outcome: this was the path followed by the European periphery.

Indeed, along with the euro, the European Union had launched the Lisbon strategy that aimed at higher growth by an ambitious programme fostering innovation, especially for lagging economies. Unfortunately the outcomes have been disappointing since the divergence between southern and northern productive systems generated by the euro have not been balanced by the Lisbon strategy. The Euro crisis came as a complete surprise to the finest experts and this is puzzling for a European integration historian. De facto, a survey of the origins of the Rome Treaty and subsequent development suggests that new European public assets, such as financial stability, or a modicum of solidarity were necessary for the long-run viability of the euro. The role of political factors has to be introduced to explain this lack of concern for imposing financial regulation that could have fostered the long-run competitiveness of each national productive system: the European commission and governments delegated the monitoring of the public deficit to international finance, and its short-termism and myopia have been fuelling cumulative real economy imbalances, the underlying cause of the severity of the Euro crisis. But then, why has the Eurozone not collapsed? Simply because of the bold move by the European Central Bank. Mario Draghi announced on July 2012 that the euro was irreversible and will be defended against speculation at any cost. This has been (transitorily) calming the storm, but simply buying time since the generalisation of austerity policies is nonetheless widening the innovation and productive gap across national economies.

2. The responsibility of an irrelevant theory for analysing the creation of a new currency

The launch of the euro coincides with the loss of influence of the Keynesian paradigm and the rise of real business cycle (RBC) models that assume that business cycles can be explained by exogenous shocks hitting a pure Walrasian economy (Lucas 1983).

Neutrality of money and automatic real economy equilibrium

This academic school has progressively gained influence in economic policy discussions, especially since many influential central banks have been using this approach in the evaluation of their monetary policy. The European Central Bank (ECB) has thus been developing the second generation of these models under the name of dynamic stochastic general equilibrium (DSGE) models (Smets and Wouters 2002). This was presented as a definitive move towards a fully scientific approach to previously highly ideological discussions about monetary and fiscal policy.

Without overestimating the influence of macroeconomists on the fate of the euro, this conversion to pre-Keynesian conceptions has contributed to the misunderstanding of many of the issues at stake. The contrast between the key features of the Eurozone and the core hypotheses of the DSGE models is striking (Table 2.1).

Table 2.1 The consequences of the new classical macroeconomics for the assessment of the viability of the euro

Hypotheses	*Mechanisms involved*	*Consequences of euro*	*Degree of realism*
1. Exogenous money created by Central Bank	• Typical monetarism • Neutrality of money in the long run	Price stability is the first objective of the central bank	In modern financial system, endogenous money creation
2. Full employment equilibrium	• Perfect adjustment through price and wage flexibility • Only voluntary unemployment	Basically no inflation/ unemployment trade off	Large and steady involuntary unemployment in many EU economies
3. Symmetric shocks will prevail over asymmetric, country specific shocks	Thus a common monetary policy will fulfil the bulk of macroeconomic adjustments	Eurozone can be viable even if it is not an optimum for monetary unification	Significant endogenous productivity at the national level
4. Rational expectations for all actors: a. Firms, households b. governments	The economic policy rule associated with the euro will affect all private and public strategies	The irreversibility of euro is crucial for its credibility	Adaptation of firms and banks… But governments play a domestic political game
5. One size fits all	Existence of generic economic adjustments common to all member states	The euro will speed up a nominal and possibly real convergence	The Single Market has generated a deeper division of labor, hence heterogeneity

First of all, the neutrality of money is central and does not help to explain the recurring bubbles generated by the low interest rates set by the central bank. Furthermore, the central bank is the only financial entity that issues fiat money, in the absence of any commercial bank or financial market. The control of money supply to maintain low inflation was supposed to embody the essence of monetary stability. By omission, financial stability was automatically fulfilled. We can imagine the dismay of these experts confronted by the diffusion of the subprime crisis to Europe, and thereby revealing the financial fragility of many banks. In this context, the monetary policy loses its efficiency because the channel of credit is broken (Draghi 2012).

Full employment and a common model for all economies

Since wages and prices are fully flexible, unemployment is voluntary in the sense that it is the outcome of a trade-off between work and leisure. Such a pattern is difficult to reconcile with the observation of millions of Europeans willing to work for the current wage but unable to get jobs, both at the time of the introduction of the euro and after 2010, the explosion of the sovereign debt crisis and its spread to banks. Clearly, the Eurozone is facing a wave of involuntary employment, in line with the gap between capacity of production and demand. If full employment were to prevail, austerity policies would boost private demand; however, the opposite has been observed since 2010. Nevertheless, surprisingly, leading economists and politicians do continue to trust and follow a failed representation of the Eurozone (Artus 2012a).This does not help to overcome the Euro crisis.

A third misrepresentation relates to the existence of generic mechanisms that are common to all the members of the Eurozone and that this is a licence to run a common monetary policy. In a sense, this postulates the homogeneity of macroeconomic adjustments for each national economy. Quite the contrary: since 2000, some truly diverging trends have been observed and this has enhanced the initial heterogeneity of national "regulation" modes. Therefore, the EU level models lose their relevance, including in terms of transmitting monetary policy: a very low interest rate does not convert into buoyant credit when the banks of some members of the Eurozone are near bankruptcy. More generally, the complementarity of innovation and export led growth in northern Europe with a domestic-demand led configuration in the south perverts the hypothesis of a common European model. Alas, the diffusion of austerity policies (Boyer 2012) prolongs the "one size fits all" illusion that has been so detrimental to past IMF programmes in Asia and Latin America.

Governments are the servants of economic rationality

There is another consequence of the rational expectations hypothesis (REH): all actors, private and public, had to develop strategies consistent with the commitments formalised in the Amsterdam Treaty. This was not too problematic for large firms that deployed their activity in response to the removal of exchange rate risk within the Eurozone. Similarly, the banks have extended their branches throughout the members of the Eurozone and diversified their portfolio by buying foreign public bonds and securities that they would not have acquired before the euro. These two moves conformed to the prognosis based on REH.

It is not quite the same for households in economies that had weak currencies: the sharp decline of nominal and ultimately real interest rates induced many people to buy houses and durable goods on an unprecedented scale. The rapid rise in house prices was fuelled by this easy access to credit and it started speculative bubbles. These were welcome since they fed the banks' profit, created jobs in the construction sector and even filled state coffers, with some countries experiencing public finance surpluses (Spain) on the eve of the world crisis. Convinced that the financial markets were efficient and that no public authority was able to detect a speculative bubble in real time, analysts and economists praised these national experiences as promising evidence of the benefits of the euro. This hype was widespread, as evidenced by the reference to the Celtic tiger or Iceland's miracle (Mishkin and Ebbertsson 2006; Portes and Baldursson 2007).

But the most serious flaw was the rationality attributed to public authorities: having accepted the pooling of monetary sovereignty, they had to undertake all the reforms necessary to work out a viable policy mix and foster a fairly ambitious reform of their national growth regime. This meant that politicians had to take all the decisions required under pure economic rationality, in the hope that greater efficiency would generate the resources to satisfy all the other demands from citizens about taxation, public goods, welfare and the fight against unemployment. In other words, the political domain had to become the main locus where the policies necessary for the success of the euro were implemented.

This complete determination of polity through the economy does not fit with the observation that the political arena deals with the accumulation of power over a given territory, whereas for the economy, it is a matter of permanent enlargement of wealth, and this process tends to cross national political borders (Théret 1992). Therefore, joining the euro exposes major differences in national political alliances and styles. In societies where an industrial commitment prevails, European treaties spur the existing public policies centred on competitiveness. In other societies, European integration might well help politicians in a "clientelist" strategy, quite alien to any concern for the long-term viability of the national style of development. If northern Europe explores the first path and southern Europe the second, this explains the oppositions and misunderstandings that permeate the numerous European summits and councils that have taken place since the Greek crisis.

The first lesson: it was dangerous to trust an irrelevant and a-historical theory to assess the epochal change wrought by the euro.

3. The benign neglect of more relevant analyses

A whole spectrum of more realistic analytical frameworks was available and could have been used to assess the consequences of the euro, since they explored the viability or the likely failure of the euro.

The Eurozone was not an optimal currency area

The first theoretical reference is, of course, the optimal currency area (OCA) theory elaborated decades ago (Mundell 1961) and revisited during the discussions on the benefits and constraints associated with the creation of a common European currency. Four features favour the viability of a currency union, defined as the ability to enjoy an efficient economic policy in terms of stabilisation of economic activity: labour and capital mobility across the region; price and wage flexibility; automatic fiscal transfer mechanisms to adversely affected regions, nations or sectors; and relatively well-synchronised business cycles. Clearly, not all these requisites were fulfilled in the European Union of the 1960s, when very low cross-national mobility of labour but increasing geographical diversification of capital portfolios, significant nominal wage rigidity and very limited redistributive impact of the European Structural Funds were the order of the day.

Keynes, Schumpeter, Minsky and Krugman: useful warnings about an excess of optimism

The relatively broad consensus on the viability of the Eurozone has been reached by excluding alternative approaches that, in retrospect, had quite rightly pointed out some, but of course not all, of the structural weaknesses of the Amsterdam and subsequent treaties (Table 2.2).

- Imagining that the Eurozone would constitute a Walrasian economy where adjustments take place via the complete flexibility of prices and wages forgets that oligopolistic pricing is the rule in leading final goods production and that nominal wage rigidity is a common feature. Similarly, households can optimise their consumption over time only if they have access to a perfect credit market. Therefore, the Ricardian equivalence principle, which states that private agents will counterbalance any public finance decision, is not an accurate representation of the majority of European economies. This brings back *the Keynesian argument*: all the European Treaties have a structural bias towards lower growth than existed under the previous European monetary system regime. Somehow, the most recent DSGE models for the Eurozone recognise that their simulations become more accurate if "non-Ricardian households in the form of rule-of-thumb consumers" are introduced (Coenen et al. 2012). This is a hidden tribute to the Keynesian consumption function, where current income is the key factor.

Table 2.2 A more accurate and fairer assessment by other approaches

Approach	*Core mechanisms*	*Consequences for euro*	*Degree of realism*
1. Keynesian Theory	Generally effective demand is the key determinant of employment	Orthodox restrictive monetary policy and limits to public deficit will imply high unemployment	Realist for the period 1993–1999, but not from 2000 to 2008
2. Neo-Schumpeterian Theory	• Innovation is the engine of growth • The knowledge-based economy is the new paradigm	• Speed up innovation via R&D and structural reforms • Growth is the condition for the success of the Euro	• Germany and northern Europe, good pupils of the Euro • Southern Europe lagging behind
3. New Economic Geography	Increasing returns imply geographical polarization	The Euro triggers a deeper division of labor within regions and countries, hence greater national heterogeneity	The productive imbalances put the Euro at risk, in absence of fiscal federalism / large labor mobility
4. Post-Keynesian Theories	Built-in instability of finance in the context of liberalization, innovation and globalization	Need to build the credibility of the euro with respect to international finance, at the cost of lower growth	A typical sequence of optimism (2002–2007) and recurring pessimism (2008–2012)

- Nevertheless, the prognosis derived from the textbook Keynesian model on the negative impact of the euro and the Stability and Growth Pact (SGP) on economic activity has turned out to be erroneous for the period 2000 to 2008. This period is better represented by post-Keynesian analyses of the impact of financial liberalisation and innovation on the recurrence of financial bubbles (Minsky 1986). Clearly, the euro was a major financial innovation with few precedents for comparison. Nevertheless, the typical pattern of liberalised markets has been observed once more: after a wait-and-see period, the euro has been perceived as successful since keeping inflation at a low level has allowed interest rates to fall. The dynamism of consumption and the housing market has fuelled a wave of optimism and generated a bubble in a significant part of the Eurozone. The subsequent period 2008–2012 followed the pattern of previous bubbles: loss of confidence by financiers and poor reactivity of European authorities triggered a double-dip recession. After all, *Keynes and Minsky were right*: credit money is not neutral and by changing domestic financial systems, the euro exposed the irrelevance of the Walrasian approach to macroeconomics.

- The *neo-Schumpeterian approach* has not been taken seriously either, in the launching and management of the euro. First, it shows that productivity increases are not exogenous since they derive from the explicit strategy of firms to secure more profits. Furthermore, product and organisational innovation are also key ingredients in the search for oligopolistic rents. Second, neo-Schumpeterian economists have argued that Europe was not only affected by exchange rate and financial volatility but it suffered from tardiness in adopting the principle of a knowledge-based economy (KBE). This explained the slow growth of the old continent and made the sustainability of generous welfare systems problematic (Rodrigues 2002). The Lisbon agenda was intended to correct this weakness in European research and innovation systems. Moreover, the Keynesian and neo-Schumpeterian diagnoses of the impact of the euro are more complementary than contradictory: their timelines or horizons differ and they agree that R&D spending is pro-cyclical, hence reactive to the nature of macroeconomic stabilisation policy. A long-lasting conservative monetary and fiscal policy thus reduces productive capacity formation and innovation, such that long-term growth is lower (Dosi et al. 2010).

This overview becomes more and more pertinent while muddling-through the Eurozone crisis. On the one hand, the perseverance with austerity policies depresses demand and distorts the crowding-out effect typical of public spending, as put forward by neo-classical theory (Boyer 2012). On the other hand, depressed productive investment will reduce potential growth and make the sustainability of the public finances of the weakest economies more uncertain. This vicious circle cannot find any easy and convincing explanation within the current macroeconomic paradigm.

- Finally, the *new economic geography* (Krugman 1991, 1993) was able to provide an interesting prognosis, against the convergence hypothesis implicit in most European strategies and the neo-classical macroeconomics. Given the importance of increasing returns to scale, typical in most contemporary sectors, and the agglomeration effects that foster innovation, the stabilisation of internal exchange rates had the predictable consequences of polarising economic activity around the already competitive regions; this was more evident the more overvalued the domestic currency when it was converted into euros. This is precisely what developments from 2000 to 2012 have highlighted: the north of Europe has maintained a strong manufacturing export basis, whereas the south has specialised in domestic services (Artus 2011). The common currency has created the polarisation of trade surplus in the north versus trade deficit in the south, and such imbalances cannot be corrected by a purely financial strategy.

Clearly, the structural weaknesses of the Eurozone could be anticipated and they were detected quite early (Boyer 1999, 2000; Crouch 2000) but they had no impact at all on policy debates.

Second lesson: an open debate involving different economic approaches would have foreseen the present imbalances within the Eurozone.

4. The euro made national economic policy regimes obsolete, but politicians did not care!

While economists were discussing tiny details within their pet models and politicians were selling the euro as a panacea and an absolute necessity, virtually nobody heard the message of a few dissenters: such a structural and institutional change totally transformed the exercise of national autonomy, so much so that some member states might be unable to cope with the new and drastic constraints imposed on their past economic policy that promised to fulfil national objectives, such as growth and employment.

Industrial and income policies were needed to replace two lost instruments: interest and exchange rates

How should a rational economic policy be decided? One school in macroeconomic modelling has proposed a useful framework (Tinbergen 1952). Basically, macroeconomic activity is largely endogenous because consumption, investment, exports, and imports are related to wages, profits, effective demand, relative prices, i.e., variables set by private agents. But involuntary unemployment is generally observed, or an inflationary boom may imperil financial and even social stability. The policy-makers can correct these trends since they control some instruments such as the taxation rates, public spending, public sector wages, interest rates and the exchange rate. An appropriate application of these instruments can achieve a better macroeconomic equilibrium. Then the policy-maker may try to set economic policy according to target variables related to inflation, unemployment or external trade equilibrium and growth. Here comes the Tinbergen rule: the number of instruments must be at least equal to the number of objectives.

In the "Golden Age", the nation state could use at least four instruments quite freely to fulfil these objectives: monetary policy, budget and tax, exchange rate, industrial/innovation policy, with the possible addition of tentative income policies (Table 2.3). With the adoption of a flexible exchange rate and the trans-nationalisation of finance, monetary policy autonomy has been limited by the intention to monitor the exchange rate somehow, and public deficits have been put under the scrutiny of financial markets. The unemployment rate has often been the adjustment variable and full employment has become more and more difficult to achieve, in particular because public authorities had largely lost full control over exchange rates.

Table 2.3 J. Tinbergen's analysis of economic policy: the euro means the loss of two key instruments and the ability to refinance public debt via the central bank

Instruments / *Objectives*	*The "Golden Age"*	*The path towards the euro*	*After the euro*
1. Inflation	Autonomous *monetary policy* Eventually income policy	Restriction on monetary policy (defence of exchange rate)	• Mainly the objective of the European Central Bank • Interdiction of the refinancing of national public debts
2. Full employment	Mainly *Budgetary policy* Sometimes Social Pacts	Restriction on budgetary policy (lower public deficit)	• Budgetary policy restricted by the Stability and Growth Pact • Structural reforms (competition, labor market)
3. External equilibrium	Adjustment by political decisions on the *exchange rate*	Exchange rates become financial market variables, tentatively controlled by the central bank	• No more formal external constraint for Member States • The euro/$/yen exchange rates as pure market variables
4. Growth	Innovation and industrial policy	Primacy of macroeconomic approach	• Enforcement of competition, as alternative to industrial policy • Supplemented by the Lisbon Agenda

However, with the adoption of the euro, the national authorities lost a second tool: a monetary policy tailored to national needs. The situation created by the euro is *radically new*. It is neither the full autonomy of independent nation states, nor is it a typically federalist configuration (Dehove 1997; Boyer and Dehove 2001). The responsibility of economic policy is now shared at two levels and *nested* in the sense that neither the *supranational rules* nor the *subsidiarity principle* has a dominant role. Clearly *monetary policy* is the full responsibility of the ECB, in charge of maintaining price stability in Europe as a whole. But the credibility of the euro and especially its exchange rate with respect to the dollar is significantly affected by the conduct of national budgetary policies. Given the fixed exchange rate system, which was irrevocably installed by the euro between the first 11 members, the Mundell-Fleming model implies that *budgetary policy* is the only efficient instrument left for national governments to control the domestic level of activity (Wyplosz 1997). Therefore, each nation state may have an incentive to hitch a "free ride" on the collective good produced by the wise budgetary policies followed by other nation states. This is the justification for the Stability and Growth Pact (SGP). This introduces yet another limit on the use of the traditional tools to stabilise each national economy. Nevertheless, under the pressure of domestic demands to reduce unemployment, many governments have violated the SGP. They then agreed in 2005 to reform it, thus breaching one of the founding principles of the European treaties (Boyer 2006).

Last but not least, there is a third loss concerning the autonomy of national policy: on top of the monetary policy and exchange rate, the European Treaty forbids the monetisation of public debt, which had been a central device during the "Golden Age". Consequently, private credit is the only channel open at the ECB, contrary to the status of other central banks, such as the FED, Bank of England or Japan. Basically, Eurozone member states issue debt in a currency they can no longer create at the national level. This is comparable with emerging countries that have to float their public debt in dollars or another international currency. This has led some Latin-American economists to compare the Argentina crisis of 1997–2001 to the evolution of Greece since 2009. There are significant differences in the two crises, one of which is that European authorities have perceived the danger of contagion to larger economies: in violation of the letter of the treaties, the ECB has temporarily agreed to the direct purchase of Italian and Spanish treasury bonds.

The illusion of a smooth transition from the European Monetary System to the euro

These last remarks point out an underestimated consequence of the euro: it implied not only a change in the economic policy mix, between monetary and fiscal tools, but also a drastic change in the institutional architecture of most national economies.

If one adopts the conceptual framework of "regulation" theory, the viability of any socioeconomic regime relies on the short- and long-run compatibility or, even better, complementarity, of five institutional forms: the monetary regime; the wage-labour nexus; the nature of competition; integration into the world economy; and finally, the links between the State and the economy (Boyer and Saillard 2000). De facto, the process of European integration has progressively altered just about all these institutional forms (Table 2.4).

The monetary regime has shifted from a large national autonomy in the Golden Age to policies largely constrained by international financial movements, and finally the members of the Eurozone agreed to pool their monetary sovereignty and create a supranational and independent European Central Bank. In theoretical terms, the monetary regime becomes hierarchically superior, and certainly exterior, to national specific arrangements. This is at odds with the past Keynesian configuration where it was subordinated to support the basic capital—labor institutionalized

Table 2.4 The Euro meant an epochal change for national modes of "regulation"

Periods / *Level of institutional forms*	*"Golden Age" 1945–1971*	*The painful decades 1972–1999*	*The happy days of the euro 2000–2009*	*The decade of reckoning 2010–...*
1. Monetary Regime/ Credit	National	Increasing constraints on national monetary autonomy	The same *European monetary policy for all members*	• The ECB's loss of efficiency confronted with national banking and sovereign debt crises • Major concern for financial stability
2. Wage-labor nexus	National	National, but changes in reaction to fiercer competition	Still *national* but *benchmarking* at the European level	Labor market and welfare reforms to restore national competitiveness
3. Nature of competition	Mainly national	Growing impact of European competition policy	Stricter enforcement of competition at the European level	Overcapacity at the world level triggers fiercer competition
4. Insertion into the world economy, exchange rate regime	Exchange rate is the outcome of political decisions	Financial markets tend more and more to set exchange rates	A single common exchange rate set by financial markets	Promotion of internal devaluations via wage austerity and welfare slimming down
5. State/ Economy Link	Large welfare State	Recurring public and welfare deficits	Diverging evolution of public deficits	Sovereign debt crisis, diverging trends across the Eurozone

compromise. This inversion of the institutional hierarchy means that this past compromise was no longer viable and actually, the wage-labour nexus has experienced many changes: de-indexing of nominal wages with respect to inflation and productivity; decentralisation and individualisation of labour contracts; recurring reforms in the organisation and financing of welfare. These pressures on the redesign of the post-WWII domestic order were especially strong, in response also to the fact that the previous oligopolistic competition at the domestic level has been challenged by the globalisation of production, the emergence of fast-industrialising economies, and the loss of control by public authorities over industrial dynamics. Overcapacity in the production of manufactured goods at world level destabilises most European economies, either because capital flows delocalise employment in search of long-term competitiveness, or because massive imports trigger a massive de-industrialisation in the weakest market economies.

In the past, periodic devaluations of the domestic currency could stop these adverse trends but this degree of freedom progressively vanished with financial liberalisation; basically, the exchange rate tends to equalise the rate of return of financial capital across nations, thus generating cumulative imbalances in external trade. The situation is still more difficult with the euro because the European currency may appreciate with respect to the dollar, even if exporting sectors and nations become uncompetitive. The only solution left is internal devaluation, i.e., reduction of indirect taxes, social contributions and finally wages.

The post-WWII socioeconomic redesign is thus over, but the new institutional architecture where monetary stability and competition are leading the macroeconomic adjustments is far from self-regulating. Unemployment becomes a residual variable, which hinders domestic demand and stirs up social conflicts and perhaps political turmoil when years of austerity policies only prolong the recession and exacerbate the sense of unfairness felt by a large fraction of public opinion.

Lastly, the second adjusting variable is public deficit and debt, which remains moderate in the structurally competitive economies, but stubbornly large for those unable to cope with the standards of the world economy. In this case, the issue at stake is not simply the restoration of a "correct" policy mix but the reconstruction of a socio-political order compatible simultaneously with the requirements of the Eurozone and the pressing social demands of citizens. Does a viable compromise exist and can it be negotiated in the face of the impatience of international finance and the reluctant solidarity of the healthier members of the euro?

The long legacy of a North/South divide in productive capacity and competitiveness

Clearly, individual societies have reacted quite differently to the pressures associated with their Europeanization, because they display contrasting innovation systems (Amable et al. 1997; Boyer 2010) and belong to different brands of capitalism (Amable 2003). This heterogeneity might be the source of a great divide.

- On the one hand, small open economies and Germany had a long experience in designing and managing domestic institutions that foster their competitiveness and successful integration into the world economy. An open social dialogue, the dynamism of entrepreneurs and political stability were the key ingredients of these "negotiated capitalism" systems and their export- and innovation-led growth. For them, joining the euro is not so difficult since large continuities prevail: organised collective bargaining to sustain competitiveness; emphasis placed on education, training and innovation; welfare turned into an asset in world competition by well-designed and patient reforms. In most cases, the reforms are anticipatory and not triggered by a dramatic and unexpected crisis. Furthermore, the actors do not think that deficit spending can solve major macroeconomic imbalances. Consequently, economics is assigned the role of shaping stable expectations.

- On the other hand, medium-sized or less- industrialised economies tend to rely more on the monitoring of the domestic market, industrial relations are more conflicted than prone to durable compromises, Schumpeterian entrepreneurs are more the exception than the rule, recurring political conflicts make it quite difficult to achieve coherence and continuity in economic policy. All unsolved macroeconomic disequilibria—high youth unemployment, specialisation in the services, obsolescence of past industrial specialisation, lagging innovation, tax evasion, inadequate welfare system—are translated into a large and permanent public deficit. For these configurations, joining the euro implies the complete redesign of most domestic institutions. The inability to devaluate means the equivalent of implementing a permanent income policy or, to use unemployment as a painful disciplinary device, a definitive upgrading of industrial specialisation; however, these are long-term strategies that deliver their benefits only after one or two decades of effort. The inability to monetise the domestic public deficit means that governments have to convince international finance that they can reimburse by generating both a trade and public surplus. In some cases this is impossible, given the legacy of the pre-euro configuration.

This analysis concludes that the North/South divide might be one of the major threats to the current configuration of the Eurozone (Figure 2.1).

Three main characteristics explain why the crisis differs in terms of profile and severity within the same Eurozone: the quality of state organization and government handling of the crisis; the degree of structural competitiveness; and the ability to control and monitor finance.

- The northern economies (Netherlands, Finland and Germany) enjoy a good fit with the evolution of the world economy, an effective and reactive state and relative, albeit imperfect, control over finance. They fare relatively well in terms of external surplus and ability to reduce their public deficit, and thus they can comply with the EU and Eurozone rules rather easily, and ask their partners to do so.
- Unfortunately, the southern economies suffer from a structural lack of competitiveness and a limited ability of the state to intervene efficiently,

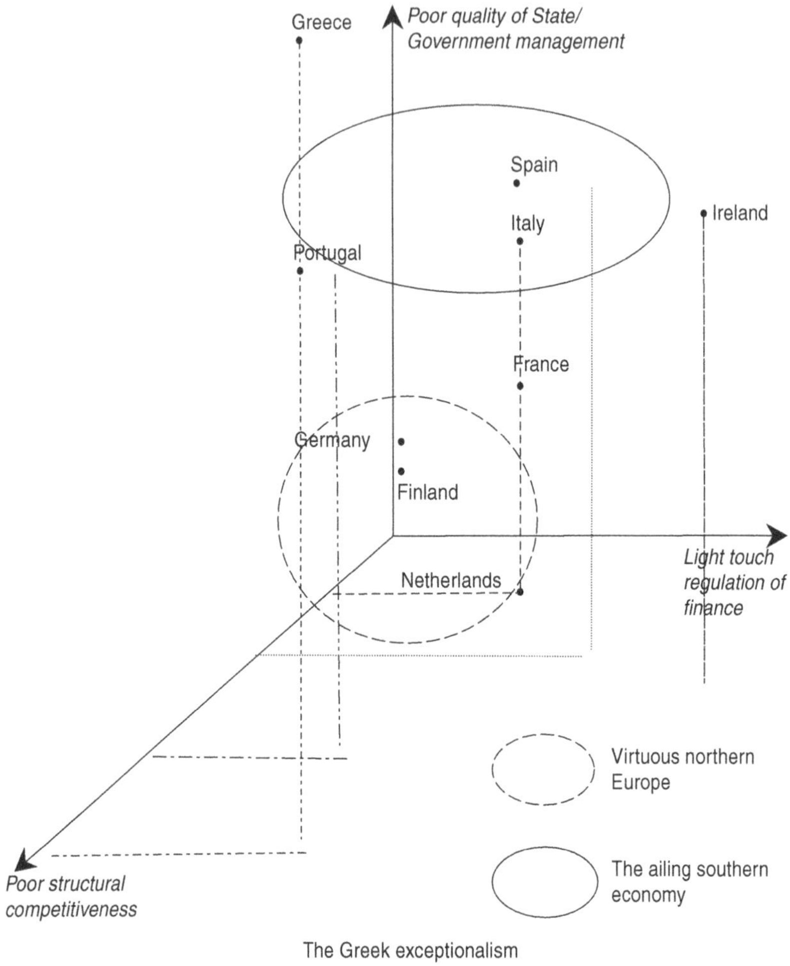

Figure 2.1 How the factors of crisis differ across the Eurozone

France as a barycenter between North and South

Ireland victim of an unwise financial liberalization

and some of them have suffered from speculative real estate bubbles generated by financial liberalisation. Given the persisting public deficits and the deterioration of their trade balances, it is very difficult from them to stick to the adjustment programmes negotiated with the EU and IMF. International finance is the referee and it is largely unconvinced that the decisions of the June 2012 European Council can be rapidly and successfully implemented and it doubts that a form of fiscal solidarity will in fact prevail before a series of defaults.

The heterogeneity of the Eurozone is still greater if we consider three hybrid configurations: France is the intermediate case between north and south; Greece is an exceptional case of clear and largely irreversible insolvency, and Ireland is a failed tiger perverted by careless financial liberalisation, but well able to bounce back to a viable export-led regime.

Lesson three: In the weakest economies, policy-makers have not perceived the radical institutional changes required by a durable integration into the Eurozone.

5. The poor implementation of the Lisbon strategy against the straitjacket of european treaties

At the very same time as the euro was launched, technical change experts (Soete 2002) highlighted a structural limit to growth revival in the old continent. The diverging trends observed between the United States and European innovation systems were putting the welfare state at risk, as it had to cope with population ageing, obsolescence of workers' skills, persistent mass unemployment. Furthermore, the emergence of China and India as major players in the world economy and recurring demands by citizens for more security added other strains to the so-called European Social Model.

A relevant diagnosis: innovation was the Achilles Heel of Europe

This diagnosis convinced the European Commission to launch a special programme, which was adopted by the heads of state at the March 2000 European Council, held in Lisbon. The *Lisbon Strategy*, as it is known, had three major components. Its objective was to promote growth and employment by maintaining a highly competitive European economy. Its originality was to couple innovation with the preservation of social cohesion, as a compromise between market liberalisation and a social democratic approach under the umbrella of a Schumpeterian view of innovation. Since this was not explicitly prescribed by the European Treaties, a new intergovernmental procedure was invented. The open method of coordination (OMC) was conceived as a device to overcome the present distribution of competences between member states and Brussels and promote at the national level the structural reforms required to fulfil the Lisbon objectives.

Unsurprisingly, the most severe critiques of the Lisbon strategy recognized that the general diagnosis was, and still is, relevant and the overall strategy is on the right path (Kok et al. 2004; Pisani-Ferry and Sapir 2006; Aghion et al. 2006) and technical change scholars continue to support the Lisbon Strategy (Lundvall and Lorenz 2011). Since the mid-2000s, before the Euro crisis, the common feeling was nevertheless that the strategy had basically failed, and that is why it had to be redesigned. Actually, the 2005 spring European Council made the reformed Lisbon Strategy a key component of its policy (Rodrigues 2004).

Poor economic outcomes, but promising institutional innovation?

Generally speaking, economists tend to diagnose a clear failure, whereas political scientists and sociologists have a far more positive assessment. After all, they do not consider the same components.

The economists focus on outputs and inputs. European growth has been sluggish and job creation disappointing, and the gap with the United States has been widening. Nor is the picture satisfactory in terms of input. The R&D/GNP objective of 3 percent in 2010 is probably out of reach for Europe as a whole and the welfare reforms have been difficult and partial, especially in France, Germany and Italy. They are also the countries that failed to increase their innovation effort.

Other social scientists (Zeitlin 2005; Zeitlin and Pochet 2005) are more interested in the method and they find a significant learning/experimenting process that could perhaps overcome some veto points in the reform of national welfare systems (Obinger et al. 2005). On the one hand, they recognise that National Employment Action Plans are frequently formal exercises in window dressing but on the other hand, they note a significant change in the cognitive maps and agenda of decision-makers, by national interactions at national and European levels. For the authors under review, the OMC is a very promising institutional innovation that could be quite helpful, at least in the long term, to overcome some of the deadlocks, exemplified by the fate of the European Constitution. By contrast, economists regret the weak enforcement of the Lisbon Strategy, the lack of clear methodology in assessing the National Reform Programmes and generally the poor involvement of national stakeholders (Pisani and Sapir 2006).

The mid-term review in 2004–2005 had clearly pointed out some limits of the current organisation and triggered a reform of the Lisbon agenda (Rodrigues 2006). Basically, it was recognised that strategic objectives were blurred, the inflation of measures and priorities was detrimental, and some basic mechanisms, as well as financial incentives, were missing regarding the implementation of the agenda. However, the most fundamental issue is a return to a "one size fits all approach" (Table 2.5).

Nevertheless, the reforms have been mild, partial and too marginal to overcome the original sin of OMC (Boyer 2009). This soft intergovernmental governance could not overcome the dominance of domestic polity in the design of difficult reforms and still less could it reduce the innovation gap between northern and southern Europe that opposes highly and poorly competitive productive systems (see Figure 2.1 above).

Table 2.5 Lisbon Strategy and OMC: limitations clearly recognized, not really corrected

Criticism	*Reply*	*Possible reforms*
1. Too many guidelines	1. A response to the complexity of modern economies The expression of political compromises	1a. Reduce the number of guidelines 1b. Replace by mechanisms combining items
2. Lack of policy instruments to implement the strategy	2. On the contrary a promising method for overcoming institutional and political deadlock	2a. Design explicit hard rules at the Community level 2b. "Blame and share" as incentives to reform
3. Lack of political will, a technocratic exercise	3. Unequal across countries Common to many European issues	3a. Better marketing, repackaging of the Lisbon strategy 3b. Explain the political objectives more clearly
4. Low democratic accountability	4. More involvement of diverse stakeholders than for other European policies (ECB, competition)	4a. Extend the diversity of stakeholders at the national level 4b. Develop another concept of democracy
5. Little justification of a Eurozone dimension of benchmarking	5. Benchmarking as a learning process, a method to overcome institutional deadlock	5a. Either an unambiguous re-nationalization of reforms 5b. Or taking into account the Lisbon strategy in the re-design of European instruments (for example SGP reform)
6. Fuzzy criteria in the assessment of National Reform Plans	6. This is only the first stage of a learning process	6a. Use the employment/growth diagnostics 6b. Build a genuine methodology
7. The same reform might have different, sometimes opposite, effects in different countries	7. It might be an exceptional case	7a. Contextual benchmarking 7b. Take national diversity into account

The relevant coordination level for structural reforms: more the Nation State than European Union.

The Lisbon Strategy raises another central issue concerning the level of governance that is appropriate to foster the institutional reforms required to fulfil its main objectives. The OMC assumes that coordination among member states is an important factor in the redesign of economic institutions. If, for instance, it is assumed that part of the macroeconomic problems are related to a rather restrictive monetary policy that takes into account the fact that labour markets are perceived to be too rigid, then a successful reform to reduce the structural employment in one country may induce a change in the European policy mix, especially if this reform takes place in a large country. There are other forms of *cross-border externalities*. Actually, a successful redesign of a national system of innovation is expected to benefit the other economies via the conventional positive spillover associated with technical change. From a theoretical standpoint, this should mean that in the long run the related competences should at least be shared between the national and the European levels. According to this view, the Lisbon process would be a method to overcome the present distribution of competences, as established by existing European treaties.

The experience of recent years suggests that even if these externalities exist they are quite weak and unable to trigger the emergence of a virtuous circle by which the lagging countries would emulate the more successful ones, a process which would induce a progressive acceleration of European growth and job creation. Quite the contrary, the abundant literature on capitalist diversity is now confirmed by research on the complementarities between labour market and welfare reforms, innovation policy and the conduct of the policy mix. The problem is that these complementarities are mainly if not exclusively national. Hence, a major difficulty of the Lisbon process: the will to cope with *cross-border externalities* disregards the fact that the crucial issue is frequently one of coordinating and sequencing *domestic reforms* (Figure 2.2).

One of the major failures is thus to have fed an illusion: benchmarking would be enough to promote an easy catching up by lagging national innovation and production systems. Quite the contrary, northern economies have thrived and improved their structural competitiveness, whereas southern ones have been anaesthetised by the inflow of credit and confusing bubbles with productive modernisation.

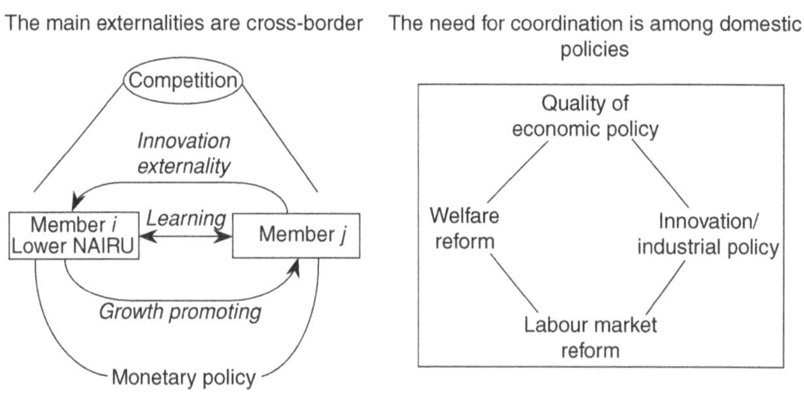

Figure 2.2 The need for coordination: across member states or among domestic policies?

Lesson four: The polarisation of specialisations across the Eurozone has not been alleviated by an active innovation and industrial policy and this is the underlying origin of the crisis.

6. In the globalisation era, low inflation does not imply financial stability

As already mentioned, the cognitive maps of the architects of the euro did not really consider how much financial innovation and globalisation had changed the objectives, instruments, and effectiveness of central banks. For monetarists, the only source of financial crisis was inflation and this conception has hindered the viability and resilience of the Eurozone.

Another example of dramatic underestimation of the break generated by the euro

The policy-makers have worked to eliminate the previous source of crisis, i.e., internal exchange rate volatility, and they even tried to anticipate and overcome some of the most likely fragilities of the new institutional design, for instance by forbidding free-rider national fiscal policies. Nevertheless, they seemed to forget that public mismanagement is not the only factor involved in the financial fragility of the Eurozone. The private sector, especially the banks, might adopt quite risky strategies, such as fuelling a real-estate boom, pushing securitisation or using huge leverage effects, and thus provoke a typical Minsky financial crisis. This is precisely what happened in Spain and Ireland. Back in 1997, the Asian crisis had already shown that very sound public finances could not protect against massive entries of capital and then their abrupt stop. Paradoxically, the cognitive reference of the builders of the euro was more the German hyperinflation of 1923 or the 1980s and 1990s Latin American sovereign debt than the new risks associated with financial globalisation and their hype effects on the "animal spirits" in the private sector. Again, the basic postulate of a "naturally" stable market economy—a convenient hypothesis for model builders—has hidden the perception of the dangerous path followed by the Eurozone after 2003. Indeed, in October 2011, the European Council recognised the need for a set of macroeconomic indicators to capture the imbalances generated within the private sector, including trade balance, real estate prices, deterioration of competitiveness and excessive credit, but it was a little late.

In retrospect, in the mid-2000s, the European policy-makers had convinced themselves that the European Union had finally achieved its purpose and that no new initiative was necessary (Figure 2.3). The project of the founding fathers was to prevent any repetition of the two world wars that had resulted in the self-destruction and afterwards the decline of the old continent. Peace was the primary public good to be sought. If it was impossible to get it through a Europe of defence, the other road was through the establishment of orderly economic relations between Germany, France,

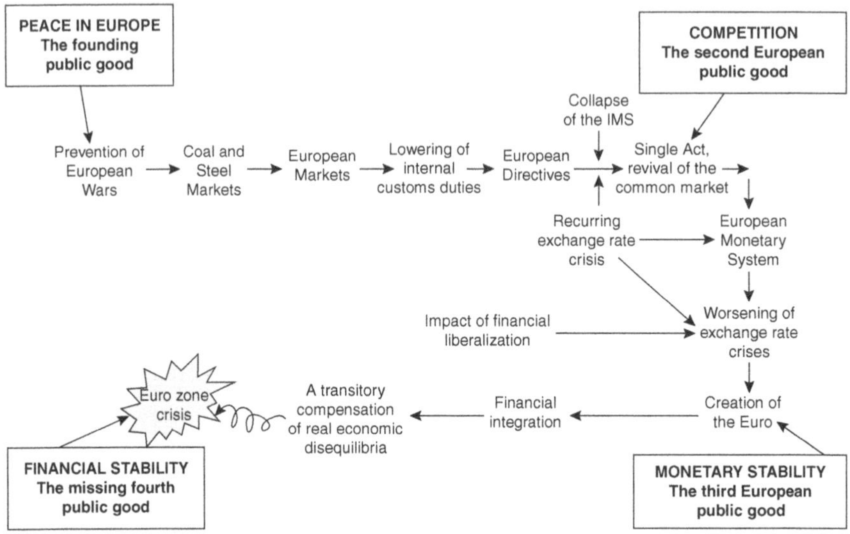

Figure 2.3 Half a century of European integration: building European public goods out of recurring crises.

and all other nations involved in these recurring conflicts. Nevertheless, a common market requires rules to maintain fair competition: it was elevated to the status of basic European public good, justifying a progressive and patient extension of European level competences (Boyer and Dehove 2006).

A dramatic weakness in the epoch of globalisation

But the process has to be re-launched with the rise of exchange rate volatility and its impact on the fairness of competition in the Single Market. After a long period of experimentation, a growing number of European elites became convinced that a common currency was necessary to continue to benefit from the deepening of inter-European trade. Hardly anybody realised that this could be a leap into a radically new configuration. It was the merit and the strength of German representatives that led to extending the approach of ordoliberalism into the relations between Brussels and national entities. The viability of monetary integration without fiscal solidarity and political union could be ensured by compliance with a set common rules designed to prevent any opportunist national behaviour that could bankrupt the Eurozone. Thus German conceptions were responsible for organising the European Union, but there was no transposition of German federalism, since an institutionalised redistributive system, equivalent to the one created among *Länder*, was not proposed.

This genuine "prudential federalism" was supposed to render financial and political federalism unnecessary. But when unanticipated sources of fragility appeared, what to do? What if the rules are not followed by all?

Should policy-makers accept a financial meltdown just to better enforce the rules that have been violated and thus prevent moral hazard from generating another crisis? But will the European Union still exist? Europeans had to recognise painfully what is clear to North Americans: it is difficult to defend the euro in the absence of a lender of last resort, with a tiny balanced European budget and no clear political leadership.

The dangerous path followed from March 2010 to July 2012 shows that financial stability was the next public good needed to preserve the cohesion of the EU; however, it was rather late. So late, that now the next step is a form, however limited, of fiscal federalism, simply to guarantee the European Stability Mechanism and the European financial entity in charge of managing the direct bailing out of some ailing European banks.

Lesson five: Monetary stability may be associated with financial instability and a major crisis: specific financial regulations were required to sustain the euro.

7. Delegating eurozone monitoring to international finance: a losing bet

It was to support the single European market in reaction to the large volatility induced by financial globalisation that the exchange rate was first stabilised and then a number of countries pooled their monetary sovereignty with the creation of the euro. For their part, the European treaties instituted an independent European Central Bank and entrusted it with the goal of maintaining low inflation, as monetary stability was perceived as the essential condition for the credibility, therefore the viability, of the euro. The fixing of the irrevocable exchange rates between member countries of the euro area was designed to promote trade between member states and promote the diversification of the financial portfolio.

The surprising reasoning of international finance: all public debts are now equivalent, from Germany to Greece

After the introductory period, marked by great uncertainty, the single currency had achieved its objectives, such as convincing the international financial community to agree to the same interest rate for all national public debts within the Eurozone, from 2002. While Greece, Portugal and Spain had to pay very high interest rates until the late 1990s, joining the euro granted them the same favourable treatment as that accorded to Germany (Figure 2.4). But this complete convergence of interest rates on all public debts stemmed from an erroneous economic analysis and a misreading of the European treaties.

- *A priori* membership of the euro eliminates a first risk factor since parity is fixed once and for all, as soon as the drachma, escudo, and peseta were replaced by the euro. However, it should have been considered that under

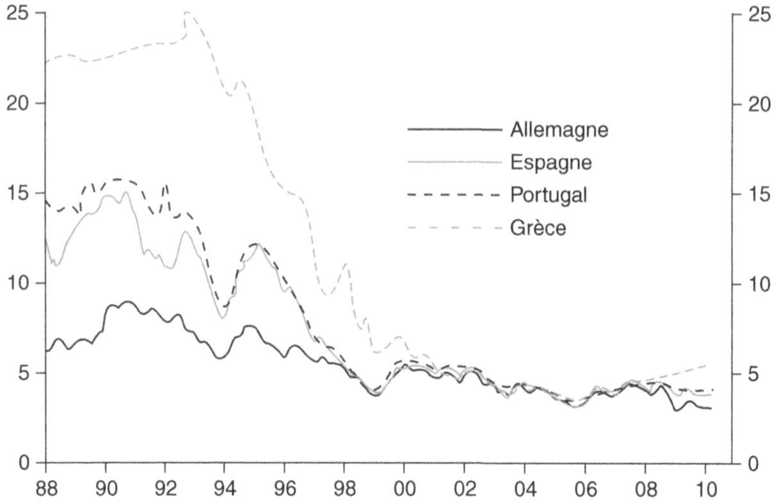

Figure 2.4 Convergence of 10-year treasury bonds interest rates.

Source: Patrick Artus (2010), "Quelle perspective à long terme pour la zone euro?", *Flash Economie*, no. 158, 12 April, p. 4.

the EU treaties some members of the euro could find it impossible to maintain the economic competitiveness of their economy, in the absence of periodic devaluations, which was the preferred instrument in earlier decades. In this regard, the experience of Argentina which established a currency board with an irreversible and complete equivalence between the peso and the dollar, collapsed dramatically in 2001. It showed that a constitutional guarantee did not have the power to contain macroeconomic imbalances accumulated over a decade, precisely because the rigidity of the exchange rate had severely penalised national competitiveness.

- A second consequence was expected and it turned out to be wrong: joining the euro would bring a quasi-convergence of inflation rates across the area. But the statutes of the European Central Bank only involve maintaining low inflation for Europe as a whole. This does not preclude some countries, because of their specialisation in sectors sheltered from international competition, particularly those of southern Europe, from experiencing higher inflation than average. In the period 2001–2007, the yearly average inflation rate ranged from 1.1 percent in Germany to 4.1 percent in Spain and 3.2 percent in Greece (Sapir 2012). As a result, over time the production costs of the southern and Irish economies diverged from the rest of Europe, leading to a deterioration of their trade balances (see Figure 2.5, infra). However, this was not initially an obstacle to their growth as the redeployment of the portfolio of European banks throughout the euro area offset this imbalance of trade until 2007, at least. Yet this divergence of inflation rates was not corrected over the years and it manifested itself through

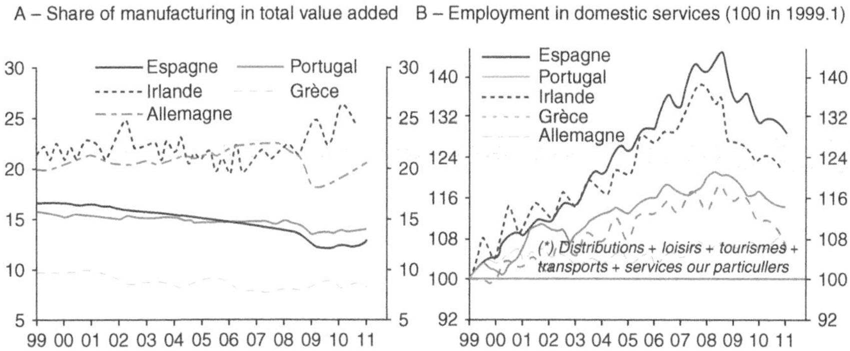

Figure 2.5 Deepening intra-European specialization: manufacturing in the north, services in the south.

Source: Patrick Artus (2011) "Pourquoi n'a-t-on pas vu, de 1999 à 2007, les problèmes de l'Espagne, du Portugal, de l'Irlande, de la Grèce?", *Flash Economie*, no. 534, 9 July, p. 5.

a contraction in manufacturing and tradable services, which built up a systemic dependence on a large, permanent entry of credit from abroad and, to a lesser extent, of capital from northern European countries in surplus, especially Germany.

- However, a third error in the analysis of international finance is still more puzzling since it affects allegedly quite rational actors: traders do not take into account the prohibition by the European treaties of any fiscal or financial solidarity between member countries of the euro area. Furthermore, joining the euro did not mean that public finances, for example in Greece, became as strong and well managed as those of Germany. Failing to take this feature into account is all the more surprising since it was common knowledge that the Greek political authorities had to resort to various accounting tricks and sophisticated financial instruments in order to remove part of the public debt from the state's balance sheet. Moreover, the Mediterranean countries admission to the Eurozone was the subject of considerable controversy because many analysts and politicians stressed that some of these countries had not built up a production system and an institutional structure that could support their long-term integration in the euro area. Ultimately, the decision was based more on political than economic argument: the European Union could not exclude Greece, birthplace of democracy.

Nominal convergence, but diverging economic specialisations and domestic growth regimes

Yet another erroneous analysis and prognosis should be stressed again. Many opponents to the euro anticipated that if a monetary policy only focused on price stability interacting with the constraint implied by the SGP then Europe would become a slow growth zone and the least competitive countries, i.e., those of southern Europe, would grow even more slowly than the European average. In fact, the opposite was observed from 2001 to 2008 because plummeting interest rates stimulated the purchase of homes and durable goods, and therefore demand in these countries. Meanwhile, the north specialised in manufactured goods which it exports to the south and to emerging economies, and thus contributed to balancing Eurozone external trade, with a positive impact on the credibility of the euro. In contrast, other economies specialised in domestic services, generally non-tradable (Figure 2.5).

Trade balance surpluses in the north, deficits in the south

A structural complementarity therefore emerged between these two sub-areas in terms of specialisation, supply/demand equilibrium and flows of credit but this meant divergence between high value added and skills economies and those limited to more traditional production. This internal imbalance was barely noticed in the early 2000s, whereas the competition with new industrialising countries means that this productive divide is still acute. Lastly, the real estate and stock market bubbles, observed for instance in Ireland and Spain, artificially and temporarily accelerated national growth. As domestic production systems whose competitiveness was deteriorating could not meet the boom in domestic demand, trade deficits widened for all these countries, especially when the euro appreciated against the dollar and other currencies. Indeed, Germany, the Netherlands and other northern European countries generated a growing trade surplus, which ensured the viability of the euro as an emerging international currency, but accentuated the internal imbalances within the area (Figure 2.6).

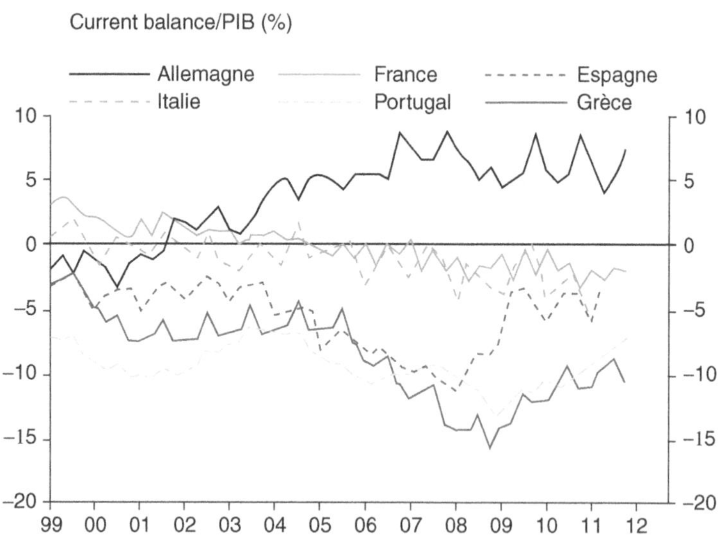

Figure 2.6 Polarization of external balance within the Eurozone.

Source: Patrick Artus (2012), *Flash Economie*, no. 347, 21 May.

The ambiguous blessing of euro credibility: more trade deficit in the south

The euro solved internal exchange volatility but did not deal with the issue of the exchange rate regime. In the context of the external and internal liberalisation of capital flows, the ECB could not monitor the euro/dollar/yen exchange rate and simultaneously control inflation, its primary objective.

Initially, going for a rather simple monetarism led to a rather optimistic assessment: if European inflation is under control, then the equivalent of a purchasing power party equilibrium exchange rate would prevail and ensure, quasi-automatically, the competitiveness of the Eurozone.

Unfortunately, the gross trans-border flows of capital have grown far faster since the 1980s than world trade and even foreign direct investment (FDI). Consequently, the external capital account position has tended to lead the evolution of the exchange rate, a long way from a rate that could ensure a medium-long term trade balance equilibrium and competitiveness of each domestic specialisation. Two years after the launch of the euro, 2002 saw the start of a long period of its appreciation against the dollar, with its value nearly doubling just before the crisis (Figure 2.7).

This move helped to kerb European inflation, in a period of rapidly rising natural resources' prices and it allowed the continuation of a neutral or slightly expansive monetary policy. But beneath the surface of this clear success, the overall competitiveness of the Eurozone was adversely affected by a negative impact on employment in the tradable goods sectors, especially in manufacturing. The high euro triggered the delocalisation of productive capacities to mainly outside, and not within, the EU. The legacy has been a very slow growth potential.

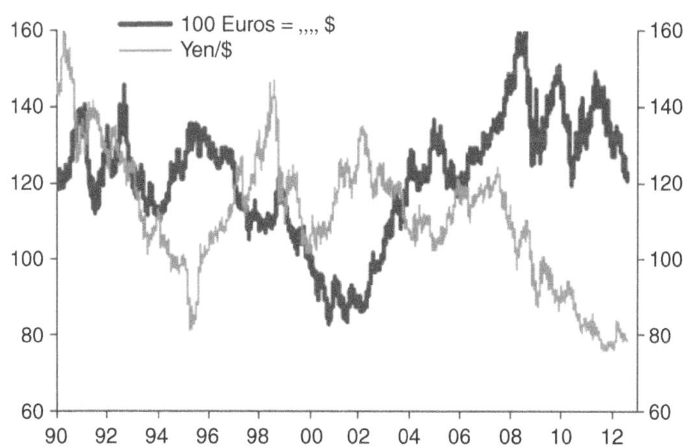

Figure 2.7 The evolution of euro/dollar/yen exchange rates.

Source: Artus (2012c), *Flash marches* no. 535, page 6.

But the strong euro has exacerbated the large productive heterogeneity that was already the Achilles heel of the old continent (Boyer 2010).

- On the one hand, the economies that follow an innovation and export-led growth pattern could cope relatively easily since many sectors and firms, being at the technological frontiers, were price makers and thus could develop clever delocalisation strategies that maintained the high-value activities at home. Germany and most Nordic countries have long been following this path. After implementing significant reforms, they fared quite well in the 2000s.
- On the other hand, other economies rely more on the domestic market and develop mainly via their sheltered sector (construction, services households, distribution) and their export sector is generally small and highly sensitive to price competition given the nature of their specialisation in standardised production in mature industries. Their deindustrialisation speeded up with the appreciation of the euro (see Figure 2.5, above).

Here are the seeds of the present European crisis: difficult sustainability of public finance largely reflects the weaknesses of domestic productive potential; the euro has not been devoid of influence in this deterioration of southern Europe's competitiveness.

Lesson six: The euro, along with full mobility of capital, has exacerbated the productive imbalances across member states, which has led to the present crisis.

8. The only defence against financial collapse: the central banker

The subprime world crisis: a brutal wakeup call from international finance

As the world economy grew at a high rate from 2002 to 2007, under the combined impact of the housing boom in the United States and the rapid development of China, the deepening of the internal imbalances in the euro area remained largely unnoticed by European authorities. Even worse, Spain and Ireland were hailed as promising models to be emulated, and they did not raise the concerns of international financiers who extrapolated the observed boom according to their typical pro-cyclical expectations training. The reversal occurred only after the collapse of Lehmann Brothers in September 2008. The sharp contraction of world trade and the deep-rooted uncertainty that blocked financial systems have forced public authorities of all political stripes to launch programmes to sustain economic activity and to give their full support to banks and bail them out. Governments definitely wanted to avoid a dramatic depression like that of 1929–1932 and thus they let the automatic stabilisers come into play: public deficits have soared. In this context, the level of public debt to GDP reached levels that were seen as alarming by international financiers, as soon as a modest recovery seemed to prevent a repetition of the 1930s. The global crisis has had the effect of exposing previously neglected imbalances: from the spring of 2010 on, the long-term sustainability of Greek, Portuguese and Irish public finances has been scrutinized by financiers and their assessment has been negative (Figure 2.8).

International financiers then suddenly adjusted their criteria for assessing the financial health of the various members of the Eurozone. Greece and Portugal first polarised their concern when they finally realised that these two countries had steadily accumulated deficits above those permitted by the SGP almost every year since joining the euro. The repercussions of the world crisis exposed a characteristic already apparent long before. This was not the case of Spain and Ireland, but they were hit by a second wave of suspicious assessments and downgrading by rating agencies, even though since their accession to the euro, the governments of both countries had maintained a prudent public finance policy, borne out by some surpluses in the years preceding the crisis. If a slimming-down of the public sector might seem suitable for Greece, it is much more dubious for Spain and Ireland since their crises derive largely from a private credit-fuelled speculative boom. Maintaining very low nominal interest rates spurred massive housing bubbles; when they burst, government deficits grew, since tax revenues fell and spending to rescue banks and welfare transfers soared. Again, one is struck by the crudeness of the models used to evaluate the financial strength of various countries. In the case of Ireland and Spain, the soaring costs of refinancing their debt are falsely attributed to mismanagement by the state whereas their crisis is largely due to errors by private actors, lured by the hype of a bubble. Capital flight to quality translates into lower interest rates on German debt. This divergence of interest rates is all the more acute the longer the period of their total convergence from 2002 to 2007 (Figure 2.9).

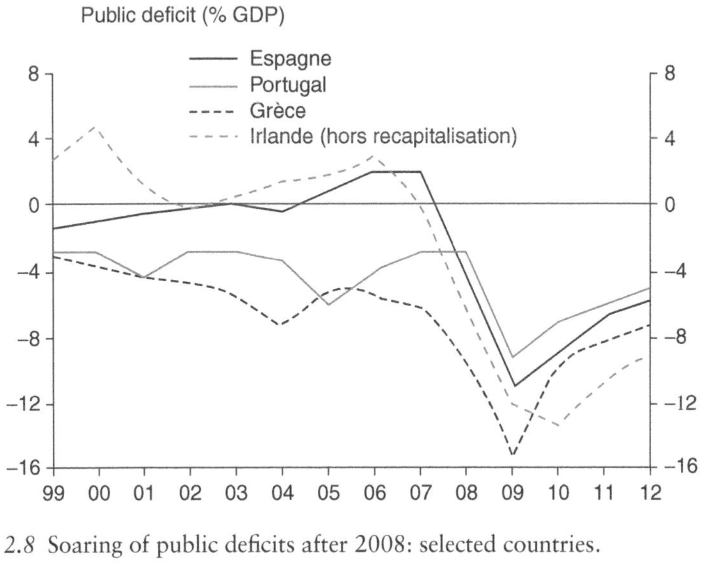

Figure 2.8 Soaring of public deficits after 2008: selected countries.

Source: Artus Patrick (2011b), L'introduction du fédéralisme dans la zone euro: les avantages et les risques, *Flash économie*, 18 April 2011, no. 284, p. 7.

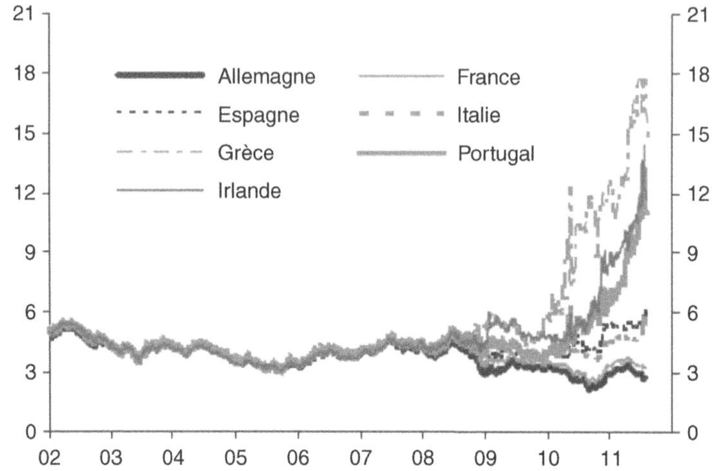

Figure 2.9 The brutal explosion of the cost of refinancing the public debt of southern Europe's economies.

Source: Artus Patrick (2011), "La crise de la zone euro nous apprend beaucoup sur le fonctionnement des Unions Monétaires; l'euro est-il sauvé?", *Flash Economie*, no. 599, 9 August, p. 5.

The July 2012 statement by Mario Draghi stops the panic

The interest rates were so high compared with growth outlook that, if they persisted, they implied default for Greece, Portugal and Ireland. In early June 2012, the most likely scenario was a victory for international finance and the break-up of the Eurozone, since the various European authorities had repeatedly shown their inability to design any relevant policies in response to the daily pressure of financial markets. This pessimistic scenario was brutally reversed by the bold words of Mario Draghi in July "*Within our mandate, the ECB is ready to do whatever it takes to preserve the euro. And believe me it will be enough [...] to the extent that the size of the sovereign premium (borrowing costs) hamper the functioning of the monetary policy transmission channel, they come within our mandate [...] We think that the euro is irreversible.*"

The ECB had to argue to defend this unorthodox monetary policy. It stated that the threat of bankruptcy of banks (and governments) was blocking the credit channel in the transmission of monetary policy to economic activity. Therefore, the ECB was ready to buy treasury bonds from Greece, Portugal, Spain, and Italy. This creative interpretation of the Lisbon Treaty was threatened by the protests of the Bundesbank and the inability to get unanimous support within the ECB council. But the aura of ECB prevailed over the sceptics and the impact on interest rates was spectacular, preventing the default of Greece and Portugal (Figure 2.10). A remarkable calm has been observed on financial markets since then, at least until the spring of 2013.

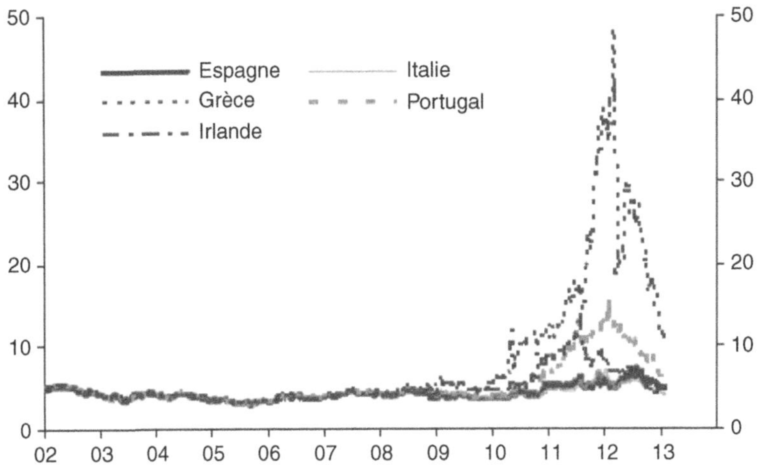

Figure 2.10 A rapid decline in the cost of refinancing the public debt of the weakest European economies.

Source: Artus Patrick (2013), *Flash Economie*, no. 118, 6 February, p. 5.

Unequal national productive capabilities erode the effectiveness of a common monetary policy

Nevertheless, credit for the ailing banks could buy time, but it was not an alternative to difficult institutional reforms of European governance, becoming less so the more adverse the impact of the diffusion of austerity policies. Consequently, if all the entities involved in the governance of the euro stuck to their traditional objectives, past strategies and instruments, no way out of the Euro crisis would emerge. Basically there was no European commissioner who could defend and implement the required industrial and innovation policy.

Two general lessons can be derived from observing this abrupt reversal of fortune, concerning the nature of European integration and the logic of liberalized financial markets.

First, this "one size fits all" approach to crisis resolution shows how difficult is it for financiers and public authorities to take into account the heterogeneity of socioeconomic regimes that coexist within the EU (Boyer et al. 1997; Amable 2003) and how serious this handicap is to the redesigning of European institutions and compliance with democratic principles, too (Höpner and Schäfer 2012).

Second, a key characteristic of financial markets has to be stressed: their evaluations, far from being based on an analytical model that seeks to understand all the factors that determine the probability of default, are in fact built on highly ad hoc and subjective perceptions that oscillate between overly optimistic in good times and completely pessimistic when the economy turns around. This pattern is typical of stock markets (Shiller 1999). They display a mimetic logic that leads to this instability, and the more they do so, the higher the degree of uncertainty (Orléan 2004, 2011). It has therefore been quite detrimental to the viability of European integration to have delegated to the financial markets the task of disciplining member states' public finances, after failing to create and implement a community-based process of a political nature, able to enforce the SGP (Figure 2.11). It was especially dangerous since the euro was conceived as a bulwark against the world instability of finance-led capitalism (Boyer 2011).

There is another irony. The euro was designed to prevent the liberalisation of capital from derailing the construction of the single European market, in response to the succession of speculations on national currencies' exchange rates. One decade later, global finance is now playing off one national public debt against another and it has thus destabilised the very foundations of the euro. If its power remains unchallenged, there is a growing risk of the euro area, at least in its present configuration, coming to an end. This is the price of abandoning a community approach: financial stability should have

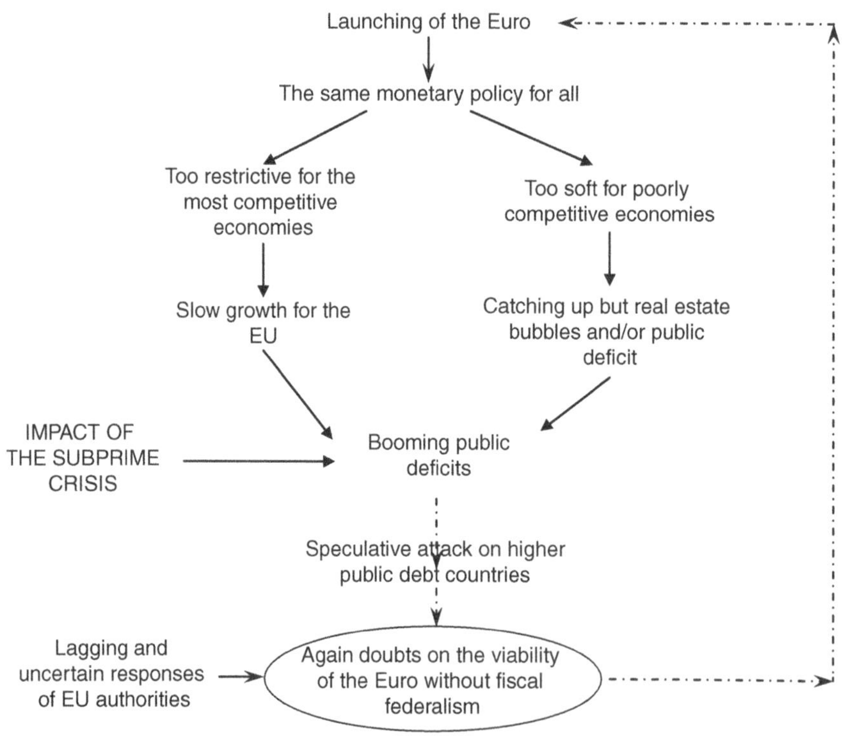

Figure 2.11 Financial speculation reveals the institutional imbalances of European governance in response to national differences in competitiveness.

been the next European public good to be implemented, especially after the failure to establish it at the world level, even after the G20 summits that followed the Lehman Brothers bankruptcy, when world leaders contemplated the possibility of a complete collapse of capitalism.

Lesson Seven: the ECB has taken the lead in the rescue of the euro but no other actor has the legitimacy and tools to develop an aggressive industrial policy at the continental level, a necessary condition for the viability of the euro in the absence of fiscal federalism.

9. Conclusion

This chapter argues against the principle of parsimony if the causes and specificity of the Euro crisis are to be elucidated. The structuring of academia, the retrenchment of polity with respect to the collective control of national economies, the progressive domination of global finance over the allocation of credit and capital jointly shaped first the rise and then the near collapse of the euro.

The neo-classical macroeconomics has convinced a majority of economists and politicians about the built-in stability of a market economy. Thus, the related economic models used to assess the impact of the euro were based on hypotheses that make any crisis impossible: the structural stability of macroeconomic equilibrium is only rocked by exogenous real shocks; the neutrality of high-powered money; full rationality of expectations; no involuntary unemployment and no bankruptcy, and last, but not least, the same model for all. This exclusive emphasis on pure and universal market adjustments disregarded two major stylised facts featured in contemporary capitalisms: the geographical polarisation of innovation and productive capabilities, on the one hand, and the primacy of financial globalisation, on the other.

Actually, it was a rather poor starting point from which to analyse a wholesale change in the economic policy mix and in the degree of autonomy of national "regulation" modes. The loss of monetary and exchange rate policies called for other instruments to be mobilised such as innovation and industrial policy, social pacts, or income policy. Some northern countries had already developed these instruments and they went through the Euro crisis rather smoothly. Nevertheless, others could not forge such a strategy in the eye of the storm. This gap makes the cohesion of the Eurozone problematic in the absence of solidarity and fiscal federalism.

Thus, politicians and macroeconomics have downplayed the heterogeneity of Eurozone members in terms of productive specialisation, economic policy styles, and political and legal conceptions. Furthermore, the deepening of the social divide between groups that gain from internationalisation and the euro and those who are afraid they may lose by it jeopardises the governability of domestic democratic systems by referring to rules negotiated at the European levels that are to be implemented whatever domestic public opinion may say, for instance, via a referendum on the European treaties.

The responsibility of financial deregulation and globalisation are deeply involved in the present turmoil. Most governments have been happy to remove from the political arena unpopular decisions in terms of capital allocation and economic restructuring. Initially, they feared that product and labour market liberalisation would strengthen economic constraints, thereby leading to slower growth and social protests, but the innovative dynamism and internationalisation of finance have removed the inter-temporal income constraints from households, firms and states. Furthermore, finance has entitled less competitive economies to enter the euro, providing instruments to hide and/or transfer the related risks. Lacking the political authority and will to enforce the excessive deficit procedure, the European entities (the Council and the Commission) have happily delegated this task to international finance. Hence, the irony of seeing first an extremely permissive finance and, then, an extremely overly pessimistic appraisal of the viability of the euro. This pathological pattern, typical of liberalised finance, has turned a local/limited crisis (Greece) into a radical uncertainty about the future of the euro and it has exposed the political and institutional limits of the European Union itself.

3 Convergence and imbalances in the EMU—the case of Portugal

Fernando Teixeira dos Santos

1. Introduction

The subprime crisis that began in the summer of 2007 was the trigger for a deeper financial and economic crisis, still unresolved. The intervention of public authorities to stabilise and rescue the financial system and to smooth the contractionary effects of the financial crisis deteriorated the fiscal position of governments in Europe and in other continents. The increase in public deficits and debts had specific consequences in the EU, particularly in the euro area. The reason for this is related to the weak coordination of economic policies within the EMU which, during the first 10 years of the euro, was unable to smooth the significant disparities among its member states in terms of competitiveness, potential growth and living standards. Imbalances remained and accumulated within the euro area generating significant surpluses in more competitive economies and increasing the level of indebtedness in less developed and less competitive economies. The emergence of the so-called sovereign debt crisis emphasised that the euro area was neither prepared to prevent nor to solve a crisis of this dimension. Markets became more averse to sovereign risks and reduced their willingness to be exposed to such risks in countries whose debt levels were considered to be too high and likely to become unsustainable. As a consequence, several euro area member states faced difficulties in obtaining the necessary financing under current market conditions and were forced to ask for financial support from the EU and the IMF. Adjustment programmes imposing fiscal targets and structural reforms were designed, enforcing very strict conditionality and surveillance on these countries.

Soft economic governance, absence of fiscal instruments aimed at crisis resolution together with slow policy reaction from the EU decision-making institutions contributed to the momentum of the crisis. The EU was slow to understand that the crisis was not a simple liquidity crisis, but rather a solvency crisis for which there were no instruments able to respond. Slow to understand the implications of the sovereign debt crisis on the banking sector and the build-up of a negative loop between them, spreading and aggravating the scope of the crisis. Slow to understand that, without EU fiscal instruments and policies supporting countries subject to the conditionality of adjustment programmes, there is a recessionary austerity bias in EU policy.

The contractionary effects of this bias jeopardise the achievement of fiscal targets, compromise the prospects for debt sustainability, and undermine the political and social support required for the full success of such programmes. The initial programme designed for Greece was neither successful nor credible. Greece had to restructure its debt and an additional financial package was needed.[1] Difficulties in the implementation of the programme are apparent, economic and social costs in terms of output loss and unemployment are high, risks of political and social unrest are sizeable, and there is the perception that it takes much longer than expected to meet the projected targets in the programme. Similar difficulties are being faced by Portugal. The austerity imposed under the adjustment programme caused an unprecedented recession with a sharp increase in unemployment. This recession has created difficulties in meeting the fiscal targets and public debt increased beyond initial projections. In the meantime, political and social conditions deteriorated undermining the support and the credibility of the programme.

These difficulties clearly point to the fact that within the EMU, there is a need for stronger fiscal institutions and policy instruments. Imbalances in some of the euro area member states are mirrored by imbalances of the opposite sign in other member states. This requires a coordinated adjustment policy involving all members of the euro area. Focusing on individual member states' adjustment leads to an austerity-trap situation that affects the performance and stability of the euro area as a whole and, ultimately, the credibility of its institutions.

In the following section, this chapter analyses the economic governance framework of EMU and its inability to promote the real convergence of its economies. The effects of the crisis on euro area member states is analysed in Section 3. In Section 4 the focus is put on Portugal in the context of its historical imbalances. The implications of the crisis in Portugal and the difficulties concerning the implementation of its adjustment programme are analysed in Section 5. A brief conclusion closes the chapter.

2. EMU, macroeconomic imbalances and the (dis) coordination of economic policies

The creation of the European Monetary Union (EMU) aimed at the establishment of a macroeconomic framework in which member states would benefit from higher nominal stability in their economies, and improved coordination and governance of their economic policies. This macroeconomic environment would promote higher integration of markets, namely financial markets, and improvements in competitiveness, growth, employment creation and the well-being of its citizens. Together with the nominal convergence required to launch the euro, the EMU was expected to provide for greater real convergence of the participating economies.

After ten years, this has not been the case. Figures 3.1 and 3.2 clearly show that disparities in productivity remained significant and that asymmetries in GDP per capita levels have increased between 1999 and 2008.

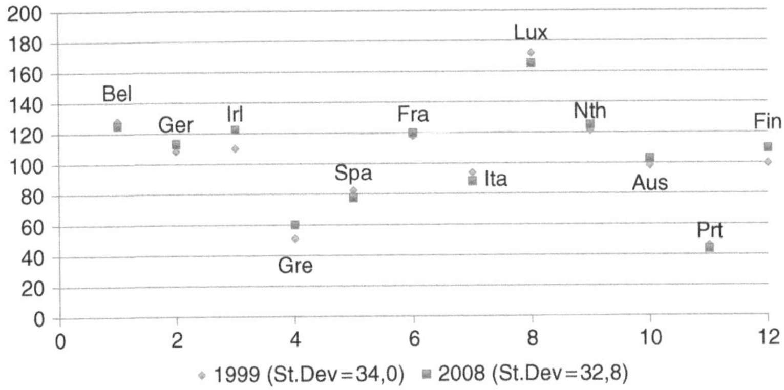

Figure 3.1 GDP per hour worked in the Euro area (EA12=100).

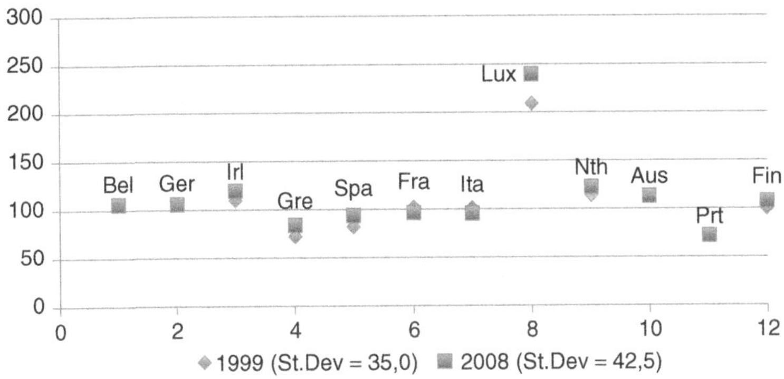

Figure 3.2 GDP per capita in Euro area countries.

Disparities among countries regarding competitiveness, growth potential, flexibility and competition in their markets, were not smoothed. On the contrary, they persisted, leading to important imbalances within the euro area. Figures 3.3 to 3.5 illustrate this fact, emphasising the contrast between the peripheral members of the euro area (Portugal, Spain, Greece, Italy and Ireland) vis-à-vis the other members in central and northern Europe (Germany, France, Austria, Netherlands, Belgium, Luxembourg and Finland).[2] The behaviour of the real effective exchange rate emphasises the difference regarding competitiveness developments. Peripheral countries, due to higher wage and price increases, experienced an appreciation of the real exchange rate, namely after the introduction of the Euro when they became unable to use the nominal exchange rate to offset negative developments affecting their competitiveness. The current account balance reflects the resulting imbalances within the euro area. While the peripheral countries accumulated deficits, the central/northern members accumulated surpluses which implied a significant accumulation in foreign financial assets and, thus, an increase in their net international investment position.

Such imbalances within the euro area would have required a coordinated policy response aiming at their correction. Surplus countries should have conducted more expansionary policies, and deficit countries should have promoted savings and structural reforms to improve competitiveness in their economies. The absence of an effective coordination of national economic policies in the euro area, together with the lack of national commitment, allowed for the persistence of those imbalances. Indeed, the economic governance of the euro has been asymmetric. On the one hand, there is a single monetary and exchange rate policy, but, on the other, there are different national economic policies aimed at national goals and subject to different national political incentives and constraints. The Stability and Growth Pact (SGP), with the imposition of rules and sanctions, intended to

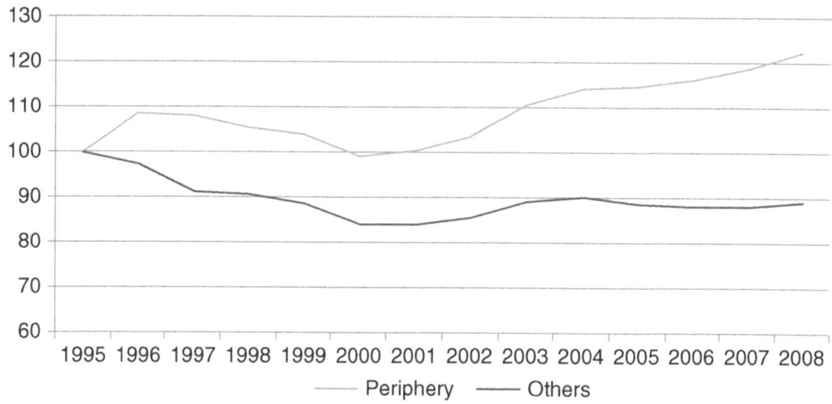

Figure 3.3 Real effective exhange rate in EA12 (1995=100).

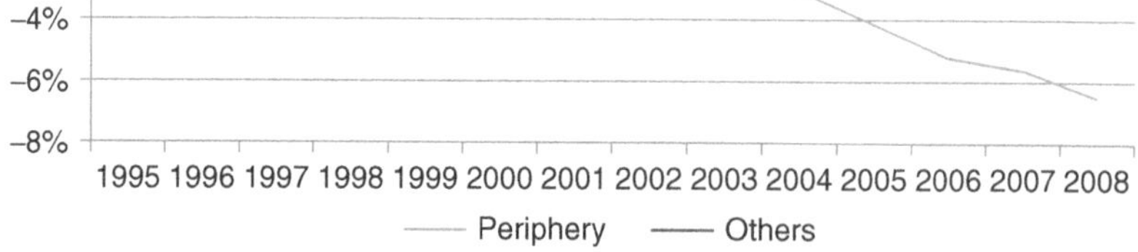

Figure 3.4 Current account in EA12 (% GDP).

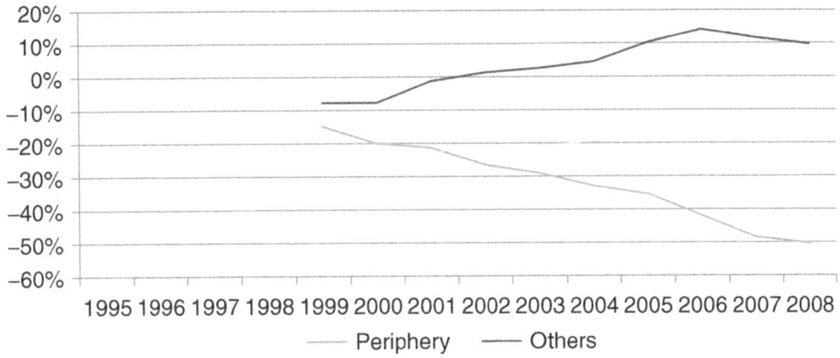

Figure 3.5 Net international investment position in EA12 (% GDP).

promote discipline in the conduct of national fiscal policies. But in what concerns other economic policies, coordination relied on a procedure involving recommendations to countries enacted by the European Council (Broad Economic Policy Guidelines). Under this framework, member states were subject to enhanced surveillance and pressure to meet fiscal targets. But that was not the case for other economic policies, namely, structural reforms to foster competitiveness, growth, and a more balanced Union among its members. They were only subject to soft coordination.[3]

Progress in the integration of European Union financial markets was important to the effective transmission of the single monetary policy to member countries. This integration eased the flow of funds from surplus to deficit countries. Markets were easy in lending to deficit economies and did not significantly differentiate among them. It is known that, when the Euro was launched, some of the member countries had public debt ratios well above 100% of GDP. However, the perspectives of improved growth raised by the launch of the single currency, within a framework of improved fiscal discipline provided by the SGP, made a scenario of default by any of its members very unlikely. Until 2008, interest rate spreads narrowed and were more the result of differences in liquidity of bond markets than risk differentiation among sovereigns.

External imbalances within the Eurozone were, thus, regarded as no big problem. Indeed, the balance of current transactions in the euro area, as a whole, has been fairly close to balance, although there have been imbalances among member states. The absence of peer and political pressure under the soft economic governance model of the euro area, together with the easy, and cheap, financing of the deficits in the weaker economies, did not generate the appropriate incentives for the promotion of the needed structural reforms. As money flowed so easily, some economies (governments and private sectors) were able to afford delaying such reforms. There was no sense of urgency in correcting those imbalances.

3. The asymmetric consequences of the current financial and economic crisis

The subprime crisis of 2007 was a trigger of a broader financial crisis with severe economic consequences. Due to deficiencies in risk assessment, to high leveraging of financial institutions and to regulatory and supervisory failures, financial institutions were exposed to high-risk assets which implied substantial losses and failures. Difficulties in assessing counterpart risks led to a loss of confidence in financial markets, a quasi-paralysis of interbank money markets, and a credit contraction with negative impacts on economic activity.

At EU level, authorities soon expressed their concerns on the financial and economic consequences of the crisis and defined a coordinated policy response.[4]

The coordinated response of policymakers aimed at the following major goals:

- stability and the recovery of confidence in the financial system. This involved initiatives to reform the regulation and supervision of financial activities, such as the creation of the European Systemic Risk Board, the creation of EU-wide regulatory authorities in the banking, insurance and securities markets, legislative initiatives such as Solvency II, the Capital Requirements Directive (Basel III), the creation of the Financial Stability Board, etc.;[5]
- solvency and access to liquidity of financial institutions. State money was made available for capital injections and state guarantees were provided as collateral for refinancing operations of banks. Central banks improved their cooperation aimed at the better coordination of their interventions in monetary markets;
- to promote a fiscal stimulus to counteract the recessionary effects of the financial crisis. This was the case, for example, of the European Economic Recovery Plan launched at the end of 2008, and the Recovery Plan presented by President Obama in early 2009.[6]

Public finances reflected these efforts together with the impact of automatic stabilisers (namely the fall in tax revenues). Figures 3.6 and 3.7 illustrate how general government deficits and debt-to-GDP ratios increased sharply between 2007 and 2009 in Europe and other major economies in the world. Deficits were, on average, aggravated by 5.7 percentage points of GDP in the euro area, 8.7 in the UK, 9.1 in the United States, and 6.8 in Japan. Greece, Spain, Ireland, and Portugal had an increase of 9.2, 13.1, 13.9 and 7.0 percentage points, respectively. The ratio of public debt-to-GDP jumped 13.6 percentage points in the euro area, 23.6 in the UK, 22.7 in the United States, and 27.2 in Japan. In Greece, the public debt-to-GDP ratio increased by 22.5 percentage points, by 17.6 in Spain, by 39.8 in Ireland, and by 15.3 in Portugal.

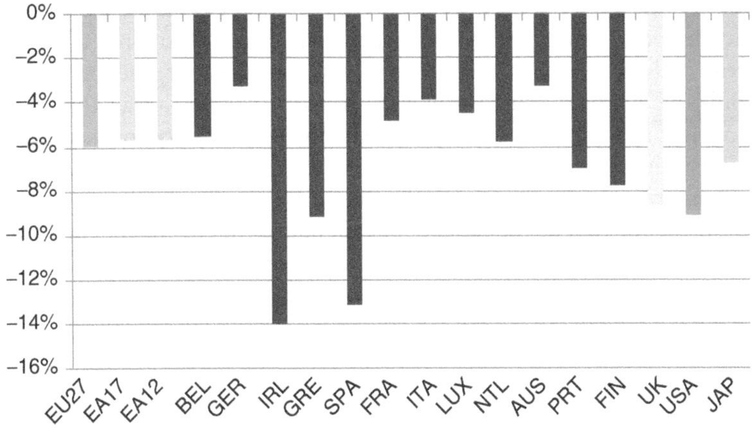

Figure 3.6 Change in general government balance 2007–2009.

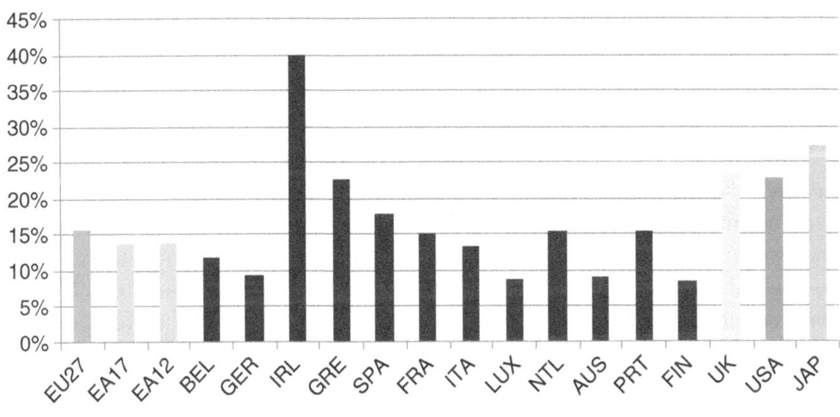

Figure 3.7 Change in general government gross debt 2007–2009.

When the Euro was launched, several economies had high debt-to-GDP ratios. In particular, Greece, Italy and Belgium had debt/GDP ratios above 100%. For several years, the absence of EU common fiscal instruments for crisis resolution, namely the absence of a lender of last resort, was not perceived as a problem. Apparently, markets believed that the monetary union, together with the integration of financial and monetary markets, would promote the convergence of their economies in terms of competitiveness and growth potential. However, the deterioration of fiscal positions in the euro area member states triggered a strong reaction from the markets[7]. With the emergence of the Greek crisis, markets became aware that, within the monetary union, without a lender of last resort and without domestic monetary and exchange rate policies, countries with high general government deficits and debts would not be able to correct their imbalances in a timely manner and to ensure a sustainable path for their public finances. Markets realised that the "no bailout, no default and no exit" trilogy foreseen in the treaties is inconsistent and believed that it would be broken. With the Greek crisis, it became clear that the EU, particularly the euro area, had no means to help Greece in the resolution of its crisis. Member states had to coordinate and to mobilise a set of bilateral loans to provide Greece with financial resources.[8] The conditionality imposed on the Greek authorities and the financial conditions of the loans in terms of maturity and interest rate were very strict. It was apparent that Greece would have great difficulties in meeting such demands in the given short period of time.

The perception from markets that the EU/Euro area was not prepared to respond to such a crisis, the perception that the rescue package for Greece could hardly be implemented successfully, compromised the attempt to prevent the contagion of the crisis to other member states, namely to those with higher deficits and debts—Portugal, Ireland, Spain and Italy.[9] Ireland requested financial assistance in November 2010. Portugal requested such support in April 2011. In February 2012, a second package was decided for Greece. Spain and Italy have been under market pressure, namely regarding the robustness of their banks. In mid-2012, Spain and Cyprus asked for financial support to recapitalise their banks.

An abrupt change in the markets' assessment and pricing of risk has occurred during the crisis. Markets started differentiating among euro area countries in a way they never did before. This is clearly reflected in the evolution of the spreads on the 10-year sovereign bond yields. Prior to the subprime crisis started in 2007, markets appeared not to differentiate sovereign risks across euro area member states. This differentiation became evident after the failure of Lehman Brothers, and became even more significant after the Greek crisis broke out (see Figure 3.8). Markets became increasingly concerned with the sustainability of sovereign debts. Spreads started reflecting the reaction of markets to the levels of public debt and to the interest rate/growth differential.

Figures 3.9 and 3.10 illustrate the relation between the average spread on 10-year sovereign bond yields, vis-à-vis the corresponding German yield, and the average debt-to-GDP ratio, and between that average spread and the average interest rate/growth differential in the euro area's initial member states.[10] The figures illustrate these relations for the periods from 1999 to 2007 and from 2008 to 2012. They clearly show the mentioned change in market behaviour.

All in all, the impacts of the crisis were uneven across countries. The crisis has been an asymmetric shock affecting the financial conditions of sovereigns. As monetary and financial conditions became highly differentiated across countries, markets were segmented, namely in what concerns the peripheral member states. The progress achieved thus far, regarding the integration of the euro area monetary and financial markets was destroyed. This

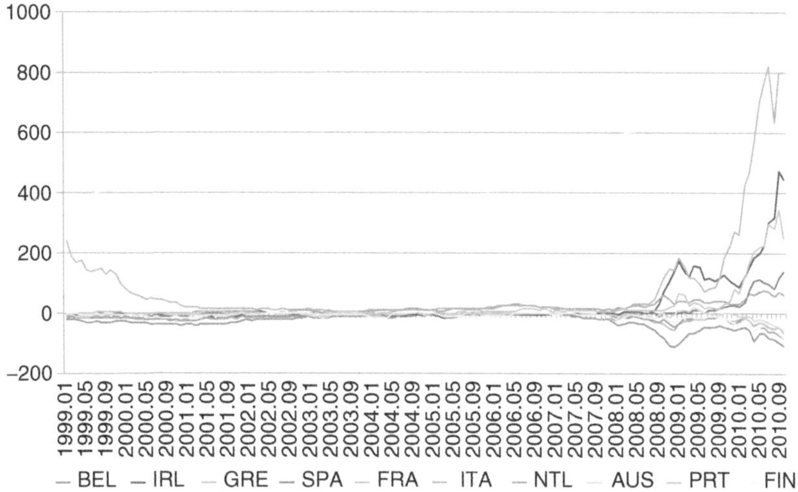

Figure 3.8 Monthly spread of 10-year government bond yields vis a vis the German 10-year bunds.

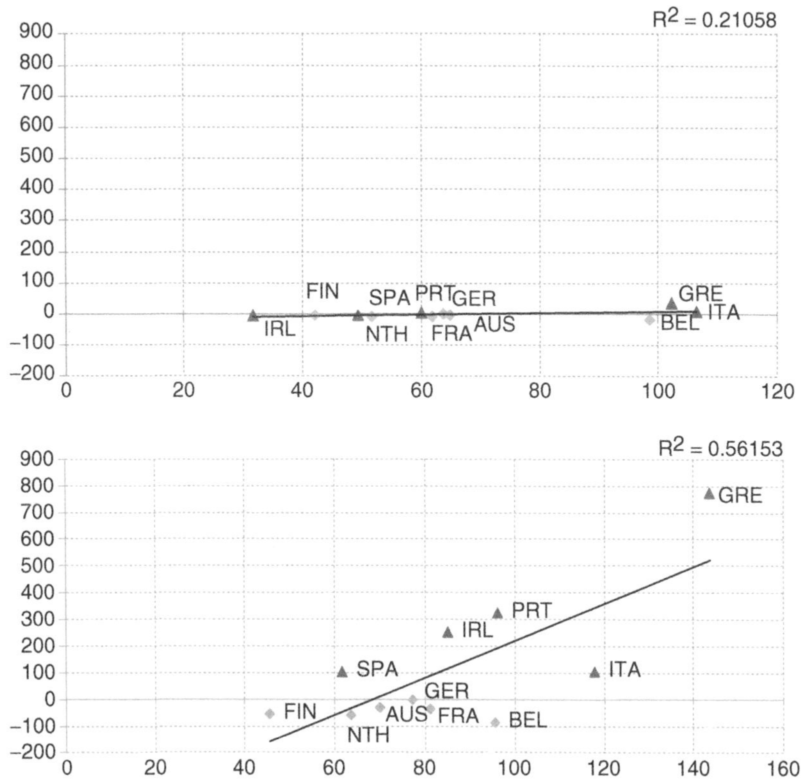

Figure 3.9 Debt to GDP ratio (x axis) and 10 year government bond spreads (y axis).

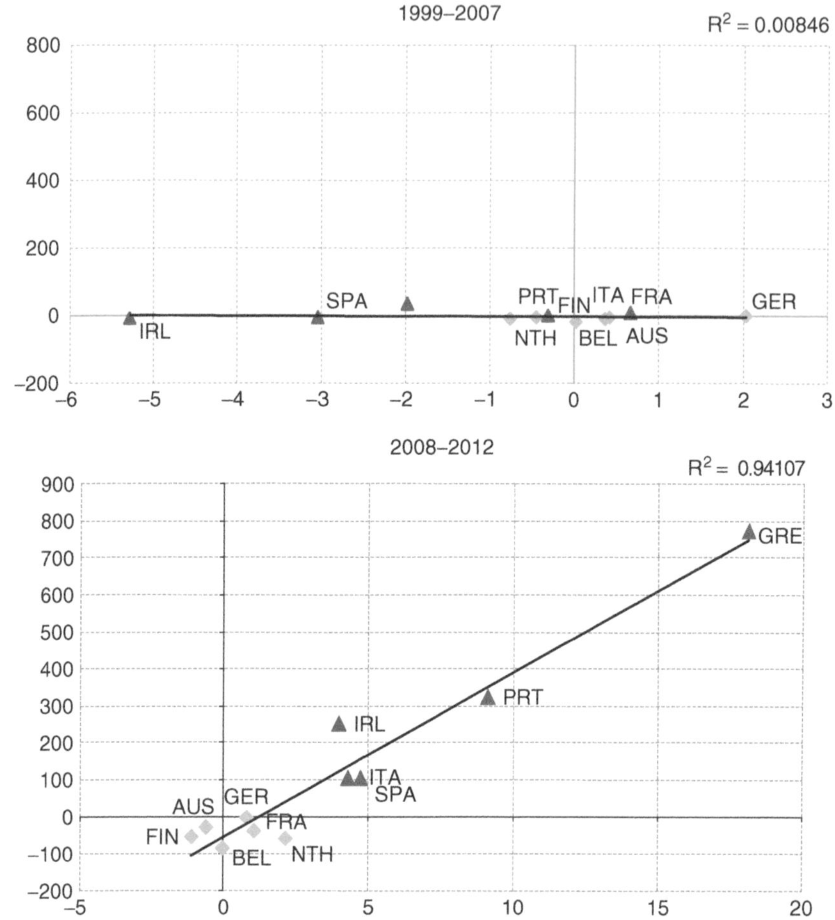

Figure 3.10 Interest rate/growth differential (X-axis) and 10-year government bond spreads (Y-axis).

segmentation has become a clear threat to the conduct of the single monetary policy because sharp differences among countries in terms of interest rates and liquidity jeopardise its effectiveness. This adds to the mentioned asymmetric effects of the crisis across EU member states.

Indeed, this should not be a surprise given the existing structural differences and imbalances in their economies, namely with respect to the levels of indebtedness. Eurozone economic governance was mainly focused on fiscal discipline. Asymmetric developments in competitiveness and growth among members have not been addressed as seriously as fiscal imbalances. The Stability and Growth Pact provided incentives for fiscal discipline, but as for competitiveness and growth only recommendations were issued. No peer pressure or incentives existed to correct such imbalances. Easy financing, soft euro area governance and lack of national commitment delayed the needed structural reforms to correct macroeconomic imbalances, improve competitiveness and foster growth. The case of Portugal is a good illustration of this.

4. Macroeconomic imbalances in portugal in an historical perspective

Since the reestablishment of democracy in 1974, Portugal has recorded significant macroeconomic imbalances. The collapse of the Bretton Woods fixed exchange rate system and oil shocks together with political, economic and social instability in the years following the April 1974 "carnation revolution" generated domestic and external imbalances in the Portuguese economy. Sharp increases in unit labour costs and increasing domestic demand, fuelled by expansionary policies and by the substantial increase of the resident population,[11] in the context of a more unstable external economic and financial environment, generated increasing deficits on the foreign current account together with fiscal deficits, high inflation, and increasing unemployment. External deficits originated sharp reductions on foreign exchange reserves forcing Portugal to negotiate two programmes of financial assistance with the IMF (1977–1979 and 1983–1985). Contractionary policies were then implemented, real wages fell sharply and the national currency (the *escudo*) was substantially devalued. With these policies, competitiveness was restored and the current account deficit was temporarily eliminated.

Figures 3.11 and 3.12 illustrate the developments in Portuguese competitiveness indicators. Figures 3.13 and 3.14 illustrate the major imbalances in the current account as well as in the fiscal position of the country for the periods before 1986 (previous to entry to the European Economic Community), between 1986 and 1998 (before joining the euro), for the period within EMU from 1999 up to 2007, and for the crisis years from 2008 to 2010.

Real unit labor costs increased sharply until 1976 leading to a significant appreciation of the real effective exchange rate. The two IMF programmes curbed real labour costs and the real exchange rate depreciated in the late 1970s and early 1980s. However, these programmes did not focus on structural reforms of the economy. Rigidities in labour, and goods and services markets remained and affected negatively the competitiveness of the Portuguese economy. Appreciation of the real effective exchange and external deficits remained during the following decades.

After joining the European Economic Community in 1986, trade deficits persisted, although lower than those recorded in the previous period. The high level of net transfers from abroad, namely remittances from emigrants and transfers from the European Community, helped by the inflow of foreign direct investment, allowed Portugal to face the needs of its external

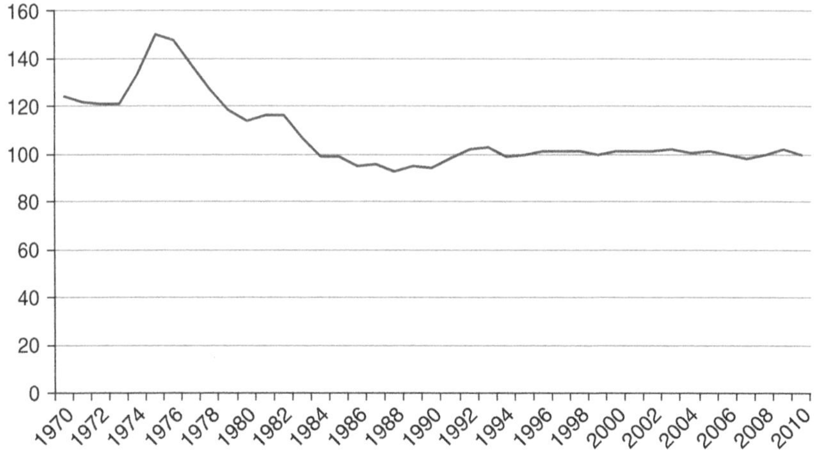

Figure 3.11 Real unit labor costs.

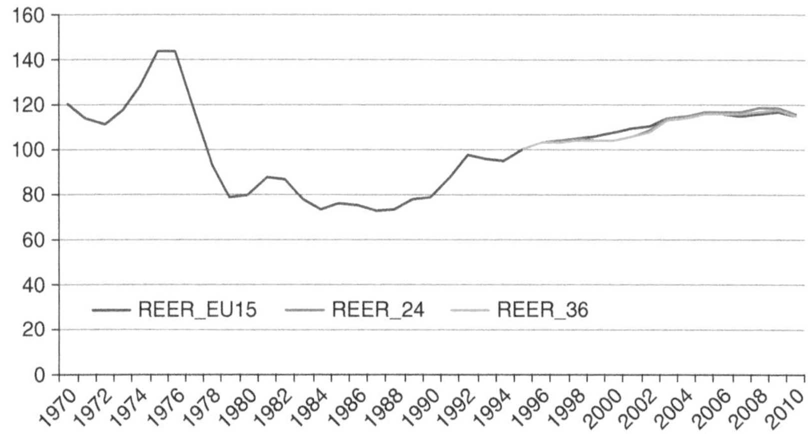

Figure 3.12 Real effective exchange rate Portugal vs. group of EU15, EU15+9 and EU27+9 other countries.

payments, namely until the mid-1990s, without substantially aggravating its external indebtedness.

The years following entry to the EC (1985 to 1990), as well as during the changeover years to the Euro (1995 to 2000), fed optimistic expectations on a sustained improvement in life standards. These expectations, together with the sharp decline in nominal and real interest rates, and the expansionary policies conducted during those periods, created an unprecedented wealth-effect with a major impact on domestic demand, namely consumption and savings.

Such expansionary policies reflected in the maintenance of high fiscal deficits in the 1980s and 1990s. Despite the discipline imposed by the Stability and Growth Pact since 1999, the average fiscal deficit between 1999 and

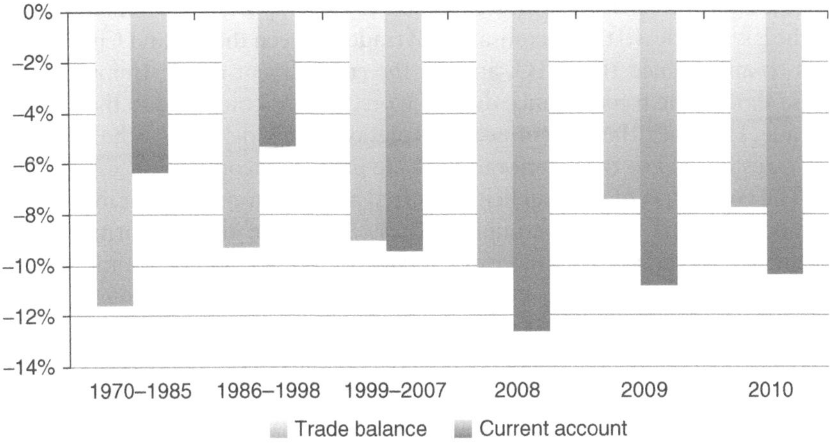

Figure 3.13 Current account (% GDP).

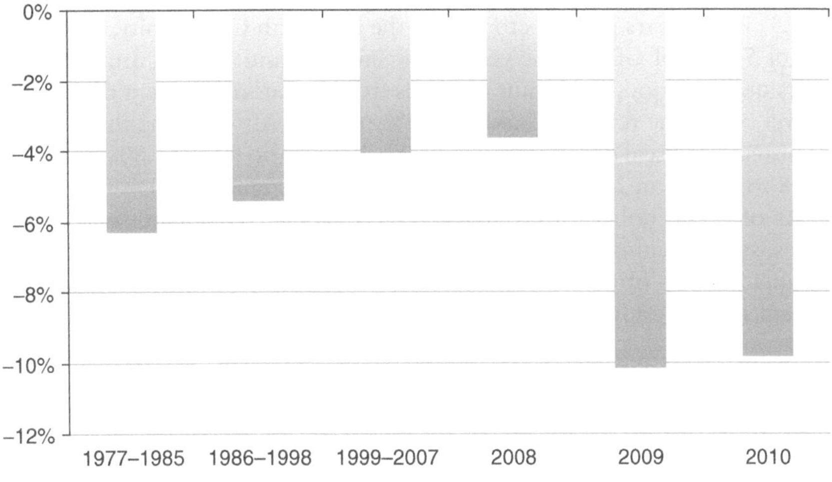

Figure 3.14 Portugal-budget balance (% GDP).

2007 was 4.1% of GDP. As of 2009, fiscal deficits increased substantially reflecting the impact of both the countercyclical policies promoted between 2008 and 2009 and automatic stabilisers.

Until joining the European Monetary Union in 1999, the devaluation of the escudo was intensively used to offset the negative effects on Portugal's competitiveness from increases in nominal and real unit labour costs above those of its partners. Since 1992, within the European Exchange Rate Mechanism, the use of exchange rate devaluations to improve competitiveness became more difficult and, finally, no longer possible within the euro area. Structural reforms to improve labour market performance and foster productivity became of utmost importance to correct these imbalances and to promote growth. In addition, after joining the euro, Portugal was subject to two important asymmetric shocks in the last decade: (i) the liberalisation of trade between the EU and China, when this country joined the WTO, and (ii) the enlargement of the Union. Despite these shocks, the trade balance did not worsen when compared to the previous decade. However, the current account aggravated its deficit due the decline in net transfers and to the deterioration in the primary income balance.

The correction of these deficits required a major improvement in the trade balance through gains in competitiveness. However, those reforms did not occur at the required pace, competitiveness did not improve, and current account deficits persisted, pushing Portuguese debt to increasingly higher levels. Indeed, in the context of the single currency, with easier access to pan-European monetary and financial markets, external imbalances reflected more and more in the increase of indebtedness. Private indebtedness increased sharply since the mid-1990s. From a level of 83.4% of GDP in 1995, private debt increased to 148.7% in 1998. When the crisis started, this ratio was 222.6% in 2007 and almost 240% in 2008. In what concerns the public debt ratio, the average of the public debt ratio increased from an average level of 32.2% in the years previous to joining the European Community, to an average of 54.9% of GDP in the years between 1985 and 1998. During the final years of this period, significant proceeds from privatisations kept this ratio at a level below the reference value of 60% of GDP. After joining the euro, the persistence of fiscal deficits ultimately raised this ratio from 51.8% of GDP in 1998 to 68.4% in 2007, and 71.7% in 2008 (see Figure 3.15).

As of 2005, policies were implemented aimed at reducing fiscal imbalances, strengthening the sustainability of public finances and improving the competitiveness of the Portuguese economy. Reforms in the social security system, in public administration, and in the labour market were implemented.

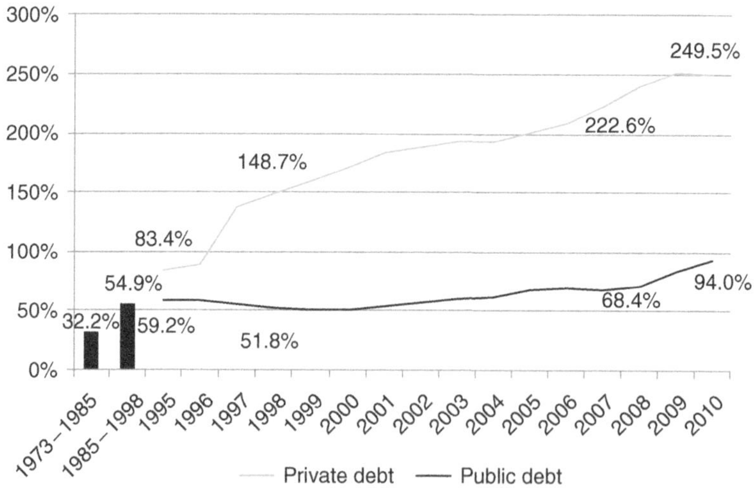

Figure 3.15 Public and private debt (% GDP).

Policies to improve the efficiency and effectiveness of the educational system, to foster research and development, technological progress and innovation were also implemented. The fiscal balance improved, the general government debt ratio slowed down, indicators on the sustainability of public finances improved, the appreciation of the real exchange rate was halted, and exports gained momentum.

5. The crisis and the portuguese/EU/IMF/ECB adjustment programme

The crisis that began in late 2007 halted the effects of these reforms and ended up having a negative effect on public and private indebtedness. The general government deficit increased to 10.1% of GDP in 2009 and 9.8% in 2010. In this year, public debt increased to 94% and private debt was almost 250% of GDP. As a consequence, the net international investment position of the country deteriorated to –107.2% (see Figure 3.16).

The impact of the crisis in Portugal is not surprising given the previously mentioned historical record of macroeconomic imbalances:

- loss of competitiveness during the two decades prior to the crisis;
- high current account imbalances;
- decline in savings and increasing private indebtedness, namely external;
- persistent fiscal imbalances, with negative effects on reputation and credibility.

These fragilities and the concerns generated by the Greek situation provided momentum to the development of the crisis in Portugal. Markets became more and more reluctant to be exposed to Portugal's risk and spreads on government bonds reflected these concerns (see Figure 3.8, above).

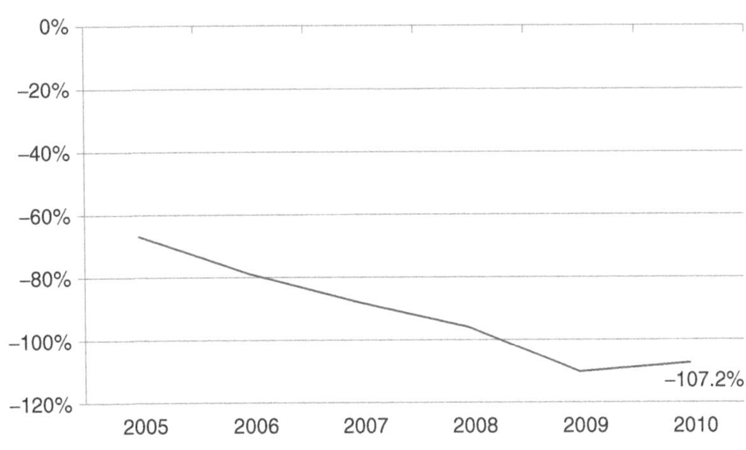

Figure 3.16 Net international investment position (%GDP).

The high pricing of sovereign risks imposed by the markets had a significant contagion effect on the financial sector. Banks have recorded significant imparities/haircuts on their holdings of sovereign debt with important effects on their profitability and solvency. Banks' ratings have been negatively affected, limiting their ability to refinance their activity and, consequently, constraining liquidity. The contagion of the sovereign debt crisis on the financial sector has imposed the need for banks to recapitalise and deleverage their balance sheets.

Portugal endeavoured to avoid the contagion effects of the Greek crisis. In May 2010, immediately after the "rescue package" for Greece was decided and the European Financial Stability Facility (EFSF) was created, Portugal announced more ambitious fiscal targets for 2010 and following years, speeding up the process of fiscal consolidation. Additional fiscal measures were announced and implemented. The budget proposal for 2011, presented in mid-October, introduced sizeable cuts in expenditure and increases in taxes to meet such revised targets. However, the deterioration of the Greek situation pointing to an inevitable restructuring of the sovereign debt, the demands of private sector involvement in restructuring operations,[12] and the rescue of Ireland in November, increased the pressure on the "next weak piece" in the ongoing euro area "domino effect": Portugal.

The Portuguese authorities intended to frame their response strategy within a "comprehensive strategy" to preserve financial stability that was being designed at the Eurogroup level.[13] In the context of enhanced surveillance, involving the Commission and the European Central Bank, Portugal demanded an assessment of its fiscal situation and the design of fiscal measures and structural reforms aiming to improve fiscal and growth prospects. The Portuguese authorities, with the cooperation of the Commission and the ECB, defined a programme of fiscal and structural measures intended to prevent the worsening of market conditions for Portugal and enabling the country to ensure its access to market financing. This programme had strong political support from the Commission, the ECB, and major member states. Once implemented, it would enable the ECB to intervene on secondary sovereign bond markets.

In March 2011, the Portuguese Parliament refused to give political support to the programme. Following this rejection, the prime minister resigned and an early election was called. The political instability resulting from these events, and the uncertainty it created in markets, implied successive downgrades of the country's ratings as well as of major banks. Obtaining the necessary financing under current market conditions became increasingly difficult and the exposure of banks to Portugal's risk became unbearable.[14]

On April 6, the government announced that Portugal would request financial assistance from the EU and the IMF. The programme agreed with the EU and the IMF will provide a total financing of 78 billion euros until mid-2014 and imposes very strict conditionality. Largely based on the rejected preventive programme, it defines a wide set of measures: (i) fiscal adjustment and sustainability of public finances, (ii) ensure the stability and soundness of the financial system, and (iii) structural reforms to improve competition, for greater labour market flexibility, to improve doing-business conditions and business environment, and to enhance competitiveness and growth in the medium/long term. The programme includes several institutional reforms on the budgetary framework improving governance, transparency, surveillance, and control of fiscal risks. Measures also target privatisation and deregulation of markets, namely in energy, telecommunication, and housing sectors, reform of the judicial system improving efficiency, and effectiveness of the court system.

The programme demands the deleveraging of the public and private sectors of the economy. Both the general government and the private sector—households, banks and non-financial companies—have raised savings and reduced their financial needs.

The fiscal policy's main targets are the reduction of the deficit to levels in line with the euro area medium term objective of a structural balance above –0.5% of GDP. In 2015, the fiscal balance target is –2.5% of GDP, corresponding to a projected structural deficit of –1.1% of GDP. Between 2012 and 2015, the deficit has to be reduced by 3.9 percentage points of GDP (2.9 percentage points in structural terms). This fiscal adjustment is of the utmost importance to ensure sustainability conditions for the debt-to-GDP ratio. According to the projections of the IMF/EU, assuming that real GDP growth recovers and reaches an average annual rate of 2% by 2020, so that annual nominal GDP growth will be around 4%, and that the interest rate on the public debt falls to 5% until 2017, the sustainability of the Portuguese public debt requires a structural primary surplus of 3% of GDP a year. Under these assumptions, the debt-to-GDP ratio will be over 110% in 2020 and more than 80% in 2030.

Figures 3.17 and 3.18 indicate the observed budget balance and debt/GDP ratio in recent years as well as the targets that have been defined for the next years. From 2009 to 2012, the budget deficit was reduced by 3.8 percentage points of GDP (a reduction of 5.3 percentage points in the primary balance and of 5.2 percentage points in the structural balance). In structural terms, the balance in 2012 fell short of the –2.4% target previously defined for the year.[15] This reflects the impact of the deeper recession on fiscal outcomes, namely on fiscal revenue and unemployment benefits, and the consequent difficulties in reaching the targets defined.

In what concerns the stability and soundness of the banking system, banks have been under a sizeable deleveraging process. Banks have improved their capital ratios. The capital adequacy ratio of banks has increased from 9.8% in 2011 to 12.6% at the end of 2012. The core Tier 1 ratio increased from 8.6% to 11.3% during that same period. However, deleveraging has had a negative impact on the flow of credit to the economy (see Figure 3.19). In the first quarter of 2013, the year-on-year growth rate of total domestic credit was –8.2% (–8.2% on credit to non-financial corporations and –4.0 to households).

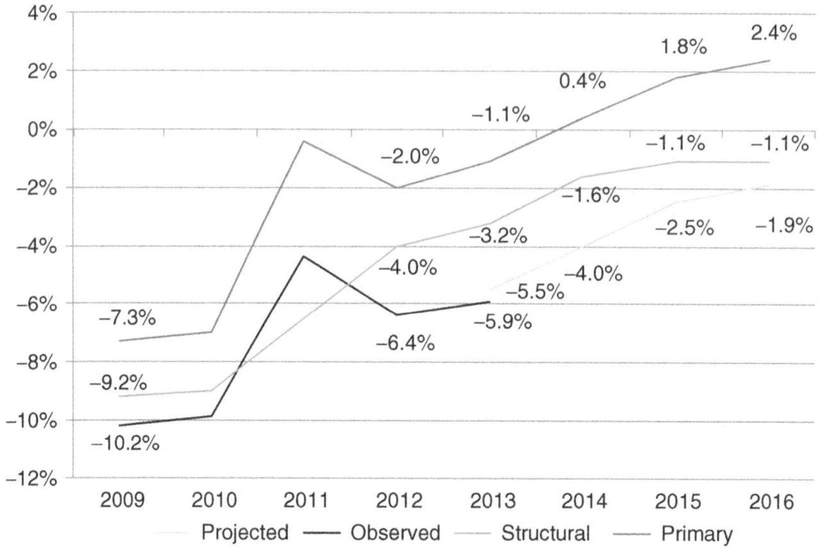

Figure 3.17 General government budget balance.

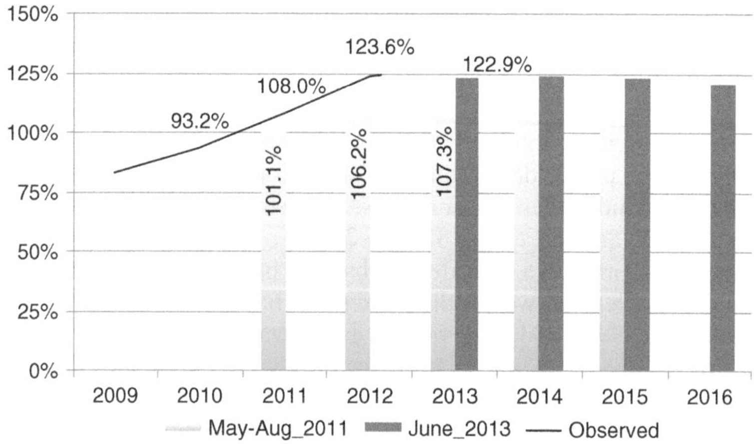

Figure 3.18 Public debt: observed vs. memorandum projections.

Fiscal policy has reduced government consumption and transfers, and taxes have been raised implying a reduction in the disposable income of households. The deleveraging of banks has been sizeable and has implied a decrease in the stock of credit. The effect of these policies on aggregate demand is illustrated in Figure 3.20. Private and government consumption declined as well as gross investment, implying the decline of domestic demand. On the other hand, net foreign demand has been fuelled by increasing exports and by a fall in imports resulting from lower domestic

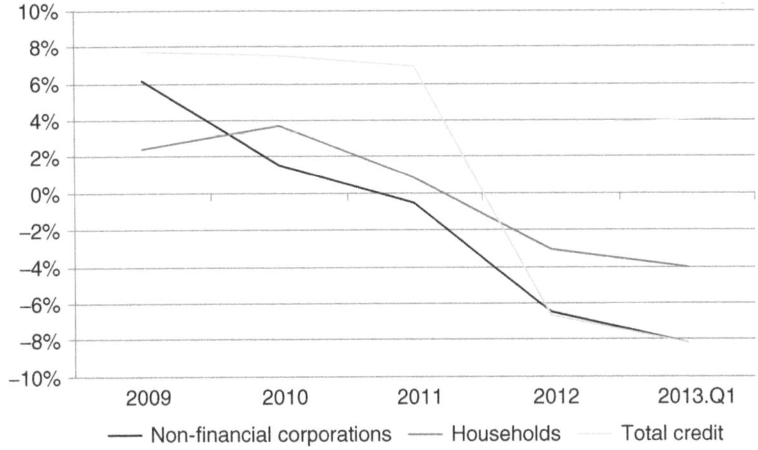

Figure 3.19 Growth of credit aggregates.

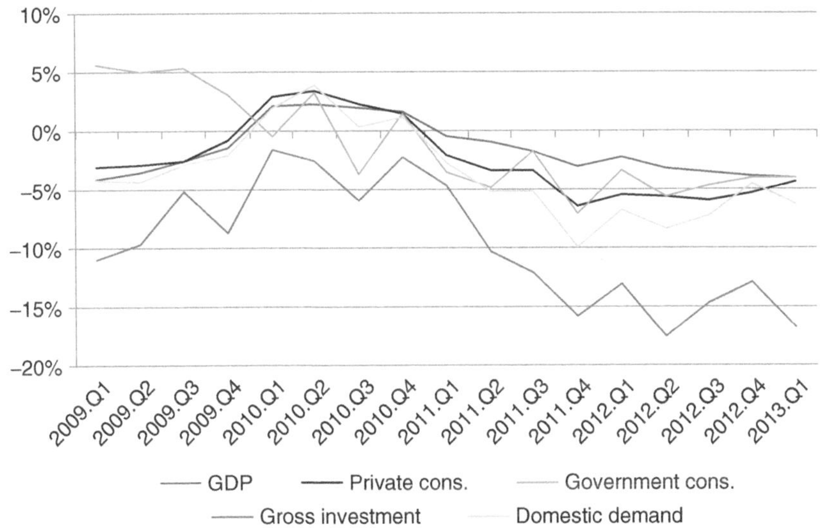

Figure 3.20 Ghange in GDP and domestic components.

demand (see Figure 3.21). This improvement in net foreign demand has not been strong enough to offset the fall in domestic demand, and real GDP has declined since 2011. As a result of the recessions of 2009 and 2011–2013, unemployment has risen sharply during this period (Figure 3.22).

Two years after the implementation of this programme, the costs are well perceived by the population. The ongoing adjustment under the conditionality imposed by the EU/IMF/ECB is accruing significant costs in terms of output loss and increased unemployment. The positive outcomes are not so perceptible yet. Difficulties in reaching the fiscal targets, reflected in its

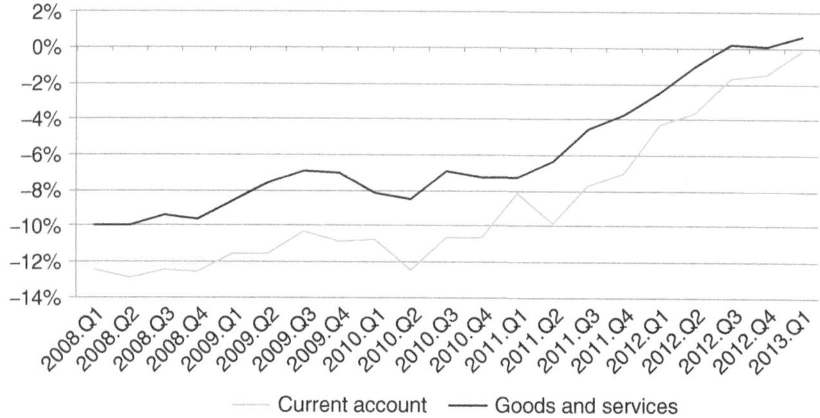

Figure 3.21 External balances.

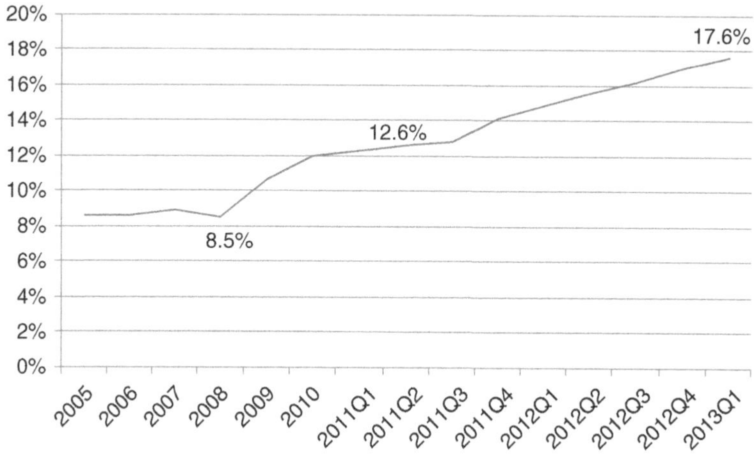

Figure 3.22 Unemployment rate.

revision and the extension of the adjustment period sustain the perception that austerity-oriented policies will remain, protracting the period of low growth and high unemployment, which is undermining political and social support to the adjustment programme.

The difficulties encountered in the implementation of the Portuguese adjustment programme clearly illustrate that countries with no national monetary policy or lender of last resort and unable to manage the exchange rate are forced into an austerity bias with high social and political costs. As long as they are part of a monetary union implying the delegation of important policy instruments to supra-national entities, they cannot be left alone bearing the costs of the adjustment. It is clear that this is a crisis affecting the euro area as a whole and its resolution cannot rely almost exclusively on national adjustment policies. The lack of euro area-wide policy instruments and institutions, namely on the fiscal side, and the absence of a lender of last resort is placing a high burden on member states. Progress towards a stronger fiscal pillar to support the euro is clearly the issue, unfortunately an issue and a challenge that EU politicians are not yet willing to face.

6. Conclusion

The European Monetary Union was unable to promote the real convergence of the euro area economies. The existing asymmetries among them when the euro was launched persisted or were even aggravated in the following years. As a consequence of competitiveness and growth disparities, macro-economic imbalances occurred within the euro area which translated as an accumulation of liquidity in surplus countries and an increase in indebtedness in deficit countries.

The economic governance framework of the Euro has focused on the single monetary policy and on fiscal surveillance and conditionality under the Stability and Growth Pact. It has neglected economic and structural reforms aimed at boosting competition and growth in member state economies.

The financial crisis had, consequently, asymmetric implications within the euro area. Less competitive economies, more indebted and with lower growth prospects, were particularly penalised by markets when confronted with the increase of their deficits and debts. Portugal was particularly affected by these events. For decades, competitiveness was undermined by unfavourable unit labour cost developments. Loss of competitiveness together with lower net transfers from abroad and higher net external payments of primary incomes have kept the deficit of its current account at high levels. In other words, national savings were short to meet the country's financing needs, and consequently, its level of indebtedness increased over time.

Persistent external and fiscal imbalances, lower growth prospects determined by non-competitive market structures and rigidities in the labour market, determined a negative assessment of the country's sovereign risk in face of the deterioration of the fiscal position occurred in 2009/2010. The change in the markets' risk pricing of Portugal slowed down the private flows of capital into the country, raising difficulties in ensuring the necessary financing under current market conditions.

Since 2011, Portugal has been implementing an adjustment programme, under the surveillance of the EU, the IMF, and the ECB, imposing strict conditionality in the conduct of national economic policies. The current account deficit has been so far eliminated and the structural fiscal position has improved. However, the prolonged and deep recession levied by the austerity-biased programme is keeping the country from achieving the projected targets. Increased unemployment and prolonged austerity is undermining political and social support to the ongoing policies. The implementation of the Portuguese programme clearly illustrates that there is a need for enhanced euro area fiscal instruments and institutions to overcome the current crisis.

Notes

1 The IMF has recently recognised that there were mistakes in the initial assessment of the Greek situation.

2 The aggregate values for the two groups of countries are a weighted average of the figures for the countries included, where the weights are the average share of each country GDP on the total GDP of the corresponding group over the period 1999 to 2008. On these imbalances, see Nils Holinski, Clemens Kool, and Joan Muysken "Persistent Macroeconomic Imbalances in the Euro Area: Causes and Consequences", Federal Reserve Bank of St. Louis Review, January/February 2012.

3 The EU intends to correct this situation, with the recent launch of the Macroeconomic Imbalance Procedure. For many years, the items in the Ecofin and Eurogroup agendas focusing on the surveillance of fiscal policies were those deserving much more attention as compared to those related to the Broad Economic Policy Guidelines.

4 "... *We agree to coordinate closely in our actions and to take into consideration potential cross-border effects of national decisions. We agree that public intervention has to be decided at national level in a coordinated framework.*" "*To protect the depositors' interests and the stability of the system, we stress the appropriateness of an approach including, among other means, recapitalisation of vulnerable systemically relevant financial institutions.*" *(Council of Economic and Financial Affairs, Luxembourg, 7 October 2008).* "*The European Council agrees on a European Economic Recovery Plan, described below. The plan will provide a coherent framework for action to be taken at the level of the Union as well as for measures adopted by each Member State, taking account of their individual circumstances. In line with the Commission communication of 26 November 2008, it is based on an effort equivalent in total to around 1.5 % of European Union GDP. It also envisages the initiation of priority action to enable our economies to adjust more rapidly to current challenges.*" *(Brussels, European Council 11 and 12 December 2008, Presidency Conclusions).*

5 More recently, major banks have been subject to stress tests and banks were required to increase their *core tier 1* capital ratios. In this context, banks, and the private sector in general, have engaged in a deleveraging process implying a slowdown, and in some cases, as in Portugal, a decline in the stock of credit to the economy. Presently, EU authorities are in a process to creating a banking union which will imply a single rulebook and a single EU-wide supervisor for major banks.

6 International organisations, namely the IMF, recommended counter-cyclical policies to promote economic growth. In December 2008, in the IMF Staff

Position Note "Fiscal Policy for the Crisis," Antonio Spilimbergo, Steve Symansky, Olivier Blanchard, and Carlo Cottarelli state "The current crisis calls for two main sets of policy measures. First, measures to repair the financial system. Second, measures to increase demand and restore confidence. While some of these measures overlap, the focus of this note is on the second set of policies, and more specifically, given the limited room for monetary policy, on fiscal policy." In March 2009, Charles Freedman, Michael Kumhof, Douglas Laxton, and Jaewoo Lee in the IMF Research Department paper "The Case for Global Fiscal Stimulus" state "Global fiscal stimulus is essential now to support aggregate demand and restore economic growth. The International Monetary Fund has called for fiscal stimulus in as many countries as possible, including emerging market and advanced economies." The OECD also recommended active policies to face the recessionary effects of the financial crisis together with structural policies to promote sustainable long term growth (see "OECD Strategic Response to the Financial and Economic Crisis: Contributions to the Global Effort," 2009).

7 Paul de Grauwe and Yuemei Ji (2013) argue that markets were led by fear and panic, pushing spreads to high levels and forcing countries to adopt austerity-driven policies with very negative consequences on their economies.

8 Curiously, in May 2010, on the same day the bilateral lending contracts were celebrated with Greece, Euro Area Member States decided to create the European Financial Stability Facility (EFSF). This was a transitory facility aimed at financing sovereigns with difficulties in accessing financial markets. In 2011, the decision was made to establish a permanent facility for this purpose, the European Stability Mechanism (ESM).

9 In October 2010, Chancellor Angela Merkel and President Nicholas Sarkozy, after a French-German summit in Deauville, stated that restructuring of sovereign debts would imply private sector involvement. This was a strong incentive for investors to move away from the sovereign debt of countries under stress.

10 Luxembourg is not included because until May 2010 there was no public debt with a maturity near 10 years.

11 Between 1974 and 1976, more than six hundred thousand people returned to the mainland from the former Portuguese colonies, representing a population increase of more than 6%.

12 These demands were coming, namely, from Germany, Finland, and the Netherlands and were supported by France in the already mentioned German-French summit in Deauville.

13 On February 4, 2011, the heads of state and government of the euro area and EU institutions issued a statement on this strategy. According to this statement, the strategy would include initiatives to reinforce the economic governance of the euro, stress tests and financial sector repair, the implementation of the European Semester and the following steps:

- Continued successful implementation of the Greek and Irish programmes.
- Assessment by the Commission, in liaison with the ECB, of progress made in Euro Area Member States in the implementation of measures taken to strengthen fiscal positions and growth prospects.

- Concrete proposals by the Eurogroup on strengthening the EFSF so as to ensure the necessary effectiveness in providing adequate support.
- Finalisation of the operational features of the European Stability Mechanism.

14 On the effects of the crisis on the private flows of capital see Silvia Merler and Jean Pisani-Ferry "Sudden Stops in the Euro Area", Bruegel Policy Contribution, March 2012.

15 These projections have been revised recently. The previous projections were more ambitious. In April 2012 (Third Review of the Programme) they were the following:

	2012	*2013*	*2014*	*2015*	*2016*
Budget Balance	–4.5%	–3.0%	–2.3%	–1.9%	–1.8%
Structural Budget Balance	–2.4%	–0.9%	–1.1%	–1.3%	–1.8%

4 We'll still be here in the long run—austerity and the peripheral growth hypothesis

Miguel St. Aubyn

1. More than a decade lost ... an appraisal

There was a time when economic growth in the European periphery was most impressive. From 1960 to 1973, Portuguese and Greek GDP per capita increased at an annual rate of 7.3 percent, and Spain only slightly lower, at 6.2 percent (see Table 4.1). This very high rate was only comparable to the other "growth miracles" of the time (e.g., Korea and Singapore) and much higher than average European growth, which, while very significant at the time, was 4.3 percent in the same period.

In this high growth convergence period, Portuguese GDP per capita increased from 42 percent of the (future) European Union average in 1960 to 62 percent in 1973. Greece would attain a historical maximum of 90 percent in 1978, with Spain reaching a peak of 92 percent in 1975.

This convergence pattern was interrupted in the mid-1970s. The first decade after the democratic transition witnessed major changes in the Portuguese, Spanish and Greek economic, social and political fabric. In Portugal, these included the nationalisation of the banking sector, later reversed, and of some major industrial and services firms, and two IMF interventions following balance of payments crises, and, in Spain, a complete transformation of a centralised state towards regional autonomy. In its turn, Greece entered the so-called "metapolitefsi" (regime change) period in 1974, after the fall of the colonel's military junta (1967–1974).

As part of what was generally seen as a kind of natural consequence of a democratisation process, Greece, Portugal and Spain were to enter the European Community in the 1980s (Greece, 1981; Portugal and Spain, 1986).

Greece was not to grow at a faster rate after European integration and divergence was the prevailing pattern until the end of the millennium. For the Iberian countries, however, entering the European Community, later the European Union was an opportunity for growth they did not miss. Access to markets, new foreign and internal investments, both public and private, fuelled by structural funding and compounded by a better-prepared workforce ignited a new convergence period that lasted until 1999. By the end of the millennium, Portuguese GDP per capita attained 70 percent of the EU average. The Spanish figure was significantly higher (just over 92 percent).

From 2000 to 2012, average GDP per capita increased at a very low (Spain, Greece) or even negative rate (Portugal) (see Figure 4.1). This includes several years of effective decline, including every year from 2009 in the Greek case. It comes as no surprise that these last few years are sometimes referred to as a "lost decade".

This period of "euro divergence", which coincided with the adoption of the single currency, is all but striking. It is a complete break with previous patterns and its full impact on expectations and economic agents' behaviour is still ongoing. In the following sections, we provide tentative explanations for this break to have occurred.

Table 4.1 Average GDP per capita growth rates

	1960–73	*1974–85*	*1986–1999*	*2000–2012*
European Union	4.3%	1.7%	2.1%	0.9%
Greece	7.3%	1.6%	1.2%	0.2%
Portugal	7.3%	1.0%	3.7%	−0.1%
Spain	6.2%	0.8%	3.0%	0.5%

Source: GDP per capita in constant 2005 US$, World Bank. http://data.worldbank.org; Ireland (1960–1999): AMECO database, http://ec.europa.eu/economy_finance/db_indicators/ameco/

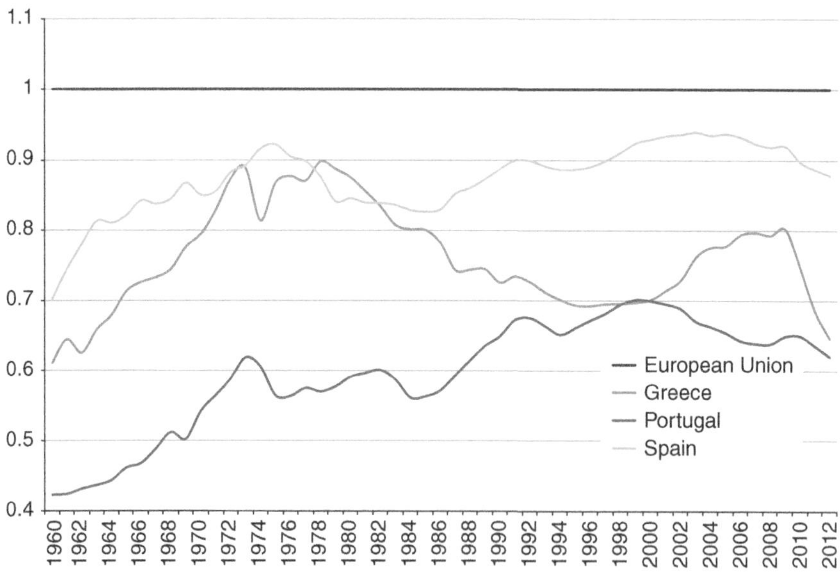

Figure 4.1 Greek, Portuguese, and Spanish GDP per capita as a percentage of the EU.

Source: GDP per capita in constant 2005 US$, World Bank, http://data.worldbank.org/

2. Why did we lose so much?

Adoption of the euro led to different developments in central and peripheral countries. In simple terms, one can associate central countries to those economies that had low interest rates before adopting the euro (Austria, Belgium, France, Germany and the Netherlands) and peripheral countries to those that had higher interest rates (e.g., Ireland, Italy, Portugal and Spain). Euro adoption led to a quick drop in interest rates in peripheral countries with macroeconomic consequences to which it would be difficult to react with the meagre available instruments.[1]

This evolution is illustrated in Figure 4.2 for the cases of Germany, Greece, Ireland, Spain and Portugal. The interest rates of peripheral countries converged to the German level at the end of the 1990s, Greece a bit later, and divergence from the latter was only evident with what would then be called the sovereign debt crisis.

One would expect from a theoretical analysis relying on theoretical general equilibrium models that such a significant drop in interest rates would lead rational economic agents to take advantage of more favourable conditions to increase their debt level. Consumption would increase and, on aggregate, the peripheral economy would incur in current account deficits that would pile up as foreign debt. In later times, of course, this would be reversed as debt is supposed to be sustainable. The impulse on aggregate demand in the peripheral economies would be consistent with a real appreciation.[2]

Real data is consistent with these theoretical insights. Figure 4.3 shows current account time series for Greece, Ireland, Spain, and Portugal. In all

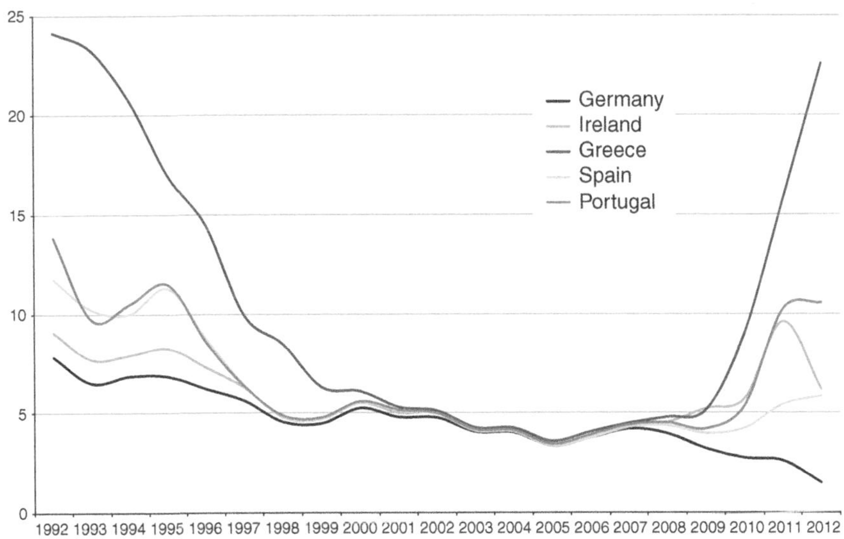

Figure 4.2 Long-term nominal interest rates.

Source: AMECO database, http://ec.europa.eu/economy_finance/db_indicators/ameco/

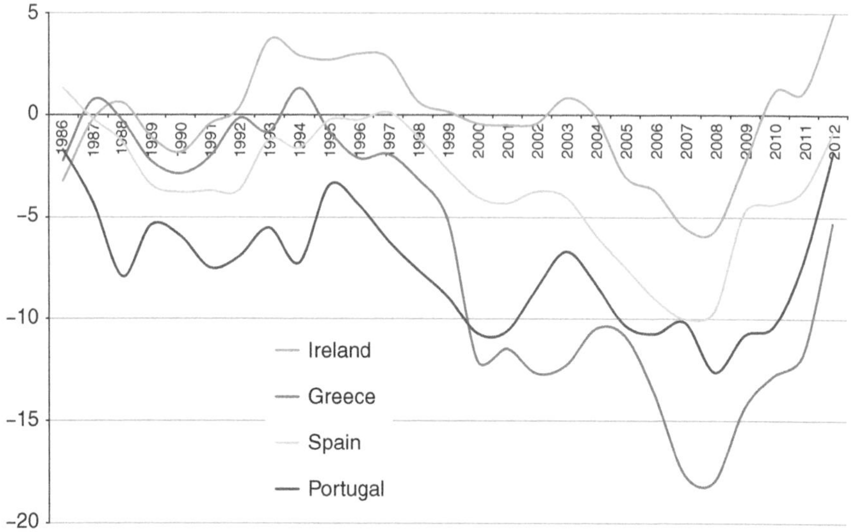

Figure 4.3 Current account as percentage of GDP.

Source: AMECO database, http://ec.europa.eu/economy_finance/db_indicators/ameco/

cases, it attained new negative records in recent times, only to approach equilibrium with the ongoing adjustment programme.

Figure 4.4 illustrates the real exchange rate time path for these same four countries in the euro periphery. In all four, substantial appreciations occurred after euro adoption (the lines follow upward trends in the chart). Interestingly enough, this real appreciation has been corrected more recently.

It is interesting to note that, while there seems to be some common patterns across peripheral countries, there are also some striking differences coming out of these macroeconomic data. Namely, Portugal differed from the Greek, Irish or Spanish case as its economy grew clearly less in the first years after euro accession (see Figure 4.1). Indeed, other than factors directly related to euro adoption, the 2008 economic and financial crisis and the sovereign debt crisis, the initial years of the third millennium brought on some additional difficulties for the Portuguese economy. This was a time of trade liberalisation, with stronger competition from third countries, including China, in the European markets. Moreover, the European Union admitted 12 new members—Cyprus, Czech Republic, Estonia, Hungary, Latvia, Lithuania, Malta, Poland, Slovakia and Slovenia in 2004, and Bulgaria and Romania in 2007.

Trade liberalisation was of particular importance for Portugal in what concerns the textile and clothing sectors, where quantitative restrictions on third country exports to the European Union imposed by the Multi-Fibre Arrangement were progressively lifted from 1995 to 2005 in accordance with the Agreement on Textiles and Clothing. According to Amador and Opromolla

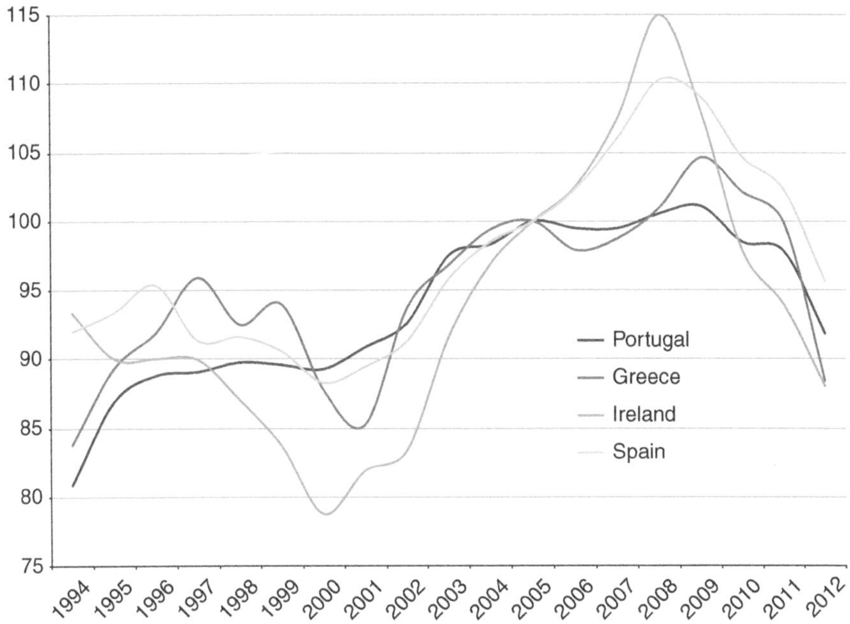

Figure 4.4 Real exchange rate based on unit labor costs.

Source: Eurostat

(2009), employees in textile and clothing industries declined from 11.6 percent of total employees in 1982 to 5.4 percent in 2006. Also, the same authors report that textile importance in industrial exports declined from 19 percent in 1982 to 8 percent in 2006, while clothing exports, after increasing from 11 percent in 1982 to 13 percent in 1992, were to decline to 4 percent in 2006.

3. The case for adjustment

Early life of the euro in peripheral countries was thus characterised by the loss of external competiveness, by high debt and, in the case of the Iberian countries and in particular in what concerns Portugal, by low GDP and productivity growth. These vulnerabilities on the verge of the 2008 economic and financial crisis were compounded by another one—the government budget front.

Euro area and some peripheral government deficits are compared in Figure 4.5. The purple line depicts the 3 percent threshold—deficits were supposed to lie below that threshold according to the European Union Treaty. The fact that in Greece or Portugal deficits were always higher than 3 percent in the period considered (from 1995) is striking in the figure. This was not at all the case for the Euro average, where the more meaningful breach (2009 and after) is the one ensuing and reacting to the economic and financial crisis.

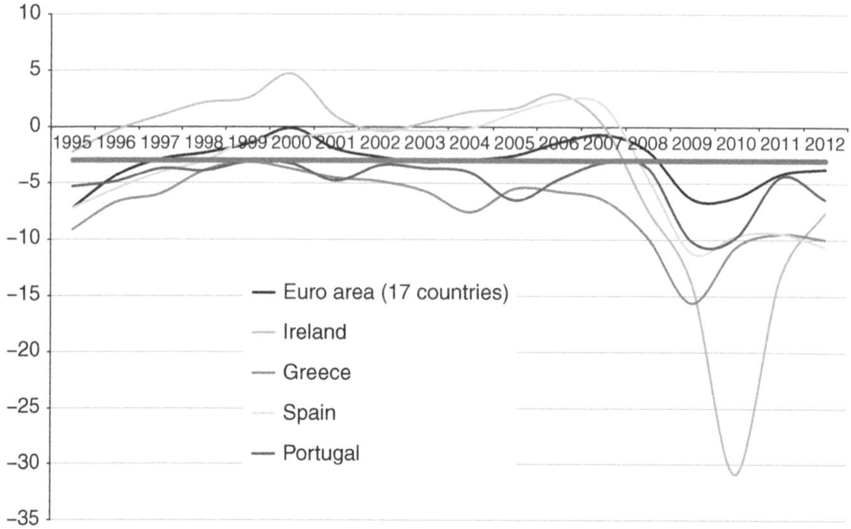

Figure 4.5 Government surplus.

Source: AMECO database, http://ec.europa.eu/economy_finance/db_indicators/ameco/

The impression of budgetary vulnerability of these two countries is reinforced if we observe how public debt progressed in the same period (Figure 4.6). In what concerns Greece, an already high public debt of around 100 percent of GDP entered an explosive path when uncontrolled deficits that reached more than 15 percent of GDP were coupled with strong recession. In the case of Portugal, a combination of low growth and deficits led to an increase in public debt as percentage of GDP starting in 2000. It increased beyond the European reference value of 60 percent in 2004. Its upward movement was accentuated after 2008 and has yet to be restrained. In its turn, Ireland, where budget surplus was the rule and with a declining public debt until 2007, has suffered a very strong decline in its budget position mostly due to the effects of the financial and banking crisis.

As is now well known, the 2007–2008 financial crisis amplified and propagated into the world economy at large. Credit was rationed, firms and families contracted investment and consumption spending, with wealth losses resulting from the price decline in housing and growing recession in stock markets. The economic crisis was, as expected, amplified across countries by the usual international trade channel.

Economic policy was to respond in an expansionary manner. Central banks cut interest rates aggressively, and governments adopted expansionary budgetary policies. In the European Union, the European Commission conceived a so-called "European Economic Recovery Plan", where a budgetary stimulus of about 200 billion euros (1.5 percent of GDP) was meant to stimulate aggregate demand. Deficit increases, well documented in Figure 4.5,

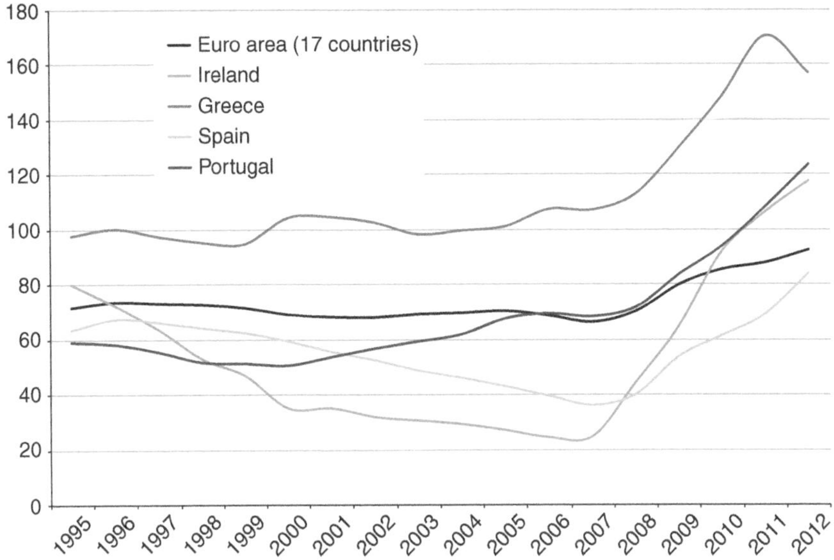

Figure 4.6 Government debt as percentage of GDP.

Source: AMECO database, http://ec.europa.eu/economy_finance/db_indicators/ameco/

were thus partly endogenous (loss of taxes due to the recession) and partly a consequence of expansionary policies.

In reality, the budgetary consequences of the crisis wrought dire consequences for some peripheral Eurozone economies. In April 2010, Greece, facing no credit in the markets, had no alternative but to ask for financial assistance from the European Union and the IMF. Greece was followed by Ireland (November 2010) and by Portugal (April 2011). The 2007–2008 financial and economic crisis had given birth to a new sovereign debt euro crisis.

Adjustment programmes rightly and inevitably emphasised fiscal consolidation, so that deficits and debt were to follow a sustainable path, ensuring a future "return to the markets".

Moreover, wage cuts were also to play a part. Internal devaluation, a replacement of exchange rate devaluation in countries lacking their own currency, would stimulate the production of tradable goods and exports by restoring external competitiveness. Public sector wage reduction was in this respect a double-edged instrumental—it helped to achieve a reduction in government expenditure and it induced private sector wage cuts.

Programmes also included a package directed towards banking and financial stability and deleverage, and another aimed at structural reforms.

4. Adjustment failures and the austerity vs. growth debate

The "austerity doctrine", as embedded in the Greek, Irish, and Portuguese adjustment programmes, has been subject to a number of criticisms. This author shares a number of them, and these are reviewed in the following lines.

1 ***Austerity adjustment programmes are designed without taking into account Eurozone architectural flaws***
i *the exchange rate problem*

As recognised from the beginning by many, the Eurozone is not close to what one could confidently call an optimum currency area. Some member countries have very different economic structures, namely the peripheral ones, like Greece and Portugal. This implies that the same monetary and exchange rate policy is not guaranteed to be suitable for all participating economies, and particularly for those in the periphery. Developments described earlier on the consequences of a low interest rate for peripheral countries highlight this aspect.

This could be mitigated if other adjustment mechanisms were available or worked properly. Wage and price flexibility is an adjustment device that would alleviate the economic and social costs of austerity programmes in a monetary union where currency devaluation is not an option. In fact, adjustment programmes rely on this type of adjustment, as the so-called internal devaluation, a surrogate for external or exchange rate devaluation, would be achieved with the proper changes in prices and wages. That is to say, nominal wages would have to fall to ensure the restoration of external competitiveness, and this would be less painful the more they respond to unemployment. Some of the structural measures included in the adjustment package are consistent with this view, namely those that aim to enhance labour market flexibility.

In a sense, the troika adjustment programmes take the Eurozone architecture as given and unchangeable, as an exogenous restriction that a country in dire straits faces. It could be otherwise. In a more encompassing view, the Portuguese, Greek, and Irish plight, as of other countries even some that are not under financial assistance, would be regarded as a manifestation of a systemic Eurozone problem. This would bring to the fore an important discussion on the role of European institutions, the European Central Bank but also the lack of its economic policy counterpart, a meaningful European Union budget, fiscal receipts, transfers and spending and a shared common budgetary policy, included. A drive towards more economic and political integration would give much-required meaning and counter value to the unavoidable sacrifices imposed on countries under adjustment.

2 ***Austerity adjustment programmes are designed without taking into account Eurozone architectural flaws***
ii *the European Central Bank problem*

As Paul de Grauwe (2011) and others have emphasised, the European Central Bank does not constitute a "lender of last resort" to Eurozone governments, differently from what happens in countries with their own currency. Those taking debt from the U.S., British or Japanese governments know that, in the event that any of these governments find it difficult to refinance themselves in the market, there is a very strong possibility that their debt will be monetised by the central bank—and they will be repaid. This is not so in the Eurozone, as the ECB is forbidden by the European Treaty to finance any government.

This design sets the scene for what de Grauwe and Ji (2013) call "panic-driven austerity". If financial markets are taken by panic, rooted in a generalised fear of not being reimbursed, then credit to a specific Eurozone government may suddenly shut down, and spreads increase in a manner not justified by economic fundamentals. In this version of self-fulfilling prophecies, governments will then have no other option but to ask for financial assistance and adopt austerity measures. These measures will then induce a recession that could otherwise be avoided.

To be consistent with this argument, the proper policy response would be to directly address the root of the problem and take immediate action on Eurozone fragilities, overcoming present asymmetries where only budgetary contraction policies seem to be allowed. Effective fiscal policy coordination should allow for solutions where some countries expand while others contract, therefore avoiding excessive spillover effects that can lead to the self-defeat of austerity (see Holland and Portes 2012; Eichengreen and O'Rourke 2012).

3 ***Austerity adjustment programmes are designed with underestimated multipliers***

There is growing literature providing empirical evidence on the idea that adjustment programmes were based on "underestimated multipliers". In other words, that the depressing effects of reducing government spending and increasing taxes were undervalued. Blanchard and Leigh (2013) present some evidence that this may not only be true, but also that multipliers may be higher when the economy is in a recession as compared to expansion times. In a report concerning the first Greek bailout (see IMF 2013a), it is mentioned that this could have been the case in that country. Also, a reason is mentioned for that to have occurred (i.e., for a deeper than forecasted recession)—the fact that structural reforms were either not fully implemented or that their effects show up slower than expected. In what concerns Portugal, some recent research also point to this asymmetry and to higher budgetary policy multipliers (see Castro et al. 2013).

These results have generally been interpreted as implying that adjustment programmes were too harsh and that a more gradual approach would have been more appropriate than frontloading.

5. The growth hypothesis

Consider the Portuguese case as an illustration of the relationship between growth and debt sustainability.

Figure 4.7 illustrates the prospective time path of Portuguese government debt under different hypotheses. Government debt, D_t, results from the accumulation of budget deficits, according to the following equation:

$$D_t = D_{t-1} - S_t + A_t$$

where S_t is the budget surplus and A_t some deficit/debt adjustments.

Budget deficits in each scenario are depicted in Figure 4.8. Government deficits under scenario A and scenario C correspond to the "troika" projections as described for example in IMF (2013b), i.e., 5.5, 4, 2.5, 1.9, 1.6, and 1.1 percent of GDP from 2013 to 2018, and 0.5 from then on. In scenario B, austerity or budget consolidation measures are more spread out over time and the corresponding time path is more linear in Figure 4.8. In this more gradual approach to austerity, a budget deficit of 0.5 percent of GDP is only achieved in 2021.[3]

We have assumed a constant interest rate on public debt equal to 3.9%. The corresponding primary surplus is depicted in Figure 4.9. Note again the more linear behaviour under scenario C as opposed to a more frontloaded approach under scenario A and B.

These three scenarios also differ in what concerns GDP growth, as is apparent from Figure 4.10.

Scenario A assumes the "troika" projected rates and a long-run growth rate of 1.8 percent. Scenario B assumes the same long-run growth rate, but the different pace of austerity is reflected in GDP growth, so that when

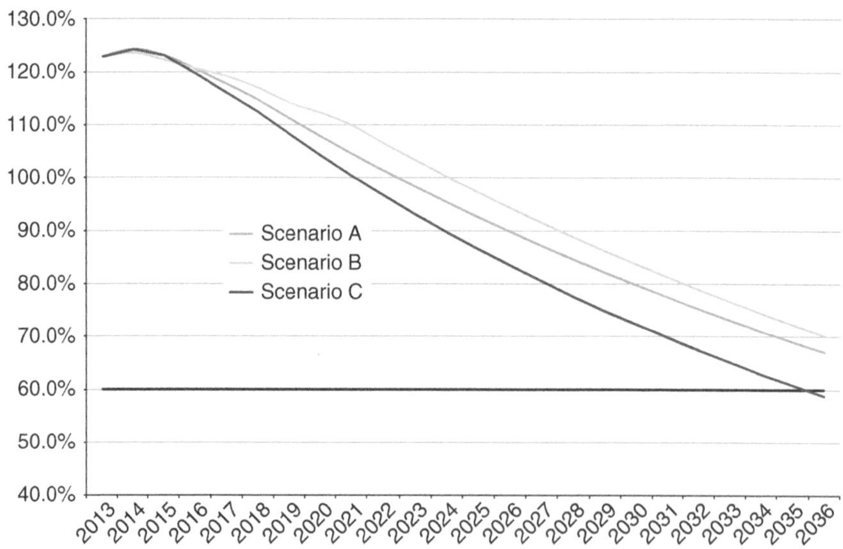

Figure 4.7 Government debt as percentage of GDP under different scenarios.

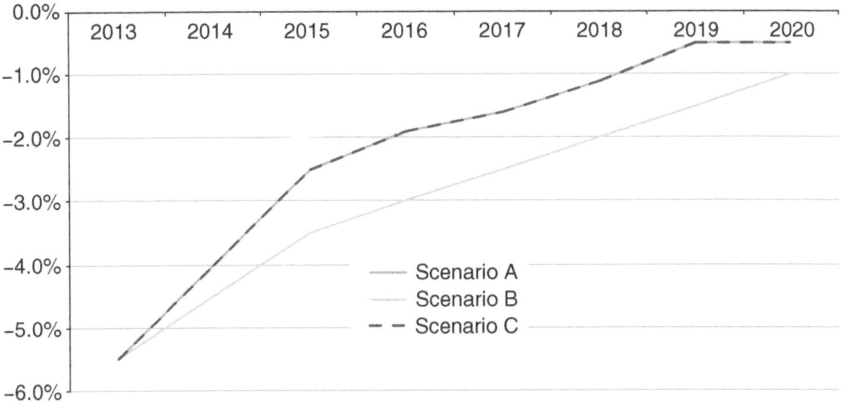

Figure 4.8 Government surplus/deficit as percentage of GDP under different scenarios.

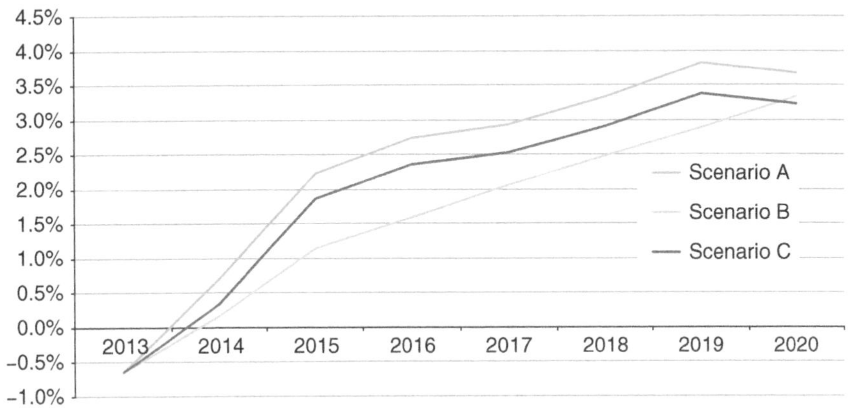

Figure 4.9 Primary surplus/deficit as percentage of GDP under different scenarios.

deficit reduction is larger (smaller), output growth will be below (above) that of scenario A, with an assumed value for the multiplier equal to 2.[4]

Under scenario C we assume a higher long-run growth rate of 2.5 percent. This is the only difference between scenario A and C.

The different government debt time paths (Figure 4.7) suggest the following important points.

1 ***Reducing the pace of austerity does not come without a price***

When comparing the yellow line to the green one in Figure 4.7, it can be concluded that the debt-to-GDP ratio is smaller in the gradual approach (scenario B) only until 2016. This is due to a higher GDP. However, the effect of a higher accumulation of debt is felt from then on, the ratio being consistently above the troika baseline. The difference between the two would be at its

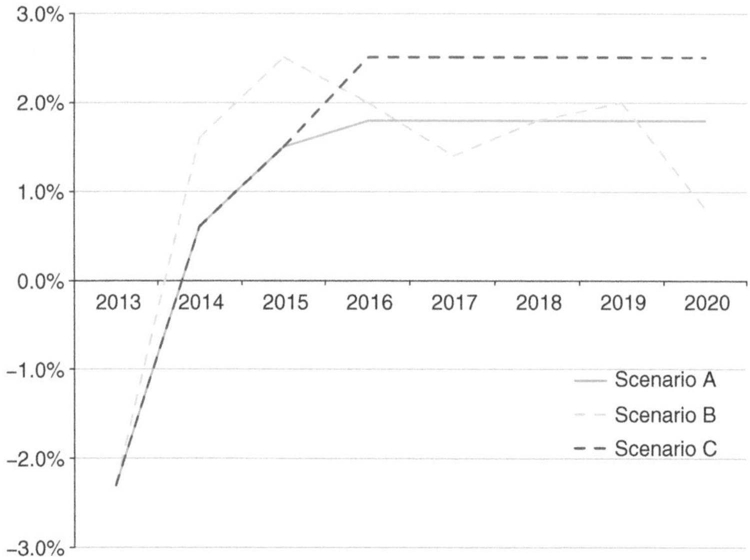

Figure 4.10 GDP real growth rates under different scenarios.

highest in 2023—in scenario B debt-to-GDP would be 103.3 percent whereas in scenario A it would be 98.3 percent. Clearly there is here a trade-off between short-run gains in GDP and employment versus a higher debt in the long run.

2 *The long-run growth rate matters*

That the long-run growth rate matters is evident when one compares scenario C to scenario A. In scenario C the long-run growth rate equals 2.5 percent, which is only slightly higher than 1.8 percent, the imbedded value in scenario A. This difference in growth equal to 0.7 percent per year leads to an 8.4 percent of GDP smaller ratio in 2036, when under the relatively high growth scenario, the 60 percent threshold is finally crossed. As a comparison, this threshold would be crossed in 2041 only in scenario A.

These simulations illustrate the important link between debt sustainability and growth. Above, we basically showed that higher growth greatly helps sustainability. However, there is arguably a link from sustainability to growth, and this idea underlines the Greek, Portuguese, or Irish adjustment programmes. In a nutshell, unsustainable public finances lead to a lack of financing, to a slump in consumption and investment, and to diminished growth prospects and expectations. Only restoring sustainability would therefore allow higher growth.

If we give some credit to both links; that is, the idea that sustainability is a pre-condition for growth and that growth itself ensures sustainability, we will have to adopt some sort of "adjustment with growth framework". Adjustment programmes in the Eurozone were designed with a complete focus on supply conditions and on structural reforms, while disregarding demand conditions, particularly at the European level. Some of those structural reforms, or at least their motivation, have more widespread support than others, as for example increasing competition, particularly in the non-tradable part of the economy, or achieving more efficiency in the public sector, whether in the health, education or the justice sectors. The main disagreement here seems to be that the dominant thought assumes too often that efficiency is to be achieved by cutting the resources available to a specific activity, without sufficient emphasis on reorganisation, which sometimes necessarily implies some public investment.

But probably the more important point concerning adjustment and growth concerns the fact that the adjustment programme was not properly contextualised in the European framework. The imbalances of the Portuguese economy are in many essential aspects shared by other peripheral economies in the euro area. They did not result simply from misplaced behaviour in the face of not completely understood new circumstances. On the contrary, they ensued from logical and even predictable reactions of economic agents to the incentives with which they were confronted. In fact, architectural flaws in the euro area are the deeper causes of the building's instability. A government that issues euro denominated debt and does not own a central bank cannot completely ensure that their obligations will be paid. This fact leads to speculative market movements that target countries "under suspicion" but not necessarily insolvent. As a consequence, austerity programmes like the ones we have come to know ensue, promoting an asymmetric adjustment of imbalances. To overcome these failures would imply important structural reforms in the Eurozone in what concerns the institutional structure and lead to a greater political union. In a wider view, adjustment programmes like those of Portugal, Greece or Ireland would be part of other important changes in the European Union, and this would give them some new meaning and more positive expectations would probably prevail.

Notes

1 Although it can be argued that expansionary budgetary policies exacerbated the interest rate shock consequences. See Gaspar and St. Aubyn (2009).

2 See Fagan and Gaspar (2008) and Gaspar and St. Aubyn (2009) for some analysis of this kind.

3 Albeit differently formulated, these scenarios benefited from discussions of the author with Paulo Trigo Pereira and other colleagues in the ISEG project "Budget Watch".

4 A value that seems plausible according to recent research (see Lopes de Castro et al. (2013)).

5 The euro crisis and the failure of the Lisbon strategy

Bengt-Åke Lundvall and Edward Lorenz

1. Introduction

When the Lisbon Strategy was launched during the Portuguese presidency it was in an era of optimism. The major problem to be tackled by the strategy was that Europe seemed to be less dynamic then the United States in terms of economic growth and job creation. Ten years later, when the European Commission published the new 10-year strategy for Europe, EUROPE 2020, the world looks quite different and Europe is in deep trouble.[1]

The financial crisis has demonstrated that the common currency that should offer stability to the countries that joined the Eurozone has become a major burden especially for countries south of Europe. In this chapter we show that there is a huge gap between how people work and learn in different parts of the Eurozone and that it constitutes one of the Eurozone's fundamental weaknesses. We argue that the original version of the Lisbon Strategy with its emphasis on the quality of jobs and on social cohesion could have helped to close this gap. But these elements were given less weight halfway through the strategy period when the perspective became narrowly focused on employment and economic growth.

In the wake of the financial crisis and the Euro-crisis, the real governance of the European Union has changed. Germany has taken on a clear leading position and sets a new agenda for Europe where the road back to economic growth for each of the member states should be stronger 'international competitiveness', For Spain, Portugal, Italy and Greece, as members of the Eurozone, this has meant mass unemployment, 'internal devaluation' in the form of lower real wages and a much less ambitious welfare state.

This chapter shows how the crisis and the crisis strategy have together increased inequality within the Eurozone both at the country level and between the north and the south of Europe. All that is left of the original Lisbon strategy is a neoliberal consensus on 'structural reform'. The long-term result is a clear decline in the quality of jobs across Europe and long-term mass unemployment in the south of Europe. The predominance of supply-side economics and the fear of what 'the market' may do to the European interest rate(s) have hindered the European Community from engaging in an active and cohesive response to the crisis.

It should be obvious that there is a need for a more ambitious and coordinated response to the crisis with a focus on strengthening knowledge creation and learning in the south. Education systems that mix and give equal weight to practical training and theoretical education and labour markets that combine flexibility with security are elements that would contribute to the 'structural competitiveness' of these countries. This could be stimulated by a kind of Marshall Plan for Europe where the transfer of funds from the north to the south would be combined with different kinds of structural reforms than normally envisaged by the IMF and the European Commission.

Section 2 discusses the new context for Europe in terms of a globalising learning economy, providing a mapping of how Europe's economies work and learn, and illustrating how income equality and inequality in access to learning relate to the uneven development of building competitiveness in the south and the north of Europe. Section 3 analyses how the Lisbon strategy contributed to objectives such as employment, social cohesion, and knowledge-based economic growth. Data is presented showing how inequality has been growing and the quality of work has been deteriorating in Europe during the crisis. Section 4 considers the relation between the European employment strategy and the monetary union. Section 5 concludes by discussing why Europe needs a different vision than that offered in EU2020 and why the 2011 'competitiveness strategy' is counter-productive and does not address the underlying structural problems of the Eurozone.

2. Europe in the globalising learning economy—How Europeans work and learn

Introducing the globalising learning economy

In the Lisbon Strategy, the references to a knowledge-based economy played an important role in signalling a new era where competitiveness requires investments in education and in research. Here as elsewhere we propose that it is more appropriate to define the current era as a globalising learning economy (Archibugi and Lundvall, 2001).

The concept of 'a learning economy' refers to a specific phase of capitalist development where a combination of factors such as globalisation, deregulation of finance, and the widespread use of information and communication technologies *speeds up the rate of change* in different dimensions. This is reflected in more rapid communication of information, shorter life cycles for new products and, not least, in a rapid change in the demand for skills and knowledge (Lundvall and Johnson, 1994).

While the term 'knowledge-based economy' refers to the growing importance of investment in knowledge, the learning economy concept signals that knowledge becomes obsolete more rapidly than before. Therefore, it is imperative for firms to engage in organisational learning and for workers to constantly engage in attaining new competencies.[2]

The learning economy is characterised by cumulative circular causation. The selection by employers of more learning-prone employees and market selection in favour of change-oriented firms accelerate further innovation and change. In this context, the key to economic success for a national or regional economy is its capacity to renew competencies in order to be able to move into activities that are less exposed to global competition based on low wages or cost-cutting measures. In the next section, we show that the opportunities employees have for learning in their daily work are unevenly distributed across the member states of the European Monetary Union.

International competitiveness in the learning economy

International competitiveness has become a key concept in the current European strategy. This is reflected in the 'competitiveness pact' that Merkel has imposed on the European Union. It is a devious concept. It applies a perspective used to understand how business enterprises compete with each other in the national economy. When a business enterprise has strong competitiveness it earns more money and grows more quickly than its competitors. Strong competitiveness may be the outcome of a successful management strategy.

At the national level, competitiveness has been linked mainly to export and import market shares and to the balance of payment. When export market shares of domestic firms increase and exports grow more than imports it is said that the competitiveness of the whole economy has become stronger. Different processes may lead to a stronger export performance.

Often the focus is on the costs of production and especially on how the national wage level develops in international comparisons. It is assumed, on the basis of a ceteris paribus argument, that a stronger growth in wages will raise costs and thereby lead to difficulties in selling commodities and services in international competition. Employers' organisations often use such a narrow definition of competitiveness as an argument for wage restraint.

But it is obvious that some of the countries that have been most successful in terms of export-led growth have been characterised by rapid growth in real wages. In Kaldor (1978), the relationship between wage increases and export growth was shown to move in parallel. This so-called Kaldor's paradox means that the value of export in the long run will reflect more effective production and more attractive products. Developing and making use of new products and processes will require increasingly high-quality research, education, organisational learning and management.

In the learning economy, the institutional setting and the organisation of the economy at different levels are crucial for economic performance. The most important institutions are those that shape and motivate people and those that shape their relationships with each other. In a primitive factory-like organisation, where workers pursue trivial tasks, management may be based on simple economic incentives such as payment per piece produced combined with detailed control of workers' time and negative sanctions for those who do not give their best.

As we are going to see below, most workplaces in Europe do not correspond to such a model of simple work. Therefore, it is highly problematic that the current strategy focused on competitiveness operates within such a narrow definition and that the macroeconomic strategy regards the workforce as a homogenous mass. 'The quality of jobs' is fundamental for work productivity and for international competitiveness but it is neglected by the macroeconomists who are in charge of the design of national competitiveness strategies.

Mapping forms of work organisation in Europe

Before the crisis, it was widely accepted that competition is knowledge based and that governments need to invest in knowledge through formal education and research. Differences in national efforts in this regard are well documented and attempts are made to use lead countries as benchmarks. But there is no corresponding attention paid to workplace learning. This is problematic since in the learning economy, the skill formation that takes place at the workplace is crucial for economic performance. And, as we shall see, international differences are huge even within Europe.

Lorenz and Valeyre (2005) and Arundel et al. (2007) develop an EU-wide mapping of the adoption of different types of work organisation. Drawing on the results of the Third European Working Conditions Survey,[3] cluster analysis is used to identify four different systems of work organisation:

discretionary learning (DL)
lean production
Taylorist organisation
traditional/simple organisation.

The two most important dimensions used to distinguish between them are, respectively, problem solving and on-the-job learning, on the one hand, and the degree of freedom that the worker has to organise his work activities, on the other. Discretionary learning involves complex problem solving and freedom to choose or change one's work methods and pace of work. A typical example would be managers, experts or skilled workers with great autonomy.

The principal difference between discretionary learning and lean clusters is the high levels of discretion or autonomy in work exercised by employees grouped in the former. Over 85 percent of the employees grouped in the DL cluster state that they have control over their work pace and work methods, whereas in the lean cluster only slightly over the population average of about 60 percent of employees said the same. This difference can also be seen in the fact that about 70 percent of workers in the lean cluster state that their work pace is determined by quantitative production targets, whereas this was only the case for about 35 percent of employees in the DL cluster.

Another difference is that such core 'lean' or 'high performance' work practices, such as team work, job rotation and the use of quality norms, are at average, or below average, levels in the DL cluster, whereas they are considerably above average in the lean cluster. Workers in automobile factories where modern management techniques are applied would typically fall in the lean category.

Discretionary learning thus refers to work settings where high responsibility is allocated to the employee who is expected to solve problems on his or her own. Business service jobs are typical examples where employees are continuously confronted with new and complex problems. Although some of the tasks take place in a team, teamwork is not seen as imposing narrow constraints on the work. Rather, teamwork may involve brain-storming by professional experts as much as collectively solving narrowly defined problems.

Lean production also involves problem-solving and learning but here the problems appear to be more narrowly defined and the space for possible solutions less wide. The pace of work is more constrained, notably by constraints linked to the use of numerical production targets or performance targets. This points to a more structured or bureaucratic style of organisational learning that corresponds rather closely to the characteristics of the Japanese or 'lean production' model.

The other two clusters are both characteriaed by lower levels of learning and problem-solving. Taylorism offers the employee very limited access to learning and little autonomy when it comes to organising daily work. This is a kind of work widely used in textile factories in the south of Europe. In the traditional cluster, task complexity is the lowest among the four types of work organisation, and at the same time constraints on the pace of work are relatively low. This category groups traditional forms of work organisation where methods are, for the most part, informal and non-codified. This kind of work may be found in small shops and in paid domestic work.

The first four columns of Table 5.1 show the frequency of the four forms of work organisation for the EU-15.[4] The figures show that the DL forms are most widely diffused in the Nordic countries and the Netherlands, and to a lesser extent in Germany, Belgium and Austria, but are barely applied in Ireland and in the southern European countries. The lean model is most in evidence in the UK and Ireland. The Taylorist forms are more present in Spain and Italy, while the traditional forms are more in evidence in Portugal and Greece as well as in Germany, Belgium and Luxembourg.[5]

Table 5.1 National differences in forms of work organization for the EU-15 (2000)

	Percent of employees by country in each organizational class				*Exposure Index*
	Discretionary learning	*Lean production*	*Taylorist organization*	*Traditional organization*	
Austria	38.8	28.1	18.8	14.3	**96.8**
Belgium	39.2	22.2	16.4	22.2	**99.3**
Denmark	58.9	22.4	8.8	9.9	**86.1**
Finland	43.6	29.6	14.2	12.6	**93.9**
France	35.6	29.4	17.7	17.4	**99.4**
Germany	40.5	20.5	15.1	23.9	**99.0**
Greece	15.5	25.5	23.1	35.9	**113.9**
Ireland	17.5	40.9	21.7	19.9	**107.5**
Italy	36.0	20.2	21.8	21.9	**101.9**
Luxembourg	32.2	32.2	12.8	22.8	**100.6**
Netherlands	56.5	24.2	7.1	12.2	**87.1**
Portugal	18.9	22.4	33.0	25.7	**112.7**
Spain	19.4	28.2	33.6	18.7	**110.3**
Sweden	49.1	23.2	9.8	18.0	**92.5**
UK	23.1	45.1	15.7	16.2	**102.5**
EU-15	35.1	28.2	17.4	19.3	**100.0**

Source: Third Working Condition Survey 2000. European Foundation for the Improvement of Living and Working Conditions.

Globalisation, transformation of work, and international competitiveness

In a globalising learning economy, it constitutes a competitive advantage if most jobs in the national economy are skill intensive and not directly exposed to competition from the rapidly growing Asian economies including China and India. Having a large proportion of workers in jobs where they continuously learn new skills while they work makes it possible to retain such an advantage.

It is in this light that the 'exposure index' presented in the last column in Table 5.1 should be viewed. The basic idea is that different types of jobs are more or less exposed to global competition—highly exposed jobs might be outsourced or disappear when confronted with competition from low-cost countries. We assume that exposure increases with the degree of standardisation of the job and with the intensity of use of low-skilled labour.

Therefore, we assume that the least exposed jobs are those involving discretionary learning while Taylorist jobs and Traditional Organisation are most exposed, with Lean Production in an intermediate position. We have calculated the index using the following formula:

$$\text{Exposure Index} = 1.0\text{DL} + 1.5\text{LP} + 2.0\,(\text{TAY} + \text{TRAD})$$

The index has been normalised so that the unweighted average for the EU-15 equals 100. A high value for the index indicates that the economy is highly exposed to low wage competition from outside Europe. Greece, Portugal, Spain and Ireland are most exposed while the Nordic countries and the Netherlands are the least exposed.[6] We would argue that *the inverse* of the exposure index provides an indicator of the quality of working life and of how capable nations are of sustaining their competitiveness in the longer term.

The differences captured by the index help us understand the background for the Euro-crisis. The fact that the economic structure is so uneven across member countries explains why they were affected differently by the crisis. In the wake of the crisis, political leaders from the north of Europe have developed a moral discourse pointing to 'lack of responsibility' and political inefficiency in the south as a background for their specific problems with unsustainable public finance. This discourse neglects that, from the beginning, the Eurozone was heterogeneous in terms of the strength of its economic structure and exposure to global competition.

Public policies and learning organisations

The learning economy needs support from an active welfare state. A fundamental inherent contradiction in the learning economy is that while it thrives on the basis of social cohesion, if left to operate on its own, social cohesion is undermined. For example, the rapid speed of change makes it increasingly difficult for low-skilled workers to find employment while the demand for skilled workers tends to outgrow supply. Such processes were reflected in the outcome of the OECD (1994) Job's Study demonstrating a tendency toward polarisation of labour markets operating in *all* OECD member countries between 1985 and 1995.

In such a context, public programmes that continuously upgrade the skills of workers, and especially low-skilled workers, are important. Expanding youth education and reforming initial education programmes to stay up-to-date in relation to changes in technology and skill demands is important but it cannot stand alone. In the learning economy, the renewal of skills that comes from absorbing new generations of workers works too slowly (the annual inflow of new entrants coming from youth education and with the most updated competences constitute only 2–3 percent of the total labour force). This implies a need to increase investments in lifelong learning, including continuous vocational training provided by employers.

This is a necessary policy to cope with the learning economy at the national level. But it is equally necessary at the European level. If the Lisbon strategy had succeeded in transforming education, organisation, work and labour market institutions in the south of Europe, it could have upgraded the quality of work and the economic structure and the Euro-crisis could have been avoided. As we shall see in the next section, this would have required a focus on building 'social cohesion' and trust. In reality, this dimension of the Lisbon strategy was gradually weakened and what was left was 'structural reform' of labour markets aimed only at more flexibility.

The social conditions for success in the learning economy: the role of equality and trust

The data referred to above on organisational models of learning in different European countries also makes it possible to develop a more dynamic and suitable indicator of inequality than the ones based on income distribution.

In Table 5.2 we present an indicator for the social distribution of workplace learning opportunities. We distinguish between 'workers' and 'managers' and we compare their access to discretionary learning in different national systems.[7] Table 5.2 shows that generally employees at the high end of the professional hierarchy have more easy access to jobs involving discretionary learning. But it is worth noting that the data indicate that inequality in access to learning is quite different across countries. In the Nordic countries and the Netherlands, the inequality in the distribution of learning opportunities is relatively moderate compared to countries in the south of Europe or those in the centre with the exception of Austria and, to a lesser extent, Germany. Italy

Table 5.2 National differences in organizational models for the EU-15 (2000) (percent of employees by organizational class)

	Discretionary learning	*Share of managers in discretionary learning*	*Share of workers in discretionary learning*	*Learning Inequality index**
North				
Netherlands	56.5	74.9	45.3	39.5
Denmark	58.9	79.1	50.0	36.8
Finland	43.6	60.2	36.5	39.5
Sweden	49.1	70.8	37.1	47.6
Centre				
Germany	40.5	61.7	31.2	49.4
Austria	38.8	59.8	34.4	42.5
Luxemb	32.2	56.7	23.5	58.6
Belgium	39.2	63.4	31.3	50.6
France	35.6	60.2	24.0	60.1
West				
UK	23.1	42.2	14.7	65.2
Ireland	17.5	30.2	12.4	58.9
South				
Italy	36.0	67.2	29.1	56.8
Portugal	21.0	39.2	16.4	58.1
Spain	19.4	45.5	13.3	70.8
Greece	15.5	26.4	12.7	51.9

Source: Third Working Conditions Survey 2000. European Foundation for the Improvement of Living and Working Conditions.

*The index is constructed by dividing the share of "workers" engaged in discretionary learning by the share of "managers" engaged in discretionary learning and subtracting the resulting percentage from 100. If the share of workers and managers were the same, the index would equal 0, and if the share of workers was 0 the index would equal 100. The analysis follows closely that developed in Lundvall, Rasmussen, and Lorenz (2008).

provides a striking example of this difference. The proportion of the management category engaged in discretionary learning in Italy is almost as high as in the Netherlands (75 percent in Finland and 69 percent in Italy), but the proportion of workers engaged in discretionary learning is much lower in Italy (29 percent versus 45 percent).

Inequality in learning and income

Sen has argued against using income distribution as an indicator when it comes to assessing well-being and the degree of inequality, and his capability perspective makes access to organisational learning an interesting candidate for an alternative indicator. On the other hand, a high degree of skewedness in income distribution may have an impact on the 'social cohesion' on which interactive learning depends.

It is therefore interesting to see to what degree international differences in access to learning are mirrored in corresponding international differences in income inequality. Table 5.3 compares the two forms of inequality for the EU 15. The data on income inequality derive from a paper by Brandolini and Smeeding (2007) on inequality patterns and refer to the Gini coefficient with respect to disposable income. Both data sets cover the year 2000.

The most striking result is that the countries with the highest degree of income inequality (UK, Portugal, and Spain) are amongst those that are most unequal in terms of access to discretionary learning, and that those countries (Denmark, Finland and Netherlands) that have the most equal

Table 5.3 Comparing income inequality with organizational learning inequality: EU-15

	Income inequality Gini Coefficient	*Ranking Income inequality*	*Inequality in Organizational learning*	*Ranking Inequality in Organizational learning*
Austria	0.257	11	42.5	12
Belgium	0.279	7	50.6	9
Denmark	0.225	15	36.8	14
Finland	0.246	13	36.5	15
France	0.278	8	60.1	3
Germany	0.275	9	49.4	10
Greece	0.334	4–5	51.9	8
Italy	0.334	4–5	56.8	4
Luxembourg	0.313	6	58.6	7
Ireland	0.260	10	58.9	5
Netherlands	0.231	14	39.5	13
Portugal	0.363	1	58.1	6
Spain	0.336	3	70.8	1
Sweden	0.252	12	47.6	11
United Kingdom	0.343	2	65.2	2

Sources: Brandolini and Schmeeding (2007: 31) and the last column of Table 5.3.

income distribution also offer the most egalitarian access to jobs with discretionary learning.

This pattern shows that income distribution tends to be more equal in countries where workers are given and take on more responsibility at the workplace. While income distribution may be of less relevance for individual welfare, there seems to be a major 'system effect' from income distribution on the degree of participation in processes of work. In an era with growing income inequality in the United States and in most European countries, this raises important questions about how increased inequality impacts on participatory learning. A fundamental cause of the weakening of the competitiveness of nations may be 'below the radar' and reflect that growing income inequality reduces the willingness of workers to take an active part in processes of organisational learning.

When bosses get better off while workers experience more work for less pay it should come as no surprise if workers become less engaged in contributing to organisational and technical change. Perception of injustice linked to not receiving a fair share of the returns from economic activity breeds mistrust between workers and employers and reinforces more hierarchical forms of work organisation based on high levels of control and characterised by less autonomy. In what follows we raise the more general issue of the relation between social capital or trust and the development of learning organisations.

How and with whom people interact will reflect the society they live in and the education system that shaped them. We argue that in the Nordic countries social capital and trust are fundamental resources that make national systems strong in terms of incremental innovation, absorption of knowledge produced elsewhere and rapid adaptation (Lundvall, 2002). Both the level of trust and the level of income equality are high in the Nordic countries. We also find that a fundamental and dynamic indicator of equality—equality in access to learning at the workplace—shows high values in the Nordic countries and the Netherlands.

In the U.S.-dominated literature, social capital has been presented as rooted in civil society and the frequency of participation in civic activities has been used as indicator of 'social capital' (Woolcock, 1998). It has been argued that big government undermines civil society and thereby also social capital. From the Scandinavian experience it is not clear that the growth of the welfare state has reduced participation in civic organizations. In fact, the levels of trust are higher in the Scandinavian countries than in countries with small government. In particular, there seems to be a correlation between general (rather than selective) social welfare programmes and generalised trust.

According to the European Social Survey, trust among agents seems to be consistently higher in the Nordic countries than in most other countries and combined with the small size of the system it results in dense *interaction* among agents both within and across organisations.

This not only gives rise to low transaction costs. More importantly, it facilitates processes of interactive learning where new insights about technologies and good organisational practices are diffused rapidly both within organisations and across organisational borders. The most important impact of high degrees of trust is *high learning benefits*. Low social distance between managers and workers and willingness to trust partners are key elements behind the relative success of the Nordic countries.

Summing up

Our results indicate that social cohesion as reflected in equal income distribution goes hand in hand with broad and democratic participation in organisational learning. Increasing income inequality may undermine the learning economy.

3. Three key relationships in the Lisbon strategy

The mid-term review of the Lisbon strategy weakened the social dimension

A shift in priorities took place a few years into the Lisbon strategy period with a weakening of its social dimension and a more narrow focus on growth and employment. This stemmed from a mid-term evaluation in 2004–2005 that argued that the strategy was 'too complex' with too many targets. Therefore it should focus all attention on employment and economic growth. This change also reflected a shift in the political landscape where social democratic governments had been substituted by more right-wing regimes.

The shift narrowed the goal of 'more and better jobs' to 'more jobs', it placed emphasis on 'flexicurity' but focused almost exclusively on flexibility. While the Lisbon Strategy, and especially the focus on social cohesion and a knowledge-based society, was generally pointing in the right direction, those in charge of implementing the policy saw 'social cohesion' more as a burden for Europe rather than as the necessary foundation for the learning economy. Therefore, implementation became increasingly lopsided and dominated by the neoliberal interpretation of 'structural reform' as imposing more flexibility on workers and their wages.

The Lisbon Strategy involved many dimensions and it is necessary to focus on some key relationships. In this section, we will discuss three central themes in the Lisbon Strategy: the creation of more and better jobs, competitiveness with more social cohesion, and the shift to a knowledge-based economy. In each of these areas, we intend to assess the success of the Lisbon Strategy in achieving its targets and in making the Eurozone more sustainable.

More and better jobs? Or just more jobs?

In several respects, the Lisbon Strategy may be seen as a follow-up, as well as a broadening and revitalisation, of the European Employment

Strategy (EES) that was established in 1996. A new element was the increased emphasis on the role of knowledge and innovation. But raising the employment rate through labour market reform remained a central goal over the 2000–2010 period, and the widespread use of the Open Method of Coordination (OMC) was inspired by procedures already practised within the EES.[8]

The employment strategy was in its turn inspired by the OECD Job's Study that emphasised the lack of flexibility in Europe's labour markets as the major reason for unsatisfactory job creation and economic growth. The specific design of the strategy reflected a mixture of neoliberal and social democratic ideas. The Commissioner in charge, Allan Larson, former Minister of Finance in Sweden, played an important role in designing and implementing the EES.

Perhaps the most consistent aim of the Lisbon Strategy has been to increase the employment rate in member countries. This objective has wide support across the political spectrum, which suggests that high employment rates can be the outcome both of a Nordic welfare strategy and of a neoliberal strategy. This is also an area where there has been some positive development in terms of approaching the target of an average employment rate of 70 percent. The EU employment rate thus increased from 62 percent in 2000 to 66 percent in 2008 before it dropped back again to less than 65 percent as a result of the crisis.

In the Lisbon Strategy the objective was originally 'to create more and better' jobs. But while the quantitative dimension was easy to measure it was not possible to agree on an indicator for better jobs (Raveaud, 2007). One option that was considered but rejected was to define good jobs as 'standard jobs' and bad jobs as part time or 'fixed term' jobs. This proposal was vetoed by the UK and the Netherlands on the grounds that non-standard jobs should be seen as stepping stones to standard jobs.

We propose that the international comparisons of the frequency of jobs offering employees access to learning with high levels of discretion and scope for exploring new knowledge developed in Section 2 above may be regarded as a more suitable indicator of quality of jobs. A major advantage of this indicator is that it links quality of jobs to the knowledge-based economy perspective. In Table 5.4 we extend the analysis presented in Table 5.2 and show how the different forms of work organisation evolved over the period of the Lisbon agenda.

The results show an increase in the DL forms of slightly less than 2 percent during the first half of the Lisbon period counterbalanced by a fall in the traditional forms. The results for 2010, however, show that there was a sharp fall in the frequency of the DL forms after the 2008 financial crisis and the considerable decline in output and employment which accompanied it. This decline was compensated by an increase in the more bureaucratic lean forms and to a lesser extent by an increase in the Taylorist forms of work organisation. Although an analysis of the

Table 5.4 Frequencies of forms of work organization by survey wave: EU-15

Wave	*Discretionary learning*	*Lean Production*	*Taylorism*	*Traditional*	*Total*
2000	35.1	28.2	17.4	19.3	100.0
2005	36.8	28.6	17.8	16.8	100.0
2010	31.8	31.3	18.6	18.3	100.0
Pooled	34.1	29.6	18.0	18.3	100.0

Source: European Conditions Surveys 2000, 2005 and 2010. European Foundation for the Improvement of Living and Working Conditions.

causes for these changes goes beyond the scope of this chapter, the data is consistent with the idea of a positive relation between the quantity and quality of jobs rather than a trade-off. The share of the DL forms increased during the period up to 2005, characterised by an increase in the average employment rate for the EU-15, only to decline during the latter part of the Lisbon period, when the employment rate also fell. Moreover, from the cross-section perspective, it is interesting to note that only the Netherlands, Denmark, Sweden, Austria, and Germany reached the target employment rate (70 percent). These are also the economies where the share of workers engaged in jobs that offer discretionary learning is amongst the highest (see Table 5.2).[9]

Flexicurity with little security

The Lisbon Strategy documents have increasingly referred to the concept of 'flexicurity' as a goal for the labour market institutional set-up. In the Commission documents this concept has been substituted by the less popular requests for 'more flexibility' in labour markets. This seems to go against the tendency to narrow the agenda toward a neoliberal strategy. But a closer look at the use of the concept indicates that the definition used differs from its original meaning.

Flexicurity has been associated especially with the Danish and Dutch labour market institutional set-ups. It combines few restrictions on employers hiring and firing of workers with tax-financed unemployment insurance that is quite generous, both in terms of replacement rate and especially in terms of the duration of the unemployment benefits. The Commission's evaluation document refers to the endorsement of the flexicurity principles by the European Council in December 2007 and argues that, 'a majority of Member States have now developed or are developing comprehensive flexicurity approaches' (European Commission, 2010: 16).

Providing empirical evidence to evaluate this claim is problematic given the lack of consensus on relevant indicators for measuring levels of flexicurity. Here we simply provide data on changes in two key dimensions of flexicurity: the generosity of unemployment benefit expenditure and changes in legal restrictions on firing employees. For the former dimension, we use the data available on Eurostat's electronic database for national expenditures on unemployment protection. The figures include both 'passive' expenditures providing income maintenance and 'active' expenditures for training the unemployed in order to improve their chances of finding employment. The measure we present in Figure 5.1 is the level of expenditures per unemployed person as a share of GDP per capita. The results show that in the majority of the countries the generosity of unemployment protection declined or remained unchanged. The two exceptions to this trend occurred in Italy, which in 2000 had the lowest level of expenditure amongst the EU-15, and in Finland. The largest drops in expenditure occurred in Denmark (over 50 percent) and Sweden (over 60 percent).

In order to measure changes in the flexibility of the labour market, we use the OECD's overall employment protection legislation (EPL) index, which measures how difficult or costly it is for employers to lay off employees. At the time of the Lisbon Strategy's mid-term review, the OECD's Employment Outlook (2004, Ch. 2, p. 63) considered the trend from the late 1980s as convergence, 'driven largely by an easing of regulation in the countries where EPL was relatively strict'. The figures presented in Figure 5.2 below show that this provides an accurate portrayal of the general trend for the period up to 2008.[10] The level of the EPL declined in 9 of the 14 nations represented and remained unchanged in 3. The only case of an increase,

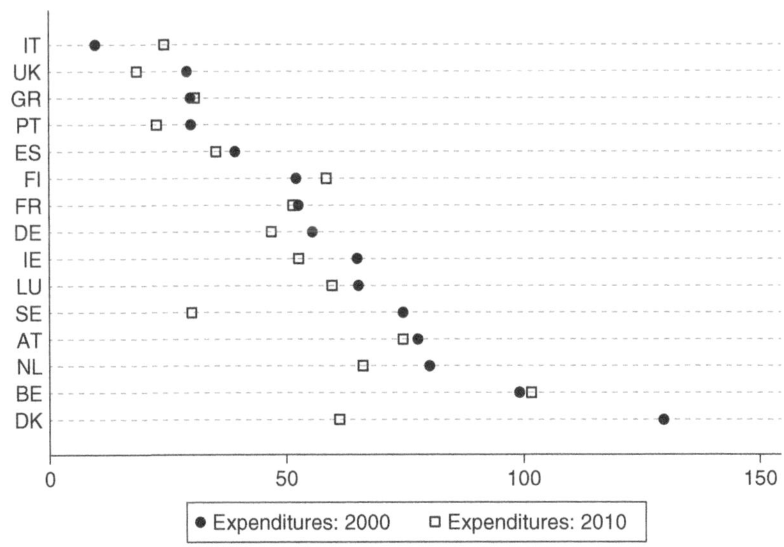

Figure 5.1 Active and passive expenditures on unemployment protection.

Source: Eurostat, http://epp.eurostat.ec.europa.eu/portal/page/portal/social_protection/introduction.

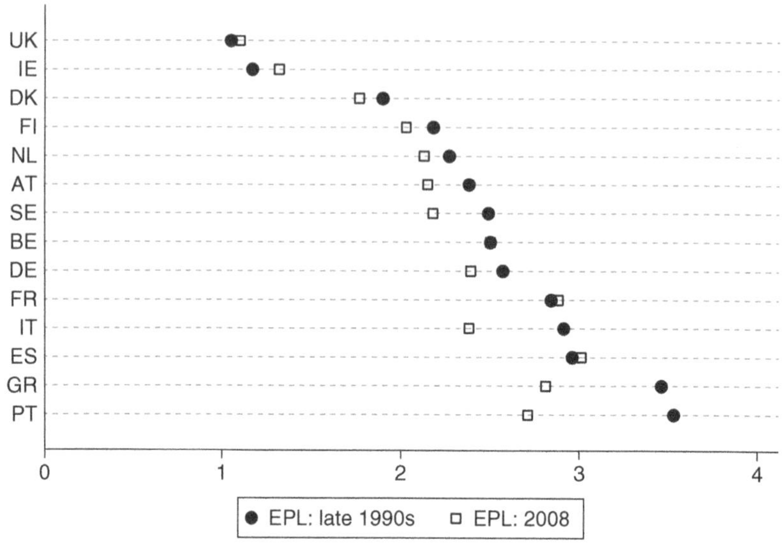

Figure 5.2 Changes in the EPL during the Lisbon agenda.

Source: OECD Employment Outlook http://www.oecd.org/els/emp/oecdindicatorsofemploymentprotection.htm.

albeit slight, in the level of the EPL occurred in Ireland, which in 2008 had one of the least restrictive labor markets in Europe.

Given the evidence presented above, it is perhaps not surprising that the Commission's 2010 evaluation report does not contain a single specific reference to success in terms of increased security for workers and definitely none to increased income security for unemployed workers. All the progress mentioned is in terms of increased flexibility. This bias is fundamental in a situation where some of the new member countries offer almost no income security for those who become unemployed. This gradual erosion of the concept of flexicurity raises concern since in its original form it was intended to bolster the learning economy (Holm et al., 2010).

Weaker competitiveness with less social cohesion

The analysis and prescription of 'structural reform' in the Lisbon agenda was a follow-up of neo-liberal ideas regarding the fundamental importance of flexible labour markets supported by the OECD and other international organisations. What was new in the Lisbon Strategy was combining this approach with the EU's historical commitment to 'social cohesion' and a strong emphasis on the importance of innovation and the 'knowledge base', Competitiveness was linked to investments in knowledge and to the upgrading of competences.

The original Lisbon Strategy recognised that the legitimacy of social policy and active state intervention in social affairs is different in Europe than in the United States. The two key concepts in the Lisbon Strategy were competitiveness *and* social cohesion. While 'structural reforms' should 'modernise' the European welfare states and make them more competitive, this should be combined with 'more social cohesion'.[11]

But there was little agreement on how the relationship between the two concepts should be regarded. In the context of the Lisbon Strategy, social cohesion and inequality can be analysed at least at three different levels. First, it signals a historical commitment to promote economic growth in the least developed regions of Europe; second, it refers to personal income distribution within nations; and third, it may refer to the reduction of poverty at the regional, national, or European level.

The patterns of 'social cohesion' have certainly changed within the EU over the last decade and to some degree this has been influenced by politics. More than a third of the EU budget is allocated to regional funds. And until the beginning of the crisis there was a certain convergence of GNP/capita across nation states and regions within Europe. Most studies on the impact of structural funds indicate that they did indeed contribute to a reduction in interregional inequality (Bouvet, 2010).

But within most EU-15 countries and for the EU-15 as a whole income distribution became more unequal. Figure 5.3 shows that the Gini coefficient

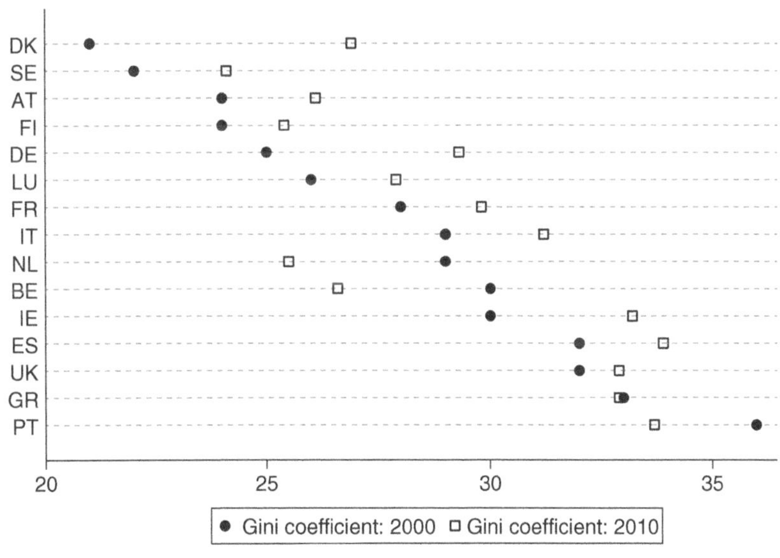

Figure 5.3 Changes in the gini coefficient during the Lisbon agenda.

Source: Eurostat, http://epp.eurostat.ec.europa.eu/portal/page/portal/income_social_inclusion_living_conditions/data/database.

increased in 12 of the 15 member states between 2000 and 2010. The largest increase occurred in Denmark which started out in 2000 with the least unequal income distribution amongst the EU-15.

Arguably, public policies may well have contributed to this weakening of social cohesion. One factor is the competition among EU member states to make the income tax system less burdensome for those with the highest incomes and for business enterprises. The argument for these changes may be seen as linked to 'competitiveness.' It is assumed that the member state that offers the lowest taxes will attract skilled workers and business activities from abroad. As a result, the effective corporate tax rate for major European countries was reduced from 29 percent to 21 percent between 1987 and 2005. The marginal tax rate on personal income was reduced from 48.4 percent to 42.1 percent between 2000 and 2008. The single country going furthest in this direction is Ireland offering a corporate tax only half of the average in the EU (12.5 percent) (Fitoussi and Saraceno, 2010). The financial sustainability of this competition toward the bottom was not seriously addressed in connection with the Commission's evaluation of the Lisbon Strategy.

One reason why the EU has not restricted tax competition among member states may be that it is seen as positive by the Commission. Reading carefully the document that evaluates the Lisbon Strategy gives the impression that the Commission assumes that 'what makes life easier for business is always good for competitiveness and economic growth'. For instance, there are several references to a few problematic countries where real wages have increased more rapidly than productivity while there is *no* reference to countries where wages have fallen behind increases in productivity (Evaluation, 2010). This is remarkable since the wage share of GNP for EU-15 has fallen from 70 percent in 1975 to less than 60 percent in 2006 (Fitoussi and Laurent, 2009: 9).

The idea that wage restraint at the national level is always for the better that dominates the evaluation report is especially contestable in the current situation where the uneven levels of 'competitiveness', both at the global and the European level, are increasingly recognised as an obstacle to re-establishing economic growth. To rebalance the uneven competitiveness between, for instance, Germany and the peripheral countries by reducing wages in the weaker economies will result in more inequality, adding to the numbers of the working poor and thus be at odds with the EU2020 goal of reducing poverty in these nations and increasing regional cohesion.

The current implementation of austerity programmes in the peripheral economies has brought the process of convergence of national income per capita within the Union to an end and, for the first time in the history of European integration, the gap between rich and poor EU countries is increasing.

The most important shift in focus of the Lisbon Strategy was thus the weakening of its social dimension in the mid-2000s. This was reflected in the fact that flexicurity became reduced to more flexibility and that more and better jobs were reduced to more jobs. Competitiveness became a goal in itself and social cohesion was neglected as a commitment. These changes were fundamental and below we will argue that they weakened the capacity of the Strategy to contribute to a sustainable Eurozone.

4. The Lisbon strategy as a scaffolding for the eurozone

Already at the time when the European Employment Strategy was designed, the strategy was presented by one of its architects, Allan Larsson (1998), as a necessary complement to the EMU and later on scholars analysed the Lisbon Strategy in this light (Begg, 2003). This perspective is especially pertinent in light of the Euro-crisis. Could and should the Lisbon Strategy have helped to avoid the current crisis where several peripheral countries have been at the brink of state bankruptcies and now remain in economic crisis?

When the EMU was established bringing together countries at very different levels of economic development, there were warnings that a monetary union without a common fiscal policy would be vulnerable to external shocks. In the United States, member states receive compensation through the federal budget in periods of slowdown and unemployment and this works as an important automatic stabiliser. The total budget for the EU is only a few per cent of the GNP as compared to about 20 percent in the United States and it cannot play this role. The Lisbon Strategy may be seen as an attempt to compensate for this flaw. There are two possible interpretations of what the Lisbon Strategy could have done to make the monetary union more robust.

The first, as highlighted by Begg (2003), is the neo-liberal strategy of 'structural reform' based on introducing more flexibility in the labour markets of the peripheral countries through, for instance, non-standard labour contracts, less protection, and increased wage flexibility based on weakening trade unions. With very high degrees of wage flexibility, external shocks could be absorbed by changes in the labour market.

A different possible interpretation in resonance with the call for 'more social cohesion' is that the Lisbon Strategy could have served to reduce regional inequality by upgrading the knowledge base and the industrial structure in the peripheral countries—aiming at better jobs less exposed to global competition in these parts of Europe. It is no accident that the countries now most exposed to financial speculation are the ones that have the weakest industrial structure with the biggest proportion of workplaces exposed to direct competition from emerging economies (see Table 5.1).

Our analysis of the globalising learning economy in Sections 2 and 3 above strongly implies that in order to be effective this second strategy would have required a much stronger focus on regional and social cohesion, reforms of labour markets and education systems, as well as massive investment in knowledge and learning.

The Lisbon agenda became increasingly oriented toward the first strategy, and while the Euro-crisis shows that this orientation did not make euro-cooperation robust, the current crisis solutions based on calls for austerity look very much like attempts to reinforce a neo-liberal model of structural reform based on increases in labour market flexibility. Despite the historical record and the severity of the current crisis facing Europe, there is little in EU2020 to indicate insight into the limitations of the first and the potential of the second to tackle the underlying structural problems of the relatively weak member states, including Greece, Portugal and Italy.[12]

5. On the insufficiency of the current national competitiveness strategies

Our conclusion is that while the general direction of the Lisbon Strategy, and especially the focus on social cohesion and the knowledge-based society pointed in the right direction, those in charge of implementing the policy saw 'social cohesion' as a burden for Europe rather than as the necessary foundation for the learning economy. Therefore, implementation became increasingly lopsided and dominated by the traditional economic focus on 'structural reform' and increased flexibility. As a result, the focus fell on more jobs but not better jobs, on flexicurity with little security and on competitiveness with less, rather than more, social cohesion (as reflected first in increased income inequality within most of the member countries and now also in increased income gaps across countries).

Second, we conclude that, even with a more balanced political approach, the combination of a hardcore monetary union and soft coordination of the policies aiming at social cohesion and innovation was preparing the ground for the current crisis. The EU2020 reproduces these problems and we are therefore not optimistic about the future of the European integration project. EU2020 puts forward important objectives for economic growth as well as for social and environmental sustainability. But the social dimension that in 2000 was 'more social cohesion' has now been reduced to 'poverty reduction', that is, narrowed down to what is typical of a (neo-) liberal view of the welfare state and there are no indications in the new strategy of an understanding of the wider policy implications of the learning economy perspective.

The Lisbon Strategy may be seen as an attempt to establish regional and political convergence in Europe with the ultimate aim of building a strong and cohesive union. But the Lisbon Strategy approach, with its emphasis on 'best-practice' and benchmarking in specific policy areas was technocratic and there are few signs that the strategy has been successful in stimulating popular participation in the project. It might have been easier to go forward with an idea of what could form the basis of a European identity corresponding to what historically formed the basis of nation-building. In a seminal paper written at the occasion of the conference on 'The European

Identity in a Global Economy', in preparation for the Lisbon Summit under the Portuguese Presidency, Manuel Castells argued that there is a need for 'a common European identity on whose behalf citizens around Europe could be ready to share problems and build common solutions' (Castells, 2002: 234).

After rejecting common religious beliefs and culture, he pointed to a constellation of values that relate to the welfare state and social protection as a promising candidate. It consists of 'shared feelings concerning the need for universal social protection of living conditions, social solidarity, stable employment, workers' rights, universal human rights, concern about poor people around the world, extension of democracy to regional and local levels…'. He proposed that if European institutions promoted these values, the 'project identity' would probably grow (Castells, 2002: 234–235).

What can be done in the current situation where Europe as a whole remains in stagnation and the south of Europe suffers from mass unemployment and growing poverty? One way forward within the existing framework would be to redefine the use of Structural Funds and vastly increase the amounts explicitly targeted to modernising education and labour markets, with a view to further develop the organisational and technological capabilities of the weaker member states.

A more radical reform would be the redefinition of the Economic and Monetary Union (EMU) so that it recognises the 'social dimension'; transforming it into an Economic and Social Union (ESU). This should be linked to reforms of the decision-making process that combine democratic participation with efficiency.

There is hence a need for a paradigmatic shift where the fear of state intervention and the belief in markets is changed into a pragmatic perspective where governments are allowed to take on the tasks necessary to promote stable economic growth. This includes establishing a much stricter regulation of financial markets. But most importantly it involves a redesign of all institutions and sector policies so that they take seriously that we are in a new phase where knowledge is the most important resource and learning the most important process.

Success would actually require a radical step forward in the process of European integration. An obvious step now debated among macroeconomists would be to move toward a fiscal union as a necessary complement to the monetary union. But this is far from sufficient to bolster the economic and monetary union and to make it stable and sustainable. There is a need to develop common policies at the European level that contribute to the kind of solidarity that was the historical foundation for the building of nation states and this includes social policy, education policy, labour market and industrial policy. Such a radical shift looks unrealistic in a situation where Germany insists on a strengthening of nationalist strategies aimed at short-term 'cost competitiveness.' But without it, the Eurozone will remain unstable and crisis-ridden because the tension between the low-income countries in the south and the high-income countries in the north will undermine its sustainability.

Notes

1 Communication from the Commission, 'EUROPE 2020 A strategy for smart, sustainable and inclusive growth', Brussels, 3.3.2010 COM(2010) 2020

2 This can be illustrated by an extreme case referred to in a report from the Danish Ministry for Education. Here it is claimed that, on average, half the skills a computer engineer has obtained during his training will have become obsolete one year after passing the final exam, while the 'halving period' for other categories of educated wage earners is estimated to be eight years (Ministry of Education, 1997: 56).

3 The Third European Working Conditions Survey on which the mapping is based was directed at approximately 1500 working individuals in each country with the exception of Luxembourg with only 500 respondents. The total survey population is 21703 individuals, of which 17910 are salaried employees. The analysis presented here is based on the responses of the 8081 salaried employees working in establishments with at least 10 individuals in both industry and services, but excluding agriculture and fishing; public administration and social security; education; health and social work; and private domestic employees.

4 See Lorenz and Valeyre (2005) for a description of the variables used in carrying out the cluster analysis. Unlike Lorenz and Valeyre (2005), for the purposes of this chapter, the cluster analysis was performed on the pooled data for the 2000, 2005, and 2010 waves of the EWCS. The pooled-data cluster solution provides an average characterisation of national differences in forms of work organization over the period of the three waves. By comparing the frequencies of the four forms of work organisation for each of the individual waves, it is possible to show how the forms of work organisation evolved over the period of the Lisbon agenda in relation to the average (see Table 5.4). The results presented in Table 5.1 above show the national frequencies for the 2000 wave.

5 In Lorenz and Valeyre (2005), logit regression analysis is used in order to control for differences in sector, occupation, and establishment size when estimating the impact of nation on the likelihood of employees being grouped in the various forms of work organisation. The results show a statistically significant 'national effect' also when controlling for the structural variables, thus pointing to considerable latitude in how work is organised for the same occupation or within the same industrial sector.

6 While a low value on the exposure index indicates that the economy is less vulnerable to 'globalisation', it also may be seen as explaining difficulties in absorbing low-skilled labour and not least labour with a different ethnical background. Workplaces with Taylorist and traditional work organisations may be seen as 'entrance points' for immigrants with low skills since they offer jobs where workers with limited communication skills can operate efficiently. It means that the integration effort in order to be successful needs to be massive and focused on upgrading skills, including communication skills, in the Nordic countries. The current high rates of unemployment among certain ethnical groups in these countries illustrates that this has not yet been fully understood among policy makers.

7 The class of managers includes not only top and middle management but also professionals and technicians (ISCO major groups 1, 2, and 3) The worker category includes clerks, service, and sales workers as well as craft, plant, and machine operators and unskilled occupations (ISCO major groups 4 through 9).

8 Maria Rodrigues, who played the role of Sherpa in the formation of the Lisbon Strategy, served as Portuguese Minister of Labour and was as such deeply involved in the EES.

9 Seen from a different perspective, the data indicate that the welfare loss of high unemployment is more important than normally considered. Higher rates of unemployment go hand in hand with lower quality workplaces. The traditional welfare perspective with a one-sided focus on consumption and neglect of the quality of work disregards this indirect but important negative consequence of the economic crisis.

10 Data on the EPL is unavailable for Luxembourg prior to 2008.

11 One of the European Union's (EU) main objectives consisted in enhancing economic and social cohesion both among and within member countries (Article 2 of the Treaty on European Union).

12 For an interesting and original analysis of the negative impact of inequality and flexibility strategies on economic growth in Europe, see Galbraith (2006).

Part II

Structural change and competitiveness in the European periphery

6 Structural and technological change in the European periphery

Argentino Pessoa

1. Introduction

This chapter deals with structural transformations in the European periphery (EP). By EP we mean the group of four countries located in southern and southwestern Europe: Greece, Italy, Portugal and Spain. Including these four economies in a group is not without controversy, because they differ in such important characteristics as geographical dimension, cultural heritage and a number of institutional aspects. For instance, Italy is one of the original founding countries of the EEC (European Economic Community) and its industrial tradition is very different from that of Portugal and Spain. Thus, EP is used here as a pragmatic criterion rather than with any normative purpose. The idea of including these countries in the EP gained some force with the sovereign debt crisis which has affected all these countries, although at different times and with varying intensity.[1]

It is well known that the EP had engaged in substantial foreign borrowing for several years, and that the turn to foreign borrowing was facilitated by the entry into the European Monetary Union (EMU). Up to the late 1990s, the EP faced much higher interest rates than the core euro-area countries such as Germany. However, after the launch of the EMU, the interest rates fell sharply as market participants considered that the value of investments would no longer be vulnerable to erosion through currency depreciation (Pessoa, 2011). These low interest rates spurred heavy foreign borrowing by both the public and private sectors. In addition, the need to minimise the effects of the 2008 crisis, together with the action of some automatic stabilisers, also helped to increase the external debt by adding a sovereign debt crisis to the slow economic growth of the first decade of the new millennium.

The combination of slow growth with the debt crisis fostered the idea that both are the result of a lack of structural change, and this conviction obsessively fed the rhetoric of structural reforms, as if they are a panacea leading to the resumption of astonishing economic growth. However, it should be noted that structural change and structural reform are two very different concepts and perception of the latter as a magic potion is more detrimental than beneficial to economic growth and structural change. It moves the economy away from the spontaneous path to equilibrium, and destroys and wastes resources. Usually it has no economic base, other than ideological fundamentalism.

It is time for Portugal and other countries of the EP to ask: is there a structural change in the European periphery? If there is, how has this structural change occurred? How is such structural change connected with technological change? What are the effects of the crisis and the proposed solutions on the catching-up process? In this chapter, we look for answers to these questions, focusing on the European periphery, considering its structural change and seeing how this has evolved into a technological change.

A good place to start is with a basic recognition of how economic growth occurs. In the literature, there are two approaches seeking answers for these questions: the more abstract in nature is economic growth theory, and the more appreciative is development economics based on the building of stylised facts.[2] Our study considers both the economic growth inputs and the most important stylised facts of economic development. Accordingly, this chapter is structured as follows. After this introduction, Section 2 distinguishes the structural change approach from the structural reforms perspective. Section 3 deals with the process of economic growth in the EP, relates it to the advantages of backwardness theory and analyses the structural change that occurred in the EP. Section 4 focuses on the main traits of technology and innovation performance in the last few decades and indicates some factors that explain the difficulties in the growth process of both core and peripheral European economies. Some conclusions are put forward in Section 5.

2. Structural change versus structural reforms

The process of economic development can be analysed by focusing on changes occurring in a country's economic structure at the same time as its GDP increases. This is the driving idea of the structural approach to economic development. The basic rationale of the structural change approach refers to a long-term, widespread change of the fundamental structure, rather than change on a micro scale or of short-term output and employment. It can be summarised as follows: 1) economic agents respond to market incentives; 2) as GDP grows incentives change; 3) the change in incentives alters the structure of the economy, at least on the levels of production, employment and demand[3]; 4) the structural transformation is not only a consequence of GDP growth but also a condition for sustainable economic growth. However, as GDP grows and structural change occurs, the effects of the latter on the former become less significant, unless a technological change occurs. Thus, the role of technical progress is crucial to the process of structural change, as suggested by Leon (1967) and Pasinetti (1981). However, given the well-known market failures associated with innovation, policy has a part to play in the early stages of technological change.

This view is somewhat different from the perspective of structural reforms, which originated with supporters of the "supply-side economics"[4]. Although the typical policy recommendations of supply-side economists are lower marginal tax rates and less regulation, they also include other reforms such as privatisation and liberalisation of capital flows. The structural reforms perspective is neatly summarised in the 10 principles of the Washington Consensus (see Box 6.1) formerly developed by the IMF and World Bank as a recipe for developing countries confronted with external accounts problems, and which consequently asked for financial assistance from these international institutions.

The basic motivation of the structural reforms approach is to replace quickly the actual economy with an "ideal" economy, without imbalances and lock-ins. Current advocates of this approach in the European Union search the EFC (Expansionary Fiscal Contraction) hypothesis[5] for theoretical support. The EFC view is based on the traditional assumption that reducing government expenditure will lessen crowding out "making room for the private sector to expand". Of course, this only happens when the economy is near full employment. Furthermore, among the conditions for the EFC hypothesis to operate are significant currency devaluation, budget improvement through significant tax increases and spending cuts and sufficient liquidity so that current disposable income does not restrain consumption. If this latter condition is not met, that is, when current disposable income constrains consumption, the result is inevitably recession.[6] Other authors, studying Denmark's fiscal contraction in 1983–1986 show that the EFC hypothesis may work, but only for large, credible fiscal consolidations, and that other reforms may have to play an important role (Barry and Devereux, 1995; Bergman et al., 2010). In addition, an IMF working paper (Guajardo et al., 2011) that studied changes in policy designed to reduce deficits found that austerity had contractionary effects on private domestic demand and GDP and concluded that other studies appeared biased towards exaggerating the expansionary effects of austerity.

Box 6.1 The ten principles of the Washington Consensus

1. Fiscal discipline
2. Reorientation of public expenditures
3. Lower marginal tax rates and broaden the tax base
4. Interest rate liberalisation
5. Unified and competitive exchange rate
6. Trade liberalization
7. Liberalisation of FDI inflows
8. Privatisation
9. Deregulation
10. Secure property rights

Source: Williamson (1990).

Although it is evident that the EFC hypothesis is far from being proved, and current European economic conditions are not appropriate for its application, both the European Commission and many governments are deeply convinced that this is the best road ahead. More recently, this approach gained new vitality with the appropriation by the European authorities of the controversial results obtained by Reinart and Rogoff (2009, 2010).

It is difficult to understand the enthusiasm for policies of this type in light of historical results. In fact, the assistance programmes for indebted countries in Africa and Latin America, supported by the IMF and the World Bank, failed to either increase economic growth or to significantly decrease these countries' debt.[7] Furthermore, in some national programmes, such as those associated with the Thatcher government (1979–1990) in the UK and the Reagan administration (1981–1989) in the United States, where the structural reforms perspective was first implemented, there were no significant positive effects on the long-run growth. On the contrary, in the United States, the severe depression and high unemployment experienced in 1981–1983 was not followed by an increase in the potential output that the supply-side proponents had advocated.

In short, because those national and adjustment programmes systematically underestimate the effects of structural reforms on the aggregated demand, they are systematically followed by unemployment and recession, while their long-run effects on economic growth are at best uncertain. The European periphery is the most recent and evident example of such erroneous views.

3. Economic growth in the European periphery

At the end of World War II, the four southern European countries had a low level of development, as shown in Table 6.1. Yet there were significant cross-national differences in income level: in 1950, real Portuguese GDP per capita was 19.79 percent that of the United States, a percentage significantly lower than that recorded by Spain and Italy.

Table 6.1 Real GDP per capita as a percent of the USA

Year	*Portugal*	*Spain*	*Italy*	*Greece*
1950	19.79	28.75	40.29	*na*
1960	25.76	39.99	56.51	35.04
1970	36.16	57.11	69.51	56.79
1980	41.52	60.59	76.53	65.40
1990	46.83	64.01	80.46	53.28
2000	49.32	64.34	72.17	52.16
2010	48.50	66.17	68.24	61.06

Source: PWT 7.1.

Note: *na* means not available.

It is well known that after World War II these countries embarked on a process of industrialisation, first using import substitution policy and next export promotion coupled with increasing openness to international trade. Industrialisation based on investment, both public and private, contributed to accelerating convergence with the economic frontier. However, in spite of this convergence process at the end of the twentieth century, important differences were still visible in the EP with Portuguese GDP per capita below 50 percent of the United States, a barrier surpassed by Italy more than 40 years earlier and by Spain and Greece in the 1960s.

Thus, the current economic difference between Portugal and the other peripheral European countries is not a consequence of the slow pace of economic growth; it expresses the low initial level of the Portuguese GDP. In fact, Portuguese growth is noteworthy in the second half of the twentieth century for showing steady progress towards convergence. Convergence as a long-run process is also visible for Spain, Italy and Greece, with some country specificities: while in Spain convergence was continuous although uneven, it came to an end after 1990 in Italy, and it is interrupted in the first decade of the twenty-first century in Portugal. In Greece, the 1990s and 2000s are marked by a decrease in real GDP per capita. In short, the convergence process in the European periphery has important cross-national differences.

Regardless of how important it was in the 1960–2000 period as a whole, the pace of economic growth of the EP has declined since the 1960s. In fact, in Portugal, Spain and Italy the pace of per capita growth has become progressively slower over the decades, culminating in disappointing rates in the 2000–2009 period (Figure 6.1). What causes such performance? Although the causes are varied, ranging from some lock-in in the structural transformation to the changes that occurred in the international division of labour, the

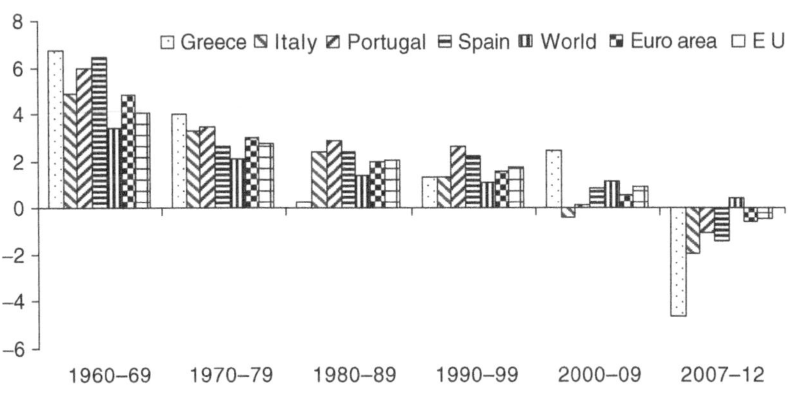

Figure 6.1 Economic growth slowdown.

Source: Based on WDI.

Note: logarithmic growth rates obtained from GDP per capita at constant prices.

effects of the 2008 crisis first and the debt crisis after that, together with the remedy used to calm down the latter, had a significant impact on the growth rate of the last decade. These factors explain why the GDP per capita downturn is much more evident in the 2007–2012 period (Figure 6.1).

The stumpy growth of the first decade of the twenty-first century prompted much rhetoric about the causes of such disappointing dynamics and numerous opinion makers came along to support the need to implement structural reforms. Simultaneously the bailout programme for the Greek, Irish, and Portuguese economies organised by the ECB (European Central Bank), EU (European Union), and the IMF (International Monetary Fund) added its authority to the domestic voices emphasising the need of such reforms. Along with the lack of structural reforms, some see the growth differences over the decades as a direct effect of policy. For instance, regarding Portugal, it allegedly performed poorly because governments used the wrong policies: government had provided incentives for consumption instead of promoting investment, or it supported investment in infrastructure instead of investment in more immediately productive activities.

Of course, these explanations are too sketchy to be taken seriously. First, because in a context of increasing openness and deregulation it needs to be demonstrated that a public policy of directing private investment contrary to market signals (Pessoa, 2012) can be effective in enhancing growth. Second, the above explanations ignore the effects of the economic integration of peripheral economies and disregard the consequences of important changes that occurred at the world economic level. However, more importantly, a solution based on this way of looking at the economy risks hampering growth rather than propelling it.

Given the increasing integration of the EP in the European Union and, later, in the euro area, an explanation for the decrease in the economic growth rate should take into account the reasons that justify the decrease of European growth. However, even though important, these reasons cannot cover up the need to determine how the structural change occurred. Hence, in the following sections, we will look at the structural change that took place in the economies of the EP, its limitations and the need for these to be addressed in conjunction with technological changes.

Catching-up effect and structural change

The economic literature contains basically two explanations for the convergence process: neoclassical rationalisation (see Barro and Sala-I-Martin, 1992) and the 'advantages of backwardness' perspective (Abramovitz, 1979, 1986). Although both approaches state an inverse association between the initial productivity levels of countries and their productivity growth rates in the long run, there is an important difference in the causal relationships each provides.

The perspective known as the "advantages of backwardness" is more adapted to the structural change approach to economic development. In fact, while the neoclassical perspective bases convergence on the low initial level of capital per worker, the "advantages of backwardness", following the leading work by Abramovitz (1979, 1986), calls attention to other factors that are absent from the neoclassical theory. In addition to the low level of capital per worker, and more importantly, the existence of a technology gap (Nelson and Phelps, 1969) between the leader and the follower countries plays the most significant role. In its simplest version, this gap indicates the possibility of profiting from advanced technologies without the cost of inventing them (Fagerberg, 1987). Nevertheless, as Pack (1993) has pointed out, it is dubious that such dividends exist for free everywhere.

Abramovitz's (1986) analysis goes beyond that simple hypothesis; he extends and qualifies the convergence hypothesis taking into account the specific societal characteristics of the countries. In his view, only the countries that possess adequate "social capabilities" can exploit the available technological opportunities, and are thus able to really converge with the most advanced economies. In addition, the pace at which the potential for catching-up is realised depends on a number of other factors, related to the "technology congruence", the pace of structural change and the rates of investment and of the expansion of demand (Abramovitz, 1986).

As demonstrated elsewhere (Pessoa, 1998), in the three decades after 1960, the two most important sources of Portuguese economic growth were investment and the use of the "catching up effect". This conclusion was based on an accounting framework that relied on the "advantages of backwardness" literature. The tendency for the Portuguese economy to converge with the technological frontier resulted in part from a technology gap (Nelson and Phelps, 1969) between Portugal and the most developed economies. It was further helped by the combined effect of several economic mechanisms associated with the structural transformation of a backward country that kindled economic development (Abramovitz and David, 2001). It is likely that this also occurred in the other peripheral countries.

Indeed, as these economies were increasingly open to the most advanced countries, they benefited from four advantages in growth potential. First, because their tangible capital was technologically obsolete when they expanded or replaced the capital stock the new equipment bought embodied up-to-date, more productive, technology. Hence, they could achieve larger improvements in the average efficiency of their productive facilities than the leading economies, which already used the state-of-the-art technology. This rationale is also valid for both disembodied technology and non-technological innovations (new forms of industrial organisation and managerial practices, routines for purchasing, production and merchandising, etc.).

Furthermore, the low level of capital per worker, considering the possibility of modernising capital stock, tended to increase marginal returns on capital and, thus to promote fast rates of capital accumulation. Additionally, given the relatively large numbers of redundant workers in farming and petty trade, with very low levels of productivity, productivity growth occurred through the shift in labour from agricultural to industrial jobs (see Figure 6.3), and from self-employment and family shops to larger-scale enterprises. This was not affected by the cost of the additional capital necessary to maintain productivity levels in the new occupations.

Finally, the relatively rapid growth resulting from the first three sources leads to fast growth in aggregate output and, consequently, in the scale of markets. This promoted technical progress, especially where it depends on larger-scale production. This sort of technical progress was able to cover up the lack of technological effort to create new knowledge through R&D activity. All the above factors, plus an industry-based import substitution policy in the 1950s and export promotion policy based on increasing openness after 1960, explain why catching-up played such an important role in driving rapid economic growth for the EP.

Of course, the pace at which the potential for catching-up is realised also depends on a number of other factors related to the changes in the national economy and in other economies to which it is connected. The political and societal changes of the 1970s contributed to increasing the "social capability" in the EP. Furthermore, the steady improvement in access to education and the expansion in school enrolment, given the initial low level of education, helped to increase productivity, generating a better qualified labour force, a key condition to boost 'social capability'.

In addition, the progressive normalization after the political changes in Portugal, Greece, and Spain in the 1970s, on the one hand, and the expectation of and actual entry to the EEC, on the other, exposed people in the EP to a more open environment and forced economic agents and their business organisations to adapt to the new context. All these changes served to increase the congruence of these economies with the technology and business administration best practice deployed in advanced countries, and therefore to counteract the tendency for the 'catching-up' contribution to economic growth to shrink as the country developed. The improvements in 'social capability' and in 'technology congruence', together with other improvements in infrastructure, have been important to reinforcing the real catching-up effect.

However, the relative contribution of the catch-up effect must decrease as the country develops, in accordance with the respective theory. In effect, according to the 'advantages of backwardness' theory, explained above (Gershenkron, 1962; Abramovitz, 1979, 1986; Maddison, 1987), as a country moves towards the technological frontier the 'advantages of backwardness' become gradually smaller. Thus, it is not surprising that the economic growth rate diminishes at the same time as the economy develops and it is likely that, in spite of some national specificity, this phenomenon occurred in all peripheral countries.

As mentioned earlier, for the economy as a whole, labour productivity growth can be achieved through technological progress and/or by moving resources from low- to higher-productivity sectors. It is basically this structural transformation that is responsible for the decreasing effect of the 'advantages of backwardness', because development makes the economy more homogeneous. In the last four decades of the twentieth century, many low-productivity economic activities shrank or even disappeared due to the effect of the progress in economic integration.

Indeed, in peripheral countries, GDP growth was accompanied by a bigger structural change seen in the structure of production. As Figure 6.2 shows, peripheral countries converge with the trend in EMU from 1970 to 2010:[8] a decline in the value-added shares of agriculture and industry and an increasing trend in the value added of services. Naturally, there are some specificities particularly affecting Portugal. Giving Portugal's initial low level of development the drop in share of agriculture's value added is significantly more abrupt and the share of industry followed a more uneven decreasing trend. Regarding the industrial value added, two countries deviate from the EMU trend more or less after 2000: Spain by excess, owing to the increase in construction, and Portugal by deficit. However, both Portugal and Spain have a manufacturing share of value added below the trend in Italy and in the EMU (Figure 6.2).

Even though 'the division of the economy among agriculture, industry and services has lost most of its relevance' (Jorgenson and Timmer, 2011: 2) in 'advanced nations', it is still useful to compare the changes in the structure of production with the structural change in employment. The process of sustainable growth is regularly associated with inter-sectoral movements as the labour force shifts from agriculture to industry and from these two sectors to services, as shown in Figure 6.3.

Although employment in agriculture fell in all countries, in Greece and Portugal the share of employment in agriculture continued to be well above the share in the other two peripheral countries, which is nearly coincident with the EMU. In Portugal the higher share of employment in agriculture, reflecting the scarce number of jobs created in industry and services, is expressed in a very low and stable agricultural value added per worker.[9] This evolution of agricultural productivity contrasts with the rising trends of agricultural value added per worker in Italy and Spain (Figure 6.3).

Jorgenson and Timmer (2011: 2) found that 'the analysis of structural change requires a radical shift of emphasis from goods production to the

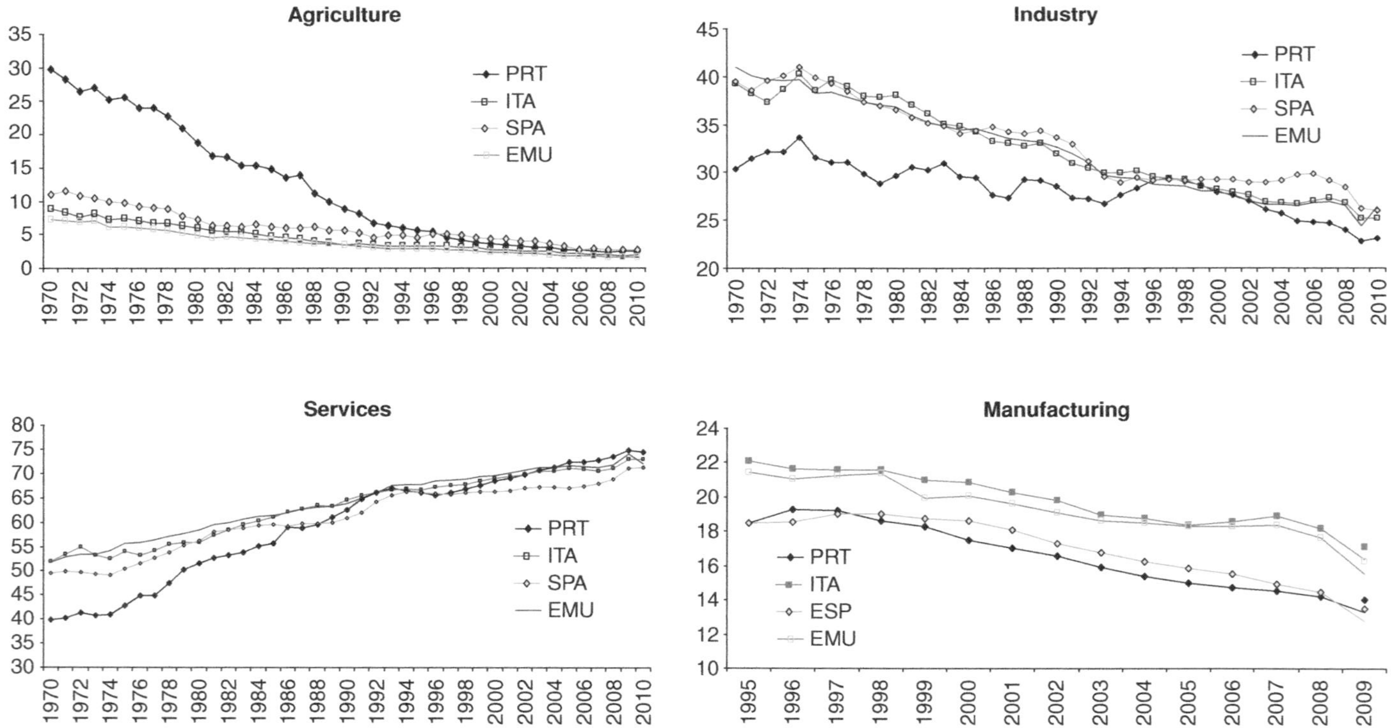

Figure 6.2 Evolution of the sectoral share of value added.

Source: Based on WDI data.

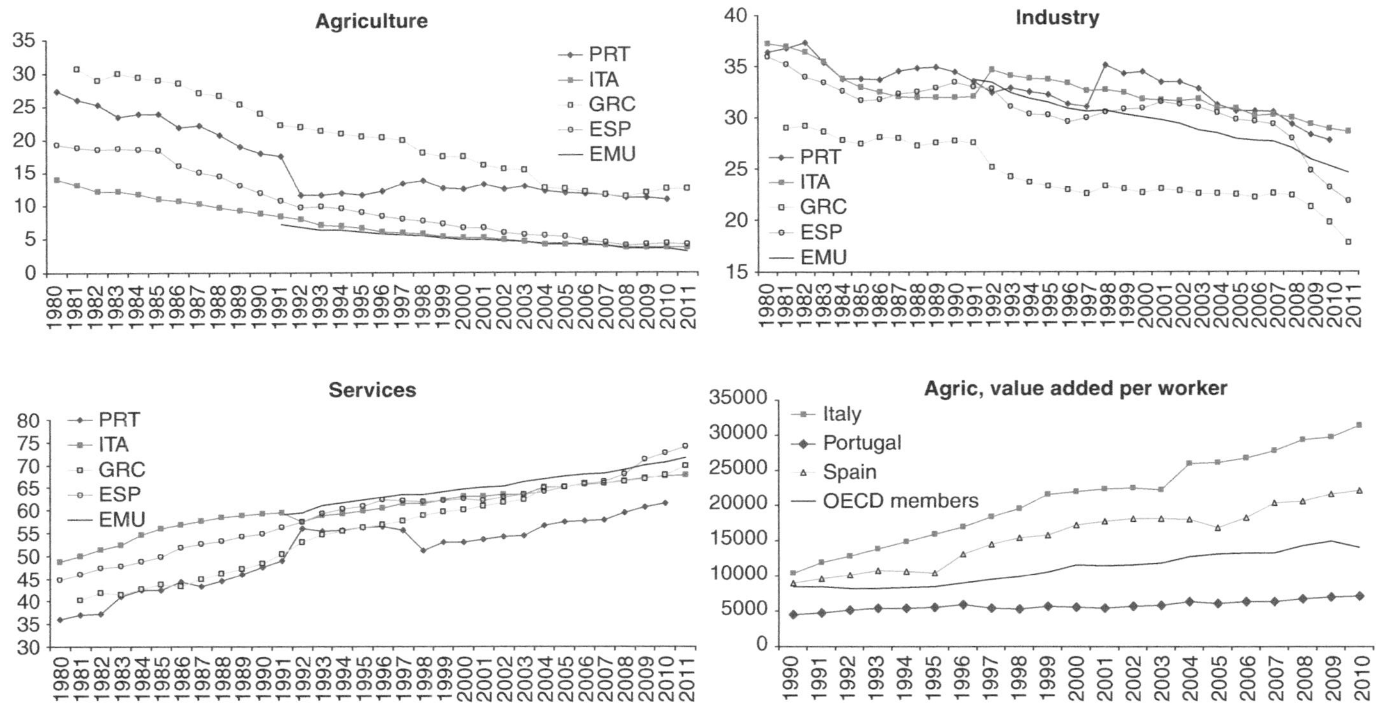

Figure 6.3 Evolution of employment by sectors.

Source: Based on WDI data.

production of services' and that there is 'substantial heterogeneity within the services sector', but 'the use of ICT capital and skilled labour is increasing in all sectors....' Since there is lack of data on services for the EP,[10] we only take into account the share of ICT service exports as a percentage of service exports, as depicted in Figure 6.4.

Figure 6.4 shows two trends, which broadly follow the tendency in the EMU: one, related to ICT goods, decreasing; the other, corresponding to ICT services, increasing. However, the decreasing trend in ICT goods is not offset by the increasing trend in services. Given the pervasiveness of ICT services in modern economies, particular attention must be paid to their production, especially in the Portuguese case where the increasing trend in ICT services was reversed after 2009.

It is likely that the change in the structure of production affects the structure of domestic demand. Figure 6.5 shows the change in the components of gross domestic product (GDP) from the expenditure side, which

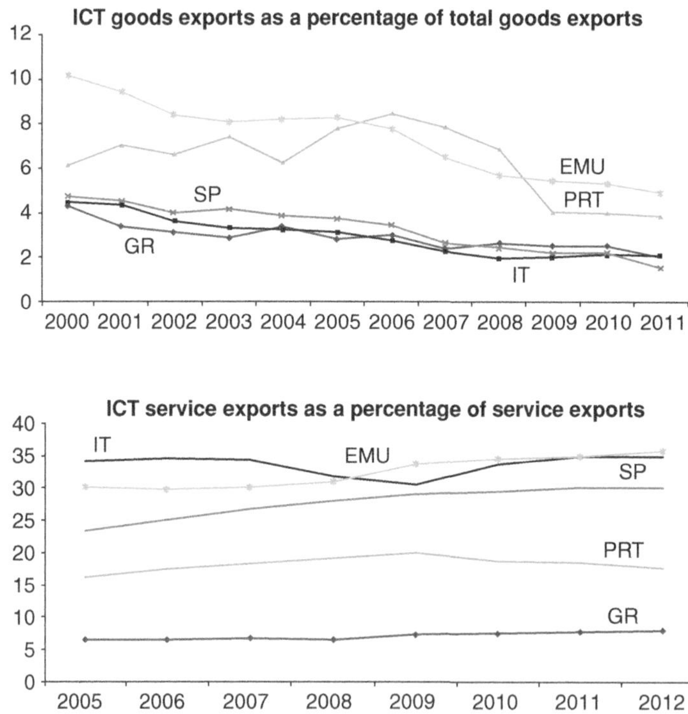

Figure 6.4 Evolution of ICT exports.

Source: Based on WDI data.

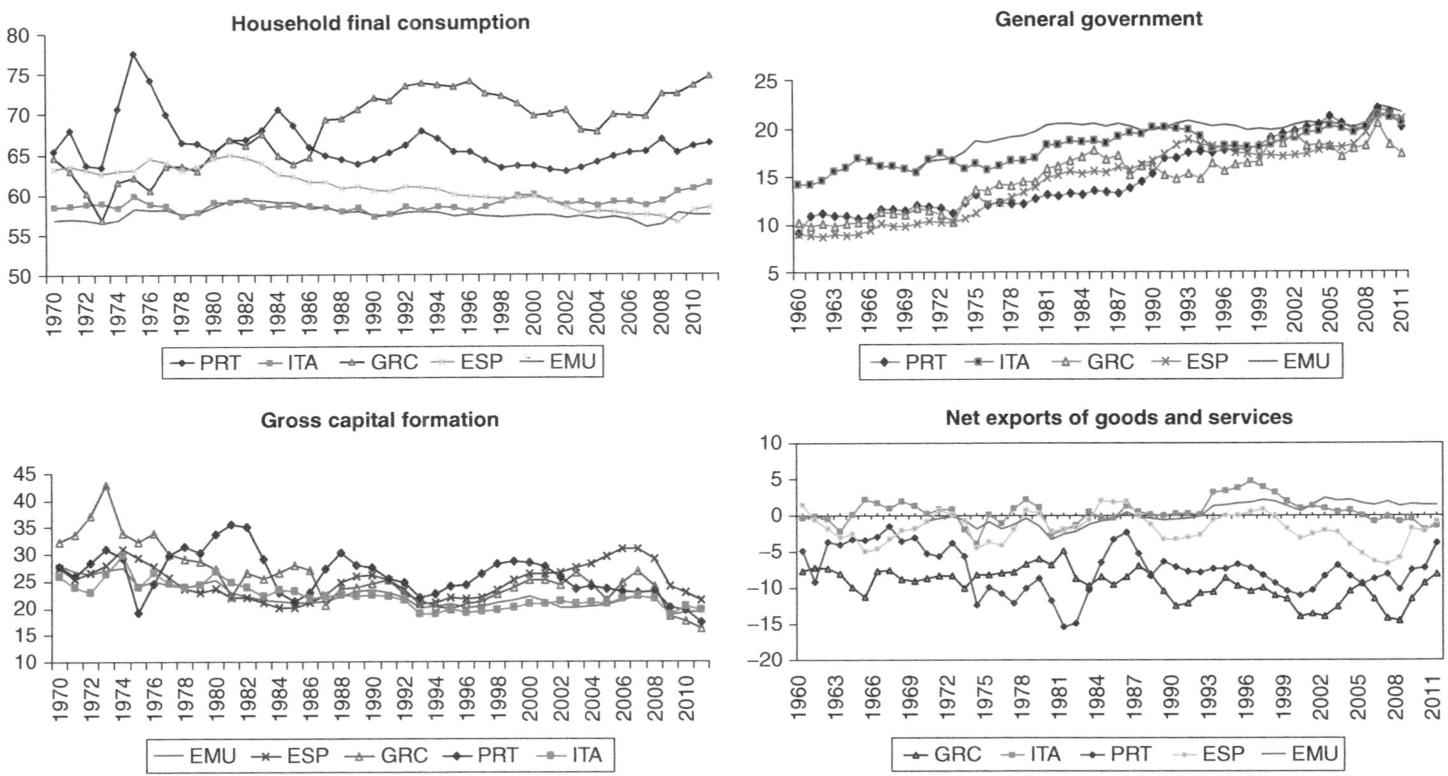

Figure 6.5 Structural change in demand.

Source: Based on WDI.

is household final consumption expenditure, general government final consumption expenditure, gross capital formation and net exports (exports minus imports) of goods and services.

As Figure 6.5 shows, the structure of domestic demand has different patterns over time. On the one hand, the share of general government consumption in GDP shows a clearly increasing trend throughout the period, catching up with the EMU share, with a faster pace in countries that initially have a weaker welfare state. On the other hand, the household final consumption share shows large variability over time. An exception to the wide variability of household final consumption is Spain, with a steady fall in the consumption share.

Figure 6.5 also shows that there was no convergence of either Portugal or Greece with the EMU in terms of level of household consumption. On the contrary, the household consumption share increased in these two economies in the 2000s and consumption continued to be higher than the EMU level. Furthermore, Italy, which followed the EMU trend in consumption throughout the 1980s, deviated from this trend and began to diverge in the mid-1990s, with this divergence intensifying after the 2008 crisis.

The large variability over time is also characteristic of the components of external demand, as summarised by the last panel of Figure 6.5: net exports of goods and services. In spite of the long-run increase of exports as a percentage of GDP in all peripheral countries, the external balance on goods and services shows a persistent tendency to be negative in Portugal and Greece, contrasting with alternating periods of positive and negative balances in Italy and Spain. The high share of household final consumption together with the persisting negative balance of goods and services in Portugal and Greece makes an analysis of saving and investment mandatory.

Figure 6.6 shows a decreasing trend in savings in the last 40 years, which was accompanied by a similar trend in investment.[11] This decline in the investment rate is very detrimental to the convergence process because, as mentioned previously, investment in physical capital was the most important source of growth for the EP in the 1960–1990 period. Furthermore, as the catching-up effect was slowly vanishing, the combination of these two effects can explain much of the decrease in the economic growth rates. Here too, there is a difference within the EP: while in Italy and Spain periods of investment exceeding savings alternate with periods of savings exceeding investment, in Greece and Portugal the share of investment has always been higher than the part of GDP saved.

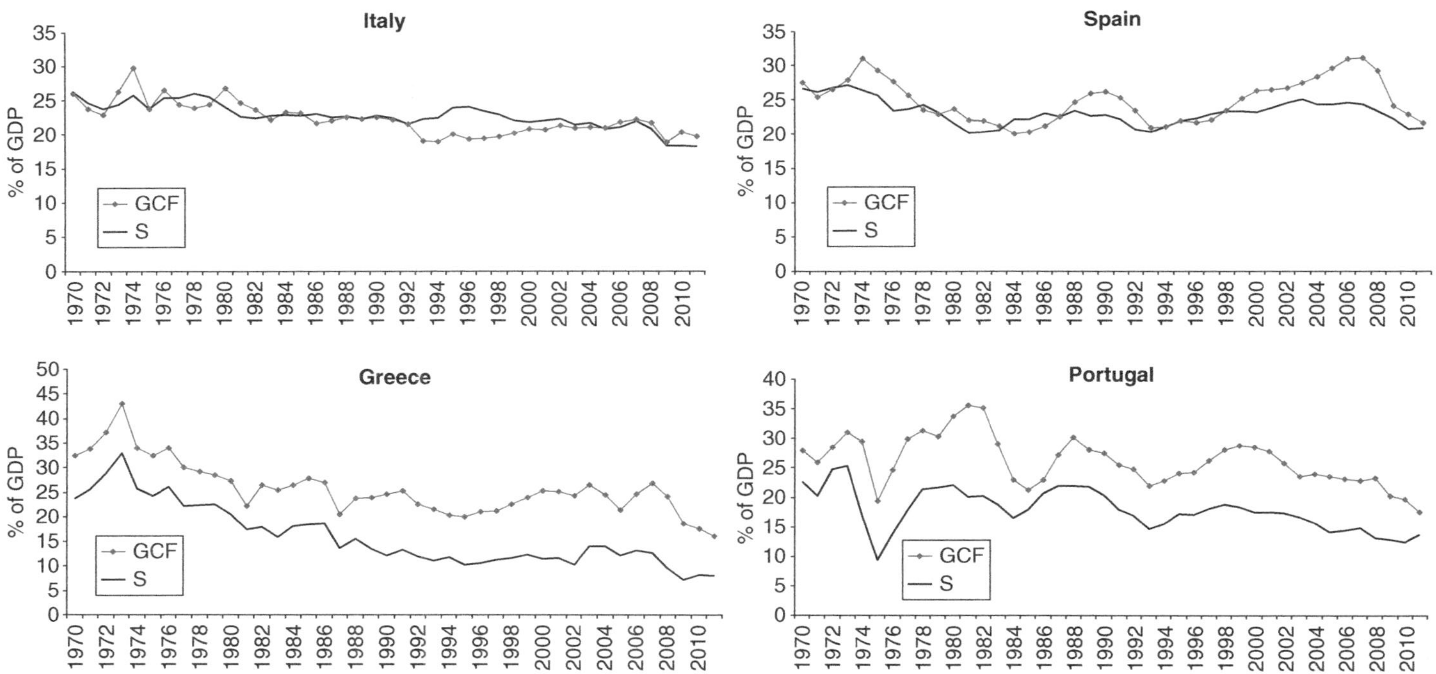

Figure 6.6 Investment and saving in periphery.

Source: Based on WDI.

The unfinished structural change

As shown in the previous section, structural change was clear-cut in the structure of production and employment, but it is less visible in terms of domestic and external demand. The share of exports in GDP has shown resistance to increase and this is reflected in the external balance of goods and services. Usually, this is explained by a lack of competitiveness of the economy, which is associated with numerous factors, ranging from low flexibility of the labour market and the high level of unit labour costs to fiscal competitiveness. This explanation amounts to assuming a structural reforms approach.

A structural change perspective should look at other economic problems. One important but usually ignored factor is firm size and its evolution over time. Peripheral countries have a distorted structure with an excessive share of very small firms. As shown in Table 6.2, in Portugal, Italy and Spain more than 93% of firms employ fewer than 10 persons while the share in Germany is only 82%. In peripheral countries, the number of firms employing 50 persons or more is less than 1%. This structure has large indivisibilities with negative effects on the improvement of productivity. It reduces the possibility of benefiting from scale effects, thus preventing, for instance, the use of professional management or the internalisation of services that can improve the position in the value added chain.

Why should this happen in peripheral countries? Because there is an employment fallacy—that micro firms create more employment—public incentives are biased in favour of micro firms. Of course, they create more employment. But the question is: why? It is because micro firms are less productive. It is normal for a micro firm to have low productivity, but the best firms grow and become more productive as they do so. This increase in the capital-labour ratio means less employment but it is an essential

Table 6.2 Enterprises in the non-financial business economy by size class of employment (%)

	Portugal	*Italy*	*Spain*	*Germany*	*Austria*	*EU 27*
From 0 to 9 persons employed	94.92	94.63	93.79	82.27	87.43	92.45
From 10 to 19 persons employed	2.87	3.46	3.56	9.85	6.95	4.08
From 20 to 49 persons employed	1.49	1.32	1.85	4.86	3.68	2.14
From 50 to 249 persons employed	0.63	0.50	0.68	2.55	1.60	1.02
250 persons employed or more	0.09	0.08	0.12	0.47	0.33	0.19

Source: Author's calculations based on Eurostat (2013) data.

condition for increasing output per capita and, by increasing aggregate demand, to then generate more employment.

Not only is the entrepreneurial structure biased towards micro firms but, in addition, the self-employed labour force is considerably higher than the EMU level (Figure 6.7).

Here we have something like the employment fallacy mentioned above. Because the economy creates few employment opportunities, individuals should create their own jobs. However, if this solves the individual's problem it pushes productivity down. If a structural reform is needed, it is here: taxes that diminish disposable income and aggregate demand should not be used to artificially maintain jobs in micro firms or to support self-employment.

The biased structure of firms and the high weight of self-employment are both important barriers to increasing productivity and show that a policy of flexibility of the labour market has not succeeded in increasing productivity. Although a policy of flexibility and deregulation of the labour market can increase productivity in a large firm by inducing reorganisation, in a micro firm the possibilities of increasing productivity in this way are very limited. In a period of stagnating or diminishing demand, while a large firm can react by cutting costs, for the micro firm this usually means shutting the doors and adding to unemployment.

For economies with a high concentration of micro firms, as is the case of peripheral countries, an increase in productivity implies that the structural change must go on. This change needs two conditions: first, there must be no artificial barriers to increasing the size of firms, unless this increase hurts competition; second, there must be incentives to introduce new products, new production processes or other types of innovation, whatever their form. Hence, proceeding with structural transformation now means changing the focus towards technological change.

Figure 6.7 Self-employment.

Source: Based on WDI.

4. The need for technological change

The causes of long-term growth are complex and over-simplified models and imperfect sets of indicators are often used to explain them. A single methodology is unlikely to unearth all the growth factors. Thus, econometric analyses must be complemented by historical studies that use a range of theories and approaches. This combination of analyses is the best way of searching for 'common features and patterns' (Kuznets, 1959) in the comparative experience of nations of differing size, location and historical heritage in order to establish regularities in structural change. Following Kuznets (1959), we use such regularities, generally known as stylised facts, to explain the best way of driving economic growth in the European periphery.

The literature on causes of economic growth contains a number of quantitative studies that are not contradicted by historical analyses and that report empirical results highlighting the following stylised facts: 1) TFP (total factor productivity), usually interpreted as the main effect of technical progress, is the most important contributing factor in economic growth (Solow, 1957; Dennison, 1962); 2) Innovative activity, as measured by R&D (research and experimental development) expenditure and patenting, is closely associated with the level of output and income per capita at country level (Fagerberg, 1987; Fagerberg and Srholec, 2008); 3) there are significant positive correlations between productivity at firm and industry level and the amount of R&D which firms and industries perform (Griliches, 1987; Nadiri, 1993; Gault, 2003); 4) R&D is positively correlated to growth, mainly via private business R&D (Guellec and van Pottelsberghe de la Potterie, 2001); 5) although public R&D has limited direct positive effects on productivity, it does have important effects on stimulating business R&D (Guellec and van Pottelsberghe de la Potterie, 2001, 2003); 6) countries with higher levels of innovative activity have a higher share of world trade (Fagerberg, 1988); 7) social rates of return to R&D are consistently higher than private rates of return (Bernstein and Nadiri, 1991; Griliches, 1992), indicating the existence of spillovers and increasing returns to scale.

Regarding R&D, the performance of the EP has been very poor, even though it has been covered up by investment in physical capital and by the other factors included under the umbrella concept of 'catching up.' However, when the effect of these factors vanishes the need for R&D to contribute more to economic growth becomes evident. In fact, when we look at figures for research inputs, the gap between EP and the OECD average is manifest (Figure 6.8). If we look at the GERD (gross domestic expenditure in research and development) as a percentage of GDP we see an evident discrepancy both in the past and in the present: in 1981, the EP R&D intensity varied from 0.15 in Greece to 0.86 in Italy, contrasting with 1.90 in OECD. In the business sector, the discrepancy was even more striking: in that year, the BERD (business enterprise expenditure on R&D) as a percentage of value added in industry ranged from 0.06 in Greece to 0.65 in Italy, contrasting with 1.78 for the OECD average.

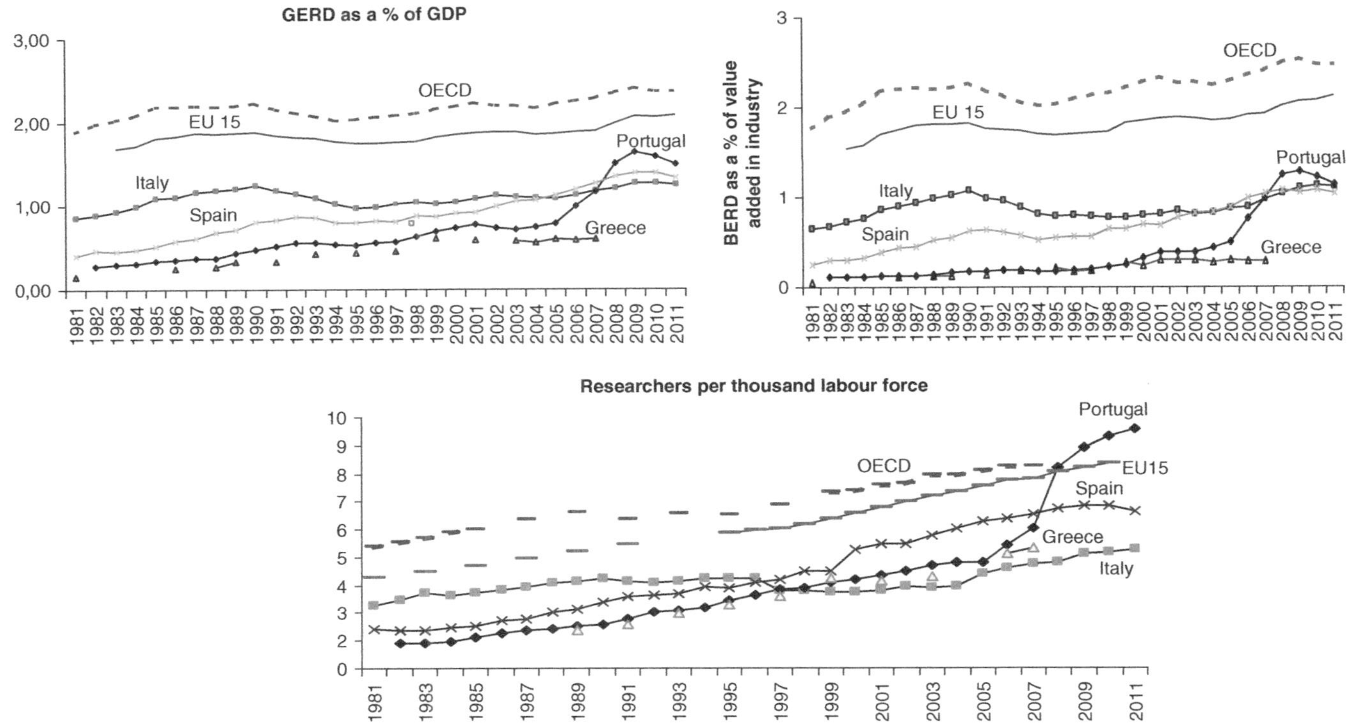

Figure 6.8 R&D and researchers in the European periphery.

Source: Based on MSTI (OECD).

However, not only is the initial level low, the evolution over time is also poor. Although countries' behaviours differed in the 1980–2011 period, the main picture that emerges from Figure 6.8 is one of inability to come close to the more advanced economies: the EP has not converged with either the OECD or the EU 15 averages. Portugal constitutes the sole exception, which is more noticeable in the period after 2005, in GERD and BERD.

With respect to human resources engaged in studying and exploring new ideas, the EP has been characterised by scarcity: in 1982, the number of researchers (FTE) per thousand labour force fluctuated between 0.92 for Portugal and 2.47 for Italy, far from the 4.54 OECD average. Moreover, in terms of R&D outlays, the evolution from 1981 to 2011 of the number of researchers was very poor, particularly in Italy which was overtaken by the other EP countries. Although these countries show more regular increasing trends in the number of researchers (FTE) per thousand labour force, they are still very far behind the most advanced economies. The sole exception is Portugal, which shows an outstanding performance in this indicator, particularly after 2005, this also being the case with R&D outlays.

In fact, the Portuguese performance is noteworthy in the European periphery context in R&D outlays and human resources. Whereas before 2000, Portugal and Greece were tied in last place in the ranking of peripheral countries, well behind Spain and Italy both in GERD and BERD, after 2000, Portugal significantly increased the share of R&D outlays in GDP and, particularly after 2005, it accelerated and overtook all the other peripheral countries. Even more significant is the increase in the number of researchers (FTE) per thousand labour force. Beginning with a figure similar to Greece, Portugal surpassed Italy, Spain, and even the euro area average (see Figure 6.8). What are the reasons for this outstanding performance? Before answering this question, we should consider other science, technology and innovation characteristics of the EP.

It is also apparent from Figure 6.8 that the distance from the OECD average is larger in BERD than in GERD. The low investment made in R&D by business enterprises has been accompanied by a distorted financing structure. In fact, Table 6.3 shows a distorted structure of GERD's financing in the EP compared with the OECD average. In the OECD, industry has always financed the majority of the gross domestic expenditure in R&D, in the EP countries industry has played a minority role, usually leaving the bulk of funding to the government. Italy was the sole exception to the minority role of industry in 1981, but its subsequent evolution has brought it closer to the other peripheral countries than to the OECD average. The biased financing structure of R&D towards government, which is typical of less developed economies, shows that the business sector is not sufficiently attracted by the benefits of technology and innovation.

So far we have looked at the input side of R&D. Looking at the output of researchers, measured by the number of journal articles,[12] we see an increase in the share of scientific and technical articles in all EP countries, showing a higher pace of growth in the EP than in the OECD average (Table 6.4).

Table 6.3 Percentage of GERD financed by government and by industry

Year*	Greece		Italy		Portugal		Spain		OECD	
	Gov.	*Ind.*	*Gov.*	*Ind.*	*Gov.*	*Ind.*	*Gov.*	*Ind.*	*Gov.*	*Ind.*
1981	78.56	21.44	47.21	50.08	61.94	29.96	56.01	42.79	44.14	51.70
1985	74.44	23.17	51.74	44.62	63.01	28.28	47.74	47.22	41.41	54.35
1990	57.68	21.75	51.50	43.75	61.78	27.04	45.13	47.44	36.74	57.87
1995	54.05	25.49	53.00	41.74	65.28	19.47	43.56	44.53	33.95	59.37
2000	46.59	33.05	na	na	64.79	27.05	38.64	49.73	28.31	64.20
2005	46.82	31.06	50.68	39.66	55.20	36.27	42.99	46.29	29.25	62.40
2010	na	na	41.56	44.66	44.93	44.09	46.64	42.99	31.08	60.28

Source: Based on Main Science and Technology Indicators, OECD (2013).

Notes: *na* means not available;

*or the next year, if available.

Table 6.4 Share of the number of scientific and technical journal articles in the OECD (in %)

	1985	*1990*	*1995*	*2000*	*2005*	*2009*
Greece	0.28	0.32	0.41	0.55	0.73	0.80
Italy	2.83	2.96	3.59	3.92	4.20	4.37
Portugal	0.07	0.13	0.20	0.34	0.50	0.68
Spain	1.21	1.55	2.27	2.71	3.12	3.52

Source: Own calculations based on WDI data.

This good performance in the number of scientific articles together with a poor performance in the number of researchers means that the number of articles per researcher has been persistently higher in Greece, Italy and Spain than in the OECD, at least after 1993.

The good performance in scientific and technical articles per researcher is not matched by the output of applied research, measured by patents (Table 6.5), where the progress registered was slight. Although Spain and Portugal have increased their share in the OECD both in triadic patent families[13] and patent applications filed under the PCT (Patent Cooperation Treaty), the other peripheral countries either do not show well defined trends (Greece) or their 2011 share is lower than that of 1985 (Italy). However, although Portugal and Spain show increasing trends from 1985 to 2011, the figures for the latter year remain far behind the figures for the more developed economies.

In fact, in 1985, Portugal had taken 1.5 triadic patent families, which corresponds to the insignificant share of 0.007 percent of the OECD total, and 15 years later the percentage is unchanged. From 2000 to 2011, the percentage of triadic patent families increased at a significantly higher rate. Regarding the patents filed under the PCT, the indicators for Portugal in 2000 are also very low, as shown by the extremely low shares in the OECD total. Nevertheless, although the percentage in 2011 is three times that of 2000, it remains extremely low compared with other advanced economies.

Table 6.5 Some patents statistics for the EP (figures in percentage)

Priority year	*Share in the total amount of Triadic patent families*				*Share in the total OECD patent applications filed under the PCT*			
	Greece	*Italy*	*Portugal*	*Spain*	*Greece*	*Italy*	*Portugal*	*Spain*
1985	0.007	2.246	0.007	0.149	0.01	2.08	0.01	0.13
1995	0.005	1.718	0.009	0.230	0.06	1.70	0.02	0.65
2000	0.013	1.404	0.005	0.319	0.05	1.84	0.03	0.65
2005	0.026	1.403	0.019	0.338	0.08	2.17	0.07	0.95
2011	0.017	1.365	0.022	0.372	0.05	2.04	0.09	1.14

Source: Calculations based on OECD MSTI database.

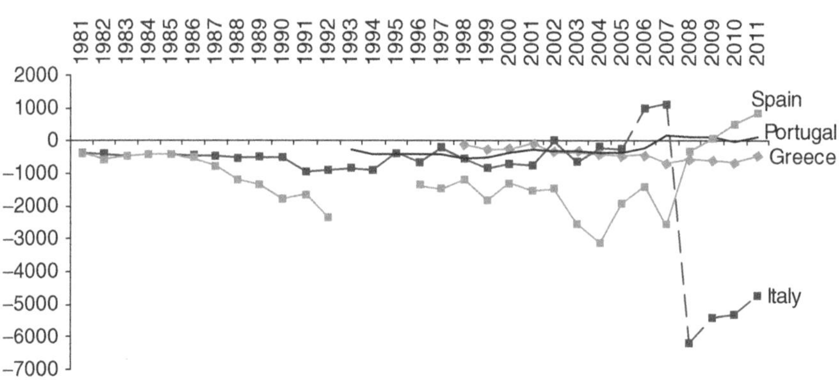

Figure 6.9 Technology balance of payments (million current dollars).

Source: Based on MSTI (OECD).

Another important domain is that of disembodied technology as measured by the TBP (technology balance of payments), which registers the international flow of industrial property and know-how.[14] Analysing the TBP of the EP we see that, despite some exceptions in recent years, it is traditionally negative, showing a chronic inability to generate receipts to pay the disembodied technology bought abroad (Figure 6.9). The most significant portion in the negative balance results from the acquisition and use of royalties and licence fees, which include payments to acquire and utilise patents, trademarks and similar rights, as illustrated by the Portuguese example (Table 6.6).

As we can see from Table 6.6, the items that contribute to the positive balance of Portuguese TBP are research and development services, technical assistance, and other technical services, but Portugal and the other peripheral countries continue to have a deficit of patents and other similar rights.

There are several reasons for the low propensity to patent in the EP, and this is not the proper place to discuss them, but the type of industrial sectors predominantly based on the supplier-dominated industries (Pavitt, 1984)

Table 6.6 The Portuguese TBP (million euros)

Year	Total			*Acquisition and use of royalties and license fees*		*Technical assistance services*		*Research and development services*		*Other technical services*	
	Credit	*Debit*	*Balance*	*Credit*	*Debit*	*Credit*	*Debit*	*Credit*	*Debit*	*Credit*	*Debit*
2006	777	946	–170	120	355	301	284	41	20	315	287
2007	1 064	938	126	197	319	421	269	42	28	405	322
2008	1 228	1 162	66	178	364	544	371	39	29	466	398
2009	1 273	1 175	98	165	390	577	346	43	28	488	412
2010	1 144	1 167	–23	42	410	592	293	40	24	470	441
2011	1 308	1 232	76	83	386	612	283	48	25	565	538

Source: Based on data from Banco de Portugal (2012).

and the firms' size prevalent in the EP bear some responsibility for such low figures. In this respect, the development of the EP's technological capacity will depend not only on the ability of researchers to increase the stock of commercially useful knowledge but also, and more importantly, on the capacity of firms to use such patented technology.

To sum up, technological change really does not exist in the EP, or if it does, it happens at a very slow pace. This pace is far short of the change that took place in the economic structure after 1960. However, for Portugal some aspects do point to some degree of change in the last few years relative to R&D outlays and number of researchers. It is now time to answer the above question: What are the reasons for this outstanding performance?

The answer points to a different approach by the Portuguese government to science, technology and innovation. First, after 2005, the government approved and implemented a Technological Plan, defining a new strategy for scientific research and science diffusion. Second, much investment was redirected to activities related to innovation. Third, the reintroduction of the fiscal incentive system aimed at business enterprise R&D—SIFIDE (Portuguese acronym for *Sistema de Incentivos Fiscais à I&D Empresarial*). Fourth, an updating of the Business Enterprise register in the 2007 Survey. Fifth, directing some European Structural Funds towards firms' innovation, which have resulted in an increase in the number of the firms performing R&D and a significant rise in business enterprise R&D.

This strategy yielded many of the expected results. In fact, Portugal experienced a significant increase in GERD as a percentage of GDP, and the increase of R&D outlays was even more significant at the business enterprise level. This rise was accompanied by an increase in human resources devoted to R&D, as was shown in Figure 6.8. Indeed, some other indications back up these findings. For instance, the EIS global index of innovation shows an improvement in Portugal's score in the EU-27 ranking, from 22nd in 2006 to 16th in 2011 (IUS, 2012). This improvement in the innovation ranking is connected to some other qualitative changes at the micro level, which constitute significant case studies on the introduction of innovative processes and products both in the science-based sectors and in supplier-dominated industries. However, the euro crisis and the way it is being solved are having an impact: there is a reversal in the ascending trend of GERD and BERD shares after 2009.

Evidently, the change in the technological pattern in the Portuguese economy did not immediately translate into benefits at the economic growth level. Besides the need to consider the necessary time lags for converting technological change in economic growth, two other facts must be noted. First, this change occurred at the same time as the EP faced new competitors and many inefficient firms went under. Second, given ongoing globalisation and the increasing integration of the EP into the euro area, it is hardly astonishing that the explanation for the decrease of the EP growth rate must also consider the reasons for the generalised decrease in economic growth in developed countries, particularly at the European level, in the first decade of the twenty-first century. As Figure 6.1 in Section 3 shows, this is the sole decade where growth in the European Union and the euro area was below the world economic level.

Why has economic growth been so difficult in Europe since 2000? The way the EMU was designed and implemented, and the concept of competitiveness adopted by the European Commission and the euro area, means that the core countries are certainly part of the answer to that question. But the fixation on the virtues of structural reforms, particularly on wage flexibility, rather than the adoption of a more dynamic concept of competitiveness based on competition involving new products and new productive processes, has contributed to losing leadership in technology and innovation. Additionally, the attempt to replace the wage-led growth model, prevailing until the mid-1990s in a number of European countries, with a profit-led model (considered the best way to turn such countries into export-led economies) is another major reason explaining the instability of GDP growth and its stumpy rate, both in the EP and in the euro area as a whole. Furthermore, the priority given to the financial markets and the globalisation of capital instead of the real economy also helps to explain the low level of investment and the high level of unemployment.

Some of the above factors have not only affected the EU and its member countries, they have also hurt the growth performance of the majority of developed countries in this century. In fact, the downturn in economic growth is not a specificity of the EP. It is generalised throughout the developed world, but within this, the euro area was particularly affected (Figure 6.1 in Section 3). Alongside the factors that are common to the developed world, including the EU, two factors are more specific to the EU periphery: the effects of entry into the EMU on the interest rate, and some 'Dutch Disease' type effects triggered by the European Funds, which jointly distorted the tradable / non tradable goods ratio. The minimisation of these effects calls for a correct exchange rate policy. However, with their entry into the EMU, the EP countries lost this possibility.

The ideology of structural reforms has proposed a substitute for the lack of the exchange rate control: the so-called internal devaluation (Pessoa, 2011) and expansionary austerity. However, the results of such a strategy are quite clear in Portugal and Greece: constant missing of economic and financial targets and a resulting recessionary spiral accompanied by increasing debt-to-GDP ratios.

Although when dealing with a crisis, theory teaches that the instruments to address the immediate problem must support a long-term view, there is real danger that the structural reforms initiated in Portugal and other peripheral countries may only seek financial equilibrium, without having any discernible long-term positive effects on the real economy. Furthermore, the present financial and economic crisis is creating severe challenges for the design and implementation of development policies, particularly in countries that are in the process of building technology and production capabilities. Because the downward spiral of economic activity does negatively influence employment, investment and production, policy-makers risk putting the wrong recipe in place, ending up by compromising growth prospects and aggravating, instead of mitigating, the effects of the crisis.

The history of earlier crises shows a contraction on the values of the GERD/GDP ratio. If the present crisis has the same outcome,[15] the timid progress registered can be entirely reversed. Moreover, when short-term and rescue policies prevail, the consensus for S&T policies tends to decline. However, if the EP abandons its efforts with S&T policy, the production structure that will emerge after the crisis will not be able to catch up with the new technologies and paradigms that will shape global production and trade. Instead of catching up, there is a risk of widening the gaps with leading countries.

5. Conclusion

This chapter focuses on structural and technological change in the EP (European Periphery). It deals with the way a country lagging far behind the technological frontier can converge with the technological and economic leaders. Inspired by several stylised facts, our point of departure was that sustained development implies structural change. However, there are limitations to structural transformation if technology does not change accordingly. Moreover, as economic growth proceeds the direction of causation between the two dynamics changes. Initially, the structural transformation pulls the technology, whereas later, it should be the technology pushing structural change and growth. Understanding this is quite important for countries lagging behind the technological and economic frontier, particularly when convergence with leaders is becoming increasingly difficult. Although EP growth in the past used the 'advantages of backwardness', when these advantages shrink, investment in R&D and innovation policy becomes crucial to further progress along the convergence path.

All R&D indicators show that the EP has been in the past, and will go on being in the future, far from the technological frontier. Although some progress has been made in some specific aspects of science and technology performance, it is virtually insignificant when compared with those associated with the structural change.

Around 2000, Portugal began a process of change in its technological performance. In fact, while the technological indicators do not show any significant convergence with the OECD average before 2000, both at the business enterprise level and in terms of the financing structure of GERD, after 2000 the situation began to change, at first slowly and unevenly, and speeding up after 2005. In fact, there was a narrowing of the gap between Portugal and the OECD average in all science and technology indicators. In addition, the structure of funding for GERD exhibited a convergence with the OECD average. More importantly, the data available showed an increase in the speed of the convergence with the more advanced countries. However, the evolution since 2009 is showing a reversal in important indicators such as those associated with GERD and BERD.

For the EP, there are still many challenges ahead in terms of R&D inputs and outputs in order to catch up with the EU and OECD level of technology. Because the main picture is still one of a lack of investment in new technologies, patenting, and so forth, it is crucial to keep the long-run horizon in science, technology and innovation policy in place. As a recent OECD report has shown (OECD, 2009), it was investment in innovation in times of crisis that allowed Finland and South Korea to become more competitive and innovative. Thus, more than Washington Consensus-like structural reforms, the EP needs to increase its efforts to initiate or develop technological transformations that complement the structural change initiated in the last century.

Notes

1 Of course, Ireland was affected by the Euro crisis, too. However, contrary to the crisis in the EP, the Irish crisis is usually seen more as a consequence of the failure of its banking system than as an effect of a structural problem.

2 Of course, there is another approach based on growth empirics. But, in our view, its reductionism is a sufficient reason to prevent it from being taken seriously per se as an inspiration for policy.

3 Fisher (1939) and Clark (1940) look at patterns in changes in sectoral employment. According to their arguments, the patterns of production are functions of income level, and resource and production changes are essential parts of development. The main determinant of these shifts is the income elasticity of demand. Goods or sectors for which there is a high-income elasticity of demand will grow in importance as income grows.

4 Supply-side economics argues that economic growth can be most effectively created through greater flexibility by reducing regulation and by lowering barriers for people to produce goods and services, such as lowering income tax and capital gains tax rates. According to supply-side economics, consumers will then benefit from a greater supply of goods and services at lower prices (Wanniski, 1978).

5 The *Expansionary Fiscal Contraction* (EFC) also known as the 'expansionary austerity' hypothesis (Giavazzi and Pagano, 1990) predicts that, under certain restricted circumstances, a major reduction in government spending that changes future expectations about taxes and government spending will enhance private consumption, resulting in overall economic expansion. The authors did not provide a model for EFC but rather described conditions under which it was observed in Denmark from 1983–1984 and Ireland from 1987–1989, a period when the world was undergoing rapid interest rate declines and worldwide growth.

6 This is recognized in one of the hypothesis' seminal texts: 'Keynesian textbook propositions seem to recover their predictive power, as witnessed by the 7 percent drop in real consumption in 1982 during the first Irish stabilization' (Giavazzi and Pagano, 1990, p. 28).

7 For instance, 29 Sub-Saharan African countries agreed to adjustment programmes conditioned by structural reforms with the IMF and the World Bank in the 1980s, but the result of those programmes was far from acceptable (see World Bank, 1994).

8 Greece is not included in Figure 6.2 because its data on value added are not available in the database used.

9 Data on value added of Greece is not available in the database used (WDI).

10 The database used by Jorgenson and Timmer (2011)—the EU KLEMS—only has data on services for Italy and Spain.

11 With respect to investment, Spain is an exception. After 1993, it shows an increasing trend due to the construction boom, which ends abruptly with the 2008 crisis.

12 Scientific and technical journal articles refer to the number of scientific and engineering articles published in the following fields: physics, biology, chemistry, mathematics, clinical medicine, biomedical research, engineering and technology, and earth and space sciences.

13 According to the OECD definition of triadic patent families, a patent is a member of the triadic patent families if and only if it is filed at the European Patent Office (EPO), the Japan Patent Office (JPO), and is granted by the US Patent and Trademark Office (USPTO).

14 The following operations are included in the TBP: patents (purchases, sales); licences for patents; know-how (not patented); models and designs; trademarks (including franchising); technical services; finance of industrial R&D outside national territory. The following operations are excluded: commercial, financial, managerial and legal assistance; advertising; insurance; transport; films, recordings, material covered by copyright; design; software.

15 For example, regarding the Portuguese economy, a first glance at the MSTI database for 2011 is not encouraging: the percentage of GERD performed by the Business Enterprise Sector is 45.9 percent whereas it was 51.24 in 2007; the GERD per capita is 379.09 vs. 408.27 in 2009; the GERD as percentage of GDP is 1.49 vs. 1.64 in 2009; the BERD as percentage of the value added of industry is 1.14 vs. 1.28, in 2009.

7 National adaptive advantages

Soft innovation and marketing capabilities in periods of crisis and change

Sandro Mendonça

1. Introduction

Economic history does not play dice. Innovation is a profound and pervasive process that has made humanity come a long way. Approaching this process also requires a panoramic awareness in order to capture techno-economic change in its different guises and details. Innovation is, indeed, a many splintered phenomenon. This study argues for the continuous development of new methodological perspectives as innovation itself continues to make history unfold. Research on innovation has to adapt as the external environment itself changes. When the economic context changes fast and violently, like during the "Great Recession" or "Little Depression" period, the reasons pushing for analytical innovation can only increase. Such efforts may uncover, for instance, deeper weaknesses in the beleaguered European periphery than those already much discussed. It may well be that such countries have been under-investing in innovation more severely than previously realised.

One purpose of innovation studies is to bring us ever-updated knowledge regarding the structure and dynamics of creative and complex economic systems. The economy, as a multivariate and evolving ensemble of knowledge and value-added activities, becomes an ever-fertile ground where genuine learning can take place among those observers concerned with the realism of their hypotheses and the appropriateness of their policy conclusions. A novelty-intensive economic reality thus calls for innovation in the working tools and raw materials themselves, that is, the concepts and data economists use to go about their trade. Innovation in theories and evidence must keep pace with the innovation phenomena themselves. There is a need to keep working and to push the boundaries of approaches and develop new ones. New combinations of intellectual devices and empirical evidence can bridge the gap between the world and our understanding of it. Like in wonderland, the innovation economics programme has to keep moving in order not to lose ground.

Our goal here is to explore ways of mapping and measuring non-technological innovation. But how to explore the softer side of innovation when innovation studies, and neo-Schumpeterian economics in particular, still suffer from a science and technology bias? One way is to focus on the more intangible side of new products made available to customers. A key observation is that new or improved products have to be "marketed", that is, the techniques and solutions for enhancing the chances of such products in the community of potential users have to be known and made attractive. Hence, one angle of analysis is to investigate how goods and services are made more persuasive. It is not enough that products themselves are better or more sophisticated. Prospective consumers have to learn about them and be convinced to try them out. The ways in which suppliers attempt to bridge the gap with the demand side may reveal important empirical information regarding the innovative activities being developed.

The goal of this contribution is thus to reflect on the ways in which the "non-functional" and "non-hard" features of innovation can be employed to understand innovation behaviour at large. In a modern economy, assets such as symbols and style, harnessed by property rights such as trademarks and industrial design, are key to the competitiveness of firms, regions, and nations. Concentrating on trademarks, this chapter studies how actors, at the country level, use non-technological innovation to build and sustain competitiveness in the dynamic contemporary globalised markets. In a multidimensional business environment, we suggest two main domains of adaptability, the technological and the marketing domains. We discuss how, as a complement to indicators such as patents, trademarks point the way to understanding the softer side of innovation and may reveal lesser known patterns among sectors and across nations.

We apply this analysis from the perspective of European periphery countries. We find that periphery countries persistently lag behind in terms of softer innovation capabilities, not only just in terms of science and technology. This has coincided with a robust performance of emergent economies, such as China, which have been strengthening in terms of intangible assets in marketing and reputation in recent years. One implication is that structural policies have to acknowledge the plural set of factors behind sustainable economic and social development for the sake of addressing the holistic fragility of the present weaknesses in the European periphery.

This chapter is organised as follows. Section 2 discusses the rationale for using trademarks as an indicator for understanding a modern economy. Section 3 presents the data and the sources. Section 4 presents the major stylised facts stemming from the analysis. Section 5, concludes by appraising how the novelty of this approach may have implications for policy research.

2. Innovation through the lens of trademarks

Studying the innovative economy

Before Schumpeter, technical change was much of a blind spot in the academic approach to the economic world. In the eighteenth century, Adam Smith indeed spoke of learning and new machinery inside a factory and, in the nineteenth century, Karl Marx discussed the transformation of the mode of production at an aggregate level. In the early twentieth century Joseph Schumpeter took us beyond inventors and initiated the economics profession on the behaviour of individual innovators and the roles of large businesses in an industrial economy. Schumpeter was the inventor of explicit innovation studies in economics. But he was also the one who was able to create a sustained and progressive research agenda.

Based on Schumpeterian theoretical foundations, several conceptual refinements were made by a number of scholars, such as Freeman (1982), Nelson and Winter (1982) and Rosenberg (1972, 1982, 1996). Neo-Schumpeterian research of the later part of the twentieth century gave maturity, depth and breath, and policy relevance to the study of innovation. These scholars took the analysis beyond single isolated actors and called attention to the institutional rules and networking practices that characterise the actual systems generating and absorbing useful knowledge. This neo-Schumpeterian tradition became a rich source of insights and methodological commitments concerning the real economy. It focuses on the sources and impacts of change, on the rhythm and direction of change, on the policies that foster and nudge actual and potential change. As these contributions accumulated it became increasingly clear that innovation was not a thing but a continuous ongoing process, a multi-actor activity, and a variegated phenomenon (see Caraça et al. 2009).

In the face of a continuously evolving environment, economic actors are pressured to respond to current impacts and future vulnerabilities. Change in the socio-economic context is characterised by short-term variability that occurs on top of an ongoing and unpredictable process of long-run structural change. Adaptability in this setting means not only protecting against negative impacts of known competitors, but also building resilience and taking advantage of trends and turns. Adaptation is done by innovating in fast-moving and rugged selection landscapes.

A creative accumulation of innovation indicators

Innovation, as a multidimensional phenomenon, has been approached with a number of different empirical indicators. Historically, innovation indicators mostly emerged as by-products of institutional and policy-making activities. Rather than being designed by social scientists and researchers, these data evolved out of established practices and routines (Smith 2004: 150). That was, for instance, the way research and development (R&D) and patents of invention started their careers as statistics on science and technology (S&T). Patent indicators were firstly used by lawyers and engineers (Mendonça 2012), whereas R&D series began to be compiled due to rising pressure by governments investing heavily in new high-tech knowledge (Godin 2005).

Hence, S&T metrics were never designed optimally as indicators. They have a number of characteristics and drawbacks as mainstream measures of knowledge-building and knowledge-using activities. There are other measures like product announcements or technological alliances but the staple of innovation studies keep on being R&D and patents (see Patel and Pavitt 1995). R&D-related figures such as financial and human resources are usually referred to as "input" indicators in the innovation process. Since publications and patents represent a scientific or technological result from previous research and shop-floor practice, such indicators are known as "output" indicators.

Innovation is itself difficult to measure. The existing indicators approach it indirectly from many angles. The idea is that the strengths of some indicators serve to compensate the shortcomings of others. Building on Patel (2000), Table 7.1 lists the main measures and statistics of innovation that have been proposed and employed in various studies. The table contrasts their key strengths and weaknesses, as well as their thematic coverage. Some indicators are suitable for certain types of firms (say, R&D and patents for big pharmaceutical companies) while others do not work well for certain types of variables (such as aggregate human capital for what is really the specific knowledge being used). Other common drawbacks have to do with the general non-coverage of non-technological innovations (Smith 2004: 153–8). This area has only recently been tentatively tackled. Explorations into less conventional areas have been tried with novel indicators, and this is the case of trademarks.

Trademarks as an economic indicator

The modern economic system is a symbol-intensive mode of production and distribution. Commercial visibility, reputation, and even fame, are sough-after strengths in increasingly competitive marketplaces. Arenas of product competition are also a pitch where many messages collide. Capitalising on this insight, marks appear today as a new consensus metric of innovation. In this state of semiotic struggle, brands and slogans provide a proxy of the level and growth dynamics of the new value of propositions and attempts at product differentiation.

The trademark indicator was proposed some time ago (Schmoch 2003; Mendonca et al. 2004) as a proxy for particular kinds of innovations, namely product and marketing. That is, new intellectual property rights registrations could indeed indicate the launch of new value propositions. But the introduction of the new products itself is facilitated by new communication actions. In a word, innovative goods and services often carry new names and logos. In the effort of introducing new products ("output" indicator) there are also activities of creativity in marketing ("soft" innovation).

Today, according to a recent survey by Schautschick and Greenhalgh (2013), there is extensive literature supporting the view that trademarks are a useful complement and supplement to the list of metrics supplying relevant information about innovative activity. This literature includes research by individual scholars (see Millot 2009) as well as official institutions (OECD 2009a; The National Science Foundation 2012: 6–54).

Table 7.1 A portfolio of innovation measures

	Nature	*Focus*	*Strengths*	*Weaknesses*	*Coverage*
R&D	*input*	Science, Technology	Captures investment in new knowledge Regular and long run data	Not detailed Underestimates mechanical innovations, software development Underestimates the performance of small and medium-sized firms	Country, sector, firms
Human resources	*input*	Science, Technology	Captures tacit knowledge Allows for some break-down by type of know-how	Deficiencies in skill categorisation	Country, sector, firms
Scientific publications	*output*	Science, Technology	Large availability of data Citation data is also abundant	Not directly related to scientific fields Far from the market	Country, universities
Patents	*output*	Technological activity	Regular and abundant data Technological classifications available	Differences in propensities to patent across industries Underestimates smaller firms	Country, sector, firms, universities, technologies
Trademarks	*output*	Product innovation, Marketing innovation	Covers smaller firms and services Captures incremental innovations Close to market	Differences in propensities to trademark across industries No information on marketing expenditures	Country, sector, firms, product classes

Regarding other output indicators, such as patents, commercial marks offer advantages that make it an attractive additional indicator, particularly to cover services (Schmock 2003; Mendonça et al. 2004; Mangani 2006; Fikkema et al. 2007), SMEs (Mendonça et al. 2004; Keupp et al. 2009), because they are closely related to the release of innovations in the marketplace (Mendonça et al. 2004; Malmberg 2005), and are especially effective in covering the developments in some specific industries (such as pharmaceuticals, software, creative industries or services based on sophisticated knowledge, cf. Schmock 2003; Malmberg 2005; Handke 2007; Livesey and Moultrie 2008; Fosfuri and Giarratana 2009; Schmoch and Gauch 2009; Giarratana and Martínez-Ros 2010). Marketing signs, moreover, are increasingly used as indicators for industry and country dynamics in a context of globalisation (e.g., Caree et al. 2011; Gallié and Legros 2012; Godinho and Ferreira 2012; Makkonen and van der Hav 2013; Sandner and Block 2011).

3. The empirics of trademark analysis

Trademarks protecting industrial personas

Trademarks are intellectual property rights that cover names, logos, slogans, and other types of distinctive signs of products and their producers. That is, they protect the corporate identity systems that are usually known as "brands". Brands are nexus of words and/or images that convey to the marketplace the presence and distinctiveness of products and/or their suppliers. Thus, as if introducing a character in an economic play and telling its tale to an uninformed or sceptical audience, trademarks are a synthesis of what an offering stands for.

Commercial emblems first appeared in the pre-modern, pre-industrial, pre-capitalistic age to distinguish producers and to allow consumers to rightly perceive the origin of the goods they acquired (Mendonça et al. 2004). By the late 1800s, marks were becoming legally enshrined in most western economies of the northern hemisphere. As mass markets developed and the new broadcasting media grew in the early twentieth century the pressure and premium for visibility became more compelling. Firms were not just competing with each other; they began to actively compete for consumers' scarce attention.

What do trademarks indicate?

Whereas R&D and patent analysis are cottage industries in innovation studies, marks have long been largely ignored. Only very recently did an empirical methodology emerge proposing and exploring the analysis of trademarks. Trademarks are now acknowledged as a proxy of strategic intent and performance in markets characterised by dynamic (non-price) competition. Over ten years of experimenting with this data has shown that firms employ trademarks to introduce new (tangible and intangible, i.e., goods and services) products and expand their reputation in a variety of markets (Schautschick and Greenhalgh 2013). For instance, competing through branded product innovations and marketing models has been a key course of action in high-tech as well as low-tech sectors (Mendonça 2012). Thus, trademarks help to track the innovation paths of firms and sectors, regions, and countries.

Trademarks can also point to marketing investments, such as patents indicate R&D spending. In this sense, trademarks may reveal a commitment to develop useful knowledge on consumer behaviour. This knowledge, however, is hardly passive. Marketing expertise is used not only to adapt but also to influence perceptions and nudge this psychological and social side of the strategic environment. Marketing management is not about just fitting to the environment, it is also about shaping its more malleable elements (Clark 2000: 6). Surely, then, trademarks are instruments for producing aesthetical impressions and emotional impacts upon consumers and may indicate innovation in branding itself as a creative activity. In this case trademarks serve as a proxy of what may be referred to as "soft innovation" (see Stoneman 2010: 279).

Trademarks are, nonetheless, imperfect indicators. Among the shortcomings, there are the different propensities to trademark across sectors and jurisdictions, for instance, or the fact that a newly registered trademark is not necessarily equivalent to a new product launch. However, while mimicking many of the patents' drawbacks, trademarks offer significant relative strengths. For research purposes, the ideal approach is to use different kinds of indicators to compensate for the partiality and bias of each of them.

The trademark data

This study makes use of the Community Trade Marks (CTM) obtained from OHIM (the Organisation for the Harmonization of the Internal Market), an official European Union (EU) institution that grants trademark rights to the 28 member states. The data is taken from 1996, the earliest year available, and the analysis is carried to the last available year, 2012. CTM applications (after some time most of them are registered) are taken as revealing initiatives to promote new offerings in the EU as a whole, or at least part of it, while keeping the option to diffuse the product more widely. So, applications are at once considered tentatively innovative (we assume) and tentatively international (we assume) attempts to capture the markets' attention to new products or to defend offerings from competing proposals.

European Union data is useful as it represents a combined marketplace for over 500 million end-consumers and over 21 million firms. With about 7% of the world's inhabitants and an output of around 20% of GDP, this is undoubtedly an interesting empirical pool for the study of trademarking dynamics. The EU expanded from 15 countries in 1996 to 28 in 2013, the companies of which may apply for CTMs for low fees. For the sake of analysis, and minimising data distortions, we will analyse only the sample of the founding OHIM members. At the OHIM, all companies file for CTMs indicating product categories (under the NICE classification system), as well as recording their firm names, country of headquarters, and administrative information.

4. Commercial trademarks and industrial progress

Major patterns and trends

When CTMs were first issued in 1996 there was an initial boom of aggregate applications. After that applications followed an upward trend, sometimes modulated by the business cycle.

Figure 7.1 presents application counts for new trademarks over time. It shows the number of total "unique" trademarks, i.e., not the number of classes to which protection was awarded. On average, three or more classes are assigned to a trademark.

Total applications grew over time, but now without fluctuations. Some of the variation may be associated with boom and bust patterns, that is, fluctuations in general economic activity. This is undoubtedly the case of the "New Economy" bubble, which is perceptible around the year 2000. A slowdown is also visible in the later part of the series, coinciding with the impact of the "Great Recession". Like in the case of patents (Griliches 1990), there is probably an administrative cycle introducing some noise. There was, for instance, a cut in fees in 2005 and an even bigger reduction in 2009, which may have contributed to attenuating the impact of

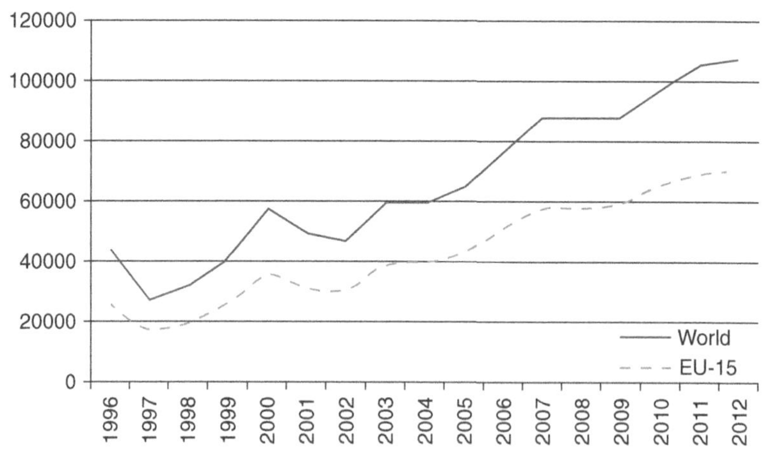

Figure 7.1 Total yearly CTM applications by world and the EU-15 aggregates.

Source: OHIM, author's calculations. All figures and tables below share the same source.

the Euro crisis on aggregate CTM applications. Also, the entry of 10 new member states in 2004 may have strongly increased the potential value of the CTM asset and hence contributed to an increase in its demand (for a recent analysis of strategic trademarking in specific sectors, see von Graevenitz 2013).

The annual number of CTM applications was above 100,000 in 2011 and, by the end of 2012, the cumulative stock of all applications was 1,1140,259, a sizable volume indeed. EU-established applicants are the most intensive users of the system. Around two-thirds of applications come from the EU-15. In terms of individual countries, Germany, the UK and Italy concentrate 60 percent of CTM applications within the EU-15 for the whole period. Large countries apply for a large amount of CTMS as shown in Figure 7.2. It is noticeable how Germany, the industrial powerhouse of Europe, is also a continental super-power in the sheer size of its trademark arsenal. Correcting for size (population and GDP), small countries come out best: Nordic countries, Ireland and Austria. Small EU-15 member states, namely Austria and the Netherlands, had the most robust growth rates in the twenty-first century.

Regarding non-European countries, the United States recently lost its position as the largest community trade marker to Germany, while Japan's application rate also declined in recent years. Meanwhile, BRICS countries have gained ground. Figure 7.3 shows the performance of the BRICS, among which the rise of China is the most notable: it took off in the mid-2000s and sustained its path from then on.

It is worthwhile also to analyse other "insurgent" nations, that is, nations from the "south", which have recently been challenging the markets of the "north." In Figure 7.4, we see Taiwan and South Korea, the so-called Tigers

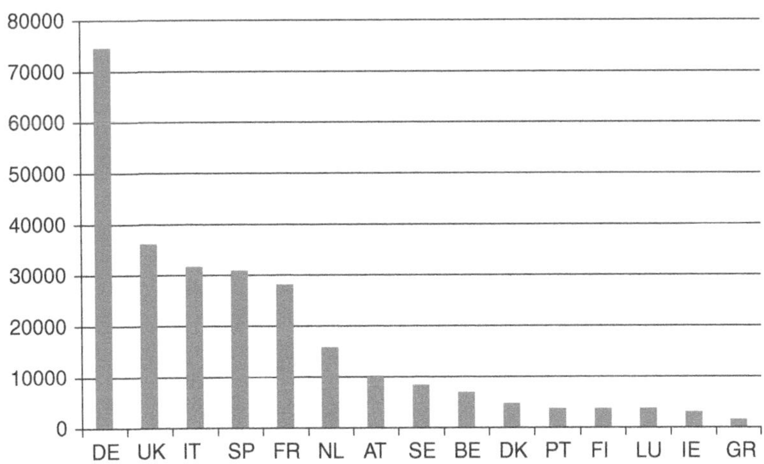

Figure 7.2 Total by EU-15 countries during 2009–2012.

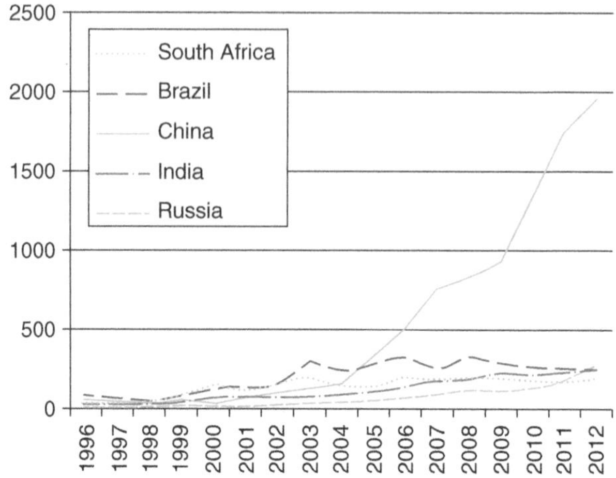

Figure 7.3 Aggregate applications for CTMs by the BRICS, 1996–2012.

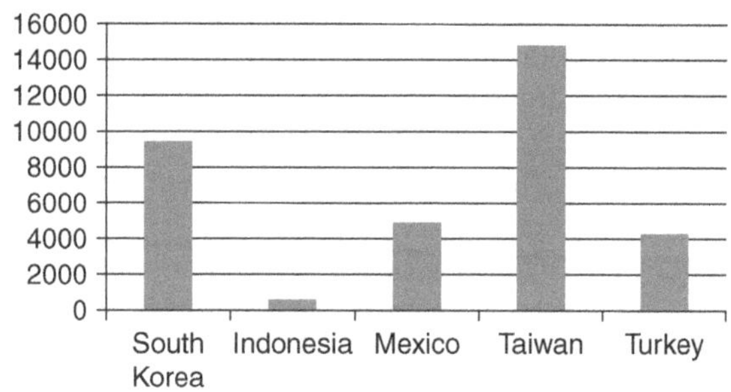

Figure 7.4 Applications for CTMs by other emergent economies, aggregate 1996–2012.

of the 1990s, displaying a large overall stock of applications. It should be noted that this performance must have something to do with the field of industrial specialisation. Indeed, the trademarking dynamics differ widely across businesses.

In terms of product category breakdown, the top ten most trademarked classes received a total of 1,630,357 applications, that is, 52.3 percent of all requested classes between 1996 and 2012. Table 7.2 shows that five of these refer to goods and the others are service classes. There are two information and communication technology classes in the top ten, which are precisely where high-performing countries such as Taiwan and South Korea have specialised for the past few decades (Fontana and Mendonça 2013).

Examining country performance in terms of product category is a worthwhile exercise. Competitiveness dynamics and structural change may be revealed in this way. As an example, Figure 7.5 shows how two

Table 7.2 Top NICE classes in total world CTM applications, 1996–2012

Rank	*Class*	*Applications*	*% of total*
1	09	307 950	9.9
2	35	242 704	7.8
3	42	214 990	6.9
4	41	168 490	5.4
5	16	161 527	5.2
6	25	142 141	4.6
7	05	108 129	3.5
8	38	104 902	3.4
9	03	94 924	3.0
10	36	84 600	2.7

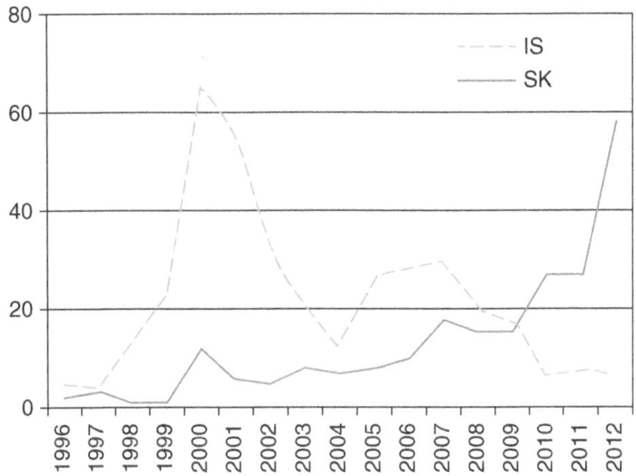

Figure 7.5 Aggregate applications for CTMs by Israel and South Korea, 1996–2012.

ICT-intensive countries have performed in class 9, which in the NICE system broadly represents electronic equipment and precision instruments. Israel and South Korea have recently shown a reversal in ICT-related areas.

So far we have seen that trademarks are requested in great numbers. We have also seen that powerful European economies tend to be strong in terms of their marketing performance. Moreover, a number of emergent countries that have pursued robust export-led industrialisation can be shown to have vibrant branding performances in the very high-tech, hard science-based sectors for which advanced countries were known for. The availability of CTM data allow us to uncover and question patterns such as these. The next section probes deeper into the forces at stake.

Goods and services under strain

Among trademark applications manufacturing goods have typically higher levels. However, service trademarks have followed a faster upward trend over time. Index numbers for the EU-15 show that the volume of applications for service trademarks in 2009, the year the crisis hit Europe, was 4.3 times higher than in 1996, whereas goods classes were only 2.3 times higher. Consequently, service classes as a whole gained "market share" from 23.8% in 1996 to 36.8% in 2009, as Figure 7.6 shows. See also Figure 7.7 for the Portuguese case.

The pattern over time points to a structural change in the aggregate economy, in line with what could be expected. Note that short-term fluctuations point to the "New Economy bubble" of 1999–2000. The volatility is clear especially in services. The onslaught of the "Great Recession" in 2008–2009 did not lead to an immediate absolute decline in aggregate EU-15 trademarking. The impact was one of stagnation, interestingly enough, simultaneously in both sectors.

High and low product sophistication over time

It is interesting that low-tech sectors are crucially important even for advanced countries. It is thus interesting to compare the scenario at EU-15 level with that of a country like Portugal. When focusing solely on industrial

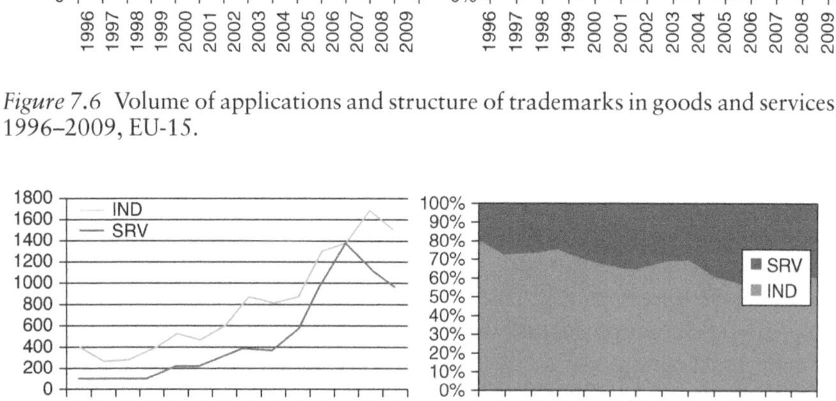

Figure 7.6 Volume of applications and structure of trademarks in goods and services, 1996–2009, EU-15.

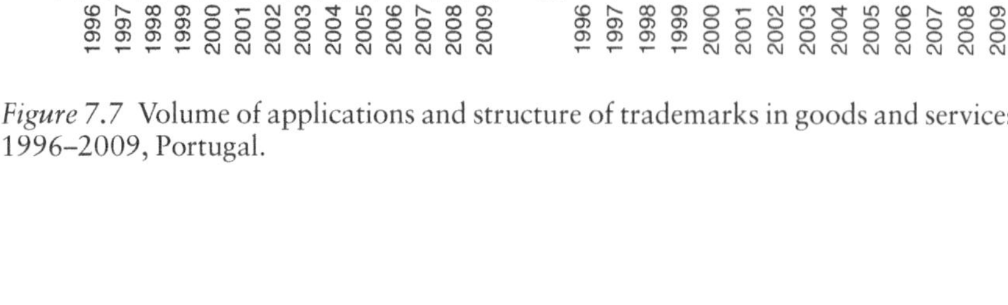

Figure 7.7 Volume of applications and structure of trademarks in goods and services, 1996–2009, Portugal.

goods classes for EU-15, the case of Figure 7.8, we see that European countries show a predominant trend for applications in areas of traditional goods. That is, "Low-tech" trademarks count for the largest proportion within the classes of tangible products for these countries. In 2009, low-tech CTMs reached 45.6%, not that different since 1996. Even more interestingly the two most dynamic types of goods within the EU-15 between 1996 and 2009 were the "low-tech" and "high-tech" categories.

Trademarks allocated to low-tech industrial goods are also a majority in Portugal, although with a greater weight than in the EU-15 (see Figure 7.9). This category accounted for 65.5% of goods brands in 1996 and 56.7% in 2009 (i.e., until the Euro crisis struck). This suggests a less sophisticated general profile for the Portuguese economy but a fast catch-up to the European structure. At the same time, higher-tech classes were strengthening their relative weight, although not at the expense of a decrease in the absolute number of low-tech brands.

Figure 7.10 shows that, in the EU-15, the most sophisticated services (the "High-information intensity", i.e., High-info) are more "trade-marked" than the more basic or traditional services (Low-info). The "New Economy Bubble" is clearly visible in the High-info services, while the "Great

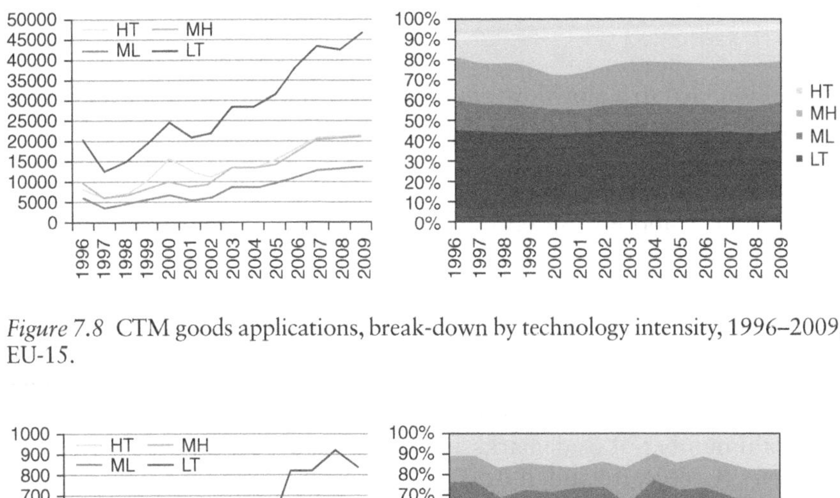

Figure 7.8 CTM goods applications, break-down by technology intensity, 1996–2009, EU-15.

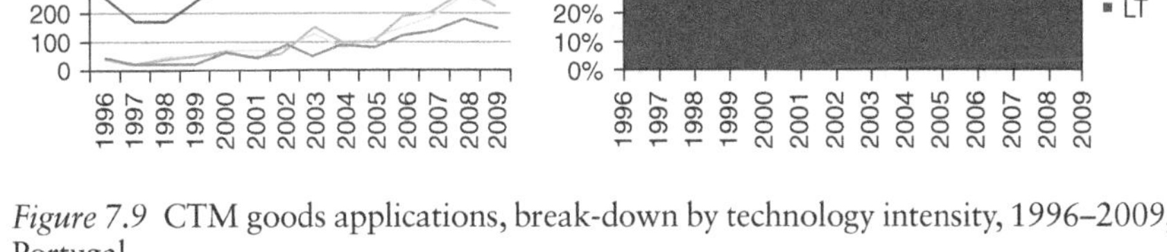

Figure 7.9 CTM goods applications, break-down by technology intensity, 1996–2009, Portugal.

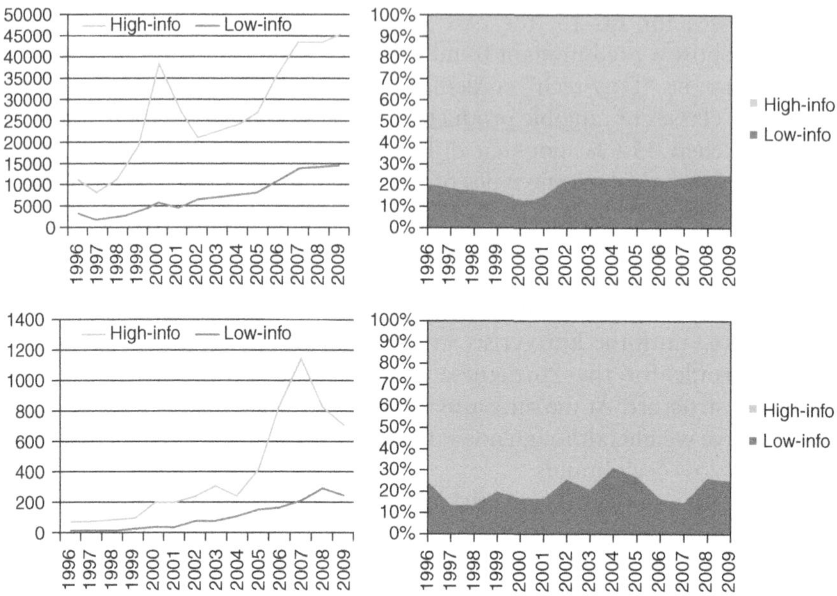

Figure 7.10 CTM service applications, break-down by information-intensity, 1996-2009, UE-15 (above) and Portugal (below).

Depression" led to a slowdown in both types of services. As for services in Portugal, as Figure 7.11 shows, High-info also explains an overwhelming proportion of applications for service marks (about three quarters on average during the entire period). The sharp rise in High-info growth during 2005–2006 is abruptly stopped in 2008, i.e., a year before the Low-info category suffers a contraction.

Countries and the crisis

Figure 7.11 shows what happened after the impact of the Sup-prime/Euro-crisis in terms of index numbers for groups of EU-15 countries. The total number of trademarks applied for is lowest for the "Periphery" countries (Greece, Ireland, Italy, Spain and Portugal as a whole) and highest for the "Nordic" countries (Denmark, Finland and Sweden), with the "Core" countries in the middle (Germany, France, United Kingdom, etc.). In terms of total trademark applications, Portugal was the most hit of the "Periphery" countries (in 2012, it was 13% below its 2008 level) whereas Austria and Sweden were the most dynamic of their groups (45% and 44% higher than their respective 2008 levels).

The heterogeneity of sectoral dynamics crosses with the differences in country dynamics. The crisis led to a drop in trademarking activity in Europe but also to a sharp decline in Portugal. Figure 7.12 illustrates this.

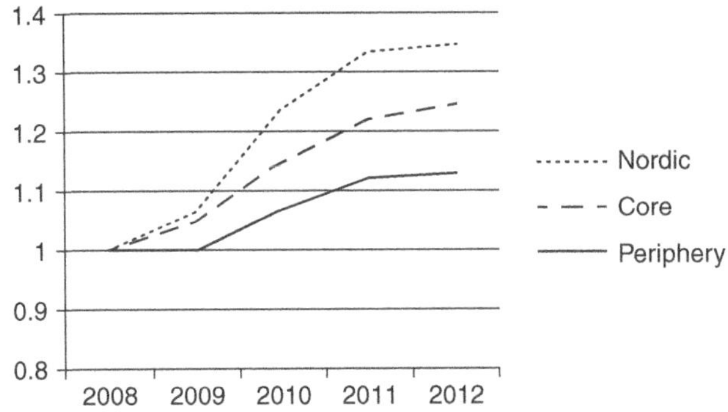

Figure 7.11 CTM applications, 2008–2012, per country group within the EU-15.

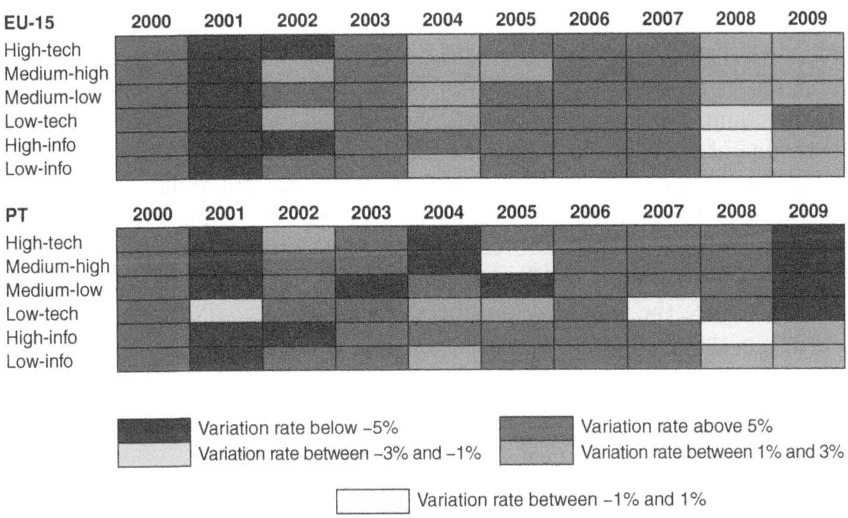

Figure 7.12 Heat map of CTM services applications, by sector, 1996–2009, EU-15 and Portugal.

We can see that the "New Economy" crisis produced negative effects in the EU-15 and in Portugal, and although widespread in terms of sectors, they were essentially short term. In contrast, the "Great Recession" hit the EU-15 and Portugal differently, and the impact is much less homogeneous across sectors, deeper and longer.

An integrated view of innovation capabilities

The following diagrams plot countries' performance along two axes that explore technological/functional capabilities (horizontal axis) and non-technological/promotional capabilities. In doing so, this analysis applies the view that innovation is not only about solving objective problems, it is also about breaking through subjective barriers, mental habits and collective inertia.

Figure 7.13 can be taken at first as evidence of CTMs as an indicator of innovation. It shows that CTM applications in high-tech goods classes are correlated with patenting performance. In other words, records of invention in the technology realm correlate strongly and positively with the investment in marketing assets in high-tech product areas. However, we can see a concentration of the periphery in the bottom left-hand corner while the crisis-resilient show up in the top right-hand corner. This pattern can be taken as complementing Mazzucato's (2013: 52) observation that the countries suffering most and longer from the Euro-crisis (such as Greece, Portugal and Italy) are those that have spent the least on science and technology. In other words, the picture suggests that "core countries" which have escaped the worse effects of the crisis have not only been those spending the highest R&D/GDP, they have also honed the soft skills needed to interpret market preferences and persuade audiences of the good quality of their products. Those countries mastering hard science and high-technology are not lost to the value of "soft power" where engaging users' needs is concerned. Good products are not enough, promotion counts in large amounts.

Figure 7.14 uses R&D intensity and CTM per capita applications to produce and partition EU-15 economies. We see the "Core" and "Nordic" countries performing above average in both domains. On the opposite corner, we see the southern periphery, namely, Greece, Portugal, and Italy. Also, it is also possible to note that the UK, Spain, Ireland, and even France

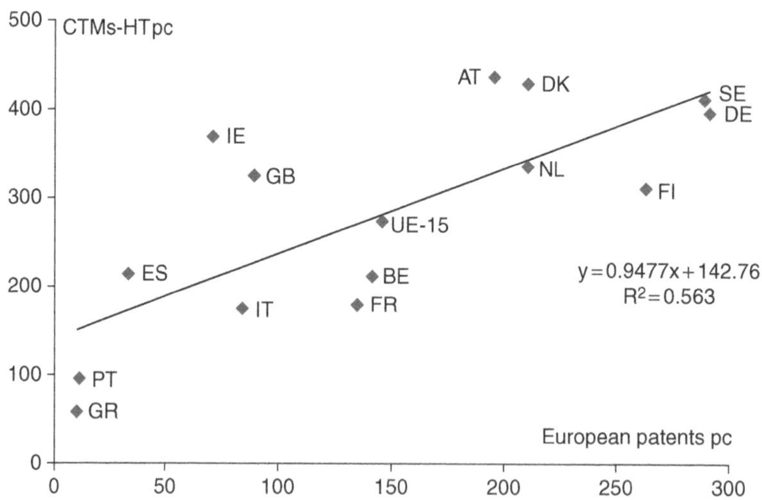

Figure 7.13 High-tech CTMs pc (applications) and European patents pc (granted), EU-15 countries for the sample period 2005–2007.

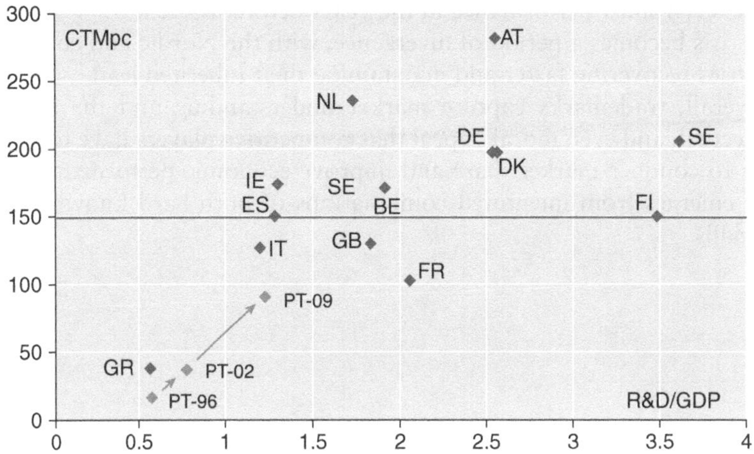

Figure 7.14 Technological and marketing capability map, 2009.

are all too near having relative weaknesses on both vectors. Just before the crisis a country like Portugal was actually "behaving" appropriately: Portugal was strengthening its knowledge base on both fronts. That is, it was actively doing the tough march toward the benchmark countries. Under the impact of the crisis, reverse gear was set in place, dissipating years of steady cumulative progress.

5. Conclusions

Trademark data are useful in providing an additional means to map and measure the adaptability of actors and groups of actors to dynamic contexts where Schumpeterian competition is the dominant mode of market dispute. Trademarks are an innovation output indicator and a yardstick to assess the marketing capabilities of economic units. Here we used Community trademark data for the period 1996–2012 at the country level. We focused mostly on the 15 member-state countries that witnessed the founding of this intellectual property right.

A number of trends and stylised facts surface that yield instructive insights regarding innovation-led change and competiveness dynamics. Both core and catching-up economies seem to build strong positions on science and technology as well as organisational and marketing knowledge bases. The current European crisis was translated into a major downturn in those countries that had below-average technology and marketing tools to withstand its impact.

Periphery countries are those with the most lack-lustre performance after the crisis that started in 2008. These countries were in a catching-up process in terms of soft innovation. Among these, for instance, Portugal, which had a very robust performance in the years before, is the most severely hit. The crisis becomes a period of divergence, with the Nordic and core EU-15 countries recovering faster and maintaining their inherited lead.

Overall, trademarks capture market understanding and the aesthetic, intellectual, and even moral appeal that competitive players have to build in order to conquer market share and improve economic performance. Resilience emerges from integrated combinations of both hard knowledge and soft skills.

8 Human capital and growth in services economies

The case of Portugal[1]

Marta C. N. Simões and Adelaide Duarte

1. Introduction

Services currently comprise the largest sector in many economies, accounting for around 70 percent of value added and employment in OECD countries (see e.g., OECD 2005; Jorgenson and Timmer 2011). This process of dynamic structural change has raised the question of whether services can be a source of sustained growth since the services sector has long been regarded as unproductive, merely operating as a complement to other sectors and traditionally viewed as composed of low productivity/stagnant activities, such that increased specialisation towards services would lead to a growth slowdown (see, e.g., Baumol 1967). However, the services sector can no longer be considered homogeneous, composed of non-tradable services with no opportunity for scale economies and improvements in productivity, known also as traditional personal services. These include, for instance, trade, hotels, restaurants and public administration. Technological change boosted the development of services such as communication, banking, insurance, and business-related services, which can be easily transported at low costs and have a high potential to increase productivity through the incorporation of technological advances. These services, which share many characteristics with manufacturing, are known as modern impersonal progressive services (see, e.g., Ghani 2010), and are also assumed to be relatively skill-intensive, so human capital and thus education play an important role in driving growth in these sub-sectors (see, e.g., Peneder 2007).

Portugal is no exception with regard to the dominance of the services sector and the Portuguese economy has become almost stagnant since the late 1990s. It is thus important to analyse the services sector in greater detail in order to understand if it contributed to the Portuguese economy's current lack of growth and whether it can help Portugal to overcome its dismal growth prospects. This concern applies also to other peripheral European countries that have recorded since the mid-1990s an increasing participation of low productivity services sectors together with weak growth and convergence performance (see Silva and Teixeira 2012). The persistence of relatively low aggregate income, low productivity levels and poor performance in Portugal and other peripheral European countries is probably linked to the strong weight of services, and especially traditional (stagnant) personal services (see, e.g., Mateus 2006; Ramos and Simões 2011; Silva 2011; Silva and Teixeira 2012). The modern impersonal progressive services, on the other hand, have registered higher labour productivity levels and growth rates. However, since these sub-sectors demand higher levels of human capital, the relatively low educational levels of the peripheral European workforce may have prevented these countries from capitalizing on the opportunities provided by modern services growth and may continue to do so in the future. For instance, Silva (2011) and Silva and Teixeira (2012) present evidence on the difficulties Portugal faces in promoting major changes towards high-skill and high-tech activities over the period 1980–2007. The authors argue that this slow change in structure may have its roots in the still relatively unqualified Portuguese workforce since "(...) a large supply of high-skilled labour seems to be a prerequisite to promote significant structural change, by enabling the adoption and creation of technology and stimulating innovation. As a consequence, education influences structure, but the inverse relationship is plausible as well." (Silva and Teixeira 2012: 21). Additionally, Silva (2011: 20) also points out that "(...) a vicious circle between low education attainment and low-tech industry structure seems to have been in place, making it more difficult to implement the modernization of the economy and promote its adaption to global competition."

This chapter provides some clues on these relationships by exploring the existence and relations of causality among service sector productivity and expansion, aggregate productivity, and human capital over the period 1970–2006 for Portugal. The main aim is to examine whether the increasing tertiary sector in the Portuguese economy constituted an obstacle or an opportunity for its aggregate productivity performance and if the expansion of the services sector is related to human capital availability. Other countries of the European periphery show similar patterns in terms of productive structure, human capital availability, and aggregate productivity performance (Mas et al. 2008; Silva and Teixeira 2012), hence, this analysis of the Portuguese case can also provide important insights for these economies.

2. Services, growth and human capital: theory and evidence from the perspective of the european periphery

The European periphery: some facts

The general picture from a few recent studies on the growth and productivity performance of the peripheral European countries (Italy, Greece, Portugal, and Spain) is one of below-average growth from the mid-1990s onwards that resulted in stagnation or even divergence relative to their northern and central European counterparts. These studies examine the role of structural change in this process and identify some interesting common features that can help explain the current crisis all these countries are experiencing, and that must necessarily be dealt with in order to restore growth and convergence to the European core. Mas et al. (2008), Silva (2011), and Silva and Teixeira (2012) give ample evidence of the slowdown in productivity growth the peripheral European countries have faced over the last 15 years. The first study focuses on the situation of Italy and Spain, the second is devoted to Portugal and Spain, while the third considers the three countries simultaneously.[2] These studies provide a detailed picture of the contribution of structural change to this trend, pointing to the rising relevance of low-productivity and low-skilled activities, namely services sectors, as an important cause of the decline in aggregate productivity, although to varying degrees given the three countries' initial differences in terms of productivity levels, quite high in Italy while similar in Portugal and Spain. According to Silva and Teixeira (2012), in 1970, Italy's real GDP per capita was almost in line with that of the EU-15, whereas that of Portugal and Spain stood at slightly over 60 percent of the average. By 2010, however, the differences across the three countries had narrowed considerably with figures when compared to the EU-15 of around 85 percent for Italy, 65 percent for Portugal, and 80 percent for Spain. In terms of performance, labour productivity growth in the European periphery declined throughout the period and at a faster pace than in the EU-15. Mas et al. (2008) provide evidence of a negative multifactor productivity (MFP) contribution to aggregate value added growth across all sectors in Italy and Spain, particularly severe in the personal (market) services sector, that additionally showed a strong increase in labour creation. On the other hand, non-market services such as education and health presented an increase in labour productivity. Using a slightly different sectoral aggregation, Silva and Teixeira (2012) also show that, contrary to the countries experiencing faster productivity growth more recently, in Italy, Portugal and Spain information and technology-producing sectors (where telecommunications are included) and market services (trade, hotels, and restaurants, transport, financial and business services, and social and personal services) have contributed little to aggregate productivity growth. In the first case, this is due to their relatively small participation in terms of total value added and employment, while registering high rates of labour productivity growth. In the latter case, the opposite applies.

As for potential causes of the increasing specialisation pattern of the peripheral European countries towards low-skill, low-productivity growth services such as distribution, and hotels and restaurants, Mas et al. (2008), Silva (2011), and Silva and Teixeira (2012) suggest that educational attainment played an important role in explaining the European periphery's slow convergence in productive structure when compared to the richer EU member states. Despite improvements, the three countries still have a high supply of unskilled workers, which hampers the adoption and creation of technology necessary for the development of high-productivity service sectors. Although not focusing on the services sector, Reinstaller et al. (2012) provide some evidence on the importance of a well-educated labour force for the convergence of productive structures in the EU, pointing to Greece and Portugal as examples of countries in a stasis in the development of their productive structures with quite low levels of product complexity and diversification. According to the authors, Spain and Greece experienced a relative decline in the complexity of their productive structures between 1995 and 2010 showing divergence from industrialised countries, where the relatively low levels of educational attainment probably played an important role. In the case of Italy's regional manufacturing industry, Hirsch and Sulis (2009) find results similar to those of Ciccone and Papaioannou (2009), pointing to the importance of human capital in fostering faster growth in high-skilled industries, which in turn leads to faster aggregate regional productivity growth. Simões (2009) also provides evidence on the importance of secondary schooling for productivity improvements in the Portuguese manufacturing industry, playing a more important role in high-tech industries. Some of the previous studies also suggest that another explanation for the European periphery's lack of convergence in productive structure is the loss of competitiveness in traditional low-tech and low-skill products, which led to an adjustment in the production structure in order to meet the needs of the changing domestic demand, especially after joining the EMU in 1999.

Theory

In many countries, the structure of production has shifted towards an increased specialisation in the services sector and away from manufacturing, traditionally viewed as the driver of technological change and hence economic growth. This dynamic structural change process has thus raised the question of whether services can be a source of sustained growth. From a theoretical point of view, earlier theories on structural change and growth predicted a negative influence of an increased specialisation in services. Baumol (1967) suggests that, due to differences in the rate of technological progress, the three major sectors grow at different rates, which means that changes in the composition of production and employment can determine important differences in the aggregate growth rate of an economy. Since the services sector was traditionally viewed as a low productivity (stagnant) sector, increased specialisation towards services would lead to a growth slowdown. Kaldor (1966) had already defended that the manufacturing sector was the engine of growth, with faster growth in the manufacturing sector leading to faster growth in overall output due to spillover effects to the other sectors of the economy.

More recent theories consider that services can also be a driver of sustained growth, as long as the change in the composition of production and employment occurs towards services sub-sectors that have benefited from what some authors call the 3Ts, technology, transportability, and tradability (see, e.g., Ghani 2010). These enable services to benefit from technological advances and become more productive as well as participate in global trade. Although value added and employment in the services sector are dominated by the so-called traditional personal services, which include activities like hotels, restaurants, and public administration, viewed as non-productive, modern impersonal services that include communications, banking, insurance, and business-related services can be an important driver of economic growth, since they take advantage of ICT, globalization and scale economies and thus benefit from higher productivity growth rates (see, e.g., Ghani 2010). For instance, Desmarchelier et al. 2013) review the literature on the importance of knowledge-intensive business services (KIBS)—such as survey, consultancy, research and engineering activities targeted at businesses—for growth due to their role as "users, diffusers and sources of innovation." They build a theoretical model with consumers, industrial firms and KIBS activities to examine in more detail the channels through which KIBS foster (or inhibit) economic growth. The authors conclude that "KIBS are ultimately a factor of economic growth. (...) industry still appears as a significant factor for explaining economic growth, even if it is via the demand of industrial firms for KIBS." (Desmarchelier et al. 2013: 17). Kapur (2012) develops a model with heterogeneous services, progressive and asymptotically stagnant services, and manufacturing, where innovation drives productivity growth and delivers different endogenous stages of growth. At earlier stages, consumer demand is directed mainly towards manufactured products and so innovation is more profitable in this sector. As income rises, demand shifts towards services, but progressive services are more productive and thus respond more to innovation. Hence, the latter should concentrate on this sector in order for the economy to maximize growth.

Ngai and Pissarides (2007) and Acemoglu and Guerrieri (2008), on the other hand, introduce some changes in the assumptions of Baumol's two-sector unbalanced growth model in terms of either the inputs considered or factor proportions. They conclude that, even with differences in total factor productivity growth across sectors, it is possible for an economy, under certain conditions, to reach a balanced growth path in the aggregate, such that structural change will have no impact on the growth rate of real income per capita.

But even the traditional (stagnant) personal services can make a positive contribution to growth, according to some authors. Pugno (2006) expands Baumol's model by considering that the consumption of services (such as education, health and culture), which the author also calls household services to contrast with business services, may contribute to human capital formation and, in this way, offset the negative contribution to overall growth due to its low productivity. van Zon and Muysken (2005) focus on the importance of health for economic growth arguing also that it is not only an important factor in final goods production but also fundamental to knowledge accumulation and thus a driver of growth.

Reverse causation from economic growth to the expansion of services is also possible, since economic growth leads to higher income per capita levels that, according to Engel's law (higher income elasticity of demand in the services sector), results in a change in the structure of demand that shifts away from manufactured products towards services (see, e.g., Echevarria 1997; Ngai and Pissarides 2007; Bonatti and Felice 2008; Foellmi and Zweimüller 2008). Adjustments in the production structure occur in response to demand-side changes so that economic growth causes structural change towards the services sector. Peneder (2003) also highlights the possibility of higher income levels leading to more investment in R&D and education, which in turn would create incentives for higher specialisation towards services industries that make greater use of these complementary institutions.

Evidence

The idea that services can no longer be viewed as a homogeneous sector characterised by low productivity/stagnant activities is well documented in a number of recent papers focusing on advanced countries. Inklaar et al. (2008), Maroto-Sánchez and Cuadrado-Roura (2009), Jorgenson and Timmer (2011), and O'Mahony (2013) provide an in-depth analysis of service sector performance based on harmonised sectoral data from the EU KLEMS[3] database. International comparability is thus ensured, namely in what concerns the use of a common industrial classification, focusing on European Union (EU) member states, Japan and the United States from 1970 onwards (see O'Mahony and Timmer (2009) for details on the EU KLEMS database). The paper by Inklaar et al. (2008) is mainly motivated by the need to better understand the slower labour productivity growth in the EU when compared to the United States since the mid-1990s. For this purpose, the authors focus on market services productivity, a major driver of productivity growth in the United States since the mid-1990s and a fundamental source of the labour productivity growth differences between the EU and the United States. The descriptive analysis is carried out for the period 1980–2004 and an aggregate of 10 EU member states that does not include Greece and Portugal, focusing on market services as a whole, which includes trade, transport, communication, financial, business, and personal (including hotels and restaurants) services. The evidence shows that since 1995 market services labour productivity accelerated in the United States (from an annual growth of 1.4 percent in 1980–1995 to 3.3 percent in 1995–2004), whereas in Europe it slowed down. The authors also highlight the fact that the differences are more pronounced in retail and whole trade and financial services. Maroto-Sánchez and Cuadrado-Roura (2009) and Jorgenson and Timmer (2011) confirm this idea, with both studies analysing the period 1980–2005. Jorgenson and Timmer (2011), for a sample of ten EU countries (that again does not include Greece and Portugal), the United States and Japan find that distribution services showed rapid labour productivity growth in these last two countries, at rates even higher than in the manufacturing sector, whereas finance and business services and personal services suffered from low productivity growth in all regions. By far the fastest growth occurred in the ICT production sector that includes post and communication services, although it was slower in Europe than in the United States and Japan. In fact, productivity in all market services sub-sectors grew faster in these two countries when compared to Europe, while in this region non-market services productivity growth was higher than in the United States and Japan, and also higher than in finance and business services and personal services. The authors thus conclude that "(...) the treatment of the services sector as a homogeneous and stagnant sector in contrast to dynamic manufacturing is completely unwarranted." (Jorgenson and Timmer 2011: 26). Maroto-Sánchez and Cuadrado-Roura (2009), using shift-share analysis, take a more disaggregated perspective in terms of services sub-sectors considering nine activities, and compare additionally their performance in the United States and the EU-15, thus including all the countries from the European periphery in this aggregate. The authors also identify important disparities in terms of productivity levels and performance across services sub-sectors and regions, with communications and transport in the European countries or wholesale and retail and financial services in the United States showing improvements comparable to those of manufacturing industries.

The former studies indicate that even across the two broad categories of services considered in this chapter, traditional personal services and modern progressive services, a disaggregated analysis reveals differences in terms of the expected productivity behaviour, with some traditional services such as trade showing good productivity performances in the United States, while for modern progressive services like finance the opposite applies in some cases. However, the level of aggregation of services sub-sectors and countries (aggregates) under analysis differs across studies. A more recent contribution from O'Mahony (2013) comparing labour productivity growth in 1995–2007 relative to 1980–1995 in the EU-10 and the United States concludes that there is (p. 13): " (...) considerable diversity within the market services sector, with both Communications and Financial services showing accelerations in output and productivity in both the EU and the USA. The main differences are in Distribution and Business Services where in the USA, productivity growth and contributions from labour composition accelerate compared to decelerations in the EU."

Early empirical analyses of the impact of services expansion on economic growth from the 1990s include cross-country studies like Dutt and Lee (1993) and time series studies such as Ansari (1992) that point to a negative impact on growth derived from increased specialisation towards the services sector. Ansari (1992) examines whether the aggregate growth slowdown in the Canadian economy from 1961–1972 to 1973–1988 can be attributed to the shift in resources from manufacturing to services. Based on the evidence of a positive influence of the growth rates and shares of output in the industrial and manufacturing sectors on real GDP growth, the author concludes for an adverse effect of deindustrialisation on growth. Dutt and Lee (1993) use data for a sample of between 57 to 98 countries to estimate growth regressions for three sub-periods, the 1960s, the 1970s, and the 1980s, and conclude that the impact of the services sector on real GDP growth depends on the period considered and the way the role of services is measured, but argue for stronger evidence in favour of a negative impact on growth. However, these studies do not differentiate across services sub-sectors and do not consider more recent periods when information and communication technologies became more important for productivity growth, especially in the services sector.

More recent studies apply panel data methodologies to study the relationship between the expanding tertiary sector and growth, taking advantage of both the cross section and time series information of the data. Peneder (2003) estimates how the share of services affects either the level of real GDP per capita or its growth rate in a sample of 28 OECD countries over the period 1990–1998. Besides some typical control variables always present in the estimation of growth regressions, the author considers as additional variables to control for the influence of structure on the level or growth of real GDP, the value added shares of technology-driven and human capital-intensive manufacturing industries, and the relative export and import shares of technology-driven and high-skill industries. The results point to a negative influence of an increasing share of services on the aggregate growth of GDP per capita, as well as on its level, and are thus consistent with Baumol's predictions. However, the impact is weak and the author stresses that it may be the case that opposite sign effects are netting out, and that in any case there may be a positive contribution from certain types of services industries that systematically achieve higher rates of productivity growth. Following up on this idea, Maroto-Sánchez and Cuadrado-Roura (2009) assess the impact of an expanding tertiary sector on overall productivity growth for a sample of 37 OECD countries over the period 1980–2005. The authors estimate a panel data productivity growth regression to test how the growth of services contributed to the evolution of overall productivity. The dependent variable is the labour productivity growth rate and the variables that control for the influence of structural change towards the services sector are the initial total employment share of services and its change. The main empirical finding is that the increase in the weight of services had a positive and quantitatively important effect on overall productivity growth. Additionally, the initial weight of services at the beginning of the period is also statistically significant with a positive sign. The heterogeneity of the services sector is taken into account by estimating the productivity growth regression differentiating between market and non-market services. The estimated coefficients are positive in both cases but the productivity growth impact of market services is stronger.

Silva and Teixeira (2011) adopt two different classifications of industries, one that takes into account the industries' skills requirements, and a classification based on technological characteristics, to assess the importance of structural change for productivity growth in a sample of 10 countries described by the authors as 'relatively less developed' in the late 1970s but that exhibited different paths of structural change from then onwards. The main idea is to test whether these differing paths in terms of productive structure towards more skilled and technology-intensive activities can explain the different growth performances registered over the period 1980–2003. The evidence suggests that a change in the high-skill industries (these include services such as communications, financial intermediation, except insurance and pension funding, real estate activities, computer and related activities, research and development, legal, technical and advertising, and education) and science-based industry shares positively influences aggregate labour productivity growth. In contrast, an increase in the value added share of supplier-dominated industries (such as hotels and restaurants) results in a decline in labour productivity growth.

Hartwig's (2012) main aim is to test the more recent view that even the so-called stagnant services can make a positive contribution to growth. The data used refers to 18 OECD countries between 1970 and 2005 and the variables of interest are the growth rates of real per capita GDP and the real per capita education and health care expenditures, with the latter serving as proxies for the importance of health and education services in the economy. The results however lend at most support to Baumol's predictions, with more expenditure on health and education Granger-causing real per capita GDP growth with a negative sign.

There is also considerable debate on whether the causality runs from services expansion to growth or primarily the other way round. Studies that explicitly examine this issue include Linden and Mahmood (2007) and Dietrich (2012). The first study estimates cointegration and causality between real GDP per capita growth and sectoral shares (agriculture, industry, services) in 14 Schengen countries over the period 1970–2004. The evidence indicates a two-way causality between the growth rates of GDP per capita and services sector share. Growth in the services sector share leads to slower GDP per capita growth but faster GDP per capita growth has a positive impact on services share growth. Dietrich (2012) computes structural change indexes using both employment and real value added sectoral shares and finds evidence to support bi-directional causality between these and the growth of real GDP in a sample of seven OECD countries over the period 1960–2004. However, the results vary across countries. Aggregate economic growth causes structural change in the largest economies, Germany, Japan, the UK and the United States, whereas the results for the other countries depend on the measure of structural change used, employment or value added. In the other direction, structural change in the form of employment causes economic growth in Japan and the United States only, with non-statistically significant results for all remaining countries.

Using data for 28 manufacturing industries from 44 countries over the period 1980–1999, Ciccone and Papaioannou (2009) provide evidence of the importance of human capital availability for structural change. The authors find a positive statistically significant correlation between initial schooling levels and value added and employment growth in schooling-intensive industries, stronger for more open economies. Faster educational attainment growth also seems to lead to faster shifts in production towards human capital-intensive industries. It is thus also likely that the availability of high levels of human capital, by facilitating technology adoption in education-intensive services sub-sectors, leads to faster value added and employment growth in modern progressive services.

To the best of our knowledge, the empirical work done so far does not explore in a comprehensive manner the linkages between structural change, human capital availability and growth in the European periphery. On the one hand, the main concern of most studies is to test whether structural change leads to a lower rate of aggregate growth as predicted by Baumol. The issue of reverse causation is usually not dealt with and the role of human capital in the process of structural change is almost always ignored. On the other hand, little attention is paid to this specific group of countries, which share some more recent, interesting common features as far as the behaviour of their productive structure and specialisation pattern are concerned. This study intends to fill this gap, focusing on the recent experience of a peripheral European country that went through important transformations in its structure of production and employment but seems to be stuck in a pattern of specialisation based on low-tech and low-educational intensity activities. Silva (2011) shows that market services have been a major contributor to aggregate labour productivity growth in Portugal but their still low weight in the Portuguese economy has prevented Portugal from capitalising on these productivity improvements. The same seems to apply to Italy and Spain, countries that according to Silva and Teixeira (2012) show similar trends to those of Portugal in terms of specialisation towards low-skill and low-tech activities, as well as maintaining relatively low educational attainment levels. Antzoulatos (2011) gives a similar picture for Greece, arguing that specialisation towards the non-tradable sector and the associated loss of competitiveness are two of the major causes of the current crisis and the severe adjustment this country is facing.

3. Productivity growth, services, and human capital in the Portuguese economy

Our variables of interest refer to the four dimensions under analysis: productivity and expansion of the services sector, aggregate productivity and human capital. Annual output and employment data from 1970 to 2006 were obtained from the EU KLEMS database (see O'Mahony and Timmer 2009), especially suited for sectoral studies. Output is measured as gross value added at 1995 prices. Employment corresponds to total hours worked by persons engaged. Labour productivity was obtained dividing gross value added by the total hours worked by persons engaged. In order to better ascertain the role of services productivity on overall productivity in the Portuguese economy, we distinguish between different services sub-sectors based on their division into two broad categories, modern impersonal services and traditional personal services. We took into account five services sub-sectors: transport and storage and communications (C); finance, insurance, real estate and business services (F); wholesale and retail trade (T); hotels and restaurants (R); and community, social and personal services (P). The first two sectors can be considered as modern progressive services and the last three as traditional personal services.

Figure 8.1 outlines the evolution of labour productivity in the Portuguese services sector over the period 1970–2006. All the services sub-sectors considered exhibit a positive labour productivity trend over the period under analysis, although at different paces. The sub-sectors that recorded the highest growth rates were transport and storage and communications (C), followed by community, social and personal services (P), hotels and restaurants (R), finance, insurance, real estate and business services (F), and finally, wholesale and retail trade (T). However, towards the end of the period, all sectors registered a productivity growth slowdown, which led also to an aggregate productivity slowdown, especially strong in the hotels and restaurants sector, wholesale and retail trade and community, social and personal services. As far as the productivity levels are concerned, finance, insurance, real estate and business services present the highest level in 1970 and again in 2006. The transport and storage and communications sector occupied the fourth position in the ranking in 1970 but since the 1990s, it climbed to the second position. In terms of aggregate productivity, in 2006, transport and storage and communications and finance, insurance, real estate and business services registered productivity levels that were, respectively, double and triple of aggregate productivity; productivity in community, social and personal services was in line with the aggregate level; and wholesale and retail trade and hotels and restaurants, especially the latter, were less productive. In 1970, sectoral productivity relative to productivity in the total economy presented more or less the same pattern across sub-sectors, except for transport and storage and communications, which was only slightly more productive than the aggregate.

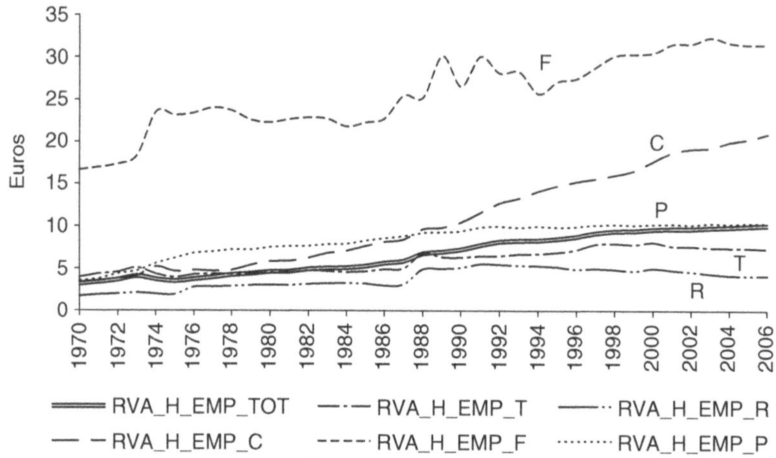

Figure 8.1 Labor productivity in the services sector, Portugal 1970–2006.

Notes: RVA_H_EMP corresponds to real value added by hour worked by person engaged in 1995 euros. TOT= total economy; T=wholesale and retail trade; R=hotels and restaurants; C=transport and storage and communications; F=finance, insurance, real estate and business services; P=community social and personal services.

Source: authors' computations based on data from the EU-KLEMS database.

The process of tertiarization of the Portuguese economy can be illustrated by looking at the evolution of the shares of the different services sub-sectors in total real value added. Figure 8.2 contains information on the real value added shares of the five services sub-sectors from 1970–2006. Considering the whole period, transport and storage and communications, community social and personal services, and finance, insurance, real estate and business services increased their participation in total value added, whereas hotels and restaurants remained the same, and wholesale and retail trade recorded a decrease. In 1970, the services sector as a whole represented around 56 percent of total value added but by 2006 its participation had increased to almost 70 percent, confirming that Portugal experienced a process of tertiarization over the period under analysis. In that same year, the services sub-sectors that contributed the most to total value added were wholesale and retail trade, finance, insurance, real estate and business activities, and community, social and personal services, representing together around 47 percent of the total. In 2006, these remained as the most important services sub-sectors in terms of value added, but transport and storage and communications almost doubled in importance, whereas wholesale and retail trade suffered a decrease. Additionally, community, social, and personal services became the second highest contributor to total value added, although towards the end of the period, there was hardly any change. On the contrary, finance, insurance, real estate and business activities, and transport and storage and communications were more dynamic in the last two sub-periods.

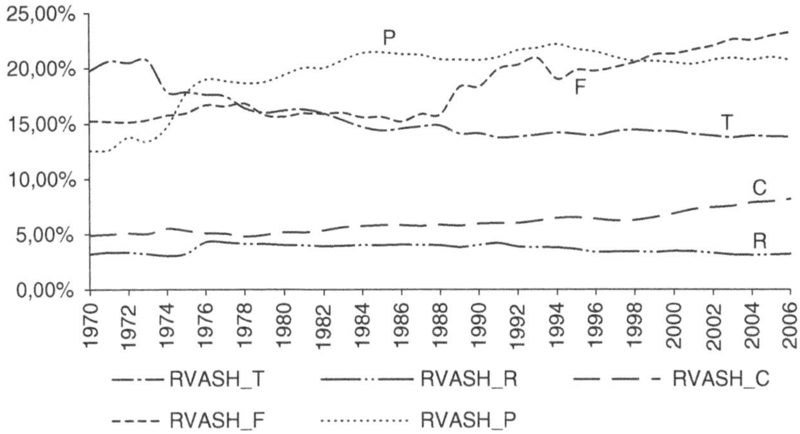

Figure 8.2 Total real value added shares of the services sector, Portugal 1970–2006.

Notes: RVASH corresponds to the share of the corresponding services activity in total real value added. T=wholesale and retail trade; R=hotels and restaurants; C=transport and storage and communications; F=finance, insurance, real estate and business services; P=community social and personal services.

Source: authors' computations based on data from the EU-KLEMS database.

Structural change towards the services sector can also be analysed from the perspective of employment. Figure 8.3 contains information on the total employment shares of the different services sub-sectors over the period 1970–2006. Employment refers to total hours worked by persons engaged. Four of the five services sub-sectors analysed increased their participation in total employment over the period, confirming the increasing importance of the services sector in the Portuguese economy. The exception is the transport and storage and communications sector, where employment more or less stagnated since the 1980s. The highest employment shares at the beginning and the end of the period are those of wholesale and retail trade, hotels and restaurants, and community, social, and personal services, with the latter climbing to the first position from the late 1990s onwards. In 1970, employment in the services sector represented slightly more than 40 percent of total employment, and by 2006 this share increased to around 58 percent.

Comparing the evolution of the different sub-sectors' employment and value added shares (Figures 8.2 and 8.3), contrary to the case of value added shares, wholesale and retail trade and hotels and restaurants increased their employment share, whereas transport and storage and communications recorded a decrease. In finance, insurance, real estate and business services and community, social, and personal services the growth rate of the employment share was higher than the growth rate of the value added share, with a higher differential in the first case.

Human capital is measured as the average number of years of education, total and by schooling level, of the working age population. Data from

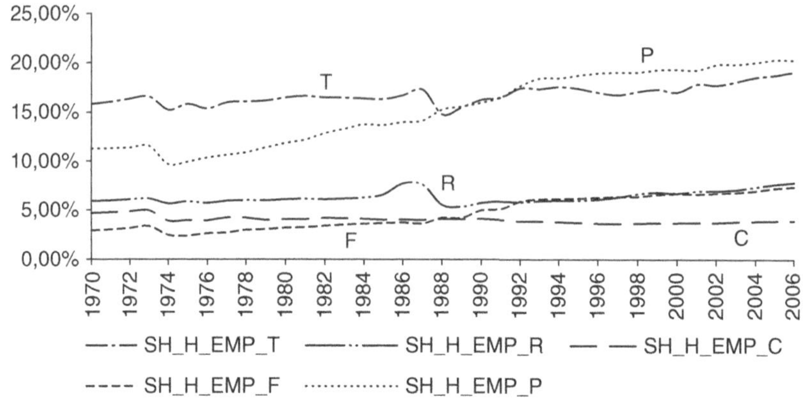

Figure 8.3 Total employment shares of the services sector, Portugal 1970–2006.

Notes: SH_H_EMP corresponds to the share of the corresponding services activity in total employment (total hours worked by persons engaged). T=wholesale and retail trade; R=hotels and restaurants; C=transport and storage and communications; F=finance, insurance, real estate and business services; P=community social and personal services.

Source: authors' computations based on data from the EU-KLEMS database.

1970 to 2001 was taken from Teixeira (2005), a human capital database specifically built for the Portuguese economy that follows Barro and Lee's methodology but presents two main advantages. First, problems related with poor data quality are mitigated due to stronger consistency of national data sources, and second, data frequency is annual, which is convenient given the time series methodologies we apply. Data from 2002 to 2006 were computed applying the human capital annual average growth rates based on the data from Barro and Lee (2012), which has data for the years 2000, 2005 and 2010. Figure 8.4 contains some summary information on these human capital variables. In 1970, Portugal still recorded low levels of educational attainment with only an average of 3.276 years of schooling per working age person. By 2006, the situation had improved considerably with 8.286 average years of total schooling. In any case, according to Barro and Lee's data, this figure is still lower than the values for countries at similar stages of development, such as Greece or Spain, which in 2005 stood at 9.891 and 9.720, respectively, and much lower than in Germany (11.845). Growth was faster at the higher schooling levels, which is not surprising given the low initial levels, but has slowed down considerably during the last sub-period.

4. Empirical model and results

We apply econometric time series analysis techniques to examine the relationship between service sector expansion and productivity performance, human capital and aggregate productivity in Portugal. For this purpose, we estimate VAR models with annual data for the period 1970–2006.

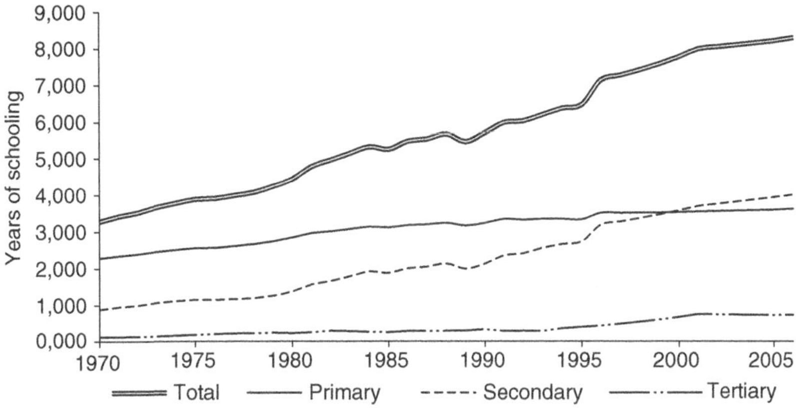

Figure 8.4 Average years of schooling of the working age population, Portugal 1970–2006.

Source: authors' computations based on data from Teixeira (2005) and Barro and Lee (2012).

The variables considered are integrated of order one, I(1).[4] We began by testing for cointegration relations and thus established long-run relationships between the variables. However, in most cases, the number of cointegration relationships obtained was the maximum possible, so that we could not reject the hypothesis of jointly stationary variables. In other situations, the error correction (ECM) term had the wrong sign. The choice of the optimal lag order also led us to reject VECM models as the basis of our econometric methodology. In fact, if we have a VAR defined in levels with *h* lags, to determine the ECM we have to impose a VAR with *h-1* lags. In our study, for most of the models estimated, *h* was equal to 1, which would lead to a VECM with only the short-term residual ECM. All these results pointed to an analysis based on the Doan-Litterman-Sims strategy that consists in estimating VAR models in levels.

We estimate VAR models with the following general form:

$$y_t = A_1 y_{t-1} + \ldots + A_p y_{t-p} + B_0 x_t + \ldots + B_q x_{t-q} + CD_t + u_t \qquad (1)$$

where $y_t = (y_{1t}, \ldots, y_{Kt})$ is a vector of K observable endogenous variables; $x_t = (x_{1t}, \ldots, x_{Mt})$ is a vector of M observable exogenous variables; D_t contains the constant as the deterministic variable; and u_t is a K-dimensional unobservable zero mean white noise process with positive definite covariance matrix $E(u_t u_t') = \sum_u$. A_i, B_j and C are parameter matrices of appropriate dimension.

Our VAR models consider four variables each: aggregate labour productivity (LY), the average number of years of education, whether total, secondary or tertiary, of the working age population, (LTH, LSH, and LHH, respectively),[5] labour productivity of services sub-sector i (LYi); and the employment share of services sub-sector i (Eir), as the structural change indicator. We began by estimating VAR models considering all variables as endogenous. However, based on the results from the impulse response analysis carried out further ahead in the paper concerning the influence of the human capital and employment share variables on the other variables of the model, which turned out not to be statistically significant in most of the models, we decided to estimate models considering those variables as exogenous. We identified the models of the first type with a capital A, and the models of the second type with a capital B. For each model A we thus have K=4 and M=0, and for each model B we have K=2 and M=2. In the second type of models, the two endogenous variables are aggregate productivity and sectoral productivity and the two exogenous variables are human capital and the sectoral employment share. In summary, we estimated ten VAR models, according to the sector considered (five in total) and the model type, A or B (see Table 8.A.1 in Appendix 8.A), models 1A-5A, and models 1B-5B.

The optimal lag order for each model was chosen using the Bayesian or Schwarz information criteria (BIC) and in most cases it is equal to one. The exceptions are models 1B and 3B where the optimal lag order is two, and model 4B with an optimal lag order of three. For all models, the absolute value of the eigenvalues of the reverse characteristic polynomial lie inside the unit circle, which indicates model stability (see Table 8.A.2, Appendix 8.A). Autocorrelation of the residuals was tested using two LM type tests for autocorrelation with one lag (see Doornik 1996). The LM test and the LMF test consider as the null hypothesis the absence of autocorrelation in the residuals of order one (see Table 8.A.3, Appendix 8.A). Models 2A, 5A, 1B, 3B, 4B and 5B exhibit autocorrelation. This might imply that the impulse-response analysis results depend on the order of the variables in the model when the Cholesky decomposition is applied, which is the case here. However, this potential problem is mitigated because the ordering of the variables in the model obeys theoretical criteria.

To identify the role of service sector productivity and structural change on aggregate productivity, and respective interdependencies with human capital, two types of causality were tested, Granger causality and instantaneous causality. In the first case, a variable X does not Granger-cause variables Y or Z if the respective lags do not appear in the equations for these variables. In the second case, X does not instantaneously cause Y or Z if, and only if, the respective residuals are uncorrelated. The logic behind this last concept is the following: if X causes instantaneously Y or Z then knowing the value of X in the forecast period helps to improve the forecasts of Y or Z (see Lütkepohl (2004)). The Granger and instantaneous causality analysis results are summarised in Table 8.1 (see also Table 8.A.4, Appendix 8.A), which highlights only the results regarding

Table 8.1 Summary of the causality analysis results – services sub-sectors influence

	Granger Causality	*Instantaneous Causality*	*Granger Causality*	*Instantaneous Causality*
Variables	LYT	LYT	ETr	Etr
Model 1A	YES	YES	YES	NO
Model 1B	NO	YES	—	—
Variables	LYR	LYR	ERr	ERr
Model 2A	YES	YES	NO	YES
Model 2B	NO	YES	—	—
Variables	LYC	LYC	ECr	ECr
Model 3A	YES	YES	YES	NO
Model 3B	YES	NO	—	—
Variables	LYF	LYF	EFr	EFr
Model 4A	YES	YES	NO	YES
Model 4B	NO	YES	—	—
Variables	LYP	LYP	EPr	EPr
Model 5A	YES	YES	YES	YES
Model 5B	YES	NO	—	—

Notes: LY=logarithm of labour productivity; E_r=employment share; T=wholesale and retail trade; R=hotels and restaurants; C=transport and storage and communication; F=finance, insurance, real estate and business services; P=other community, social and personal services.

the influence of each of the services sector's variables on the other variables considered in the specific model estimated.

According to the results presented in Table 8.1, the only sub-sector that both Granger and instantaneously causes the other variables in the respective models, either through its productivity or through its employment share, is sub-sector P, community, social and personal services (the only exception is model 5B, where LYP shows no instantaneous causality). In terms of productivity, in most of the models estimated all the other four sub-sectors show Granger and instantaneous causality (the exceptions are models 1B, 2B, 3B, and 4B). As for the employment share from the remaining sub-sectors, wholesale and retail trade and transport and storage and communications show Granger causality, whereas both hotels and restaurants and finance, insurance, real estate, and business services show instantaneous causality.

Some interesting conclusions can be drawn from this analysis. First, the services sector productivity variables seem to be more relevant than employment shares in causing the remaining variables, whether in the Granger or the instantaneous causality sense. Second, in the case of the services sector's productivity, the results are mixed, depending on the notion of causality under analysis. Nevertheless, in models of type A there is always causality in both senses. Third, among the different services sub-sectors, sector P seems to be the most influential one whether through its productivity or employment share since it presents causality in both senses, Granger and instantaneous.[6]

In order to shed additional light on the relationship and forecasting ability of the variables in our model, we also performed an impulse response analysis. The impulse response analysis showed how a shock to one of the model's endogenous variables affects the contemporaneous and future values of all endogenous variables in that same model. Specifically, we considered orthogonal shocks, which allowed us to take into account uncertainty in the variables' equations contrary to the more usual consideration of unit shocks. We always considered confidence intervals (CIs) at the 90 percent significance level, computed by bootstrapping. When interpreting the statistical significance of the different shocks, we only retained point estimates within the CI when the null is outside the CI.

Figures 8.B.1 to 8.B.10, in Appendix 8.B, present the results from the impulse response analysis for the different types of models. A shock to human capital in models of type A has no influence over sectoral services productivity or employment shares since the results are not statistically significant. The same result applies to the response of aggregate productivity except for model 2A, when there is a positive influence of the human capital shock after the 5th year. As for shocks to the services employment share, the influence on human capital and sectoral services productivity is not statistically significant (see Figures 8.B.1-8.B.5, Appendix 8.B). However, the influence on aggregate productivity is positive and lasting in model 5A that considers community, social and personal services. Regarding the responses to sectoral services productivity shocks, they do not seem to exert any influence over aggregate productivity. The influence of shocks to aggregate productivity is positive for human capital and market services employment shares; negative for non-market services employment shares and productivity.

Table 8.2 summarises the results from the impulse-responses analysis for models of Type B. The detailed results can be found in Figures 8.B.6 to 8.B.10 in Appendix 8.B. In what concerns the influence of shocks to services productivity on aggregate productivity, LYR and LYF shocks are not statistically significant. Furthermore, wholesale and retail trade, and transports and storage and communications shocks are negative, and the time duration of these shocks is generally high. If we consider jointly the magnitude of the shock and its time duration, we can say that productivity of the wholesale and retail trade sector has a strong and prolonged negative influence on aggregate productivity. As for the influence of shocks to aggregate productivity on sectoral services productivity, the main results are that the shocks are positive and have a high magnitude, although the time duration exhibits a certain degree of heterogeneity. The time duration ranges from one year in the case of finance, insurance, real estate and business services to more than 10 years in the case of transport and storage and communications and community, social and personal services.[7]

5. Conclusions

This chapter explored the linkages between the services sector's productivity and expansion, human capital and aggregate productivity in the Portuguese economy over the period 1970–2006. The main aim was to examine whether the increasing tertiarization of the Portuguese economy constituted

Table 8.2 Summary of the impulse-response results with models of type B

Models	*Impulse response variables*	*Time duration (years)*	*Maximum shock magnitude (%)*
Model 1B	LYT–> LY	9 (–)	–81 (7)
	LY–> LYT	2(+)	76 (2)*
Model 2B	LYR–> LY	———	———
	LY–> LYR	1	72 (1)*
Model 3B	LYC–> LY	1 (–)	–26 (1)
	LY–> LYC	(...)	85 (3)
Model 4B	LYF–> LY	———	———
	LY–> LYF	1 (+)	63 (1)
Model 5B	LYP–> LY	(...)	23 (3)
	LY–> LYP	(...)	44 (2)

Notes: (+), (–) denote positive and negative shocks; (...) - time duration exceeds 10 years; () – the year at which the maximum magnitude of the shock occurred; * the year refers to the point estimate with statistical significance and not to the year associated with the maximum point estimate of the shock magnitude. T=wholesale and retail trade; R=hotels and restaurants; C=transport and storage and communication; F=finance, insurance, real estate and business services; P=other community, social and personal services.

an obstacle or an opportunity for its growth performance and if the expansion of the services sector is related to human capital availability in the Portuguese economy. Since the services sector is composed of heterogeneous activities in terms of its potential for productivity improvements, we distinguished between five different services sub-sectors based on the division of services into two broad categories, modern impersonal services and traditional personal services. Given the varied theoretical predictions and empirical results on the linkages between the expansion of the services sector and economic growth, the most suitable approach seemed to be testing for the existence causality among the relevant variables. In this way we can account for endogeneity and reverse causation in the relationship.

Our findings regarding the Granger and instantaneous causality analysis indicate that community, social and personal services in Portugal seems to be the most influential sector through both its productivity and employment share since it presents causality in both senses. In terms of productivity, all the other sub-sectors also seem to Granger and instantaneously cause the other variables. As for the employment share, the only other sector that shows Granger causality is wholesale and retail trade, whereas hotels and restaurants and finance, insurance, real estate and business services also reveal instantaneous causality. The findings from the impulse response analysis point to a mixed contribution of the services sector's productivity relative to aggregate productivity. The contribution to aggregate productivity growth from wholesale and retail trade, and transport and storage and communications is negative. The contribution from hotels and restaurants, and finance, insurance, real estate and business services is not statistically different from zero. The most influential services category seems to be community, social and personal services with this sector's productivity growth contributing significantly to aggregate productivity growth. On the other hand, aggregate productivity growth seems to influence positively all services sub-sectors, with the exception of hotels and restaurants.

Except for community, social and personal services, which make a positive contribution to aggregate productivity, the employment shares of the different services sub-sectors do not seem to cause the other variables in the model, namely aggregate productivity or human capital, and the impact of shocks to these sectoral variables are also not statistically significant. These results seem at odds with Baumol's structural burden hypothesis since community, social and personal services are usually described as services activities where productivity gains are hard to achieve and would thus make a negative contribution to aggregate productivity. The mechanism of transmission in action could thus be that of human capital accumulation as community, social and personal services include education and health activities, in line with Pugno (2006) and van Zon and Muysken (2005) predictions.

The methodology applied was not able to confirm whether human capital in the form of education plays a role in driving productivity growth and expansion in the different services sub-sectors, nor is it influenced by their evolution. Nevertheless, the schooling levels identified as potentially relevant varied across services sub-sectors. For instance, secondary schooling seems to be the relevant educational attainment variable for most services categories, with tertiary schooling relevant only for finance, insurance, real estate and business services. Fruitful avenues for future research thus include a more detailed analysis of human capital availability across sectors, introducing quality issues as well as other forms of human capital such as training and experience. It can also be the case, as suggested by Silva (2011) and Silva and Teixeira (2012), that factors other than human capital availability, such as changes in international and domestic demand are the most relevant ones in explaining structural change towards the services sector in Portugal and other countries of the European periphery.

A natural extension of this research involves its application to other countries of the European periphery that share common productive structures and human capital features with Portugal. Wider international comparisons applying panel data methodologies could also yield important generalisations on the relationships under analysis.

Notes

1 We would like to thank João Sousa Andrade, the editors of the book and participants at the workshop "Structural Change, Competitiveness and Industrial Policy: Painful Lessons from the European Periphery," September 14, 2014, Faculty of Humanities, University of Porto, for their valuable comments and suggestions. The usual disclaimer applies.

2 Antzoulatos (2011) and McKinsey and Company (2012) give a similar picture for Greece.
3 Available for download from www.euklems.net.
4 Results of the stationarity tests are available from the authors upon request.
5 For each services sector we estimated VAR models using different schooling levels. We retained the model with the best estimate for human capital (see Table 10.A.1 in Appendix 10.A). The results can be obtained from the authors upon request.
6 In Simões and Duarte (2013), we also analyse the contribution of the services sector to aggregate productivity growth according to the more usual distinction between market and non-market services, as productivity is supposed to be higher in the former due to higher exposure to market forces and thus stronger competition. However, this distinction does not exactly serve the purposes of this chapter since these two classes of services sub-sectors mix traditional and personal services. As Inklaar et al. (2008), p. 170 put it "(…) there is a large heterogeneity in productivity performance across market services and pooling these industries together in econometric analysis might not be warranted." Additionally, in the EU-KLEMS database, post and telecommunication are removed from market services because these industries are aggregated with others to constitute the sub-sector "ICT producer sector," and real estate activities are considered as non-market services given the difficulties in correctly measuring the output of this industry (it mostly reflects imputed housing rents rather than sales of firms). According to our results in Simões and Duarte (2013), non-market and market services behave quite differently in terms of causality. The employment share of market services never causes the other variables in the models, whereas in the case of non-market services the respective employment share instantaneously causes the other variables. As for productivity, instantaneous causality is confirmed for both types of sectors but Granger causality is only confirmed in some models.
7 At a higher level of aggregation, the results in Simões and Duarte (2013) confirm that productivity shocks in market services and non-market services sectors contribute differently to aggregate productivity growth, as in, for instance, Maroto-Sánchez and Cuadrado-Roura (2009). In the first case, the contribution is not significantly different from zero but in the latter case the contribution is positive. Again we believe that these results are better understood by taking into consideration the behaviour of some of the corresponding subsectors and the respective potential for productivity improvements as traditional or modern services, as described in the main text. Note also that the measurement problems associated with output from real estate activities do not seem to influence our results, since even when they are considered in the non-market services group, they maintain their influence on aggregate productivity growth, pointing to the importance of education and health services (and possibly public administration) as drivers of productivity growth in the Portuguese economy. Additionally, an analysis of the evolution of labour productivity in finance and business services compared to that of real estate (that we consider as a whole in the causality analysis) reveals positive annual average growth rates over the period 1970–2010 in both sub-sectors, although higher in real estate (2.4 percent in the first case and 4.2 percent in the second), which also presents higher productivity levels from the start.

Appendix 8.A

Table 8.A.1 VAR models variables

VAR Models	*Endogenous Variables*				*Exogenous Variables*	
Model 1A	LY	LSH	LYT	ETr	—	—
Model 1B	LY	LYT	—	—	LSH	ETr
Model 2A	LY	LTH	LYR	ERr	—	—
Model 2B	LY	LYR	—	—	LTH	ERr
Model 3A	LY	LSH	LYC	ECr	—	—
Model 3B	LY	LYC	—	—	LSH	ECr
Model 4A	LY	LHH	LYF	EFr	—	—
Model 4B	LY	LYF	—	—	LHH	EFr
Model 5A	LY	LSH	LYP	EPr	—	—
Model 5B	LY	LYP	—	—	LSH	EPr

Table 8.A.2 Model stability

Models type A	*Eigenvalues*	*Models type B*	*Eigenvalues*
Model 1A	|z|= (2.1313 1.0429 1.1977 1.2977)	**Model 1B**	|z| = (1.0483 1.4125 4.4632 10.8483)
Model 2A	|z|= (1.7492 1.2666 1.2666 1.0354)	**Model 2B**	|z| = (1.3667 1.3667)
Model 3A	|z| = (1.8917 1.0282 1.0282 1.5980)	**Model 3B**	|z| = (1.0270 3.1145 3.1145 4.2645)
Model 4A	|z|=(1.8618 1.0521 1.1010 1.1010)	**Model 4B**	|z| = (1.4485 2.5411 2.5411 1.1019 1.2319 1.2319)
Model 5A	|z| = (1.5526 1.3064 1.1819 1.0573)	**Model 5B**	|z| = (2.6594 1.1519)

Notes: |z| corresponds to the absolute value of the eigenvalues of the reverse characteristic polynomial.

Table 8.A.3 Autocorrelation results with one lag

Models A	*LM and LMF statistics*	*Models B*	*LM and LMF tests*
Model 1A	LM:20.46 LMF:1.19	**Model 1B**	LM:16.18*** LMF: 4.20***
Model 2A	LM: 29.76** LMF: 1.93**	**Model 2B**	LM:6.68 LMF:1.47
Model 3A	LM: 22.01 LMF: 1.19	**Model 3B**	LM :24.86*** LMF:11.14***
Model 4A	LM: 25.22 LMF: 1.51	**Model 4B**	LM:17.35*** LMF: 4.69***
Model 5A	LM:26.45** LMF:1.66*	**Model 5B**	LM:12.43** LMF:3.30**

Notes: LM type test for autocorrelation with 1 lag, Doornik (1996), LM test and LMF test (with F- approximation); H0 = no autocorrelation of order one of the residuals. *; **; *** - significant at 10%, 5% and 1% levels, respectively.

Table 8.A.4 Summary of the causality analysis results

Variables and tests	*Models*		
	Model 1A		**Model 1B**
Causality variables	LYT $\nrightarrow$ "LY,LSH,ETr"	ETr $\nrightarrow$ "LY,LSH,LYT"	LYT $\nrightarrow$ "LY"
Granger causality	2.4409*	3.5963**	2.1546
Instantaneous causality	17.2503***	6.2121	14.3272***
	Model 2A		**Model 2B**
Causality variables	LYR $\nrightarrow$ "LY,LSH,ERr"	ERr $\nrightarrow$ "LY,LSH,LYR"	LYR $\nrightarrow$ "LY
Granger causality	2.6006*	1.5010	2.0807
Instantaneous causality	15.6732***	13.4913***	11.4080***
	Model 3A		**Model 3B**
Causality variables	LYC $\nrightarrow$ "LY,LSH,ECr"	ECr $\nrightarrow$ "LY,LSH,LYC"	LYC $\nrightarrow$ "LY"
Granger causality	2.4098*	1.5506	2.7406*
Instantaneous causality	14.1483***	8.9594**	0.0046
	Model 4A		**Model 4B**
Causality variables	LYF $\nrightarrow$ "LY,LHH,EFr"	EFr $\nrightarrow$ "LY,LHH,LYF"	LYF $\nrightarrow$ "LY"
Granger causality	9.4558***	1.9763	1.9763
Instantaneous causality	14.2036***	12.5228*	3.9648**
	Model 5A		**Model 5B**
Causality variables	LYP $\nrightarrow$ "LY,LTH,EPr"	EPr $\nrightarrow$ "LY,LHH,LYP"	LYP $\nrightarrow$ "LY"
Granger causality	2.2469*	2.7621**	11.7993***
Instantaneous causality	7.8641**	8.7994**	0.7827

Notes: In the Granger causality test the null hypothesis corresponds to, for type A models, H0= X does not Granger cause Y, Z, W. The instantaneous causality null hypothesis is H0=no instantaneous causality between X and Y,Z, W. *; **; *** - significant at 10%, 5% and 1% levels, respectively.

Appendix 8.B

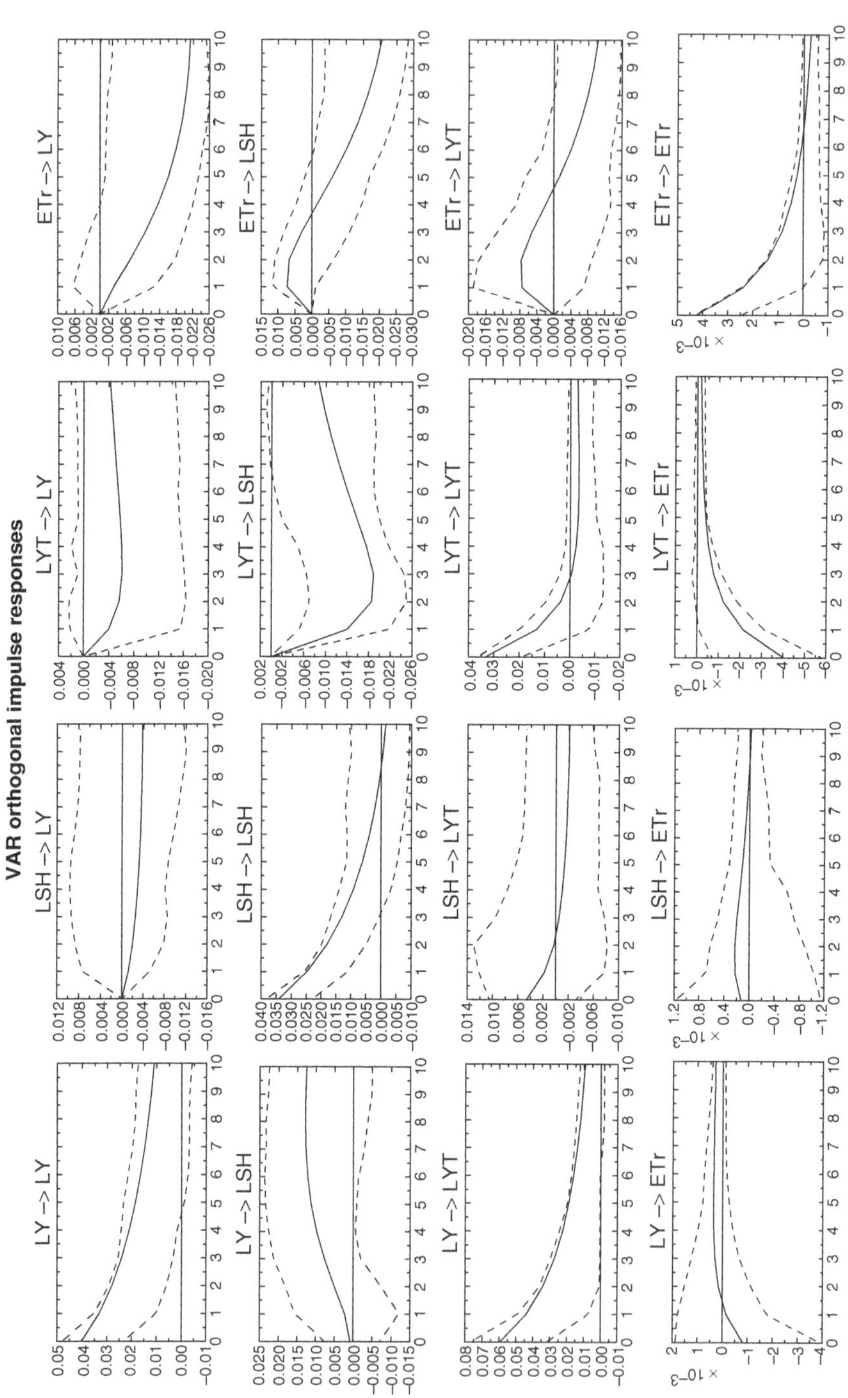

Figure 8.B.1 Impulse response analysis, model 1A.

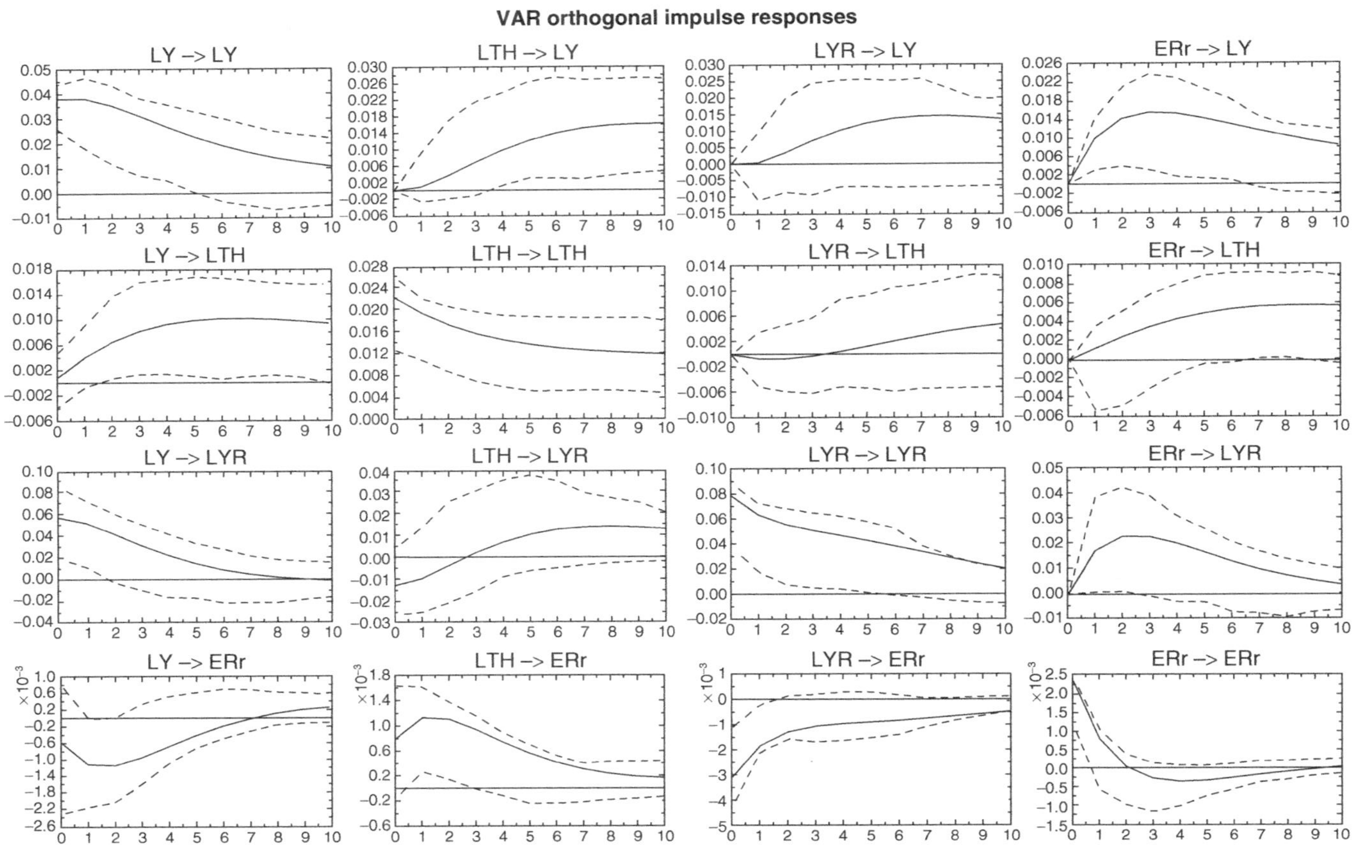

Figure 8.B.2 Impulse response analysis, model 2A.

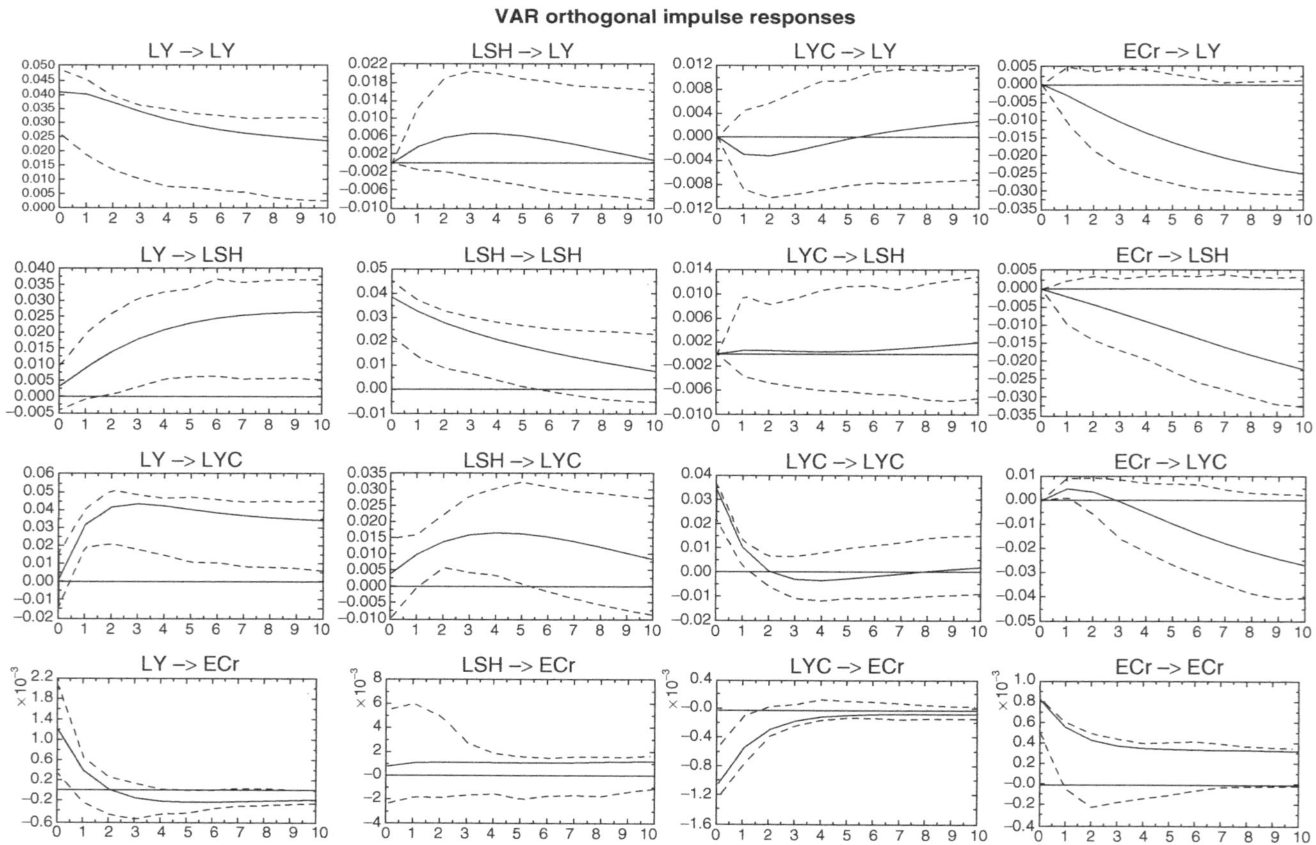

Figure 8.B.3 Impulse response analysis, model 3A.

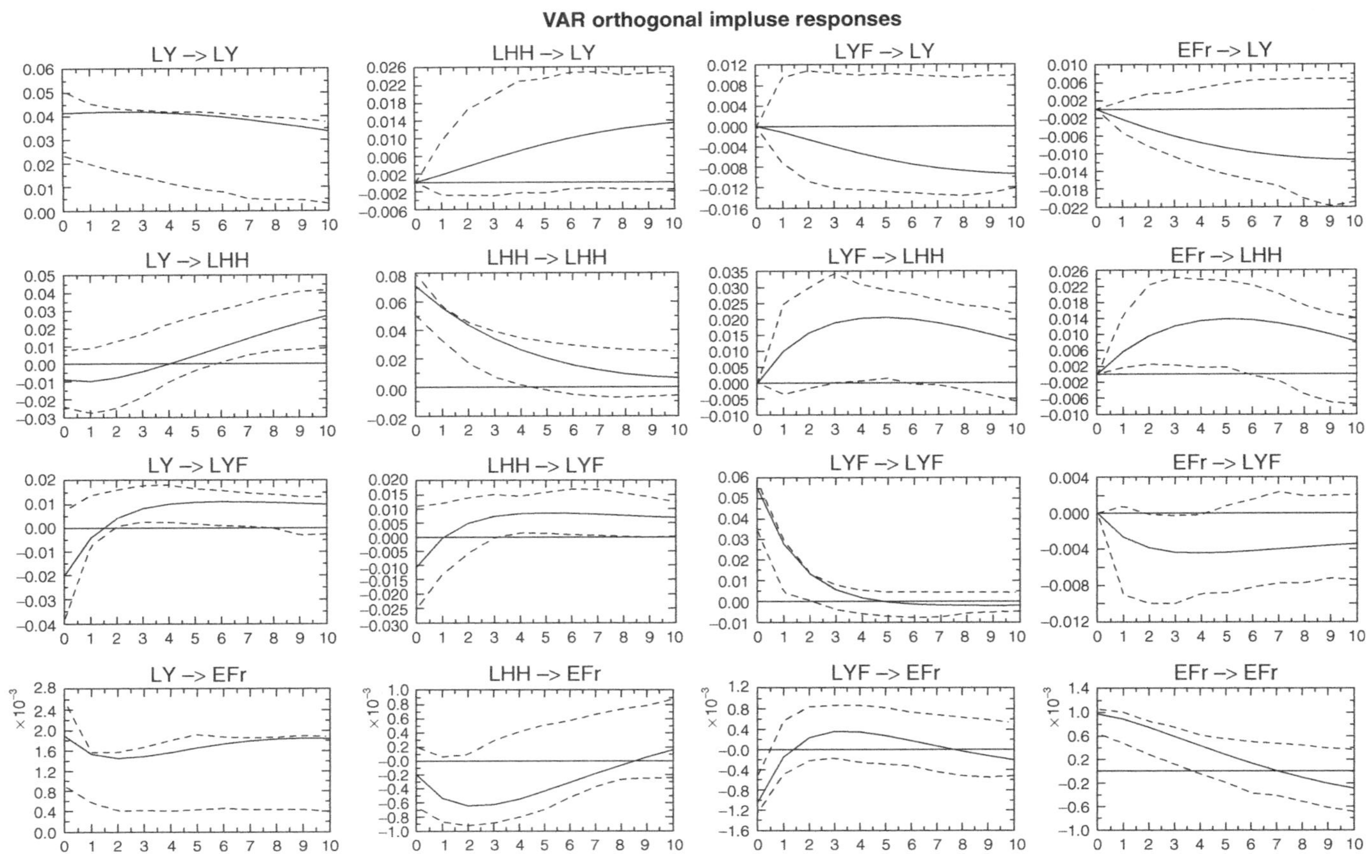

Figure 8.B.4 Impulse response analysis, model 4A.

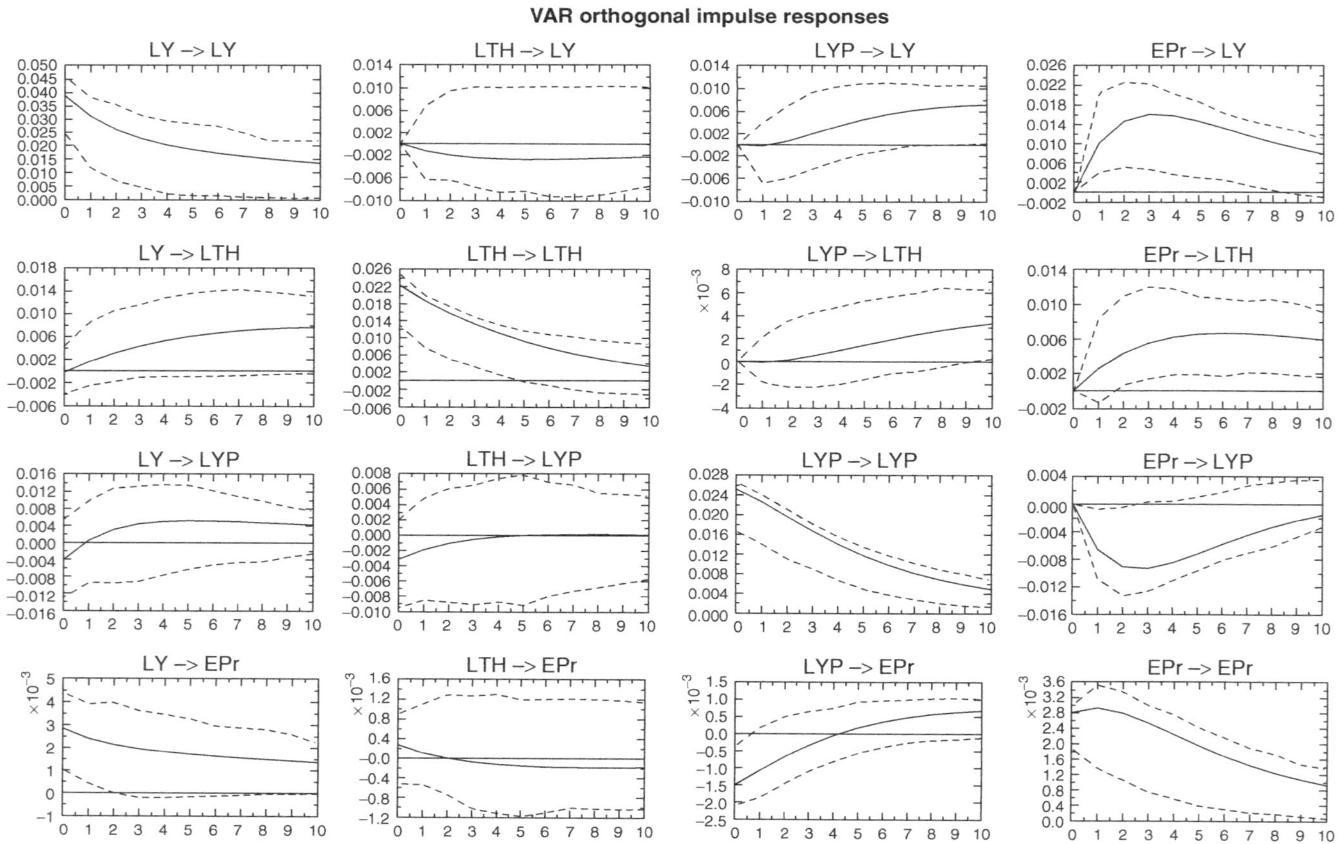

Figure 8.B.5 Impulse response analysis, model 5A.

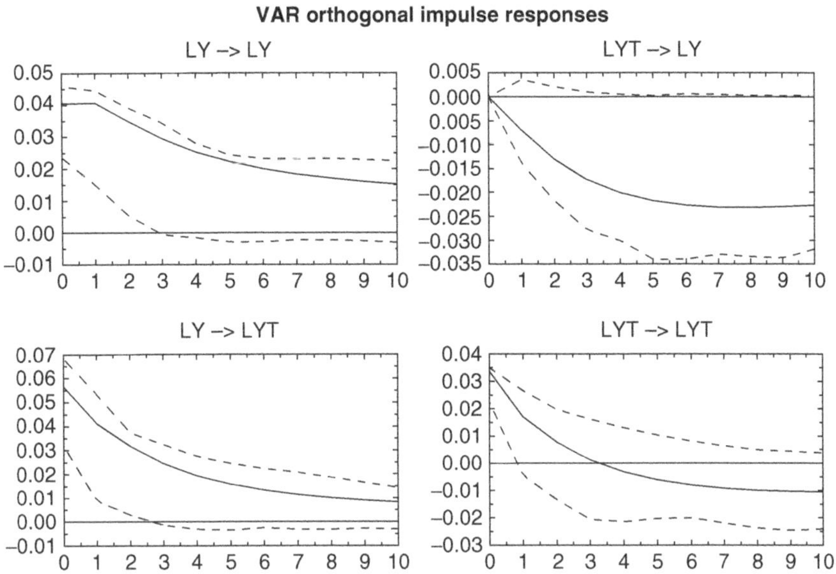

Figure 8.B.6 Impulse response analysis, model 1B.

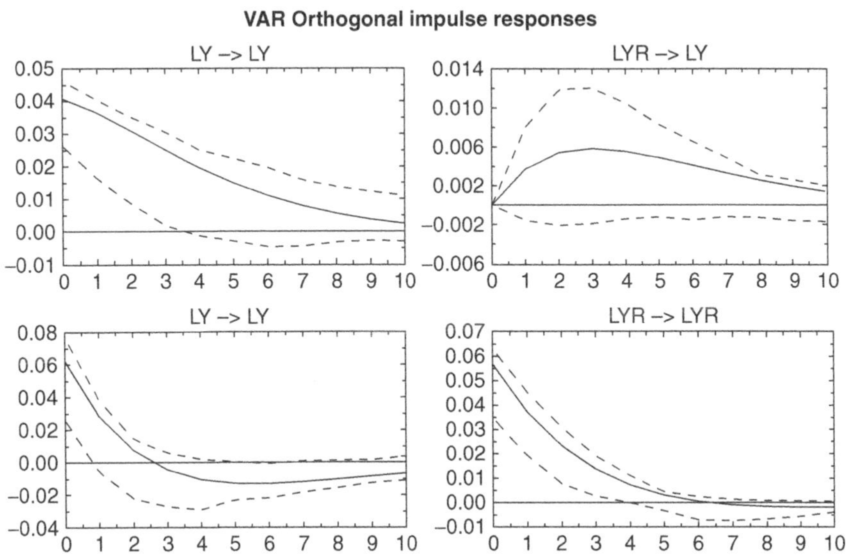

Figure 8.B.7 Impulse response analysis, model 2B.

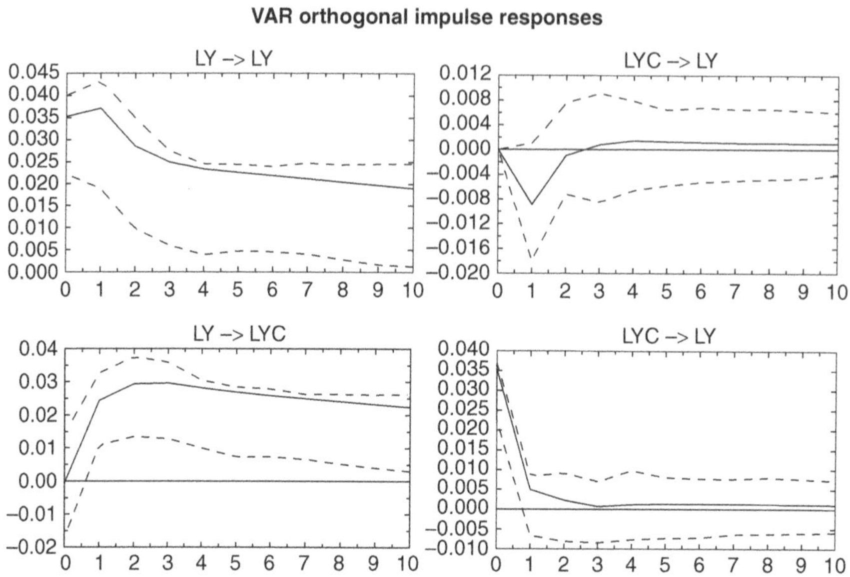

Figure 8.B.8 Impulse response analysis, model 3A.

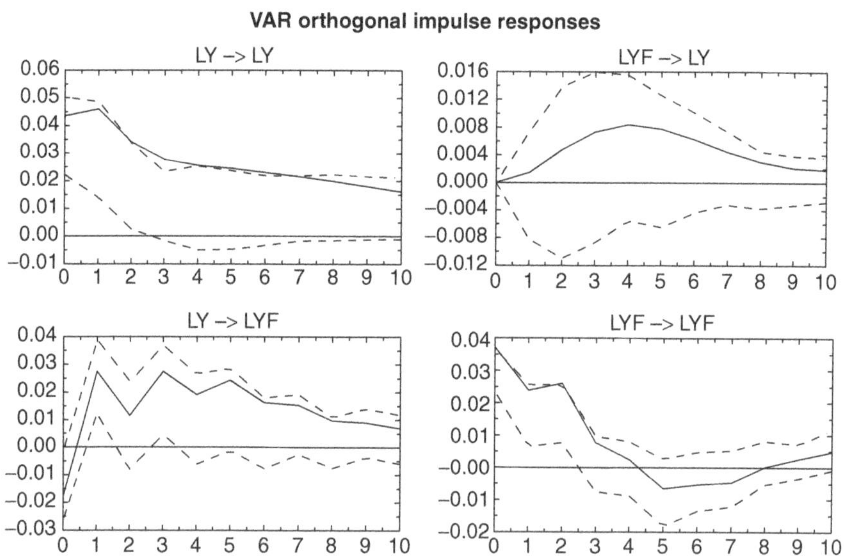

Figure 8.B.9 Impulse response analysis, model 4B.

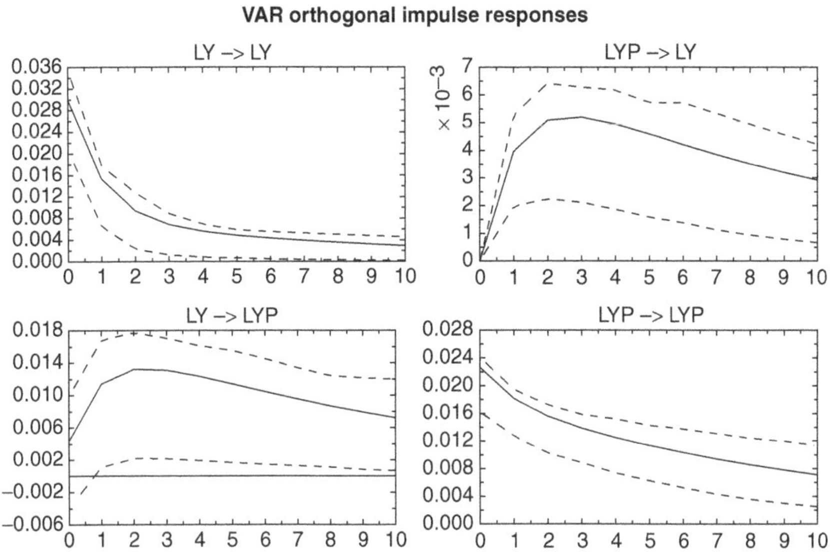

Figure 8.B.10 Impulse response analysis, model 5B.

9 Learning, exporting and firm productivity

Evidence from Portuguese manufacturing and services firms

Carlos Carreira

1. Introduction

In Portugal, as in other small open economies, discussion over the role of exports in promoting growth in general, and productivity in particular, has been ongoing for many years. Indeed, there is widespread evidence of an aggregate productivity effect through resources reallocation, namely, the expansion of high-productivity exporting firms, reconciling microeconomic and macroeconomic findings to show that more open economies grow faster (see, for example, Baldwin and Gu, 2003; Bernard and Jensen, 2004; Hansson and Lundin, 2004; Harris and Li, 2008; Gleeson and Ruane, 2009, inter al.). Since the seminal work of Bernard and Jensen (1995), a series of empirical papers have documented the superior characteristics of exporters relative to non-exporters, at least in developing countries—exporting may not be as critical for firms located in developed countries with a large domestic market, where scale efficiencies have already been achieved (see Wagner, 2007 or Greenaway and Kneller, 2007, for a survey; Martins and Yang, 2009, for a meta-analysis; and ISGEP 2008, for comparable evidence on 14 countries). Two alternative, but not mutually exclusive, explanations for this phenomenon have been proposed: (i) the self-selection hypothesis, that is, only the most productive firms can overcome trade costs and become exporters; (ii) the learning-by-exporting hypothesis, that is, firms are exposed to international competition after they begin to export and hence are able to learn and improve their performance.

In this chapter, we extend the evidence on exports and productivity by examining total factor productivity differences between exporting and non-exporting Portuguese firms in manufacturing and services sectors, and their contribution to aggregate productivity growth. Motivated by the recent heterogeneous-firm models of international trade, we ask how much of the industry productivity gains came from the reallocation of economic activity across exporters and non-exporters within industries. We also assess the productivity gap between exporters and non-exporters, the so-called exporter *premia*, controlling for other types of learning. Finally, analyses are conducted separately for the manufacturing and services sectors, given that exporting is usually more prevalent in manufacturing.

We do not examine the two alternative, but not mutually exclusive, explanations for the higher productivity level of exporters: the self-selection hypothesis and the learning-by-exporting hypothesis. This exercise has already been done for European periphery (see next section), especially by Silva et al. (2012; 2013) for Portugal.

When compared with the EU (28 countries) average, the countries of the European periphery (Greece, Italy, Portugal and Spain) have a lower degree of openness to foreign trade. As can be seen in Figure 9.1, in 2004 (the last year of our micro database), the exports per capita of goods and services in Portugal and Greece were only four thousand euros (at 2005 prices) per person, just about half of the EU average. In the case of Italy and Spain, the corresponding figures were 6.2 and 5.3 thousand euros per person, respectively (i.e., 78 percent and 68 percent of the EU average). In the Italian case, however, the level of exports at the beginning of the period under analysis was comparable to that of the EU average. This poor performance is explained by the weak real growth rate of exports: 2.7 percent (annual average over the period 1996–2004) in Italy against 6.3 percent in the EU (Figure 9.2). The real growth rate of exports for Greece and Spain was 8.1 percent and 7.2 percent, respectively, higher than the EU average of 6.3 percent. In the case of Portugal, the corresponding growth rate was 5.3 percent, almost one percentage point below the EU average.

The general picture does not change when we look at the share of exports in GDP (Figure 9.3). While exports in the EU countries rose from about 30 percent of GDP in 1996 to almost 36 percent in 2004, they tended to remain constant over the period in the European periphery (roughly 23 percent of GDP in Greece, 25 percent in Italy and Spain, and 28 percent

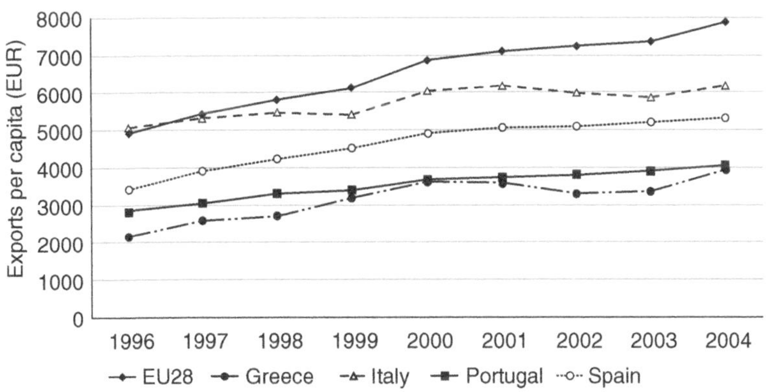

Figure 9.1 Exports per capita.

Source: AMECO database, accessed in October 2013).

Note: at 2005 prices.

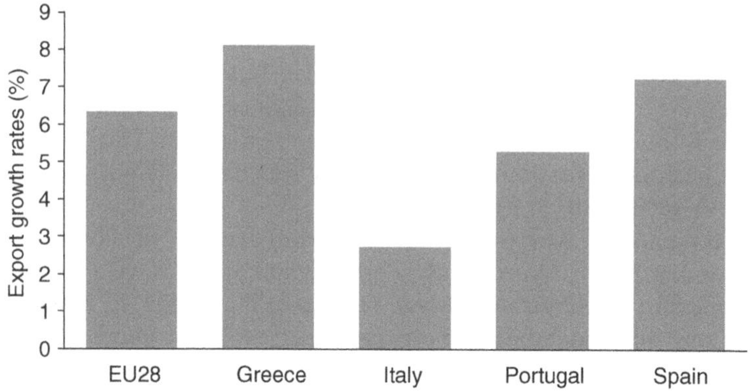

Figure 9.2 Real growth rate of exports.

Source: AMECO database, accessed in October 2013.

Note: annual average over the period 1996–2004.

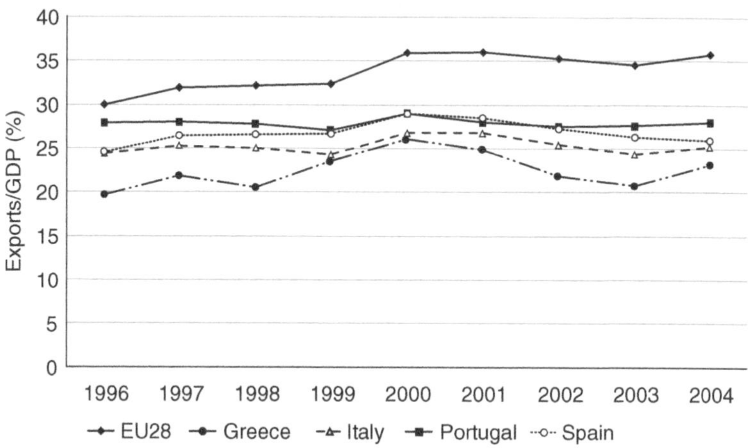

Figure 9.3 Share of exports in GDP.

Source: AMECO database, accessed in October 2013.

in Portugal). (A discussion on the pattern of Portuguese foreign trade specialisation can be seen in Chapter 10.)

The chapter proceeds as follows. Following a brief review of the background literature in the next section, Section 3 presents the dataset and variables used. Section 4 presents the results of the industry productivity decomposition exercise, and Section 5 analyses the productivity gap between exporters and non-exporters and the role of other sources of firms' knowledge. Section 6 offers some concluding remarks.

2. Exporting and productivity: theory and selected empirical findings

Theory

There are large and persistent productivity differences across firms, even within narrowly defined industries, with only the more productive firms surviving and self-selecting into export markets. A number of theoretical papers take these empirical findings as a starting point to develop models of international trade with heterogeneous firms which focus on the relationship between productivity and exports (see, for example, Bernard et al, 2003; Melitz, 2003; Yeaple, 2005, inter al.). The major point of these models is that intra-industry trade promotes aggregate productivity growth namely due to within-industry resource reallocation towards more productive firms.

Melitz (2003), for example, built a monopolistic competitive industry model where, prior to the sunk cost of entry, each firm faces initial uncertainty about the true (fixed) productivity level. Firms expand and export when they realise they are efficient and remain domestic and shrink (or even exit) when they learn they are not. The main claim of his pioneering model is that, through a combination of entry and firm selection effects, increased exposure to exporting induces inter-firm market share reallocation towards more productive firms, which raises aggregate industry-level productivity.

Bernard et al. (2003) reach the same conclusion, but with a different industrial organisation framework—we explicitly stress the impact of import competition. A reduction in trade costs induces the more-efficient domestic firms to expand and export, at the same time that it encourages more efficient foreign firms to penetrate the domestic market, thus displacing less efficient producers, which leads to an improvement in overall productivity.

On the whole, these models suggest that micro analysis is the proper complement to aggregate industry studies, as it provides considerable insight into the connection between exporting and industry productivity growth.

Major empirical findings

The heterogeneous firm trade models outlined in the previous section predict a positive impact of exports on aggregate productivity through resource reallocation. Although a growing number of authors has carried out decomposition exercises on industry productivity change to examine the contribution of *internal* and *external restructuring*—the former accounts for the change due to improvement within individual firms, the latter due to resource reallocation across firms (Disney et al., 2003; Carreira and Teixeira, 2008)—little attention has been paid to quantifying the contribution of exporters.[1] Table 9.1 compares the results of some of these rare studies: Baldwin and Gu (2003) for Canadian manufacturing plants in 1974–1996; Bernard and Jensen (2004) for the U.S. manufacturing plants in 1983–1992; Hansson and Lundin (2004) for Swedish manufacturing firms in 1990–1999; Harris

Table 9.1 Exporters' contribution to aggregate productivity growth, selected studies

Author	*Country*	*Period*	*Sector*	*Data*	*Methodology*	*Results (% of total)*				
						Group	*Within*	*Between*	*Entry-exit*	*Total*
Baldwin and Gu (2003)	Canada	1974–96	Manufacturing	ASM, small and large firms	BG, labour productivity	Total Exporters	(with+bet.)	82.9	17.1	100
						Non-Exporters		79.3	18.0	97.3
								3.6	−0.9	2.7
Bernard and Jensen (2004)	USA	1983–92	Manufacturing	ASM from LRD	Average weight, TFP	Total Exporters	58.1	41.9	-	100
						Non-Exporters	46.9	89.3	-	136.1
							11.2	−47.3	-	−36.1
Gleeson and Ruane (2009)	Ireland	1998–2004	Manufacturing	Census, all firms	BW, labour productivity	Total Exporters-	98.5	−24.4	25.9	100
						Non-Exporters	90.4	−20.4	22.5	92.6
							8.0	−4.0	3.4	7.4
Hansson and Lundin (2004)	Sweden	1990–99	Manufacturing	Statistics Sweden, ≥50 employees	Average weight, TFP and labour productivity	Total (TFP)	161.8	−61.8	-	100
						ExportersNon-	117.6	61.8	-	179.4
						Exporters	44.1	−123.5	-	−79.4
						Total (LP)	78.3	21.7	-	100
						Exporters	55.1	191.3	-	246.4
						Non-Exporters	23.2	−169.6	-	-
										146.4
Harris and Li (2008)	UK	1996–2004	All market-based sectors	FAME, representa-tive sample	FHK, TFP	Total Exporters-	22.0	21.5	56.5	100
						Non-Exporters	20.1	13.9	27.3	60.8
							1.9	7.7	29.2	38.8

Notes: FHK, BG and BW denote the decomposition methods proposed by Foster, Haltiwanger, and Krizan (2001), Baldwin and Gu (2003), and Breuning and Wong (2007), respectively. The 'between' effect also includes the 'covariance' term, when applicable.

and Li (2008) for the UK firms of all market-based sectors in 1996–2004; Gleeson and Ruane (2009) for Irish manufacturing plants in 1998–2004. Because of the different data characteristics, decomposition methods used and productivity measures, the figures across these studies are not strictly comparable. Nevertheless, the common premise is that overall exporters account for a larger proportion of productivity growth than non-exporters. The studies do not provide clear evidence on whether productivity growth was mostly derived from internal or external restructuring. The within-firm effect seems to be relatively less important for exporters where the domestic market is large, such as the United States (cf., the US, Swedish and Irish figures).

When it comes to firms' learning (i.e., within-firm effect), in recent years, an increasing number of empirical studies have focused on the relationship between exporting and productivity using firm- or plant-level data for several countries (see Wagner, 2007 or Greenaway and Kneller, 2007, for a survey). The underlying idea of these works is that firms either self-select into exporting, that is, only high-productivity firms can afford the trade costs to serve competitive foreign markets, or there is learning-by-exporting, that is, exports should improve firms' efficiency through both exploitation of economies of scale and fostering a learning process through knowledge and technology spillovers.

The main findings that emerge from fifteen years of micro-econometric research are that: (i) exporters tend to be more productive than non-exporters; (ii) firms with higher ex-ante productivity self-select into export markets; (iii) post-entry productivity growth of exporters is not necessarily higher than that of non-exporters—Table 9.2 summarises these findings for the cases of Greece, Italy, Portugal and Spain.

3. Data description

To conduct our empirical analysis, we use an unbalanced panel of Portuguese manufacturing and business service firms covering the period 1996–2004. The raw data is drawn from the combination of two statistical data sources, both run by the Portuguese Statistical Office (INE): *Inquérito às Empresas Harmonizado* (IEH), an annual business survey with information on inputs and output, required to estimate production function at firm level; and *Ficheiro de Unidades Estatísticas* (FUE) that contains generic features (activity, number of employees, age and location) on all Portuguese firms. (The unit of production considered is thus the firm.) The longitudinal dimension of the panel, required for our analysis, was constructed using each firm's unique identification code.

The IEH survey comprises all firms operating in Portugal with more than 100 employees, plus a representative random sample of firms with less than 100 employees.[2] The following filters were applied: first, due to lack of good data, firms with less than 20 employees were eliminated from the estimation

Table 9.2 Evidence on exports and productivity: the cases of Greece, Italy, Portugal and Spain

Author	*Country*	*Period*	*Data*	*Productivity difference between exporters and non-exporters*	*Self-selection hypothesis*	*Learning-by-exporting hypothesis*
Tsekouras and Skuras (2005)	Greece	1975–1996	Survey of Cement industry		Firms are forced to increase exports in order to reduce the average production cost.	
Castellani (2002)	Italy	1989–1994	MCC, sample	Labour productivity is higher for exporting firms than for non-exporters.	Labour productivity is higher in future export starters than in non-starters three years before entry.	Labour productivity growth is influenced by firms' export intensity and not simply by the presence in the export market.
Castellani and Zanfei (2007)	Italy	1996	CIS2	Companies with the highest international involvement are characterized by the highest productivity *premia*.	Productive firms will self-select into international markets.	
Silva et al. (2012)	Portugal	1996–2003	IAE and ECE, survey			A higher growth of labour productivity and TFP is found for new exporting firms.
Silva et al. (2013)	Portugal	1996–2003	IAE and ECE, survey		Evidence of a self-selection to exports is found.	

Author	*Country*	*Period*	*Data*	*Productivity difference between exporters and non-exporters*	*Self-selection hypothesis*	*Learning-by-exporting hypothesis*
Delgado et al. (2002)	Spain	1991–1996	ESEE, survey	TFP is higher for exporting firms than for non-exporting firms.	Evidence of self-selection of more productive firms in the export market is found.	Evidence in favour of learning-by-exporting is rather weak and limited to younger exporters.
Farinas and Martin-Marcos (2007)	Spain	1990–1999	ESEE, survey	TFP is greater in exporting firms.	Evidence of selection in the export market entry of is found.	No systematic differences in TFP between non-exporters and exporters after entry are found.
Cassiman et al. (2010).	Spain	1990–1998	ESEE, survey, small and medium sized		Product innovation affects productivity and induces small non-exporting firms to enter the export market.	

sample;[3] second, given the reduced number of observations, manufacture of tobacco products (CAE 16), manufacture of coke, refined petroleum products and nuclear fuel (CAE 23) and research and development (CAE 73) were also excluded; third, since the aim of this chapter is to analyse exporting firms in the services sector, we only consider the rentals and business services industry (CAE 71 to 74); and, finally, firms with missing observations or unreasonable values (negative values and outliers) were dropped from the estimation sample. For each industry, we define as an outlier a firm for which the log difference between an input and the output is in the top and bottom one percentile of the respective distribution. As a result of all these procedures, we have, for the period 1996–2004, an unbalanced panel of 9,952 firms and a total of 38,554 (year-firm) observations.

Tables 9.A1 and 9.A2 in the Appendix report the summary statistics and the correlations matrix, respectively, of the main variables used in our empirical analyses. About 35.8 percent of firms in our sample do not export at all. Furthermore, as can be seen in Figure 9.4, roughly 38.0 percent of exporting firms export less than 10 percent of their total sales, which may signal that these firms are only occasional exporters, as noted by Castellani (2002).

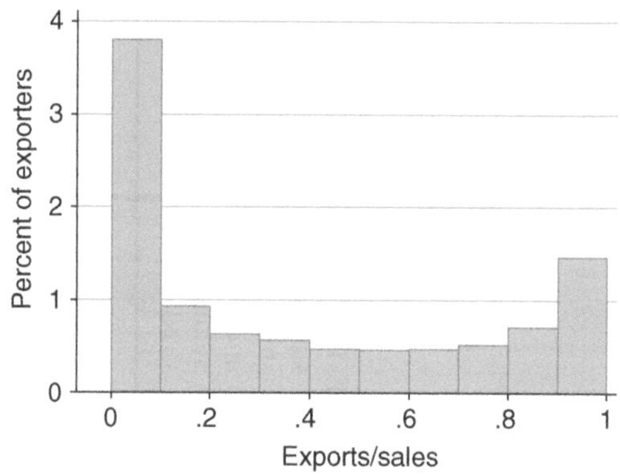

Figure 9.4 Distribution of exports as a percentage of sales.

Note: pooled yearly values of exporting firms, 1996–2004.

4. Contribution of exporters and non-exporters to industry productivity growth

Decomposition methodology

In order to quantify the contribution of exporters to industry productivity growth, we decompose changes in productivity level from years $t-\tau$ to t into two components—as in Bernard and Jensen (2004) and Hansson and Lundin (2004), we only consider continuing firms, that is, firms that exist both in year $t-\tau$ and in year t—: (i) the within-firm (own-firm) productivity effect; (ii) the between (reallocation) effect. We ignore the contribution of entering and exiting firms, a limitation of our decomposition methodology. However, our dataset is not particularly suited to that purpose because the reasons why a firm is excluded from the dataset may not be related to its failure at all.

First, we define the industry productivity level, P_{jt}, in year t as a weighted average of firms' productivity levels, that is, $P_{jt} = \sum_{i \in I} \theta_{it} a_{it}$, where θ_{it} is the output share of the ith firm in year t and a_{it} is the corresponding productivity level. Clearly, industry productivity growth can occur through changes in a_{it} or θ_{it}, that is, either through changes in the productivity level across micro units or through changes in their market shares.

We make use of the decomposition method proposed by Griliches and Regev (1995) to decompose the cross period change in aggregate industry productivity (for details, see Carreira and Teixeira, 2008):[4]

$$\Delta P_{jt} = \sum_{i \in J} \bar{\theta}_i \Delta a_i + \sum_{i \in I} \Delta \theta_i \left(\bar{a}_i - \bar{P} \right) \tag{1}$$

where $\bar{\theta}_i$, $\bar{a}_i$, and $\bar{P}$ are the average of each variable over the base and end year. The first term in equation (1), called the *within-firm effect* or internal restructuring, represents the productivity growth within continuing firms (weighted by the average shares in the industry). The second term, the *between effect* or external restructuring, reflects the aggregate productivity improvement coming from high-productivity continuing firms' expanding shares (or from low-productivity continuing firms' contracting shares).

Measurement of productivity

Firm-level *total factor productivity* (TFP) is our selected productivity measure. In order to compute the TFP, we first estimate the factor elasticity parameters of a Cobb-Douglas production function for each industry, to allow for sector heterogeneity:

$$\ln Y_{it} = \alpha_0 + \alpha_K^j \ln K_{it} + \alpha_L^j \ln L_{it} + \alpha_M^j \ln M_{it} + u_{it} \tag{2}$$

where $\ln Y_{it}$ is log real gross output of the ith firm in year t, and $\ln K_{it}$, $\ln L_{it}$, and $\ln M_{it}$ are log capital, labour and material (intermediate) inputs, respectively; α_f denotes factor elasticities, $f = K, L, M$; and u_{it} is the error term. Note that we do not impose any restriction on the sum of the three factor elasticities.

The *gross output* is given by the sum of total revenues from sales, services rendered, and production subsidies. It is deflated by the producer price index at the three-digit level. The *labour* input is a 12-month employment average. *Materials* include the cost of materials and services purchased and were deflated by the GDP deflator. *Capital stock* is measured as the book value of total net assets (excluding financial investments and cash stock).

To estimate equation (2), we assume $u_{it} = \omega_{it} + \eta_{it}$, with ω_{it} denoting a firm-specific unobserved component and η_{it} a residual term uncorrelated with input choices. Ordinary least-squares estimation produces inconsistent estimates due to the likely presence of simultaneity and selection bias: the simultaneity bias arises because input demands are also determined by the firm's knowledge of its productivity level, which makes ω_{it} correlated with the observed inputs; the selection bias is generated by endogenous exit, as smaller firms, with lower capital intensity, are more likely to exit. Assuming that ω_{it} is time invariant, equation (2) can be estimated using the least square dummy variable approach or the within transformation.[5] Consistency of the fixed effect model requires, however, strict exogeneity of the included regressors, a non-realistic assumption (Grilliches and Mairesse, 1998). To overcome this problem, we estimate equation (2) using the generalised method of moments (GMM) methodology. In particular, we employ the Arellano and Bond (1991) one-step difference GMM (GMM-DIF) estimator, which (i) transforms the panel data model in first differences to remove the individual effects, and (ii) uses lagged levels of the dependent variable and the predetermined variables as instruments for the endogenous differences.[6]

Finally, using equation (2), the (log) TFP is given by:

$$\hat{a}_{it} = \ln Y_{it} - \hat{\alpha}^{j}_{K} \ln K_{it} - \hat{\alpha}^{j}_{L} \ln L_{it} - \hat{\alpha}^{j}_{M} \ln M_{it} \qquad (3)$$

Decomposition results

The results of the productivity growth decomposition exercise are given in Table 9.3. The TFP grew on average 14.4 percent between 1996 and 2004 (i.e., 1.7 percent per annum)—the respective rates in manufacturing and services sectors were 9.2 percent and 40.4 percent (i.e., 1.1 and 4.3 percent per annum, respectively). Looking at the difference between exporters and non-exporters, the contrast between the low productivity growth among non-exporters and the strong productivity gains of exporters shows that exporters are the dominant source of aggregate productivity growth, accounting for approximately 95 percent of the TFP growth over the period 1996–2004. This contribution is even larger in the case of the services sector, where they explain the total observed gains. In the case of the manufacturing sector, the exporters represent 91 percent of the TFP growth. These figures are close to those previously reported by Baldwin and Gu (2003) for Canadian manufacturing plants, and Gleeson and Ruane, (2009) for Irish manufacturing—Bernard and Jensen (2004) for the USA manufacturing plants, and Hansson and Lundin (2004) for Swedish manufacturing firms observed that non-exporters account negatively for the productivity change, thus exporters are the only ones responsible for the growth (see Table 9.1).

Another finding that emerges from Table 9.3 is that exporters' within effect accounts for a greater share of overall productivity growth, explaining approximately 72 percent of the gains. Additionally, there is clearly a marked difference between sectors in terms of contributions to productivity growth: the within effect dominates (94 percent) in the manufacturing sector, while the between effect explains about 53 percent of the TFP growth in the services sector. Our within share of the manufacturing sector is comparable to that found by Gleeson and Ruane (2009) in Ireland. Conversely, Bernard and Jensen (2004) found that the between effect was dominant.

5. Productivity difference between exporters and non-exporters

In the previous section, we found that exporters account for a larger share of industry productivity growth, with the prevalence of the within-firm effect. A key issue now is to test whether exporters are more productive than non-exporters. We assume that a firm's TFP is driven not only by the learning-by-doing and the stock of knowledge, but also by the exposure to international trade (export, import and foreign owned), that is:

$$a_{it} = \beta_0 + \beta_L LD_{it} + \beta_Z Z_{it} + \beta_X XSH_{it} + \beta_M MSH_{it} + \beta_F FOK_{it} + \omega_{it} \tag{4}$$

where LD_{it} is a learning-by-doing index of firm i in year t; Z_{it} is the stock of knowledge, proxied by the logarithm of intangible assets (ln*INTASS*); XSH_{it} is the share of exports in total sales; MSH_{it} is the share of imports in total intermediates and capital equipment purchases; FOK_{it} is the share of foreign ownership capital; and ω_{it} is the error term.

Therefore, we assume that the hypothesis of learning-by-exporting is related to the intensity of involvement in foreign markets. Low export intensity may result from occasional exports without a clear exporting strategy, which limits the productivity gains. Thus, as in Castellani (2002), to capture the effects of the firm's exposure to international markets, we use the share of foreign sales in total sales, rather than the binary export status used in most of the previous empirical literature.

Recent empirical studies also shown that importing activities and foreign-owned firms have a positive impact on firm-level productivity (e.g., Augier et al., 2013; Muûls and Pisu, 2009; for a survey, see Greenaway and Kneller, 2007).

Following Carreira and Teixeira (2011), we assume as a proxy for the firm's production experience (i.e., learning-by-doing) the inverse of firm age (inv*AGE*)—thus the effect of experience on productivity converges to zero and we expect to find a negative and significant β_L in our regression. The rationale is that learning-by-doing is subject to sharply diminishing returns (Arrow, 1962). However, it should be noted that there is a problem with this measure: it assumes that the firm accrues a similar level of experience each year, which is unrealistic since production varies over time.

Although many early studies adopt a two-step approach—that is, first regressing output on inputs to obtain firm-level TFP, i.e., equation (1), and

Table 9.3 Decomposition of aggregate productivity growth

	Overall			*Manufacturing*			*Services*		
	Total	*Within*	*Between*	*Total*	*Within*	*Between*	*Total*	*Within*	*Between*
Average TFP growth	*1.69% per annum*			*1.11% per annum*			*4.33% per annum*		
All	0.1439	0.1113	0.0326	0.0921	0.0947	–0.0026	0.4039	0.1962	0.2076
	(100.0%)	(77.4%)	(22.6%)	(100.0%)	(102.8%)	(–2.8%)	(100.0%)	(48.6%)	(51.4%)
Exporters	0.1371	0.1039	0.0332	0.0835	0.0867	–0.0031	0.4064	0.1924	0.2140
	(95.3%)	(72.3%)	(23.1%)	(90.7%)	(94.1%)	(–3.4%)	(100.6%)	(47.6%)	(53.0%)
Non-exporters	0.0067	0.0073	–0.0006	0.0085	0.0080	0.0005	–0.0026	0.0038	–0.0064
	(4.7%)	(5.1%)	(–0.4%)	(9.3%)	(8.7%)	(0.6%)	(–0.6%)	(0.9%)	(–1.6%)

Note: TFP growth decomposition using the method proposed by Griliches and Regev (1995) at sector-level, 1996–2004. Aggregation weighted over 23 two-digit industries by firm's output. The share of aggregate productivity growth is shown in parentheses.

then estimating a variant of equation (4) with TFP as the dependent variable—, in this chapter, we test export experience directly in the estimation of the production function (see, for example, Van Biesebroeck, 2004; Bigsten et al., 2004). In fact, the estimation of equation (4) jointly with equation (2) in one step could lead to a more efficient estimator. Table 9.4 gives the productivity differences between exporters and non-exporters, the so-called exporter *premia*, controlling for other types of learning. The validity of GMM-DIF estimates depends on the absence of second-order serial autocorrelation and on the choice of the appropriate set of instruments. As expected, negative first-order serial correlation is found in the Arellano-Bond AR(1) test while the AR(2) test indicates the validity of instruments for the four regressions (at the 5 percent significance level).

As can be seen, the exporter *premia* coefficient (*XSH*) is significant at 0.01 and positive for the overall sample and manufacturing sector, but it does not seem to be statistically significant at conventional levels for the services sector. In particular, a Portuguese exporter that only sells to foreign

Table 9.4 Exporter premia

Variable	*Overall* (1)	*Manufacturing* (2)	*Services* (3)
$\ln Y_{t-1}$	0.1646***(0.0601)	0.1766***(0.0413)	0.2894** (0.1209)
$\ln K_t$	0.2548***(0.0975)	0.1631** (0.0793)	0.5124***(0.1276)
$\ln K_{t-1}$	-0.1224 (0.0795)	-0.0354 (0.0656)	(0.1063)
$\ln M_t$	0.1887***(0.0541)	0.2672***(0.0444)	0.3210***(0.0904)
$\ln M_{t-1}$	0.0839 (0.0512)	0.0816** (0.0353)	-0.1254 (0.0836)
$\ln L_t$	0.5606***(0.1110)	0.4293***(0.1163)	0.3437***(0.1068)
$\ln L_{t-1}$	-0.3859***(0.1037)	-0.2138* (0.1136)	-0.2050* (0.1133)
XSH	0.0585***(0.0129)	0.0411***(0.0109)	-0.1050 (0.0853)
MSH	0.0520***(0.0120)	0.0415***(0.0104)	0.0931* (0.0551)
inv*AGE*	-0.3487***(0.0804)	-0.2154***(0.0628)	-0.1245 (0.2780)
ln*INTASS*	0.0016* (0.0010)	0.0005 (0.0008)	0.0034 (0.0029)
FOK	0.0117 (0.0098)	0.0080 (0.0086)	0.0224 (0.0270)
Industry dummies	yes	yes	yes
AR (1) (Prob > z)	-8.55 (0.000)	-9.24 (0.000)	-4.18 (0.000)
AR (2) (Prob > z)	-0.06 (0.951)	-0.13 (0.897)	-0.40 (0.692)
Sargan test (Prob > χ^2)	146.06 (0.000)	221.20 (0.000)	64.91 (0.027)
Hansen test (Prob > χ^2)	117.29 (0.000)	176.64 (0.000)	40.56 (0.660)
Wald test	9883.95***	11281.30***	446.83***
No. of observations	18,164	16043	2102
No. of firms	4,611	3985	627
No. of instruments	79	76	58

Notes: Joint estimation of equations (2) and (4). Arellano-Bond one-step difference GMM estimators. Robust standard errors are given in parentheses. ***, **, and * denote statistical significance at the .01, .05, and .10 levels, respectively.

markets is, on average, 6.0 percent $\{=100\times[\exp(0.0585)-1]\}$ more productive than non-exporters, *ceteris paribus*. In the case of the manufacturing sector, the corresponding difference is 4.2 percent $\{=100\times[\exp(0.0411)-1]\}$. For instance, when the mean (manufacturing) firm exports 24.2 percent (26.9 percent) of sales, the respective *premia* is 1.5 percent (1.1 percent).

Conversely, a services firm that only purchases intermediates and equipment abroad is, on average, 9.8 percent $\{=100\times[\exp(0.0931)-1]\}$ more productive than non-importers, *ceteris paribus*—importer *premia* is 4.2 percent and 5.3 percent in the manufacturing sector and the overall sample, respectively. If we take into consideration the average share of imports, the productivity advantage reduces to 0.9 percent (overall sample), 0.8 percent (manufacturing firms) and 0.4 percent (services firms). Therefore, better access to imported intermediates and capital-goods raises productivity.

Looking at other sources of firms' knowledge, we found that learning-by-doing seems to impact positively on the productivity growth overall for firms and the manufacturing sector. In the case of the services sector, it does not seem to be statistically significant at conventional levels.

Table 9.5 goes a step further and looks at the specific exporter *premia* by destination markets—EU market (XEUSH) vs. other foreign markets (XOCSH). (In order to save space, only the six key-variables for the purpose of the study are shown in this table and the next ones. Complete results are available from the author upon request.) Given the additional costs of selling goods to non-EU countries, a higher *premia* for this group of exporters is expected. Indeed, in the case of exports to the other countries, the coefficient estimates for the overall sample and the manufacturing sector are larger and significant at 0.05.

Finally, Table 9.6 shows the results from estimating equations (4) with interaction terms (inv*AGE* and ln*INTASS*) to capture differences in the

Table 9.5 Exporter premia by destination markets

Variable	*Overall* (1)	*Manufacturing* (2)	*Services* (3)
XEUSH	0.0581***(0.0134)	0.0404***(0.0115)	0.0142 (0.0894)
XOCSH	0.0603** (0.0261)	0.0448** (0.0224)	-0.3399 (0.1681)
MSH	0.0519***(0.0120)	0.0414***(0.0104)	0.0649 (0.0585)
inv*AGE*	-0.3485***(0.0804)	-0.2157***(0.0629)	-0.1084 (0.2761)
ln*INTASS*	0.0016* (0.0010)	0.0005 (0.0008)	0.0033 (0.0028)
FOK	0.0117 (0.0098)	0.0080 (0.0086)	0.0229 (0.0259)

Notes: Joint estimation of equations (2) and (4). Arellano-Bond one-step difference GMM estimators. Only the key-variables for the purpose of the study are shown in table (see Table 7.4). Complete results and tests are available from the author upon request. Robust standard errors are given in parentheses. ***, **, and * denote statistical significance at the .01, .05, and .10 levels, respectively.

Table 9.6 The role of absorptive capacity in learning-by-exporting

Variable	*Overall*			*Manufacturing*			*Services*		
	(1)	*(2)*	*(3)*	*(4)*	*(5)*	*(6)*	*(7)*	*(8)*	*(9)*
XSH	0.3370***	0.0189	0.4641	0.2137***	−0.1375	0.0633	−0.1720	0.6461	0.5312
	(0.0893)	(0.2355)	(0.3018)	(0.0676)	(0.1771)	(0.2247)	(0.4400)	(0.5926)	(0.6533)
inv*AGE* × *XSH*	−4.3278***		−4.4084***	−2.5801**		−2.5438**	1.0636		3.9057
	(1.3838)		(1.4133)	(1.0137)		(1.0257)	(7.1088)		(6.9708)
ln*INTASS* × *XSH*		0.0039	−0.0119		0.0176	0.0146		−0.0760	−0.0892
		(0.0232)	(0.0267)		(0.0175)	(0.0203)		(0.0587)	(0.0644)
MSH	0.0515***	0.0520***	0.0513***	0.0442***	0.0417***	0.0443***	0.0929*	0.0946*	0.0941
	(0.0123)	(0.0120)	(0.0124)	(0.0114)	(0.0106)	(0.0116)	(0.0549)	(0.0573)	(0.0589)
inv*AGE*	1.2718**	−0.3499***	1.3056**	0.8005*	−0.2297***	0.7743*	−0.1378	−0.1543	−0.2085
	(0.5008)	(0.0812)	(0.5171)	(0.4208)	(0.0666)	(0.4285)	(0.2946)	(0.2843)	(0.3025)
ln*INTASS*	0.0008	0.0006	0.0039	−0.0001	−0.0048	−0.0045	0.0034	0.0073*	0.0080*
	(0.0010)	(0.0062)	(0.0071)	(0.0009)	(0.0053)	(0.0062)	(0.0028)	(0.0044)	(0.0047)
FOK	0.0123	0.0114	0.0132	0.0095	0.0064	0.0082	0.0243	0.0404	0.0506
	(0.0112)	(0.0099)	(0.0115)	(0.0104)	(0.0089)	(0.0107)	(0.0291)	(0.0314)	(0.0356)

Notes: Joint estimation of equations (2) and (4). Arellano-Bond one-step difference GMM estimators. Only the key-variables for the purpose of the study are shown in table (see Table 7.4). Complete results and tests are available from the author upon request. Robust standard errors are given in parentheses. ***, **, and * denote statistical significance at the .01, .05, and .10 levels, respectively.

impact of export experience on TFP for different levels of knowledge. The capacity of a firm to absorb external knowledge depends on its own knowledge ('absorptive capacity of firms', after Cohen and Levinthal, 1989), a fact that our results generally seem to confirm for the overall sample and the manufacturing sector.

6. Conclusion

In this chapter, we provide a detailed analysis of the total factor productivity differences between Portuguese exporters and non-exporters over the period 1996–2004, in the manufacturing and services sectors, and their contribution to aggregate productivity growth.

Despite some limited micro evidence of trade-induced aggregate productivity growth, especially for the European periphery countries, to our knowledge, this chapter is the first study that assesses the contribution of exporters to Portuguese aggregate productivity growth. We decomposed aggregate productivity growth into within-firm (own-firm) and between (reallocation) effects. We found that exporters are the dominant source of industry productivity growth—they accounted for almost 95 percent of TFP growth—and there is clearly a marked difference between sectors—the within effect dominates in the manufacturing sector, while the between effect explains a large proportion of growth in the services sector.

Our results also suggest that exporters in Portugal, like exporters in several developed as well as developing countries, are more productive than domestically oriented firms. However, the capacity of a firm to internalise knowledge from international markets seems to depend on the firm's knowledge. Finally, our results pointed to a learning-by-importing effect, that is, importing foreign intermediates and capital raises total factor productivity at the firm level.

Knowing the contribution of exporting to productivity growth provides policy-makers with an extra incentive to focus on helping firms develop their exporting activities. Moreover, trade-liberalisation reforms could be made more effective in terms of raising productivity if accompanied by specific aids for firms to acquire knowledge (e.g., training programmes, hiring of skilled personnel, and developing RandD activities). Finally, since external restructuring was especially important in the non-manufacturing sector, government policy aimed at sustaining exports needs to take account of the different channels through which productivity growth occurs across different sectors.

7. Appendix. Summary statistics

Tables 9.A1 and 9.A2 report the summary statistics and the correlations matrix, respectively, of the main variables used in our empirical analyses. Most variables exhibit strong variability, as shown by the large values of

Table 9.A1 Descriptive statistics

Variable		*Overall*					*Manufacturing*					*Services*				
		Obs.	*Mean*	*SD*	*Min*	*Max*	*Obs.*	*Mean*	*SD*	*Min*	*Max*	*Obs.*	*Mean*	*SD*	*Min*	*Max*
ln*Y*	Log output	38554	14.958	1.316	11.046	21.454	33752	14.983	1.314	11.675	21.454	4802	14.784	1.316	11.046	19.764
ln*K*	Log capital	38554	14.897	1.441	9.706	22.181	33752	14.940	1.395	10.179	21.426	4802	14.589	1.694	9.706	22.181
ln*L*	Log labour	38554	4.272	0.937	2.996	8.917	33752	4.243	0.901	2.996	8.917	4802	4.471	1.140	2.996	8.892
ln*M*	Log material	38554	14.346	1.545	8.255	21.254	33752	14.452	1.486	9.270	21.254	4802	13.602	1.730	8.255	20.274
XSH	Share of exports	38554	0.242	0.343	0	1	33752	0.269	0.354	0	1	4802	0.046	0.150	0	1
XEUSH	to EU	38554	0.198	0.304	0	1	33752	0.222	0.315	0	1	4802	0.031	0.116	0	1
XOCSH	to other count.	38554	0.044	0.119	0	1	33752	0.048	0.123	0	1	4802	0.016	0.079	0	1
MSH	Share of imports	38554	0.163	0.223	0	1	33752	0.181	0.228	0	1	4802	0.040	0.118	0	1
inv*AGE*	Inverse of age	37795	0.082	0.096	0.006	1	33063	0.076	0.092	0.006	1	4732	0.125	0.110	0.008	1
ln*INTASS*	Log intangible assets	38554	8.655	4.528	0	20.378	33752	8.862	4.439	0	20.378	4802	7.200	4.866	0	19.806
FOK	Share of foreign capital	38554	0.077	0.256	0	1	33752	0.074	0.253	0	1	4802	0.094	0.278	0	1

Note: Pooled yearly values, 1996–2004.

Table 9.A2 Correlation across covariates

	lnY	*lnK*	*lnL*	*lnM*	*XSH*	*XEUSH*	*XOCSH*	*MSH*	*invAGE*	*lnINTASS*	*FORKSH*
ln*Y*	1										
ln*K*	0.9078*	1									
ln*L*	0.7229*	0.6369*	1								
ln*M*	0.9548*	0.8830*	0.5783*	1							
XSH	0.2197*	0.1909*	0.2912*	0.2291*	1						
XEUSH	0.1921*	0.1500*	0.2752*	0.2003*	0.9392*	1					
XOCSH	0.1418*	0.1667*	0.1357*	0.1479*	0.4807*	0.1503*	1				
MSH	0.3625*	0.3267*	0.2275*	0.3831*	0.2703*	0.2636*	0.1050*	1			
inv*AGE*	−0.0711*	−0.1118*	−0.0239*	−0.0934*	−0.0003	0.0077	−0.0206*	−0.0490*	1		
ln*INTASS*	0.4737*	0.5430*	0.3355*	0.4728*	0.1471*	0.1180*	0.1222*	0.2061*	−0.0365*	1	
FOK	0.2785*	0.2392*	0.2222*	0.2482*	0.1961*	0.1945*	0.0678*	0.2967*	0.0137*	0.1056*	1

Note: Pooled yearly values, 1996–2004.

* denotes statistical significance at the .05 level.

standard deviations relative to their mean (Table 9.A1). The mean firm in Portugal with 20 or more employees (i.e., in our sample) has 72 employees, produces 3,135 thousand euros and exports 24.2 percent of its sales—most of these exports go the EU, 19.8 percent. Clearly, on average, manufacturing firms have a higher propensity to export than services firms, 26.9 and 4.6 percent, respectively.

Notes

1 See, for example, Foster et al. (2001), Disney et al. (2003), Baldwin and Gu (2006), and Carreira and Teixeira (2008), for an analysis of the manufacturing sector in the US, the UK, Canada and Portugal, respectively.
2 The sample is representative of the Portuguese sector disaggregation (at three-digit level), both in terms of employment size and sales.
3 We note that firms with less than 20 employees represent 71 percent of Portuguese manufacturing firms, but only 16 percent of total employment (average over the period; source: OECD database).
4 The most commonly used methodologies are Griliches and Regev (1995) and Foster et al. (2001). Alternative methods can be found in Foster et al. (2001) and Baldwin and Gu (2006).
5 The random effects model is rejected in favour of the presence of fixed effects by both Hausman and robust Hausman tests at the 1 percent significance level (see Wooldrige, 2002).
6 Regressions were performed using the Stata, *xtabond2* procedure (Roodman, 2006). The results presented in the paper are robust to fixed-effects, Olley and Pakes (1996), Levinsohn and Petrin (2003) and GMM-System methods. These results are available from the author upon request.

10 Productive experience and structural transformation

The cases of Portugal, Spain, Greece, Italy and Germany

Miguel Lebre de Freitas, Luis C. Nunes and Rui Costa Neves

1. Introduction

In this chapter, we compare the specialisation patterns of four south European countries as of 2005, taking Germany has a benchmark. The comparison addresses the current export diversification, an estimate of the income content of exports, and the consistency of the specialisation patterns. Then, we assess the extent to which the different productive experiences, as reflected in the current specialisation patterns, are more or less favourable to the development of comparative advantages in "upscale products", that is, products with higher income content than the country average—a process coined as "structural transformation".

The analysis draws on methodologies proposed by Ricardo Haussman and co-authors.[1] These methodologies were used to analyse the Portuguese case in Lebre de Freitas and Mamede (2011) and are now being explored in other dimensions, as part of a broader research project (Lebre de Freitas et al. 2013; Nunes et al. 2013; Nunes et al. 2014). The descriptive analysis implemented in this chapter as well as all the estimates used draw from this research.

The methodology to assess the value content of products directly follows Hausmann et al. (2007). Basically, a PRODY index is estimated as a weighted average of the per capita incomes of the countries with Revealed Comparative Advantage (Balassa 1965) in that product, with the weights being proportional to the RCA index. PRODY indexes are then weighted by the share of the corresponding products in each country's nominal exports to compute the average income content of export baskets (EXPY).

The methodology to assess how valuable a country's productive experience with one product is to start producing other goods was first proposed by Hausmann and Klinger (2006, 2007), and Hidalgo et al. (2007). Basically, an outcome-based measure of "relatedness" is assigned to each pair of products, which is estimated as the likelihood of a country in the world having revealed comparative advantages in both products. The underlying concept of "relatedness" is consistent with a broad interpretation of a country's "capabilities", including availability of land, climate, technical knowledge, non-tradable producer services, infrastructure, and so on.

In the works of Haussman and co-authors, "relatedness" between each two products is estimated as the conditional probability of a country having RCA in one product, given that it has RCA in another. In this article, we use estimates from Lebre de Freitas et al. (2013), where conditional probabilities are instead computed with PROBIT estimation. Another difference refers to the calculation of the "relatedness" of a product with a country's current specialisation pattern. Haussman and co-authors built a measure called "density", given by the *proportion* of product *j*'s overall relatedness to other products that is accounted for by the products in which the country is currently specialised.

Following Lebre de Freitas et al. (2013) (as well as Nunes et al. 2013), we use instead the total (*absolute*) relatedness of product *j* to the products in which the country is specialised. Nunes et al. (2014) using panel data for the period 1962–2000 confirm that these two novelties improve the forecasting power of the density measure with respect to future comparative advantages.

As stated above, the indexes used in this article are from Lebre de Freitas et al. (2013). The raw data used there to make the underlying calculations and indexes includes cross-country export data at the product level (HS-4) from the UN-COMTRADE database and GDP per capita levels (in PPP) from the International Monetary Fund, World Economic Outlook Database. All data refers to 2005 and covers 1245 products and all countries in the sample with population larger than 2 million (totalling 93).

This article is structured as follows. In Section 2, we compare the current specialisation patterns of Portugal, Spain, Italy, Greece, and Germany in terms of value content (EXPY), sectoral composition and also in terms of "consistency" of the export basket. In Section 3, we assess how helpful the current productive experiences are for the process of structural transformation. Conclusions and final remarks are presented in Sections 4 and 5.

2. Comparing the current specialisation patterns

How diversified?

As a first approach to the current specialisation patterns, we compute, for each country, the number of products in which it has Revealed Comparative Advantage (that is, RCA>1). As shown in Table 10.1, Italy and Spain are highly diversified in terms of exports, with a number of products with RCA>1 comparable to that of Germany. In this sample, Portugal and Greece reveal more concentrated specialisation patterns, but still rank 18th and 25th, respectively, in terms of diversification in our sample of 93 countries.

How valuable?

In Table 10.1, we break down the products in which each country has revealed comparative advantage, by five classes of PRODY (details in the legend). Figure 10.1 offers a visual overview of the data in Table 10.1.

Table 10.1 Number of products with RCA>1 by level of PRODY

PRODY Level	*Germany*	*Greece*	*Italy*	*Portugal*	*Spain*
VH - [23.1, 37.0]	141	18	84	22	47
H - [18.8, 23.1]	148	47	112	60	111
A - [14.5, 18.8]	118	65	127	60	108
L - [9.7, 14.5]	73	75	116	98	115
VL - [1.1, 9.7]	25	71	59	66	74
Total	505	276	498	306	455
Percentage of total:					
VH - [23.1, 37.0]	27.9%	6.5%	16.9%	7.2%	10.3%
H - [18.8, 23.1]	29.3%	17.0%	22.5%	19.6%	24.4%
A - [14.5, 18.8]	23.4%	23.6%	25.5%	19.6%	23.7%
L - [9.7, 14.5]	14.5%	27.2%	23.3%	32.0%	25.3%
VL - [1.1, 9.7]	5.0%	25.7%	11.8%	21.6%	16.3%
Memo(EXPY)	20.6	15.1	18.4	16.4	18.3

Source: Own calculations using UN COMTRADE and IMF data.

Note: The classes of PRODY correspond to the five quintiles in the PRODY series. These are "Very High" : (VH, top 20%), "High" (H), "Average" : (A), "Low" (L), and "Very Low" (VL, lowest 20%).

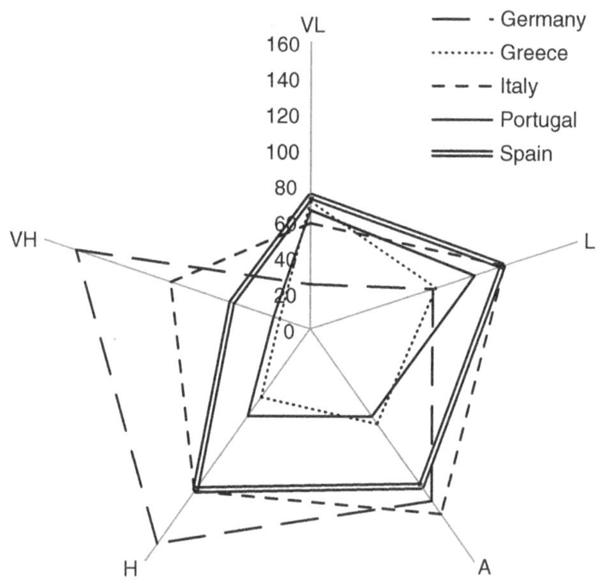

Figure 10.1 Current specialization patterns by level of PRODY.

Source: Own calculations using UN COMTRADE and IMF data. Note: The classes of PRODY correspond to the five quintiles in the PRODY series. These are "Very High" (VH, top 20%), "High" (H), "Average" (A), "Low" (L), and "Very Low" (VL, lowest 20%). We count the number of products, which have RCA>1; in these classes to create this figure.

We observe that Germany has clearly a pattern of specialisation biased towards products with "High" and "Very High" PRODY values, which account for more than half of its specialisation pattern. In contrast, more than half of the products in which Portugal and Greece are specialised have "Low" and "Very Low" PRODY values. Finally, Spain and Italy have rather flat distributions around the "average", with three quarters of their specialisation pattern ranging from "Low" to "High".

Unsurprisingly, Germany stands out in this sample as the country with higher average income content in the export basket (EXPY 20.2, comparable to the PRODY class H), followed by Italy (18.4) and Spain (18.3). All four south European countries have EXPY values comparable to the PRODY class A – "Average". In our sample of 93 countries, Greece (the country with lowest EXPY in this group) ranks 36th.

Which sectors?

In Table 10.2, we compare the specialisation patterns of the countries in our sample in terms of product categories. The product categories are obtained by grouping the 1245 products into chapters, using the HS-4 accountancy standard. Each chapter range in terms of product codes is described in the second column of Table 10.2.

According to the table, Germany has more than half of the products in which it is specialized belonging to the categories of "Machinery and transportation" and "Chemicals". Portugal and Greece have more than half of their revealed comparative advantages in products related to natural resources ("Agricultural, mineral, wood") and "Textiles, clothing, and footwear" (TCF). Italy and Spain are intermediate cases in this group, with Spain revealing strong comparative advantage in agriculture goods and Italy having a sizeable specialisation in TCF.

How consistent?

By consistency of a specialisation pattern, we mean the extent to which the products in which a country is current specialized are "related" to the other products in which the country is currently specialized.

Relatedness between each two products is estimated as the conditional probability (PROBIT) of a country in the world having RCA in these two products at the same time. Relatedness of a product to the country specialisation pattern is measured by the sum of the conditional probabilities involving this product and all other products in which the country has RCA>1. This sum is labelled "pure density". We consider that a product is "related" to the country core of "capabilities", as reflected in its specialisation pattern, if the corresponding "pure density" measure exceeds a critical value of 10, which was chosen so as to include 90 percent of the products in which the countries in the sample have RCA>1.[2] Note that this notion of relatedness is

Table 10.2 Products with RCA>1 broken down by product category

Category	*Chapter of HS*	*Germany*	*Greece*	*Italy*	*Portugal*	*Spain*
Agricultural products and food	01-24	42	75	51	49	95
Mineral products and oils	25-27	12	18	13	13	27
Chemicals, plastics, rubbers	28-40	120	39	70	42	80
Wood, wood products, paper	44-49	31	11	23	25	27
Hides, leather and textiles	41-43, 50-60, 63	29	41	81	41	51
Clothing and footwear	61-62,64-67	0	14	35	32	13
Stones, ceramic, glass	68-71	32	14	25	24	22
Metals	72-83	87	38	73	41	59
Machinery	84-85	93	14	78	20	38
Transportation	86-89	19	4	13	10	22
Miscellaneous	90-97	40	8	36	9	21
Total		505	276	498	306	455
(Share of Total Exports)		(73.5%)	(84.3%)	(75.2%)	(82.2%)	(76.4%)
Memo (percentage of total):						
Agricultural, mineral, wood		16.8%	37.7%	17.5%	28.4%	32.7%
Textiles, clothing, footwear		5.7%	19.9%	23.3%	23.9%	14.1%
Machinery, transportation, misc.		30.1%	9.4%	25.5%	12.7%	17.8%
Chemicals		23.8%	14.1%	14.1%	13.7%	17.6%
Metals, stones, ceramic, glass		23.6%	18.8%	19.7%	21.2%	17.8%

Source: Own calculations using UN COMTRADE data.

consistent with a broad interpretation of "capabilities", including availability of land and climate, technical knowledge, non-tradable producer services, infrastructure, access to markets, specific regulatory requirements, and so on.

Consistency of a country's specialisation pattern is then measured as the proportion of products in which the country has Revealed Comparative Advantage that lie at "Pure densities" exceeding this critical level. A high consistency level in terms of this indicator will be interpreted as indicating that most of a country's revealed comparative advantages have been developed inside its core of capabilities.

Figure 10.2 compares the consistency indexes thereby obtained for the 5 countries under analysis. Germany tops this sample, with a consistency index of 98.2 percent. Thus, Germany is not only the country that specializes in products with higher PRODY, it also achieves a very high consistency level in its specialisation pattern, ranking first in our sample of 93 countries. Italy and Spain also achieve very high consistency levels. Portugal has a reasonable consistency level (ranking 23rd), but Greece approaches the world average, ranking 34th only.

3. How helpful are the current specialization patterns?

How many upscale products are within reach?

We now explore the extent to which the current productive experience helps a country to develop comparative advantages in products with higher PRODY than the country average, EXPY ("upscale products").

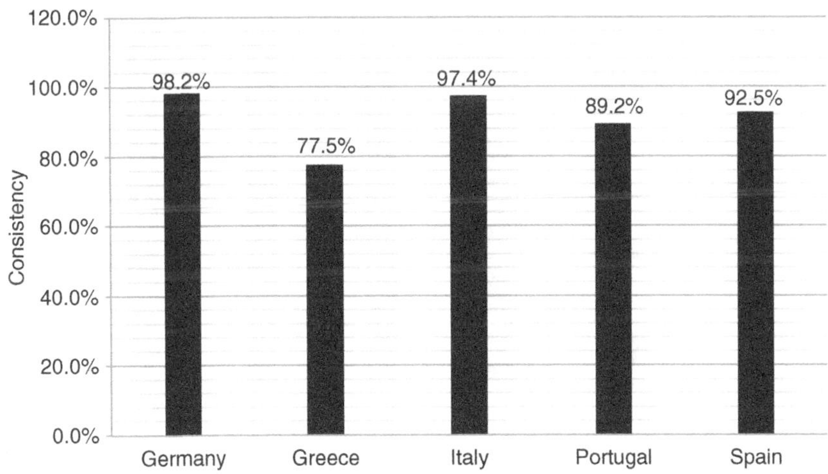

Figure 10.2 Percentage of products with RCA>1 and "pure density">10.

Source: Own calculations using UN COMTRADE data. Note: In our sample of 93 countries, Germany ranks 1st in terms of consistency; Italy ranks 2nd, Spain ranks 13th; Portugal ranks 23rd and Greece ranks 34th.

To this end, we first compute the number of products with "pure densities" higher than the critical value of 10 that the country *is already exporting* but in which it did not achieve RCA>1. The "upscale opportunities" thereby identified are plotted in Figure 10.3. The Figure shows that the number of upscale opportunities does not differ much across the south European countries, ranging from 256 to 275. The country with less upscale opportunities in the south European group, Greece, ranks 16th in this dimension in our sample of 93 countries.

Germany, in contrast, has only 122 upscale products within reach. This is not surprising: Germany has little scope for structural transformation, because most of its specialisation pattern consists already of products with high and very high income content. Taking this into account, we complement the information above, by assessing the proportion of upscale products that are still available (that is, exporting products with a higher PRODY level than the country's EXPY and with RCA<1) at a "pure density" higher than 10. We label this measure as the "coverage ratio". This indicator (plotted in Figure 10.4) gives an idea of the fraction of the *remaining* upscale opportunities for each country that are within reach.

Interestingly enough, Germany emerges in this sample as the country with less upscale opportunities, but which covers more than 80 percent of the upscale products in which it has still not developed comparative advantages. This suggests that the productive experience achieved by Germany is very favourable to start producing other valuable goods. This case contrasts

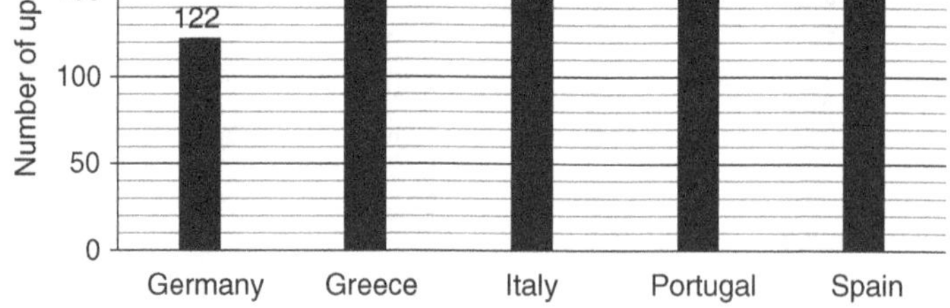

Figure 10.3 Number of upscale products with RCA<1 and "pure density">10.

Source: Own calculations using UN COMTRADE data. Note: Number of products that the country already exports but with RCA<1, with PRODY higher than the country EXPY and at "pure density higher than 10". Looking at the full sample of the 93 countries, Germany ranks 44th in the number of upscale product opportunities; Greece ranks 16th, Italy ranks 13th. Portugal and Spain present the same number of opportunities and both rank 8th.

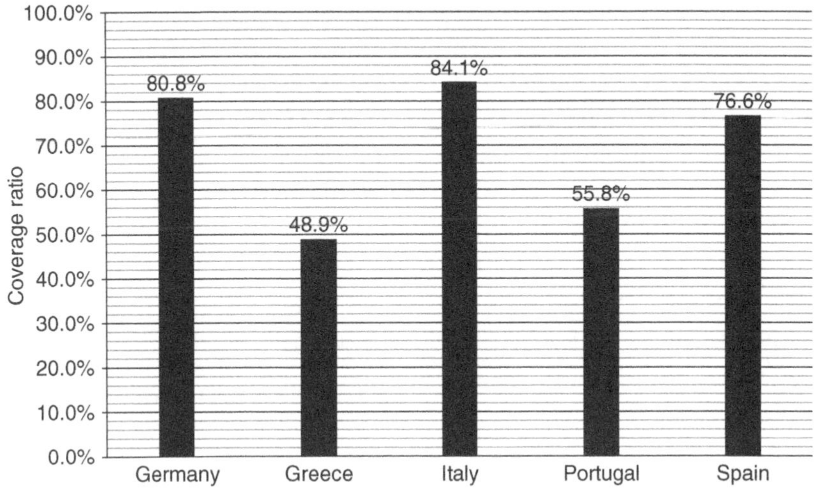

Figure 10.4 Coverage ratio (percentage of upscale products with RCA<1 with "pure densities" >10).

Source: Own calculations using UN COMTRADE and IMF data.

with Portugal and Greece, where upscale opportunities cover only about one half of the upscale products that are still available.

How close are the upscale opportunities?

In Table 10.3, upscale opportunities for each country are broken down by classes of "pure density". To recap, a high "pure density" means that the product at hand is very close to the country's core of capabilities. The lower bound of pure density in the table is the critical value 10.

As shown in the table, the only countries with upscale products lying at pure densities above 50 are Germany, Italy and Spain. These countries also have a significant number of upscale opportunities at pure densities between 30 and 40. In contrast, Portugal and Greece have more than 90 percent of their upscale opportunities at "pure densities" between 10 and 30, hence somewhat distant from the respective core of capabilities.

Although the information in Table 10.3 suggests that Portugal and Greece may lack the productive experience to implement immediate upscale moves, this conclusion should not be understated. In the case of Portugal, for instance, more than 60 percent of the products with RCA>1 lie in the range of pure densities below 30 (Lebre de Freitas et al. 2013). Thus, setting a "pure density" threshold at 30 would be equivalent to accepting as upscale opportunities only potential new products that are as close to the country's core of capabilities as the top 40 percent in the set with RCA>1. Clearly, such a threshold would be too demanding.

Table 10.3 Upscale opportunities by class of "pure density"

Pure-Density	*Germany*	*Greece*	*Italy*	*Portugal*	*Spain*
>=50	10	0	26	0	11
[40,50]	18	0	31	2	26
[30,40]	20	3	32	23	55
[20,30]	31	50	67	73	69
[10,20]	43	203	104	177	114
Total	122	256	260	275	275
Percentage of total:					
>=50	8.2%	0.0%	10.0%	0.0%	4.0%
[40,50]	14.8%	0.0%	11.9%	0.7%	9.5%
[30,40]	16.4%	1.2%	12.3%	8.4%	20.0%
[20,30]	25.4%	19.5%	25.8%	26.5%	25.1%
[10,20]	35.2%	79.3%	40.0%	64.4%	41.5%

Source: Own calculations using UN COMTRADE and IMF data.

How valuable are the identified upscale opportunities?

We now turn to the question of how the identified upscale opportunities compare in terms of PRODY. First, we look at absolute values (PRODY). Table 10.4 breaks down the number of upscale opportunities for each country by classes of PRODY. According to line (ii), Germany stands out as the country with more upscale opportunities in the "VH" category (almost 70 percent). Italy and Spain have slightly more than half of their upscale opportunities in this segment. Portugal and Greece, in turn, have more upscale opportunities in the "H" category.

In the interpretation, it is important to note that countries cannot by definition have upscale opportunities at PRODY levels lower than the country's EXPY. Hence, no country in this group has upscale opportunities in "VL" or "L" PRODY products. By the same token, Germany can only improve its EXPY by specialising in products with at least a High PRODY level.

To address this limitation, in line (iii) of Table 10.4, we compute "coverage ratios" per class of PRODY. For instance, Germany has 85 upscale opportunities in "VH" products, in a total of 105 products that are still available, which yields a "coverage ratio" of 81 percent. Italy and Spain also exhibit high "coverage ratios" across the various PRODY categories. In contrast, Portugal and Greece show much lower "coverage ratios" in the "VH" class (49.8 percent and 45.3 percent, respectively). The results in line (iii) of Table 10.4 also point to roughly uniform "coverage ratios" across the PRODY classes: that is, the degree to which the current productive experience helps a country develop comparative advantages in upscale products does not seem to depend on the PRODY value of the intended products.

Table 10.4 Upscale opportunities broken down by PRODY level

	PRODY LEVEL	*VH*	*H*	*A*	*L*	*VL*	*Total*
Germany	Number of upscale opportunities (i)	85	37	0	0	0	122
	Percentage of total upscale (ii)	69.7%	30.3%	0.0%	0.0%	0.0%	100.0%
	Coverage ratio (iii)	81.0%	80.4%	0.0%	0.0%	0.0%	80.8%
Greece	Number of upscale opportunities (i)	90	102	64	0	0	256
	Percentage of total upscale (ii)	35.2%	39.8%	25.0%	0.0%	0.0%	100.0%
	Coverage ratio (iii)	45.3%	54.8%	46.4%	0.0%	0.0%	48.9%
Italy	Number of upscale opportunities (i)	132	120	8	0	0	260
	Percentage of total upscale (ii)	50.8%	46.2%	3.1%	0.0%	0.0%	100.0%
	Coverage ratio (iii)	80.5%	88.9%	80.0%	0.0%	0.0%	84.1%
Portugal	Number of upscale opportunities (i)	100	115	60	0	0	275
	Percentage of total upscale (ii)	36.4%	41.8%	21.8%	0.0%	0.0%	100.0%
	Coverage ratio (iii)	49.8%	63.5%	54.5%	0.0%	0.0%	55.8%
Spain	Number of upscale opportunities (i)	149	108	18	0	0	275
	Percentage of total upscale (ii)	54.2%	39.3%	6.5%	0.0%	0.0%	100.0%
	Coverage ratio (iii)	74.5%	79.4%	78.3%	0.0%	0.0%	76.6%

Source: Own calculations using UN COMTRADE and IMF data.

Notes: The classes of PRODY correspond to the five quintiles in the PRODY series. These are "Very High" (VH, top 20%), "High" (H), "Average" (A), "Low" (L), and "Very Low" (VL, lowest 20%). (i) Number of products that the country already exports but with RCA<1, with PRODY higher than the country EXPY and at "pure density higher than 10".

Which sectors?

We will now look at the sectors corresponding to the upscale opportunities identified for each country. In Table 10.5, we provide the number of upscale opportunities, broken down by product category.

For the five countries in our analysis, most upscale opportunities are identified in non-traditional sectors, like "Machinery, transportation, misc." and "Chemicals". The fact that this is true for countries like Portugal and Greece, even though these countries have the majority of their core of capabilities in traditional sectors, is suggestive of a favourable path in the process of structural transformation.

To further examine this question, Figure 10.5 assesses how each country's comparative advantages would look in terms of product categories, had the upscale opportunities identified above materialised. The visual inspection

Table 10.5 Upscale product opportunities broken down by product category

Category	*Chapter of HS*	*Germany*	*Greece*	*Italy*	*Portugal*	*Spain*
Agricultural products and food	01–24	6	12	12	12	7
Mineral products and oils	25–27	3	1	4	1	0
Chemicals, plastics, rubbers	28–40	33	53	75	55	68
Wood, wood products, paper	44–49	8	11	18	17	13
Hides, leather and textiles	41–43, 50–60, 63	4	16	6	12	11
Clothing and footwear	61–62,64–67	0	2	1	2	1
Stones, ceramic, glass	68–71	10	15	21	15	18
Metals	72–83	14	42	28	46	42
Machinery	84–85	17	67	39	72	70
Transportation	86–89	2	9	10	9	5
Miscellaneous	90–97	25	28	46	34	40
Total		122	256	260	275	275
Memo (percentage of total):						
Agricultural, mineral, wood		13.9%	9.4%	13.1%	10.9%	7.3%
Textiles, clothing, footwear		3.3%	7.0%	2.7%	5.1%	4.4%
Machinery, transportation, misc.		36.1%	40.6%	36.5%	41.8%	41.8%
Chemicals		27.0%	20.7%	28.8%	20.0%	24.7%
Metals, stones, ceramic, glass		19.7%	22.3%	18.8%	22.2%	21.8%

Source: Own calculations.

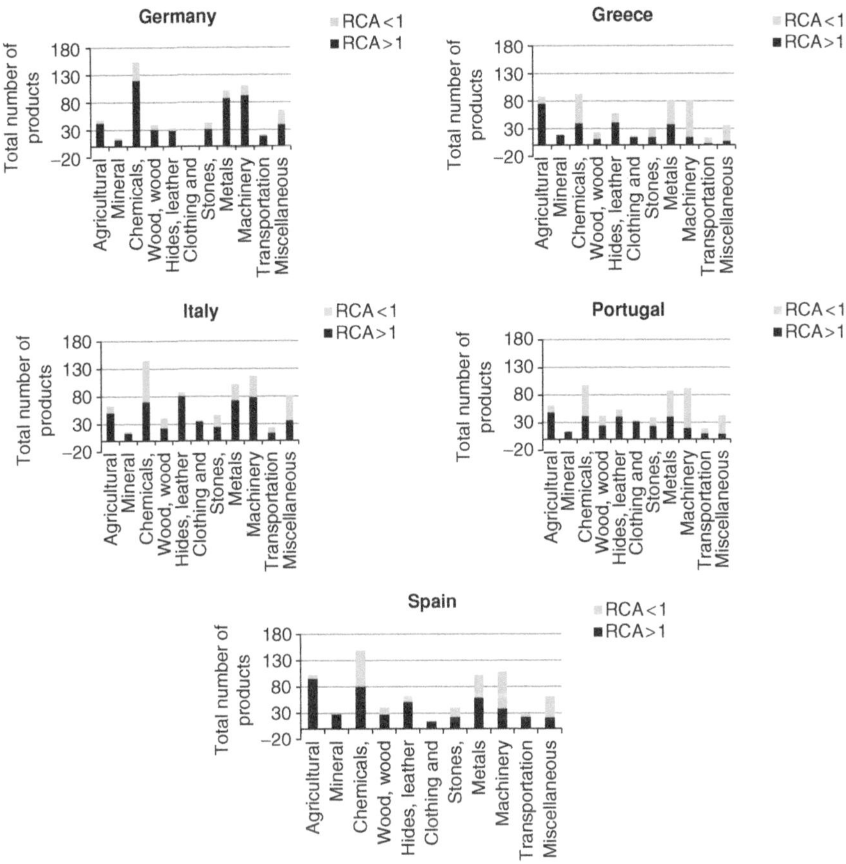

Figure 10.5 Adding the upscale opportunities to the countries' specialization patterns.

Source: Own calculations using UN COMTRADE and IMF data.

of these figures suggests that Germany's pattern of specialisation would not change much in relation to what it is now. This is confirmed by chi-square tests of the null hypothesis that the new distribution across product categories would not change compared with the current one (Table 10.6). As can be seen in Table 10.6A, the corresponding p-values equal 0.98 regardless of whether we use a 5 or an 11 sector disaggregation. Significant changes, in contrast, are found in all the other countries as the corresponding p-values are all below 5 percent.

The finding in Table 10.6 raises an interesting question: would the new patterns in these countries converge to the pattern in Germany? To answer this, we conducted a series of chi-square tests comparing Germany's pattern of specialisation, both current and future, against the future patterns of specialisation of each of the four southern countries. The results of the tests are presented in Table 6B. Interpreting, they point to significant differences

Table 10.6 Chi-square tests of equal patterns of specialization (p-values)

Part A: Current vs. Future

	Germany	*Greece*	*Italy*	*Portugal*	*Spain*
11 sectors	0.98	0.00	0.03	0.00	0.00
5 sectors	0.98	0.00	0.01	0.00	0.00

Part B: Other Countries in the Future vs. Germany

	Greece	*Italy*	*Portugal*	*Spain*
vs. Germany - Current				
11 sectors	0.00	0.00	0.00	0.00
5 sectors	0.00	0.00	0.00	0.00
vs. Germany - Future				
11 sectors	0.00	0.00	0.00	0.00
5 sectors	0.00	0.00	0.00	0.00

Part C: Between Countries Comparisons

Using current patterns with a 11 sectors disaggregation

	Germany	*Greece*	*Italy*	*Portugal*
Greece	0.00			
Italy	0.00	0.00		
Portugal	0.00	0.01	0.00	
Spain	0.00	0.04	0.00	0.00

Using future patterns with a 11 sectors disaggregation

	Germany	*Greece*	*Italy*	*Portugal*
Greece	0.00			
Italy	0.00	0.00		
Portugal	0.00	0.03	0.28	
Spain	0.00	0.46	0.00	0.01

Using current patterns with a 5 sectors disaggregation

	Germany	*Greece*	*Italy*	*Portugal*
Greece	0.00			
Italy	0.00	0.00		
Portugal	0.00	0.15	0.00	
Spain	0.00	0.01	0.00	0.00

Using future patterns with a 5 sectors disaggregation

	Germany	*Greece*	*Italy*	*Portugal*
Greece	0.00			
Italy	0.00	0.00		
Portugal	0.00	0.56	0.17	
Spain	0.00	0.26	0.00	0.04

Note: A p-value > 0.05 means that the null hypothesis of no difference in distributions is not rejected.

in comparison to the German pattern in all cases. Summing up, these tests suggest that Greece, Italy, Spain and Portugal have significant opportunities to undergo a process of structural transformation towards a new pattern of specialisation that does not necessarily follow the direction of the German case.

Finally, we investigate if the opportunities for structural transformation will lead to similar patterns of specialisation in the four southern European countries. As before, we base our conclusions on the results of chi-square tests of equality of the distributions between two countries. These are presented in Table 6C. For the 11-sector decomposition, we conclude that *current* specialisation patterns are significantly different among all pairs of countries.[3] In contrast, when the same analysis is performed in terms of *future* patterns of specialisation, we do not find significant differences between Greece and Portugal, and between Italy and Portugal (and also between Greece and Portugal at a 1 percent significance level). If the comparisons are made with a 5-sector disaggregation, we find similar results: whereas in terms of current patterns we do not find a significant difference for one pair only, namely Greece-Portugal, in terms of future specialisation patterns, there are several cases where no difference is found, namely Greece-Portugal, Greece-Spain and Italy-Portugal (and also Portugal-Spain at 1 percent). All in all, these tests suggest that the opportunities for structural transformation in the four south European countries point to a regional convergence in their patterns of specialisations, towards something that will be different from that of Germany.

4. Main conclusions

In this chapter, we compared four south European countries in terms of their current specialisation patterns as well as their upscale opportunities, defined as the products which these countries already export but in which they did not develop comparative advantage, which are simultaneously "related" to their current core of capabilities and have a higher value content (PRODY) than the country average (EXPY).

The analysis reveals that the four south European countries have relatively diversified export baskets, with Italy and Spain ranking at the top, close to Germany. In terms of the average value content of the current export basket, Italy and Spain reveal higher EXPY levels than Greece and Portugal, but not as high as Germany.

As for as the product categories of the current specialisation pattern, Portugal and Greece have more than half of their revealed comparative advantages in products related to natural resources ("Agricultural, mineral, wood") and "Textiles, clothing, and footwear". Italy and Spain are more similar to Germany, in the sense that a greater proportion of their revealed comparative advantages take place in sectors of machinery, transportation, and chemicals. Still, Spain has significant comparative advantages in "Agricultural, mineral, wood" while Italy relies significantly on exports of "Textiles, clothing, and footwear". In terms of consistency of the current specialisation pattern, Italy and Spain rank at the top of our sample of 93 countries, coming close to Germany. Portugal ranks 23rd and Greece lags behind, ranking 34th.

We then examined the extent to which the current productive experience helps a country to develop comparative advantages in products with higher PRODY than the country average, EXPY ("upscale products"). In this dimension, the four south European countries have more than twice the upscale opportunities of Germany. This reflects the fact that Germany is already a high EXPY country, so it has less upscale products available. Still, Germany achieves a rather high "coverage ratio" in terms of the remaining products within reach.

In terms of the overall sample, the number of upscale opportunities of the south European countries (between 250 and 275) compares well with the other countries. For instance, Greece, the country with less upscale opportunities, ranks 16th in the sample of 93 countries. This is suggestive of a quite useful productive experience for the process of structural transformation in the four South European countries, despite the difference in the current specialisation patterns.

Assessing the upscale opportunities in terms of values is not a simple exercise, because upscale opportunities for countries with higher EXPY imply by definition products with higher PRODY. Unsurprisingly, Germany has only upscale opportunities in products with High and Very High income content, while the south European countries can still improve the average income content of their export basket developing comparative advantages in products with Average income content. Still, Germany manages to have within reach 80 percent of the possible products with VH and H income content (same for Italy), which reveals a rather valuable productive experience. In contrast, Portugal and Greece have only half of the possible upscale opportunities for VH products within reach.

As for the sectoral composition of upscale opportunities, an interesting result was obtained: regardless of how different the current specialisation patterns are, most of upscale opportunities for the four south European countries lie in the categories of "Machinery, transportation, misc". and "Chemicals". This does to some extent suggest that the possible materialization of these upscale opportunities would deliver a pattern of specialisation more similar to that of Germany today. This assumption is however rejected by the data: a simple non-parametric analysis reveals that an hypothetical materialization of the upscale opportunities identified would impact significantly on the specialisation pattern of the four south European countries (hence, there would be scope for "structural transformation") but the specialisation structures would remain different from that of Germany. Comparing the specialisation patterns of the four south European countries, we found that they would become more equal than they are now, suggesting scope for regional convergence in specialisation patterns.

5. Discussion

Before concluding this chapter, we should elaborate briefly on the implications of this study for the main theme of the book: industrial policy.

In a word, *there are none.*

Basically, we explored an outcome-based methodology to identify the products that are more likely to be related to a country's core of capabilities, as reflected in its specialisation pattern. Hidalgo et al. (2007), Hausmann and Klinger (2006, 2007), as well as our preliminary results, point to the case that the products thereby identified are indeed more likely to become part of a country's specialisation pattern than the products identified as "less related" to the country's capabilities. But even if this methodology proved helpful to identify the products in which countries have latent comparative advantages, this is not to say that the materialization of such comparative advantages would be dependent on public intervention or that, even if it were, such intervention would be desirable at all. In fact, our method is silent regarding the different types of externalities (technological, pecuniary, self-discovery, etc.) or coordination failures underlying the production of each individual good, so it provides no guidance to distinguish goods whose production entails social benefits on top of private benefits from goods whose latent comparative advantage is basically explained by availability of correctly priced inputs in the market.

What we know is that, since we are focusing on products in which countries have already accumulated a minimum level of productive experience (that is, products that countries are already exporting), the eventual externalities were not so as to prevent the activity to spring up in the first place. Of course, there is the possibility that—for one reason or another—some of these activities are being carried out at a suboptimal level from the social point of view. However, such a possibility should be assessed on a case-by-case basis using an appropriate methodology—hopefully balancing the costs of intervention—which will necessarily be very different from the one used in this study.

Notes

1 Hausmann et al. (2007), Hausmann and Klinger (2006, 2007), and Hidalgo et al. (2007).
2 For the details on the methodology and discussion, see Lebre de Freitas et al. (2013).
3 The only exception would be no significant difference between Spain and Greece but only at the stricter significance level of 1%.

Part III

Policy issues

11 Industrial policy in times of crisis

The case of Greece

Tassos Giannitsis and Ioanna Kastelli

1. Introduction

For many years it was acknowledged that the European South (plus Ireland) had managed to be very successful in catching-up. However, the analysis of the knowledge basis of these countries showed that their progress, as measured by the Innovation Performance Index, had been much slower and revealed considerable vulnerabilities to the development of a robust knowledge-based economy (Veugelers and Mrak 2009). The catching-up countries indeed achieved significant GDP per capita convergence, but this process was based to a considerable extent on increasing debts or on policies that led to bubbles and invisible debt accumulation processes. Qualitative changes and policies targeting structural issues were sluggish, although performance differed in each country. This disparity between catching-up in terms of GDP and lagging behind in terms of production and knowledge-related capabilities is particularly relevant not only for explaining the vulnerability of the European South and the broader imbalances in the European economy, but also for designing efficient production-enhancing policies.

In Greece, during the last few decades, we can identify different cycles regarding policies to enhance the productive base. The period to the end of the 1970s was characterised by high protectionism coupled with major shifts from agricultural to industrial production. In the early 1980s, public policy in Greece attempted to actively support both the traditional industrial basis of the country and foster the development of emerging industries (biotechnology, industrial engineering, information technologies), while at the same time following a defensive approach concerning the most vulnerable, declining and even inefficient sectors and firms. However, most of these attempts failed to achieve a significant outcome. This failure had a negative consequence: the political de-legitimisation of the state regarding industrial policy interventions.

After the mid-1980s, instead of trying to address the deficiencies of the policies adopted, public policy followed a dual-track approach: on the one hand, interventionist approaches to enhance or to transform the productive base were largely abandoned and public policy moved gradually towards a liberal and demand-driven (Keynesian) course through investment and other incentives; on the other hand, public policy followed a strong interventionist and defensive approach regarding the broad area of State-related activities.

The latter often took the form of extensive formal or informal regulation of, and intervention in, numerous relations between firms, activities and the public domain (central state, local authorities, other public entities). However, this policy had a negligible impact on the productive base or in shifting the traditional production patterns to more competitive economic activities, and instead led to systemic rigidity that accentuated the adverse impact of the crisis.

In fact, the productive base was characterised by poor competitive structures and its increasing exposure to competition after Greece's entry to the European Community (1981) further weakened them. A significant number of manufacturing firms, especially the larger firms in different sectors, which constituted the core of the Greek industrial system, could not survive. It has been estimated that between 1978 and 1984 the number of medium and large companies diminished, while the number of micro firms increased significantly (Giannitsis 1988). This contradicted the expectation that EC membership and the abolition of protectionist measures would be harmful to SMEs and would mainly favour the bigger firms, which would be able to successfully deal with the new competitive pressures (Hummen 1977). The agricultural productive base was also significantly weakened. In fact, the inflow of large agricultural subsidies provided a boost to farmers' incomes, but had rather weak effects on the modernisation of this economic sector.

In view of these effects, various incentives and subsidies have been introduced by successive governments with the aim of supporting new investment, innovation, technological complexity, restructuring and regional development. However, each time the existing economic interests persuaded governments to abandon such discretionary policies and to extend incentives to all industries and even to traditional service activities (e.g., hotels), which consequently were deprived of any incisiveness. As a result, the competitiveness of the industrial sector declined and productive transformation was delayed. Despite technology policies, R&D expenditure never exceeded 0.6 percent of GDP, whereas business R&D expenditure has always fluctuated around 0.15 percent of GDP, with a negligible impact on the real economy.

In times of crisis and due to the crucial need for new engines of growth, the transformative adjustment of broader parts of the productive base has to be brought to the top of the policy agenda. A policy approach which seeks to preserve the physical, human and social capital built over the years, prevent past capacity-building processes from being wiped out and create conditions for sustainable growth is the key to a successful industrial policy. It could establish the link between growth, the productive system, competitiveness and adjustment policies. The rationale of such a policy is based on the hypothesis that without structural changes in Greece's productive base, deep imbalances will continue to function as a pro-crisis element and prolong the structural barriers to growth.

2. The rationale of an industrial policy to enhance the productive base

Industrial Policy is defined very differently by various authors. In our analysis, following scholars who argue for a systemic approach to industrial policy and relate it to restructuring (Rodrik 2004, 2007a; Bianchi and Labori 2011; Lall 2004; Aiginger 2012), we consider that in the context of globalisation and economic crisis, policy initiatives should aim to:

a improve the structural competitiveness of the economy and in particular to enhance technological capabilities,
b shift production towards more knowledge-intensive activities,
c promote new linkages and interconnections among actors,
d secure resources to boost investment and redress activities in regions that were severely affected by the crisis, and
e create new employment opportunities.

An active or targeted policy aimed at enhancing Greece's productive base should address three broader issues, as described in the following subsections.

The crisis and the rationale of industrial policy

The key policy questions for Greece and the European South include how to overcome the crisis, what kind of changes are necessary for the transition towards a sustainable post-crisis landscape, and if there is a role for industrial policy in this process. To answer these questions, it is necessary to understand the underlying cause-effect relationships behind the crisis. Typical analyses of the crisis focus on macro-issues, public deficits and debt, bubbles or financial factors. In fact, most interpretations regard the Greek as well as the euro area crisis as a macroeconomic issue and an outcome of macroeconomic mismanagement (insufficient macroeconomic and fiscal coordination, a neglect of sovereign default risk, absence of a lender of last resort, inappropriate monetary policy, insufficient banking regulation, absence of discipline, etc.).

However, this is a partial approach because it disregards significant additional parameters of the crisis. Besides its macro-economic parameters, the crisis has also been triggered by endogenous structural factors and it is the interplay between macro-imbalances and structural (or micro) factors that has determined the specificity of the crisis in Greece.

Indeed, in addition to domestic macroeconomic mismanagement and the institutional mismanagement of the Eurozone, the crisis was also the outcome of the long-term accumulation of structural weaknesses, policy choices, and broader social and political attitudes and behaviours. The crisis was a mix of a fiscal, structural, competitiveness, and political crisis, both at the national and European level, although to a different extent for each player. The direction of causality between indebtedness and the crisis is not univocal. The two main drivers of the crisis in Greece—fiscal and competitiveness imbalances—were in many ways closely related to the development of the productive base of the economy, indicating a circular causal relationship between the crisis and the system of production. The crisis undermined the system of production but at the same time the long-term erosion of the productive base made the economy more vulnerable to the destabilising effects of the crisis. In effect, the weakening of the productive base forced governments to try to mitigate the potential adverse implications by increasing public spending and deficits, using debt as leverage for growth. With the crisis, many established economic relations became unsustainable and broader economic and political relations have been destabilised.

The production structures in Greece were marked by the following changes after the two oil crises of 1973 and 1979:

- a continuous contraction of the agricultural and industrial sector, whose share declined from 49.7 percent (1970) to 16.8 percent (2011) of GDP, coupled with an expansion of service activities (including the public sector);
- a gradual decline in the production of tradable goods and services due to the contraction of agriculture and industry, as well as to the fact that a large part of tertiary activities were weakly related to technology and innovation and were not producing services used directly or indirectly in the tradable sector;
- a continuous deterioration in competitiveness over a longer period (1980–2009);
- a loose income policy adopted after 2000, which led to a widening gap between Greece and the Eurozone in terms of inflation, export prices and unit labour costs, undermining the competitive basis of the economy.

As a result, Greece is characterised by a deficient pattern of production in manufacturing, reflected in the low similarity indices of its export structure in comparison to Spain, Portugal, and Ireland, and the weaker competitiveness of the sector (Giannitsis et al. 2009). The shift in the manufacturing base from simpler to more technology-intensive types of production and exports, as reflected in the share of exported goods and services in GDP, was relatively slow.

This is one of the reasons why, although international markets can offer opportunities for recovery, the Greek productive system has failed to reap the advantages of globalisation and capture increasing market shares, especially in high value-added segments. This is a result of specific features related to entrepreneurship and the National Innovation System (NIS).

New ventures, according to the Global Entrepreneurship Monitor surveys, although achieving one of the highest percentages among innovating economies, have also reached one of the highest rates of business foreclosure every year. Shortcomings in entrepreneurship, coupled with the fact that new ventures are not creating high numbers of new jobs, is evidence of new business activities with low potential for contributing to growth.

Furthermore, the lack of knowledge-intensive production features is related to shortcomings regarding the creation and exploitation of knowledge, innovation performance and the feeble interactions among actors in the Greek NIS. In fact, innovation and technology policy during the last 25 years introduced new elements into the Greek NIS (strengthening of R&D infrastructure, promotion of cooperation and diffusion of knowledge, development of human resources, and creation of knowledge-intensive firms). Despite these supply-side initiatives, innovative performance was one of the weakest in the EU and the responsiveness of the business sector was mainly driven by funding opportunities and not based on strong incentives for transformation. All R&D and innovation indicators show reluctance, especially of the business sector, to improve its competitive position through R&D activities, but also its weak capacity to build endogenous capabilities based on imported foreign technology. According to different evaluations of national funding programmes, it is acknowledged that there was a mismatch between the programmes' objectives and the capabilities required from the participants for these objectives to succeed (e.g., technological, managerial, linkage, marketing, and other competencies needed to develop an innovation or absorb transferred technology). In addition, there is a low demand for highly qualified personnel from the private sector, although there is an overabundance of highly educated young people (Lambrianidis 2011). Policy failure regarding productive transformation, the adaptation to new competitive pressures, the development of technological and innovative capabilities, and the attraction of foreign direct investment in technologically more sophisticated tradable products and services, was probably one of the most decisive differences between Greek policy and policy in many other European countries.

Therefore, the lack of modernisation, differentiation and complexity of the productive base, combined with Greece's international specialisation in low or low to medium technology goods and the preservation of a competitive position determined by low qualified labour and low wages, leads to a continuous deterioration of the Greek position vis-à-vis world competitors.

From Table 11.1 we can see that about 80 percent of Greek exports are concentrated in agricultural, low and low to medium tech products, while the share of medium- to high-tech exports is around 11 percent, far below the corresponding figures of the other two South European countries. In addition, Greece's competitiveness lags substantially and persistently behind that of the other countries (see Table 11.2).[1]

Table 11.1 Export structure of Greece, Portugal and Spain (2011)

Product group	*Greece*	*Portugal*	*Spain*	*Ireland*
Agricultural products-raw materials	9.7%	7.2%	8.5%	10.06%
Low tech products	18.9%	26.1%	18.4%	8.46%
Low to medium tech products	51.8%	31.1%	26.4%	3.82%
Medium to high tech products	11.2%	28.6%	38.7%	42.65%
High tech products	5.5%	5.1%	5.4%	34.29%

Source: Eurostat.

Table 11.2 Evolution of competitiveness (Balassa indices [(1)]) by product groups

Product groups	*Years*	*Greece*	*Spain*	*Portugal*	*Ireland*
Agricultural products-raw materials	1994	-0.450	-0.453	-0.606	0.413
	2002	-0.529	-0.350	-0.607	0.293
	2006	-0.428	-0.366	-0.455	0.360
	2011	-0.423	-0.245	-0.416	0.331
Low tech products	1994	-0.169	0.083	-0.108	0.135
	2002	-0.266	0.097	-0.068	0.036
	2006	-0.291	0.015	-0.010	-0.025
	2011	-0.159	0.088	0.054	0.054
Low to medium tech products	1994	-0.135	-0.090	0.129	-0.363
	2002	-0.357	-0.237	-0.129	-0.532
	2006	-0.443	-0.342	-0.232	-0.639
	2011	-0.211	-0.233	-0.182	-0.555
Medium to high tech products	1994	-0.813	-0.017	-0.429	0.046
	2002	-0.758	-0.089	-0.197	0.251
	2006	-0.734	-0.149	-0.223	0.366
	2011	-0.581	0.003	-0.152	0.460
High tech products	1994	-0.840	-0.275	-0.455	0.342
	2002	-0.657	-0.348	-0.404	0.47
	2006	-0.619	-0.388	-0.391	0.377
	2011	-0.579	-0.330	-0.361	0.586
Total	1994	-0.382	-0.068	-0.198	0.118
	2002	-0.498	-0.128	-0.195	0.247
	2006	-0.502	-0.213	-0.211	0.215
	2011	-0.316	-0.100	-0.153	0.308

Source: Eurostat, (SITC Rev.3, 2-digit classification).

Note:[(1)] The index has the following form: (X – M): (X + M) (X = exports, M = imports).

Under these conditions, the weak capability of the business sector to create a sustainable and competitive productive system, the ineffectiveness of public policies, the extent of the crisis and its negative impact on the real economy, as well as the crucial role of growth for successful strategies to overcome the crisis are interrelated and highlight the need for a more active policy to enhance the productive system. In fact, over the last few years, the productive system has faced a deterioration of all macro variables: slumping demand, reduced salaries and profits, severe liquidity tightening and increasing borrowing costs, high country risks and political instability. The crisis has had a very destructive impact on Greece's productive base and microstructures, leading to a shrinking of its real economy and affecting its future growth prospects. As a result, knowledge-based investment and investment in general have been significantly constrained because of the economic and political uncertainties, the risks and the cost of capital.

The long recession in Greece presents a big risk for middle- and high-knowledge–intensive firms, for the viability of existing firms, as well as the birth and expansion of new types of business activities. As a result, in contrast to the Schumpeterian concept of 'creative destruction', the crisis caused wider 'destruction' effects, making the exit out of the crisis longer, harder and more complex.

To deal with the present situation and to enter a path of stable and self-sustained balance between macro-stability and recovery, policy should consider a broad range of key issues extending from economics to politics, social values, expectations, potential or actual social reactions and social attitudes, and the economic behaviour of the business sector. Consequently, the rationale of an industrial policy as part of a wider strategy for overcoming the crisis is double edged. On the one hand, such a policy has to tackle the structural (production related) causal factors which led to the crisis, but on the other hand it also has to address the adverse structural consequences of the crisis or of erroneous policy decisions during the crisis.

Despite these effects on the productive system, European and Greek policies have focused mainly on fiscal consolidation and macro-adjustment. Recovery is expected to result from consolidation and deregulation policies regarding wages and the labour market.

As it is, Greece needs a sustainable growth rate of at least 3 percent in the long-term just to service its debt. Otherwise, fiscal consolidation will crumble. This growth rate will not be achieved on the basis of the country's existing production structure and the policies and practices of the past. The growth rates of the past were the result of a growth-cum-debt process that was unsustainable. A new strategy is needed to regain stability and competitiveness. This strategy needs to reinforce innovation, middle and high skill-oriented activities and export orientation.

It is argued that the description of the problems does not imply that industrial policy would be an efficient instrument to deal with the issue. However, the significant failures of the policies of the past show that something went wrong and it is extremely important to change course, to avoid similar mistakes and to develop efficient policy approaches. There are two questions which need to be answered: first, why and what kind of public policies; and second, is the public sector able to implement the necessary policies efficiently? Neither of these questions can be answered *in abstracto*. The answer depends on the specific realities, choices and interests in each particular country.

Industrial policy as an instrument to overcome the trap of low-wage cost competitiveness

The internal devaluation policy that has been imposed on Greece through the Memoranda is based on the false assertion that the loss of competitiveness can be counterbalanced simply by wage cuts. Such a policy is confusing the different forms of competitiveness (structural, cost, demand, technological, etc.) and their impact on the trade balance of a country. It was estimated that by the end of 2013, Greece's cost competitiveness would be restored to the level of 2001–2002. However, the deterioration of Greek competitiveness was indeed a result of adverse cost competitiveness and weak structural and technological competitiveness. In addition, efforts to restore the country's competitiveness have been partly counteracted by the changes in the exchange rate of the euro. In the long term, the important appreciation of the euro had a particularly strong negative impact on Greek exports. The exchange rate between the euro and the dollar appreciated by about 6.2 percent between the period May–December 2010 and October 2013, impacting on competitiveness. The inefficiency of the Troika's policy became readily apparent, since despite the significant wage cuts, Greek exports increased only marginally. To the extent that the country's productive system and competitive advantages remain stuck in low-wage products and services, Greece will find it difficult to compete with other low-wage countries on less sophisticated production lines and to break away from the low-wage trap.

Consequently, although cost competitiveness should be restored, in the longer term the question is how to overcome the country's weak structural competitiveness. This brings us back to the central question of industrial policy: the productive transformation of the economy. The crisis cannot be overcome and growth and improved levels of welfare cannot be achieved by remaining within the downward spiral of an internal devaluation policy. Competitiveness and development are not linked only to monetary factors, but also to structural, technology, knowledge and production-related factors. Industrial policy is precisely the kind of policy that can break the vicious cycle of a continuous depression, despite (or because of) the implementation of a restrictive fiscal policy.

The European rationale for the enhancement of productive capabilities

As a result of the crisis, the Eurozone has actually lost a fundamental dimension of its rationale. The common currency was introduced with the aim of lowering costs and increasing the competitiveness of European production. In fact, during the 2000s, capital costs were significantly reduced. However, the crisis brought the individual countries back to a stage before the EMU. Many countries in the South are faced with much higher interest rates than the core Eurozone countries. Moreover, in many of these countries very often banks are just unable or unwilling to lend at all. Hence, for the crisis countries the euro area failed to provide one of its most critical benefits. This asymmetry erodes the very basic rationale of the common currency. High capital costs are expected to negatively affect production-enhancing policies and hence convergence processes within Europe. In contrast, the crisis initiated an era of deeper intra-European divergence and a profound divide between member countries in terms of competitive conditions, the evolution of which cannot be forecasted.

Consequently, the rationale of an industrial policy emanates not only from national policy considerations, but also from a concern with the sustainability of the European system. The present experience shows that the qualitative aspects of an economy and the degree of convergence or divergence within Europe have a broader impact on the stability and the sustainability of the common currency itself. It also shows how important it is for Europe to reduce not only its internal macroeconomic divergences, but also its productive and technological divergences.

The persistence of large intra-EU productive gaps impacts the stability of the euro and the integration process, from an economic, social and political point of view. It has been estimated that countries that were more severely affected by the crisis had a lower manufacturing base, a greater degree of erosion of this sector over previous years, and larger current account deficits at the start of the crisis (Aiginger 2011). Once the crisis hit, growth capabilities, debt and current account deficits became the proxies financial markets used to assess the ability of a country to service its debt. The issue becomes particularly relevant for the present period since, after nearly 30 years of convergence, the European Union experienced a deep setback, with GDP per capita in the crisis countries falling to their levels of about 10 or 20 years before. The rise of euro scepticism and of far-right political parties during the crisis is the most apparent expression of the non-economic risks generated by such developments. Consequently, rebalancing and growth are crucial issues today, not only from an economic perspective, but also to protect democracy, social values and European cohesion.

3. Inside the box of industrial policy

The complexity of the crisis and the national structural weaknesses suggest that policy has to efficiently tackle multiple issues, and success depends on the parallel progress on many relevant fronts. Three lessons of the last few years are that: a) fiscal consolidation coupled with high negative growth rates is associated with very high economic, social and political costs, and that, conversely, under conditions of very high indebtedness, growth without sustainable fiscal management is utopic; b) high and increasing unemployment significantly destabilises the social and political environment; and c) the possibility of efficient macro and structural policies are eroded if growth, employment and the reduction of poverty and inequality cannot be achieved.

In this context, industrial or targeted policy should also take the time dimension into account. It is important to distinguish policies and measures that have a short-term impact from those which have a medium- or long-term impact. The effects of an industrial policy are by definition of a long-term nature. However, in the short to medium term it is necessary to enhance the credibility of policymaking and to prevent the appearance of a political and/or social gap, which would undermine the creditability of medium- to long-term policies. In the following we distinguish eight issues, which under the present conditions should constitute priorities for an industrial policy:

To enhance the productivity of existing firms and production processes within both the entrepreneurial and the public sector

Higher productivity would reinforce firms' competitive position in both the foreign and the domestic market, would remove the pressure to use wage and salary cuts as an instrument to enhance competitiveness, employment and profits and to create liquidity and investment opportunities. Increased productivity would also improve the public deficit and the imbalances in the pension system. Infrastructure, information, networking, bureaucratic procedures, systematic support through agencies and incentives, especially on issues of quality control, transport systems, innovation and technical change, protection of intellectual property and tax administration, are some examples of possible instruments which could improve the productive structures of the country.

Policies targeting productivity in the broader public sector (government, local authorities, public enterprises, and public service organisations, such as hospitals, pension funds and education institutions) would have a beneficial impact on the productivity and the competitiveness of the business sector as well, since many of its inputs are offered and priced by public entities. It would also diminish the public deficit and indirectly improve macro-imbalances.

It could also be argued that an improvement in the productivity of the public sector could induce broader positive changes to the extent that it could generate:

- a wider rationalisation of political decision-making processes;
- a different mix between the systematic preference of governments for the short-term at the expense of longer-term societal considerations;
- a substantial reduction of corruptive red tape and the creation of more stable and credible institutions, which by themselves constitute a crucial competitive advantage and a significant driver for growth.

To enhance the export-orientation of firms

In times of recession, growth cannot be expected to result from a quick recovery of domestic demand. In contrast, a reorientation of domestic firms towards international markets could be seen as an answer to the domestic demand constraints and generate positive effects on GDP. Obviously, such a shift of activities is not determined only by the choices of firms, but also by structural factors. In this respect, higher production standards should be adopted, networking should be expanded, profit margins adjusted and quality factors enhanced.

An export-oriented policy would imply a more complicated and efficient approach than in the past, but could lead to some initial significant results within one to two years. It seems that a number of firms have already succeeded in increasing their export orientation. However, the macroeconomic impact of this change is still weak and in the short term will remain limited. Greece's export ratio (exports of goods and tourist receipts as a proportion of GDP) is around 11 percent and an impact of a one per cent increase in the export ratio on GDP would require exports to increase by more than 20 percent per year, taking into account the fact that higher exports would also drive up imports, whose share in the production of exported goods exceeds 50 percent.

The need to go beyond productivity and to enhance production patterns

Cost and efficiency-related policies might enhance competitiveness and productivity, but this is a necessary although not sufficient condition for growth and export expansion. Productivity could be largely irrelevant if it concerns products and services facing low and stagnant demand patterns. Such specialisation patterns are inappropriate for securing a satisfactory and macroeconomically relevant domestic or international market share.

The problem behind the present macro-imbalances has a dual nature: on the one hand, it is a problem of weak productivity which, as mentioned previously, can be enhanced through efficient policies; on the other hand, it is a problem related to the transformation of the productive base, upgrading simple, low-cost production processes and moving towards more technologically advanced production processes. In effect, productivity growth and the diversification of production should be seen as interrelated elements in a growing economy. A winning strategy depends on many elements, such as more innovative and technology-intensive production processes, a range of qualitative improvements concerning existing products and services, a deep reform of the education system, a policy favouring the growth of firms in terms of size, developing sophisticated knowledge services for innovative new firms, restricting underground activities, combating public inefficiencies and facilitating the formation of a general attitude enabling reforms, and enhancing growth, employment and incomes.

The broad range of all these factors indicates that a targeted policy towards creating competitive and sustainable productive structures cannot be but the outcome of a longer chain of interlinked public actions, where the success of each determines the success of the others. In other words, we are faced with a general equilibrium rather than a partial equilibrium question. What matters is the capacity to transform patterns of specialisation, to change and to set priorities around promising new activities and thus avoid ending up with failed state interventions.

The issue is that proactive policies are subject to similar risks of failure as horizontal ones. As has been noted, "markets can malfunction both when governments interfere too much and when they interfere too little" (Rodrik 2004). Apart from the well-known problem of public failures, such policies are subject to an inherently high degree of uncertainty and unpredictability in foreseeing what a country will be good at producing or where the advantages can lie. Successful specialisations can rarely be anticipated. Even countries with very similar levels of technological capabilities and factor endowments have followed very different specialisation patterns as a consequence of different historical evolutions, entrepreneurial initiatives and policy responses (Giannitsis and Kager 2009).

In technologically advanced economies, path dependencies could facilitate such shifts and policy decisions. However, path dependency is only partially helpful in providing guidance to technologically weak countries, in particular when the goal is to transcend existing productive structures. Path dependencies in a country like Greece, and the configuration of its technology and innovation subsystems, indicate that the potential spectrum of new industrial specialisations is not easily predictable. The policy implication is that risks cut both ways and characterise both types of policies: policies targeting ambitious projects for which capabilities and supportive conditions are insufficient, as well as policies which do not facilitate specialisation in specific new technologies, precisely in the belief that the external conditions make such a strategy risky.

The need for competitive micro-structures

Production, exports and competition are the outcome of micro-structures associated with a country's firms. The range of relevant determinant factors is broad and extends along the whole value chain of a firm and/or activity. Besides the specialisation patterns, the structural weaknesses of the Greek productive system are related to the particularly small number of medium- and larger-sized companies, the comparatively low absolute size of these companies, the low value added in industrial activities, the low degree of networking, the weak integration of most of these firms in the global value chain, the absence of any kind of R&D and innovation activities, their weak management structures and the low survival capability of a very large number of small- to medium-sized firms.

From an industrial policy perspective, it is crucial to design policies that enhance the accumulation of knowledge and the evolution of firms, and support firms, institutions, and processes which facilitate cumulativeness over time. In this respect, firm size and critical mass have a decisive impact on the outcome. With regard to size, what is crucial in industrial dynamics is less the distinction between small, medium and large, than the capacity to compete internationally and to grow. Firm size matters to the extent that it can trigger competitiveness, employment, and growth. The crucial factor is the capacity of firms to change, to stay and improve their market position, to grow and contribute to the competitiveness of their economy. What is needed is the entrepreneurial capability for a quantum leap to surpass the minimum thresholds below which the survival of a firm is at risk. Success depends greatly on the right institutional and economic environment, one that is conducive to growth and influences firms' innovative behaviour.

The geographical fragmentation of production processes resulting in the emergence of global value chains (GVCs) is of particular importance for firms and especially SMEs for the following reasons:

i As there is a high and increasing import dependency of exports, the challenge is to formulate strategies and policies on how to take position in the upper and lower part of the value chains (R&D, design, management, sales services, etc.). Firms that possess technological and organisational capabilities and advanced skills and invest in intangible assets and innovation will capture larger shares of value added.

ii The emergence of GVCs may offer new opportunities to SMEs that very often lack the necessary production scale, the expertise and capacity to engage in international trade. They expand their business opportunities across borders, although reaching international markets is not easy for SMEs. Of course, the exposure to international markets creates important challenges also in terms of management, finance and the ability to upgrade and protect in-house technology (OECD 2007).

The above issues point to important considerations in terms of policy. Creating and strengthening linkages of local SMEs with firms that are already engaged in GVCs, innovation policies, initiatives for coordinating public and private strategies concerning FDI, are potentially appropriate fields for industrial policy intervention. Industrial policy should address the issue of upgrading industrial activities, not only in the sense of increasing production efficiency in terms of cost reductions through, for example, cutting wages, but especially in climbing up the value chain and/or broadening the capabilities within the same functions or in additional functions along the value chain (Morison et al. 2008), fostering innovation, learning and technological capabilities.

Consequently, if globalisation to some extent erodes the factors and processes that build competitive advantages at the national level, industrial policy can foster the development of nation-specific assets and the development of endogenous capabilities that will enable the exploitation of market niches at the global level as well as the use of basic knowledge to generate competitive solutions. In addition, this is also important for attracting FDI as multinational corporations are investing in areas or regions with specific local advantages (Athreye and Cantwell 2007).

The upgrading of low- and medium-tech activities

European policies have long focused on fostering the development of high technology (HT) sectors since, due to high uncertainty and development costs, externalities could prevent private actors from investing in these areas. Low technology (LT) sectors have been largely ignored in the policy discussions or are considered as "archaic hangovers from an earlier era of capitalism" (Scott 2006).

Recently, however, it has been argued that LT industrial sectors can be very innovative and knowledge intensive (Smith 2002; European Commission 2006). Unlike high technology sectors, the nature of such technological change is characterised by established developmental paths and fixed technological trajectories that are dominated by incremental innovations (Hirsch-Kreinsen and Schwinge 2011). Due to high persistence and stability in these industries, entrepreneurial activities and a successful deviation from established practices and technological paths opens up strong opportunities for building competitive advantage and gaining profitability (ibid). At the same time, competitive pressure and strong path dependency stimulate innovative behaviour to overcome these constraints. Innovation and growth in traditional sectors is to a large extent shaped by technological advancements of suppliers, many of them coming from high- or medium- to high-tech industries. In addition, the pace of technological change is fast and capital-intensive, with a short time for the amortisation of the innovation cost by profitable sales, especially for high-tech industries. The modernisation of traditional activities to become more knowledge-intensive opens new market opportunities for technologically more advanced activities.

Furthermore, for countries like Greece, the company-specific knowledge and the capabilities in low- and/or medium-tech firms are of particular importance. Low and low to medium technology sectors represent over 80 percent of manufacturing production, value added, exports and employment, but their competitiveness is weak and has tended to deteriorate. At a global level, some of these activities became knowledge-intensive, while others succeeded in associating existing products and new qualities. Today, many of these sectors are producing with radically different techniques than those that were used some decades ago (textiles, naval construction, construction materials). It became apparent that in many cases path dependency did not prevent the incorporation of strong elements of new knowledge over time.

In addition, empirical research has shown that the performance of low-tech industries differs according to their level of development and knowledge characteristics, such as educational attainment, R&D, innovation, licensing, and so on (Coedhuys et al. 2013; Kastelli and Caloghirou 2014). Furthermore, despite the lower performance of low-tech vis-à-vis the high-tech sectors, there were larger differences in productivity between innovative and non-innovative firms in low-tech sectors than in high-tech sectors, implying that firms adopting new knowledge in low-tech sectors have a significant potential to enhance their market position (Halpern and Muraközy 2010). These processes point to catching-up strategies whose success depends on the firm's absorptive capacity (its capability to assimilate and exploit knowledge) and the productive, organisational and linkage competencies of the technology adopters or users.

Policy design could follow two directions:

i The modernisation of traditional sectors through the diffusion of new technologies and knowledge-intensive applications in order to respond to demand in new ways (more efficiently and/or with higher quality solutions). In this sense, suppliers can play a crucial role through the use of new technological advancements.

ii The focus of research in providing solutions to transform traditional sectors into knowledge-intensive users. This might prove beneficial to the research system as well, as it would link research to sophisticated demand.

Effective policy initiatives can then be designed targeting the upgrading of managerial and technological capabilities and the development of knowledge-intensive activities within low-tech industries. Equally, clustering and networking can bring about specialisation and the division of labour between firms that benefit from scale economies, can reduce the unit cost of knowledge-intensive business services and facilitate knowledge flows. A broader policy aimed at SME's and the extroversion of such firms also has to be supported by the EU, especially in view of the fundamental obstacles in the crisis countries. The question cannot be tackled from a business-as-usual approach from the EU. The crisis has shown how disappointing the outcome of such policies has been. Only specific efficient programmes and tools can support a transformation of the productive fabric in these countries towards more competitive and growth-enhancing production structures.

The need to consider active public policy as a value chain

Public policies to enhance the production base of the economy risk remaining ineffective if they are disconnected from broader targets or from a broader coherent policy concept. We know of many examples, related mainly to technologically weak systems, in which incentives, research programmes, R&D, innovation, or networking projects, often based on best practices, were introduced randomly and without any coherence, and which ultimately had a very weak or negligible impact on economic performance.

The issue is that public policy involvement per se does not guarantee a successful outcome. As has been extensively documented, it is important that public policy enhances the factors surrounding entrepreneurship and innovation. Efficient public policy requires a successful combination of a range of crucial parts of the whole value chain, such as management of knowledge, priority setting, strategic thinking, long-term policy design and management approaches, and not simply innovation-related aspects. Otherwise the result might be insignificant, fragmentary and temporary, and the impact on crucial economic variables (productivity, competitiveness, growth) will be quite weak.

The priority of investment and foreign direct investment

Investment and foreign direct investment are key drivers of GDP and productivity growth, in particular during a crisis period. The wage and pension cuts reinforced the recessionary effects and reduced domestic demand. Due to these factors, the idle productive capacity in all sectors, which in some cases reached 40–50 percent, allows an increase in production within existing possibilities. Consequently, investment cannot be expected to increase significantly before recovery establishes a climate of positive expectations and improves the financing of entrepreneurial investment. In addition, very few investment projects could have a visible impact on growth if they simply target the stagnant domestic market. In contrast, export-oriented activities in technologically more sophisticated production areas attracting foreign direct investment (FDI) are not constrained by these factors and could help reinforce the tradable sector, enrich the productive spectrum, enhance the technological basis of the economy, and act as a driver of growth both in the industrial and the services sector.

Financing industrial development

Financial resources are an essential element of industrial development as they determine investment possibilities and create opportunities for growth.

The current economic crisis in Greece has been marked by a drying up of market and funding liquidity, which has aggravated the recession and had serious implications for the operation and survival of firms and social welfare. Restructuring the productive system in the absence of financial resources is a contradiction in terms.

The current economic crisis has upset the dynamic relation between technology, production and economic performance through a drop in income and demand. In addition, financial distress creates very negative conditions for investing in technological development. This effect, combined with globalisation, contributes to job losses, restricts firms' turnover and shrinks financial resources to the supply side that could generate further technological development and growth.

The further reduction of the manufacturing share in GDP combined with the financial constraints that severely affect the economy as a whole, and the business sector in particular, are likely to further reduce research and innovative activity and lead to the dangerous pitfall of brain drain.

The problem today, particularly in Greece, is how to boost the virtuous circle of technological capability building, capital accumulation and improvement in production capabilities, leading to economic growth. On the one hand, anti-crisis policies are calling for fiscal consolidation, but on the other hand, technology policy and the agenda for an integrated industrial policy are calling for investment in human resources, research and innovation and capability building. Even if this investment is supposed to come from the private sector it remains difficult to see how it will find the necessary financial resources, given the sharp decline in demand, lack of liquidity and the reluctance of banks to lend in a restrictive macroeconomic environment. Given this, one possibility for industrial policy is to stimulate other funding mechanisms such as venture and seed capital and to redistribute financial resources (e.g., from tax evasion) towards activities that will raise competitiveness. Support should be centred not only on high-tech ventures but also knowledge-intensive entrepreneurship in more traditional sectors.

In order to provide financial resources to foster investment opportunities, one major condition would be for European initiatives, for example, of the European Investment Bank, to provide guarantees, as the domestic banking system is in a vulnerable position for taking risks. At the same time EU resources from Structural Funds should be directed towards the modernisation of the productive base and the improvement of technological, organisational and managerial capabilities, openness and liquidity (in the short run).

4. Concluding remarks

In the previous sections of this chapter we stressed the importance of the productive capabilities of a country as a determinant of the depth and impact of the crisis. We argued that the lack of a purposeful government policy coupled with the failure of approaches based solely on markets co-determined the gradual erosion of the production base of the country and accentuated the macroeconomic imbalances during the crisis. We also argued that there was a need to develop a different mix of macro and structural policies, which should comprise farsighted targeted policy concepts, secure greater state autonomy and break with the dominance of rent-seeking, powerful interest groups.

However, the success of an industrial policy aimed at the reinforcement and transformation of the country's productive base implies the possibility of transcending the established dichotomy of market and state failure.

The question of industrial policy is in fact a question of the relationships between the state and the market, and policy may be faced with the dilemma of market and state failure. We know that the failure of the one does not guarantee the success of the other and that often we are constrained by two different types of deficiency. However, the issue exceeds the dichotomy of market vs. state failure. In countries like Greece, the possibility to act efficiently is a measure of the systemic capabilities (or failures) to transcend the hindrances of lagging behind and to change the course of the economy in the long term. Under the influence of the policies followed in the past, the course of the Greek economy and other crisis countries evolved in a way that proved to be disastrous during the crisis.

A structural reason for this failure is related to the myopia of all relevant players: the markets, the governments and the agents. National and European policy assumed that the rational behaviour of the markets and self-correction mechanisms were sufficient to ensure the desirable growth and evolution of Europe and its member states. In this regard, there was sharp criticism of the short-termism of (financial) markets. It also proved that policy has followed even more myopic and short-term decisions, with disastrous results for the societal interests that had to be protected. The outcome today is a split Europe: the Europe in crisis, the Europe in hidden crisis and the rest of Europe.

Industrial policy as we have discussed it and any form of policy targeting are by definition medium- or long-term approaches. In the case of Greece, such a policy is in sharp contrast to the underlying established political and private interests and practices. Consequently, the theoretical rationale of an industrial policy is by itself not a guarantee of success. The implementation of such a policy is faced with the multitude of deficiencies and failures of the governance system and its capability to overcome established patterns of behaviour, to understand the radical changes caused by the crisis and to implement serious policy changes aimed at dealing with the present impasses. The assumption that state restructuring could occur as a response to the imperatives of the economic pressures and that the policy issues can be limited to the economic sphere is at best questionable (Purcell 2002: 299). The state authorities operate according to a more political rationale in which even during the crisis period the collective interests are not necessarily primary (ibid, pp. 300). The political priorities of the governance system are concentrated on the interests of the political system and the benefits of the main clientele (unions, big capitalist agents, public servants, specific professional groups), despite the fact that under the current conditions the urgent question is how to identify and implement crucial changes and overcome the crisis.

In essence, growth, macroeconomic stabilisation and the sustainability of the public debt depend on an extensive reform of the highly inefficient public sector. Inefficiency is a systemic factor that is diffused more widely in the logic of the socioeconomic system. Change could succeed only if a broader consensus on the need for a paradigm change can be established, and not because some partial policy approaches, such as industrial policies, need to be implemented.

As a consequence, the issue transcends the question of the efficiency and appropriateness of industrial policy and has to do with the broader issue of governance, which is crucial for any policy. Efficient and sustainable economic and productive patterns are a direct function of efficient policies. Hence, the question is how can the governance model and the prevailing values, attitudes, ideological prejudices, and balances of interest that led to the collapse of the economy be transformed into new types of policy thinking and acting.

In the past decades, stronger and weaker forms of industrial policy or of other state interventions have been exploited by the political system and its clientele to extract benefits disassociated from the public interest and the implicit goals of these interventions. In many of these cases the issue was not that policymaking was so misused, but that many policy approaches (interventionist or neutral) failed because of that.

Very often, industrial policy was centred on the defence of crumbling firms and industries, and delayed instead of facilitating the restructuring process. Incentives, investment subsidies, public procurement policies and tax measures often also simply favoured the black economy and tax evasion, enhancing incomes but not productive capabilities. Advocates of neoliberal policies would perhaps maintain that this shows the inappropriateness of public interventions and the high risks of state failure. This would be half of the reality. The other half is that in the absence of any action, risks, high societal costs and failures are equally present and the impact of the crisis has made this more obvious than ever. Liberal policies failed to enhance the productive base and this had a crucial impact on the extent, the duration and the implications of the crisis. Consequently, state inefficiency determines the outcome, whether in the framework of so-called "neutral" or of more active policies.

The question is not only how to choose between the market and the state but also which state. It is not enough to have a consensus on the broader changes that are needed if we disregard the changes in the structure of the state, which has to implement such changes. Industrial, technological, institutional, productive and other changes might succeed or fail depending on the specificities of the particular policies and governance systems. The question is how to be selective, what risks have to be taken, how public policies can efficiently support activities, but equally, how we can anticipate timely and efficient policy discipline in order to avoid picking the losers.

A final remark is that the success of a policy aimed at enhancing the structure of production of a European crisis country does not depend solely on national choices. It is co-determined by policies and institutional constraints related to the European anti-crisis policies. After more than thirty years, European policies have failed to diminish the divergence between the North and the South and establish in the European South solid, resilient and efficient economic structures, which are vital for competition in today's world. The present crisis is an opportunity to reflect on what went wrong, what was insufficient, why European policies should particularly consider the problems of the South and what specific aspects should change.

To continue as in the past encapsulates social and political risks in parts of Europe, which might impede efforts to overcome the institutional and economic deficiencies of the present situation in Europe.

Notes

1 The improvement in competitiveness in 2011 was mainly due to the dramatic drop in investment, the reduction of production that depended heavily on imports, the important decline of imported fuels and the severe contraction of incomes and demand for imported goods. At the same time, exports increased marginally.

12 The Italian economy, the economic crisis and industrial policy

Michele Di Maio

1. Introduction

This chapter presents an analysis of the most important aspects of the Italian economy in the midst of the current economic crisis and discusses the country's past and current approach to industrial policy (IP). Our focus is on the characteristics and evolution of the manufacturing sector and on how this has influenced the country's competitiveness and structural change dynamics. We made this choice because, although other aspects of the economy are also important, we believe that the current difficulties of the Italian economy are deeply rooted in the dynamics of the industrial sector. We supplement this analysis with a discussion on the historical and current characteristics of IP in Italy and how these should be modified to give IP a positive role in helping the economy to overcome the current economic crisis.

There are two main motivations for this chapter. The first one is the economic importance of Italy. Italy is the seventh largest economy in the world; it is the second largest industrial country in Europe and the fifth at world level (UNStats 2012). As shown in Table 12.1, even if things are changing rapidly, with new competitors emerging and old ones becoming stronger, Italy is still among the top players in the global economy. It follows that it is important to understand how and to which extent Italy is reacting to the current crisis because this will also have an impact on world trade.

The second motivation for this chapter is the potential usefulness of the analysis of the Italian case for other countries in the European periphery. A preliminary step in this direction is to correctly evaluate how much the current difficulties of the Italian economy are related to the crisis and how much they are instead the results of previous weaknesses of the Italian economy. For this reason, this chapter presents a stylised historical overview of the evolution of the Italian economy and its IP from the 1950s to today. In particular, our aim is to understand if and how much the weakness of the Italian economy is caused by the type of IP implemented in the country in these decades and how, in this case, it should be modified to favour structural change and sustained growth.

In this chapter, we adopt a broad definition of IP: IP includes all the policies aimed at favouring the restructuring of existing industries and the development of new ones (Bianchi and Labory 2011; Cimoli et al. 2009; Di Maio 2014). In this sense, IP is obviously not just state aid or (horizontal) R&D support policies. Instead, it is understood as a set of measures designed

Table 12.1 World top 10 manufacturers (percentage world value added, 2010)

	1990	*2000*	*2010*
China	3,2	8,3	18,9
United States	22,8	26,0	18,2
Japan	17,7	17,7	10,7
Germany	9,6	6,7	6,0
Italy	5,3	3,5	3,0
Brazil	1,7	1,7	2,8
Korea	1,4	2,3	2,7
France	4,4	3,3	2,6
United Kingdom	4,5	3,9	2,3
India	1,1	1,2	2,2

Note: Manufacturing refers to industries belonging to International Standard Industrial Classification (ISIC) divisions 15-37. Value added is the net output of a sector after adding up all outputs and subtracting intermediate inputs. It is calculated without making deductions for depreciation of fabricated assets or depletion and degradation of natural resources.

Source: UNStats (2012).

to favour structural change and a particular development path. This interpretation of IP is clearly in accordance with the one adopted in the other chapters of this book. The adoption of this definition implies a broad set of instruments and objectives being ascribed to IP. For this reason, following Cimoli et al. (2009), we argue that IP naturally includes policies belonging to different domains, thus: i) innovation and technology policies; ii) education and skill formation policies; iii) trade policies; iv) targeted industrial support measures; v) sectoral (competitiveness) policies; vi) competition regulation policies. While all these sets of policies are important to correctly describe the IP of a country, special attention will be paid to innovation polices, given their strategic importance in the current world economy.

Our definition of IP embraces a very large set of policies but it does not include all those that may impact on the manufacturing sector, such as exchange rate policy and labour market policies. Our choice is motivated by the need for a compromise between a broad definition able to capture the multiple aspects involved in the concept of IP and a reasonable number of different policy measures to be considered as part of it. A precise definition of the contours of IP—to clearly distinguish it from the country's general overall development strategy—is in fact a necessary condition for discussing the features, changes, and results of the different industrialisation strategies pursued by Italy in the last 50 years.

Our analysis will mostly focus on the last 20 years. There are several reasons for choosing this timespan. First, the world has changed greatly in the last two decades. For instance, since China entered the WTO the rules of the game and the players in world trade are not the same anymore. Second, this period gives us a sufficiently large time frame to provide a perspective on structural change and competitiveness issues. Third, this is the period that more or less coincides with the European Single Act of 1986, which was an important step in the creation of the Single European Market. This is quite a relevant event for our analysis since one of its consequences was a severe limitation on the possibility to use traditional IP instruments (including credit policy, trade policy, measures to support 'national champions', etc.) at the national level. Finally, during this period the EU member countries adopted the euro, which many see as one of the causes of the current crisis.

The chapter proceeds as follows. In the next section we provide a brief description of the current state of the Italian economy and discuss two anomalies that have characterissed its evolution in the last three decades. Section 3 examines the historical and current characteristics of IP in Italy, emphasising its weaknesses and potentialities. In particular, we discuss the evidence concerning the recent evolution of IP in terms of budget size and composition. Section 4 describes how the approach of the European Commission to IP has changed in the last decades and how this has influenced the behaviour of all member states, Italy included. We also consider how the WTO agreements and the rise of new world powers have influenced what characteristics IP should have. Finally, in Section 5 we present some concluding remarks.

2. The Italian economy: characteristics and anomalies

According to the European Union Report *Member States Competitiveness Performance and Policies 2011*, manufacturing contributes 16.1 percent to Italy's total value added against 14.9 percent for the EU on average. Italy is relatively specialised in labour-intensive sectors, such as leather, clothes and apparel, and in high-tech sectors, such as fabricated metal products, domestic appliances, machinery and automotive, motorcycles and bicycles. Traditionally, Italy has also a comparative advantage in marketing-driven sectors, namely, luggage and handbags and high-quality food and beverages. It is this double nature that makes the Italian case an exception in the European context.

The recent economic and financial crisis had a strong impact on the Italian economy. Manufacturing production fell by around 25 percent during the crisis and it is still 17.4 percent lower than its previous cyclical peak. At the same time, not all the current difficulties of the Italian economy originated with the crisis. In fact, the decline in economic performance started before that. In the last decade, Italy has experienced a decline in cost and price competitiveness. Nominal unit labour costs increased by 31 percent between 2000 and 2010, compared to an increase of 14 percent in the EU-27 and 20 percent in the euro area. Labour productivity per hour worked has declined over the last decade and is now only marginally above the EU-27 average and about 13 percentage points below the euro area average (EC 2012).

Overall, the current situation of the Italian economy shows a mixed picture in terms of international competitiveness. While the Italian economy still features elements of strength in some high-skill (mechanical) sectors, its performance in knowledge-intensive sectors is weak and does not seem likely to improve in the short term. Next, we describe the two anomalies of the Italian economy and their role in determining the current situation of the country's industrial system.

The two anomalies of the Italian economy

The Italian economy can be characterised by two anomalies that have played an important role in shaping the country's current economic situation. The first is the trade specialisation pattern. The second is the size distribution of Italian firms.

The trade specialisation anomaly. There is widespread consensus that economic growth is to an important extent determined by a country's export performance and that the strength of this link depends on the sophistication level of its specialisation pattern (Dosi et al. 1990). These arguments have fuelled the debate about the possibility that the recent weak performance of the Italian economy is due to its misdirected pattern of specialisation. In fact, Italy is characterised by a peculiar "trade specialisation anomaly" (Onida 1999). This consists of: a) strong comparative advantages in low-skilled and labour intensive sectors, which implies that the Italian trade specialisation pattern is more similar to that of an emerging economy than of countries with comparable levels of per capita income, and b) a very high degree of persistence of this peculiar pattern of specialisation (De Benedictis 2005). In fact, the persistence of the specialisation pattern per se is not uncommon for developed countries. What is distinctive of the Italian case is that the persistence is associated with an anomalous (with respect to other developed countries) specialisation pattern. Interestingly, for a long period the anomaly did not prevent Italy from recording significant economic growth. Yet, it seems that more recently it has finally become a problem for the economy. Di Maio and Tamagni (2008) suggest that an explanation for this can be found in the evolution of the level of sophistication of world trade. Their analysis provides an empirical characterisation of the sophistication of the Italian specialisation pattern and of its evolution from the early 1980s to recent years. They show that, in the last two decades, the entry of new competitors (in particular, emerging countries) along with a vast worldwide redistribution of production has significantly changed the relative gains of exporting in each specific sector. In the face of these dramatic changes, the Italian specialisation pattern has changed little, while the sophistication level of its export vector has been decreasing. The analysis reveals that by the late 1990s, the sectors where Italy has been, and still is, highly specialised, are characterised by an inter-temporal reduction in the value of their PRODY index. This is an index whose value is higher the more the sector/product is present in the export vector of advanced countries.[1] This result possibly explains why the "trade specialisation anomaly" was not a problem in the past whereas now it is. World trade is rapidly evolving but Italy is stuck with its traditional structure of comparative advantages, marked by strong specialisation in sectors which in the last years have become less and less sophisticated, and, thus, less and less able to sustain growth.

While the diagnosis is clear, the main challenge is to understand why no attempts have been made (or why these have been unable) to modify the specialisation pattern towards a more sophisticated export vector. There are several possible explanations. For instance, De Nardi and Traù (2005) argue that the numerous exchange rate depreciation episodes reduced incentives for firms to upgrade their products. Bottazzi et al. (2008) suggest that this is due to the (behavioural) reluctance of Italian firms to translate productivity and profitability into higher growth. Saltari and Travaglini (2006) instead argue that the cause could be the labour market reforms implemented in the second half of the 1990s that favoured cost-saving strategies rather than favouring productivity growth. Finally, Fagiolo and Luzzi (2007) suggest that a possible explanation is the inability of the credit market to sustain the best performing firms. While there is probably no single cause, all of them point to the absence of an effective in IP that could counter the trade specialisation anomaly and sustain structural change and growth.

The firms' size distribution anomaly. As in other EU economies, the vast majority of firms in Italy are SMEs (99.9 percent of companies and 81.3 percent of employment). One difference with respect to other EU countries is that Italy has a higher share of micro-companies, with less than 10 employees (47.4 percent of employment, compared to the EU average of 29.8 percent). Moreover, the prevalence of SMEs is even stronger in the South, where the average number of employees per enterprise in the manufacturing sector is 5.8 compared to 8.5 nationally (EU 2012). While these data can be interpreted as showing the presence of a strong entrepreneurial spirit in Italy, they also raise some concerns as to the overall competitiveness of the economy in relation to its innovation possibilities.

In fact, this situation is not new. The decline in the presence of large firms in the Italian economy started in the 1970s. Again, this process did not create problems for a long time, especially in the economy of the North. Since the beginning of the 1980s, the organisation of production in the traditional sectors in the Northern regions has progressively evolved towards a situation characterised by the prevalence of SMEs, often organised in districts. Somewhat surprisingly, the districts expanded in number and size and consolidated over the years. The recipe for the success of the districts lays in the combination of the high competence of the entrepreneurs and employees, the flexibility provided by the family-ownership structure and the fruitful interaction with other firms in the district. This successful mix enabled the SMEs in these districts to gain national and international leadership in specific market segments. For a long time, industrial districts have been the backbone of the Italian economy and have contributed to counter economic and industrial decline. In the long run, however, this system started showing its weakness due to the characteristics of the SMEs: low internationalisation, low level of investment in R&D, lack of managerial culture prevalence of small projects, and difficulties in scaling up production. In the South, SMEs were suffering from the same weaknesses in terms of innovation and potential growth but, in addition, their ability to cooperate was significantly lower: as a result there were fewer districts and on average they were smaller than in the North.

A comprehensive evaluation of the industrial district experience suggests that the idea that "small is beautiful" has its limits and these can be very significant in the long run. In fact, in those years, IP was unable to induce SMEs to develop and change to overcome the small-size anomaly. On the one hand, IP failed to provide incentives and programmes able to induce SMEs to upgrade their product and production processes. On the other hand, SMEs showed little interest in using the available policies, especially those supporting R&D and innovation, because of the small scale of their activities. In fact, the SMEs' behaviour largely explains the extremely low investment in R&D and innovation activities in Italy.

3. Industrial policy in Italy: historical evolution and current characteristics

As we have seen, the current state of the Italian economy shows some serious difficulties. In this context, it is natural to ask what role, if any, IP could play in favouring structural change and economic recovery. In this case, which characteristics should IP have to be effective? Is the current Italian IP able to play this crucial role? To attempt to answer these questions, we start by looking at the historical evolution of IP and its current characteristics and how these have influenced and, in turn, been influenced by the two anomalies of the Italian economy.

IP has a long history in Italy that dates back at least to the "economic miracle" period (1950–1970).[2] After World War II, the Italian economy was still largely agricultural and characterised by high unemployment and large regional disparities. In the following two decades, the Italian economy recorded significant GDP growth and the industrialisation of the North of the country began (Silva 2008). Rota (2013) argues that during the "economic miracle" period there were two distinct phases of IP, each with its own characteristics. In the 1950s, the leading instruments for IP were the state-owned enterprises (SOEs) and public holdings. In the 1960s, the major instrument for sustaining the growth of the manufacturing sector was instead the (government controlled) credit system. Government intervention therefore contributed to creating and strengthening the metal production and chemical industries in the South and the metal production and mechanical industries in the Centre-North.

The industrialisation strategy adopted in the 1960s deeply influenced the evolution of the Italian economy in the following decades. Indeed, the divergence in the regional development between the North and the South and the economic slowdown of the 1970s can both be attributed to that strategy. In the South, the development model was centred on the establishment of capital-intensive, large-scale industries such as chemicals and metal production. These sectors increased employment in the region and created the conditions for a certain amount of technology transfer. But they were sectors dominated by a few large firms which remained isolated entities, and only a few of them were able to created backward linkages with the local SMEs. In the Centre-North, the development of the mechanical and the metal production industries led instead to a more diversified and balanced industrial structure: these sectors were populated by numerous small firms which interacted both as competitors but also to create various forms of cooperation. Most importantly, SMEs were often integrated in the production cycle of large firms and in several cases they evolved together. As a consequence, in the South a few large (state-owned and private) companies had a significant political influence whereas the SMEs were absolutely marginal to the political and economic decision-making. In the Centre-North, the situation was very different. SMEs had a strong political influence because they had adopted an organisational structure that also facilitated their coordination in terms of political representation, namely, the district.

The deep differences between these two industrialisation models clearly emerged in the 1970s. In those years, drastic changes in the dynamics of wages and in the prices of raw materials and energy became common. These shocks were absorbed differently by the two models. The South was the most adversely affected given the inability of large firms to react quickly to these shocks. The Centre-North was able to adapt better to the new macroeconomic scenario, thanks to the flexibility of the SME system. In these circumstances, the government started to use competitive devaluation as an instrument of IP. This measure marked a deep change in IP perspective with regard to the activism of the 1960s (when IP was intended as planning, in the broad sense) and was particularly favourable to the SMEs in the Centre-North rather than to the weak and sparse SMEs in the South.

The large regional disparities did not disappear in the 1980s, indeed, if anything they increased. While income and industrial activity increased in some areas of the South, other areas suffered from widespread poverty and underdevelopment. It also became clear that the industrialisation of the South would have been extremely difficult and possibly would never take place (D'Antonio 1993). The situation was very different in the other parts of the country. In that decade, the Centre-North experienced high growth rates and in the Eastern regions, primarily along the Adriatic coast, there was a significant increase in manufacturing production. Again, most of this positive performance was due to the activity of the numerous SMEs established in those regions. This positive dynamic continued until the mid-1990s. Then, as we will see in Section 4, things started to change.

To understand the evolution of the Italian industrial structure, it is important to also look at the political and institutional part of the story. From the 1950s to the end of the 1970s, the development strategy and the IP were decided by the central government. At the time, IP was considered part of planning policy and its purpose was to allocate production and to direct domestic demand. In fact, decisions concerning IP were taken by two different ministries that were often in conflict: the Ministry of Industry, established in 1948, and the Ministry of State Holdings, established in 1956 (Silva 2008). The creation of these two ministries actually institutionalised the private/public-sector dualism that had characterised the Italian economy since the end of World War II (Prodi and Di Giovanni 1993). In those decades, IP was no different from those in other European countries in terms of objectives, but it did differ in terms of efficiency. In general, IP was marked by low efficiency and red tape, and was often subject to the influence of lobbies. In the 1970s, differences between the characteristics of the Italian IP and those adopted by other European countries started to emerge. While other countries were using IP to encourage mergers and strategic alliances, to create large conglomerates able to compete in the oligopolistic European markets, the priorities of IP in Italy were still to bailout firms in crisis and enlarge the sphere of action of the public sector. Silva (2008) argues that if any role was played by IP in those years in relation to industrial development in Italy, it was a negative one. In his view, IP has often been used to protect large firms that instead would have needed more competition. Although it reduced the costs of the structural adjustment in that period, this strategy caused a slow, inevitable decline of very important pieces of industry.[3] Prodi and De Giovanni (1993) argue that in fact IP seemed to be designed to serve political objectives rather than foster structural change. Another important trait of the Italian industrial development process in those years was the use of SOEs as an instrument to reduce unemployment and regional inequalities (and to increase political support for the ruling party) (Leon 1993; Gros-Pietro 1993).[4] This schizophrenic and ineffective approach to IP continued in the 1980s, rendering Italy unable to exploit the trade and technological opportunities that were emerging at the world level. As a consequence, at the beginning of the 2000s, the Italian industrial structure was characterised by: a) an international trade specialisation in products intensive in low-skill labour; b) a large presence of SMEs; c) few large firms able to compete at the world level; d) few new large firms being established. These elements motivate a serious concern about the competitiveness and the future prospects of the industrial sector in Italy.

IP in Italy has gone through several changes since the beginning of the 1990s. Two are particularly important. First, the country's autonomy in the design of IP has been severely limited by the strict guidelines issued by the EC. Second, it has changed where decisions on the design and implementation of IP are taken. Nowadays, most of the decisions on IP are taken by local governments (the Regions), especially regarding the measures aimed at supporting SMEs. This decentralisation of IP management implies that the effectiveness of the different measures and programmes now *also* (but not only) depends on the efficiency of the individual regions. A paradoxical consequence of this change is that pinpointing responsibility for each specific policy is now, in many cases, less clear than in the past, making policy evaluation even more difficult. Furthermore, the magnitude and target of government intervention has significantly changed in the last decade. Figure 12.1 reports government disbursements for IP in Italy for the period 1999–2011. As can be seen from the graph, between 2002 and 2011 the total amount of government disbursements has decreased by almost 70 percent. It is interesting to note that, in the period under consideration, there was a drastic reduction in the amount of non-repayable disbursements under state aid. For a long time these formed the majority of government measures, especially with respect to firms in the Mezzogiorno. Nowadays this measure represents only 27.5 percent of the total (compared with 59 percent in 2005) and 38.7 percent of the total resources for the Mezzogiorno (the figure was 80 percent in 2005). It is also interesting to look at the changes in the objectives pursued by state aid. As shown in Figure 12.2, the general support for the accumulation of capital (General) has decreased significantly, halving in size. The main objectives have become support for R&D (which increases from 14 percent to 43 percent) and for internationalisation activities (from 3 percent to 12 percent). As we have said, another important change in the IP concerns the increasing importance of the Regions in terms of the amount of resources provided, now standing at 32 percent of the total. Still, there are large differences across Regions, depending on a number of elements, among which the specialisation pattern of the region, the type of measures implemented, the ability of the Regions to access European Funds, and so on. In

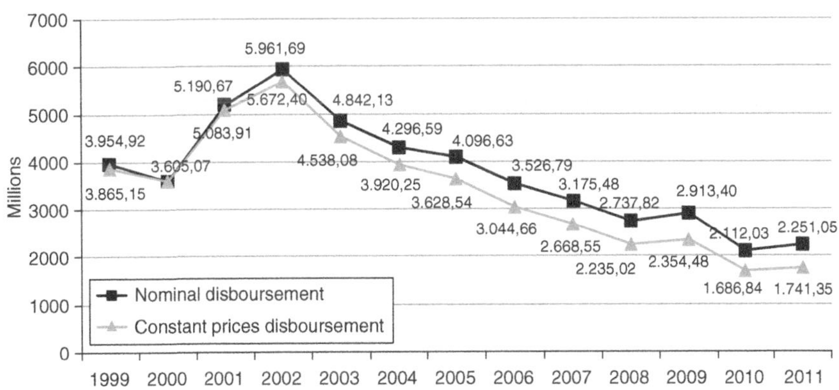

Figure 12.1 The evolution of government disbursements for industrial policy in Italy (millions of euro), industry and services to production, 1999–2011.

Source: Brancati and Maresca (2013) using data from the MET Dataset.

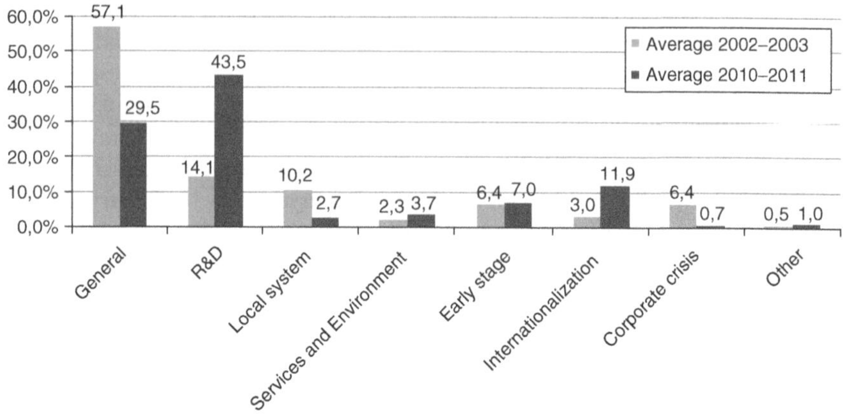

Figure 12.2 Distribution of government disbursements by objective, average 2002–2003 and 2010–2011, percentages.

Source: Brancati and Maresca (2013) using data from the MET Dataset.

fact, a divide between the North and the South regions again emerges: in the former, most of the intervention takes the form of measures to support private R&D and exports, while in the latter most of the measures are directed at supporting capital accumulation (General). The differences across regions in terms of product specialisation also explain the regional differences in terms of state aid objectives.[5]

The general framework for IP in Italy is currently provided by Industria 2015. The program was launched by Minister of Industry Pierluigi Bersani during the second Prodi government in 2006. The main objective of the programme was to bring back industrial development as one of the government's priorities. The IP strategy designed in the programme is based on two main pillars. The first is deregulation in the service sector (e.g., insurance companies, banks, distribution, etc.). The objective is to promote more competition in those sectors in order to stimulate productivity improvement in the overall economy. On the whole, the effect of this action has been modest, largely because those measures faced strenuous opposition from the lobbies of the to-be liberalised sectors. The second pillar is a national innovation policy strategy. The government's goal was to improve the coordination of the different regional innovation policies and to create five Industrial Innovation Projects (Energy Efficiency, Sustainable Mobility, New Life Technologies, New technologies for the "Made in Italy," Innovative Technologies for Cultural Goods). While the Prodi government did not last long enough to see the results of this strategy (and thus a detailed evaluation is not possible), there is a general consensus that the first signs were positive. The implementation of programme is now ongoing and has also been confirmed as a priority by the current government. However, progress in the actual disbursement of funds appears to be quite slow.

A particularly important domain for IP is that of innovation, because of its potential impact on the process of economic change and its role as a source of positive externalities. It is exactly for these reasons that the EC in fact allows some room for government intervention to help domestic firms when this takes the form of support for their innovation effort. According to the Innovation Union Scoreboard 2010, Italy is below the European average in terms of innovation, in particular concerning private R&D investment (0.65 percent of GDP) (EU 2012). The share of high-tech exports is also lower than the European average, a fact in line with the peculiar product specialisation of the Italian industry as we discussed in the previous section. The Italian regional divide is even more evident when it comes to innovation activities: for instance, the level of R&D expenditure in the South is one third lower than that in the Centre-North. Recently, some attempts have been made to improve the effectiveness of innovation policies in Italy.[6] Some new instruments are now available to support private firms' research projects and attempts have been made to ease the access to financing in the field of industrial research, and to facilitate contacts between private firms and the Ministry for Education, University and Research. In April 2011, the National Research Programme (NRP) 2011–2013 was presented after a long process of consultation with all the stakeholders.[7] Interestingly, the NRP defines the major objectives for the Italian research system as increasing R&D expenditure, improving competitiveness in key technological areas, encouraging cooperation between companies and public research institutions, improving analysis and evaluation of research programmes and bodies. One of the main goals of the NRP is to rationalise and reinforce a number of already-existing measures and projects, such as the Technology Districts, the National Technology Platforms and the National Excellence Poles. Furthermore, 14 priority projects (*Progetti bandiera*) have been identified, most notably in relation to key enabling technologies, energy and space (EU 2012).

Another strategic domain of intervention for IP is SMEs. The measures promoting SMEs emanate from both the Regions and the central government, and in fact represent a significant share of the total resources of state aid. One of the main objectives of the measures to support SMEs is actually to foster their dimensional growth since firm size is strongly correlated with export-orientation and innovation. The financial structure of Italian SMEs, which are relatively less capitalised than those in other countries, is an important factor limiting dimensional growth. This situation is made even more complicated by the fact that the Italian venture capital and private equity markets remain relatively underdeveloped, which makes Italian SMEs more reliant on short-term borrowing than those in other EU countries. To address these problems, in 2010 the Italian government created the Italian Investment Fund (*Fondo Italiano d'Investimento)* to provide risk capital to SMEs. Another strategy adopted by the government to overcome the problems related to the small size of firms has been to favour cooperation between firms. This is the aim of the "network contract" (*Contratto di Rete*) which encourages firms to collaborate on specific projects, such as R&D and internationalisation activities. While these measures are likely to be steps in the right direction, the firms' size anomaly which characterizes the Italian economy needs a more comprehensive intervention.[8]

4. A new economic context for IP: the European Union, the WTO, and the new world

The future evolution of IP in Italy will depend not only on the domestic political and economic equilibrium but also on the behaviour of a number of other actors, including the European Commission (EC), the WTO and the new emerging economies.

The EC approach to IP has changed drastically in the last three decades. Until the 1970s, the main objective of IP in Europe was to save industries in decline, and national champions were strongly supported by state intervention, often through public ownership. Starting from the 1980s, the globalisation process forced European countries to devise a new approach to IP, which found its final form in the Bangemann Report (EC 1990), then included in the Maastricht Treaty (Labory 2006). Since then, the EC has adopted an approach favouring government intervention through the use of (only) horizontal policies. The Maastricht Treaty put the IP of the member states under much stricter control, leading to a reduction in the type and extent of measures and the type of interventions that could be adopted. In particular, the creation of the Common Market in 1993 formally marked the end of the use of traditional IP tools, such as protectionist trade policy and direct transfers and subsidies for domestic firms. The strong effort made by the EC to reduce the possibility for governments to support domestic firms has been most visible in the push to reduce state aid and liberalise government procurement (Silva 2008). In line with this strategy, in the 1990s the EC forced Italy to significantly reduce the amount of direct disbursements to domestic firms (Ninni 2007). It is interesting to note that the market-oriented approach to IP of the EC in the last decade is also contained in the rules that regulate the WTO. For instance, the Agreement on Subsidies and Countervailing Measures strictly forbids the use of any specific subsides (see Belloc and Di Maio 2012). Moreover, since 1996 the Government Procurement Agreement (GPA) imposes the non-discrimination of foreign firms competing with domestic ones for any government procurement contract. Thus, two of the most traditional trade policy measures that had been most widely used to sustain economic growth are now banned by the WTO, exactly as they are banned by the EC.

While the EC's approach to IP in the last decades has been quite restrictive, there are now several signs indicating that this attitude is in fact changing.

This can be seen first of all in the larger room for decision left by the EC to individual member states with respect to IP design. While the emphasis of the EC remains on favouring competition, direct government support to improve firms' competitiveness—especially in new sectors—is no longer excluded *a priori*. In fact, in recent years, most of the European countries have increased expenditure for IP (Ninni 2007). Rota (2013) notes that the most recent economic events—from faster globalisation to the slowing down of economic growth in advanced countries and the difficulties of the world's financial system—have sharply refocused the attention on sector-based issues and on the possibility of a major role for national states in the promotion of development and economic growth.

The need for a deep rethinking of IP also derives from the fact that the world economic context has been continuously evolving and is now quite different from what it was some decades ago. The two most relevant differences are: the rules of world trade, and the international division of labour. Regarding the first, it is sufficient to note that the numerous multilateral, bilateral, and regional trade agreements have significantly curtailed the room available for using trade policy as an instrument to promote industrial development. The second important change relates to the characteristics of the global economic environment and in particular the new international division of labour. The level of competition in global markets has increased enormously, which is also due to the emergence of new world-level competitors: large developing countries such as China, India, and Brazil are now leaders in labour-intensive manufacturing. As we have seen, Italy is suffering much more from this new situation than other developed countries due to its trade specialisation anomaly. This new competitive environment requires the IP to embrace a different set of instruments and measures from the ones used in the past.

5. Some concluding remarks

The last few years have been characterised by a profound world economic crisis that had a particularly strong impact on the Southern European countries. Most governments have responded to the crisis by focusing on reducing the public debt and implementing the so-called 'structural reforms'—typically changes in the regulation of labour and product markets which aim at increasing the flexibility and cost-competitiveness of the economy. An alternative view on the strategy that should be implemented to react to the crisis suggests instead that what is needed is structural change and technological upgrading. In this case then, the view is that that finding a sustainable path out of the present crisis requires addressing the challenges of productivity growth and competitiveness in the long run.

Italy is one of the countries that have been most affected by the recent economic recession. In fact, the crisis added to the country's already difficult economic situation. In the last two decades, the performance of the

Italian economy has been quite poor as measured by almost all economic indicators. While Italy still has a diversified and in some instances globally competitive industrial base, its overall growth potential is now becoming a source of concern. The negative effects of the two anomalies of the Italian economy (i.e., the trade specialisation anomaly and the firms' size distribution anomaly) on the future economic perspective of the country are becoming increasingly evident. Moreover, the economy suffers from a large and persistent (if not growing) North-South economic divergence and by the co-existence of very different (and sometime conflicting) regional economic models.

Given the historical and current structural difficulties of the Italian economy, it appears evident that the strategy and type of measures that the government—following other European governments—has recently adopted to overcome the crisis are not enough to restart a process of inclusive growth. Our analysis suggests that what it is needed instead is a set of measures that—taking into consideration the specificities of the Italian economy—would favour structural change and technological upgrading, which would allow the country to respond to future economic shocks and downturns.

We have argued that, in this context, IP has to play a central role. In fact, we believe that a large part of the difficulties of the Italian economy in the face of the current crisis is related to the characteristics and weakness of its IP. There is no doubt that a better IP alone would not prevent the crisis from impacting the economy if the crisis originates in the macroeconomic architecture of the Eurozone—as is convincingly argued by Boyer (this volume). But this would be asking too much to an IP: even the best designed IP would not be able to solve all the problems that emerged with the crisis, simply because not all the important domains of intervention that should be considered are part of IP (such as exchange rate policy, financial regulation, etc.). Nonetheless, whatever the origin of the crisis, a radically different and more effective IP would have allowed the Italian economy to have a more effective reaction. Moreover, we argue that by fostering structural change IP will help to reduce the risk of future crises by creating the conditions for the country to adapt more quickly to the changing environment.

To better understand to what extent IP could play a role in promoting growth in Italy, in this chapter we have described the historical evolution of IP in Italy and its current characteristics, so as to identify weakness and potentialities. Our analysis has shown that historically, IP in Italy has been marked by low efficiency and red tape, and has often been often captured by political objectives. Our analysis has also shown that it is not possible to underestimate its current weaknesses: most of the measures that are currently part of IP appear to be uncoordinated and fragmented. At the same time, potentially effective measures turn out to be only partly implemented or are delayed by lack of resources and complex decision-making procedures and practices.

Why then, given the historical negative experience and the shrinking space for implementing IP, do we argue that Italy needs an IP (and probably more today than ever)? There are two main reasons for this. First, the elimination of the two anomalies of the Italian economy requires a structural change that only an active IP can bring about. For instance, the reduction of the trade specialisation anomaly could be achieved by promoting investment in high-tech and high-skill intensive sectors. The measures needed to achieve this are naturally within the domain of IP. At the same time, the mitigation of the firms' size distribution anomaly requires measures that encourage firms to grow and that stimulate active cooperation between firms. Here, too, the required measures are part of IP as we have defined it. Second, almost every other country in the world uses IP to support their domestic firms, especially in innovation activities. Italy cannot do less than its competitors: Italy should provide its firms with all the instruments needed to enable them to start from a situation that is no worse than that of their competitors, even if this intervention turns out to be more difficult and possibly more costly than in other countries because of the two anomalies of the Italian economy (prevalence of SMEs specialised in low-skilled products).

While we have argued in favour of IP, we have also stressed that to be effective, IP has to be significantly different from what it was in the past. The world has changed; there are new rules, new actors and new challenges ahead. First of all, this means that IP must comply with the constraints emanating from the WTO agreements. One important implication of this is that it is no longer possible to adopt a protectionist approach to trade policy. In fact, the WTO regulations now allow trade policy interventions only in the form of selective subsidies, to promote: (i) domestic R&D; (ii) regional development; (iii) environmentally friendly activities. At the same time, the EC also severely restricts governments' possibility to support strategic sectors (with the important exclusion of support for firms' innovation and research activities). In general, there is still some room for direct measures to support structural change and the industrialisation process, but governments have to design their IP to explicitly take the new constraints into account.

As for the characteristics essential to an effective IP for Italy, we have argued that first of all it should be designed with the two anomalies that characterise the Italian economy in mind: the trade specialisation anomaly, and the firms' size distribution anomaly. Both these anomalies have important implications in terms of which measures can realistically be implemented and which are the most effective strategies for doing so. At the same time, Italy's IP has to be designed to take into account the various requirements of firms in the different regions. It follows that, in addition to the sectoral and technological dimensions, the regional dimension should be taken into account as well, in the design of the policies for sustaining economic growth. Finally, IP should be tailored to the new and different needs of firms. Italian firms are now definitely exposed to more competition than in the past and each firm is facing a different type of threat, depending on its specific characteristics. The design of the new IP therefore needs to take into full account firms' heterogeneity. This implies that the correct measures to be part of the IP may only be identified through a continuous dialogue between the private sector and the government.

The aim of the analysis presented in this chapter was not to provide conclusive solutions to the numerous problems affecting the Italian economy, but to try to redirect the discourse and to ask the right questions, such as: What are the causes of the current difficult situation? Should achieving the budget balance equilibrium be the main objective of the government? How to restart a process of structural change and economic growth? Which could be the role of IP in this process? What characteristics should IP have to be effective, given the actual conditions of the Italian economy? While we have only provided preliminary answers to all these questions, we believe that the exercise of trying to change the perspective with respect to the dominant view is useful, especially when the situation is very complicated. In fact, asking the right questions is the first step to finding the right solution to any problem. We hope this chapter makes a useful contribution to this enormous but urgent challenge.

Notes

1 Specifically, the PRODY index is, for each traded sector (product), the weighted average of the per capita incomes of the countries that are exporting in that particular sector (product). Sectors are therefore ranked in terms of their productivity/income content, hence the name of the index (Hausmann et al. 2007).

2 For a detailed description of the content and characteristics of IP in Italy between 1950s and 1990s, see Spadavecchia (2007).

3 Silva (2008) notes that possible causes for this are wrong financial and investment decisions and a conflicting approach to industrial relations by the top management of large corporations (e.g., Edison, Montecatini, Olivetti, FIAT, IRI). However, these managers could not be removed because they controlled the financial markets and because of the ownership structure of these companies (family or state control).

4 On the complex theme of public and private-sector interaction in each phase of Italian industrial development, see Coltorti (1993).

5 It is obvious that regions (for instance, Calabria and Sardinia) in which the specialisation pattern is characterised by low-skill intensity are misaligned with respect to the full set of interventions that are directed at supporting R&D. For a detailed analysis of the regional dimension of IP, see Brancati and Maresca (2013).

6 The literature on the effects of the innovation policies in Italy in recent decades is quite limited. The few existing studies find the effect of public policies on supporting innovation is weak (Evangelista 2007; Merito et al. (2010).

7 The thematic working groups covered a vast range of topics including: environment, health, life sciences, energy, agriculture, nano-sciences and new materials, 'Made in Italy', ICT, aeronautics and space, sustainable mobility and transport, cultural goods, construction.

8 Albeit few in number, there are also successful examples of measures to support SME activities through effective IP. One of these is the case of the Emilia-Romagna region, discussed in Bianchi and Labory (2011).

13 Assessment and challenges of industrial policies in Portugal

Is there a way out of the "stuck in the middle" trap?

Ricardo Paes Mamede, Manuel Mira Godinho and Vítor Corado Simões

This chapter provides an assessment of the industrial policies[1] that have been adopted in Portugal since joining the European Economic Community (EEC) in 1986. The aim is to understand what has been achieved and what are the existing shortfalls and their implications in terms of future challenges. The evidence shows that although industrial policies provided a wide array of measures addressing Portugal's structural weaknesses, they have not been sufficient to push the country out of what we call the 'stuck in the middle' trap into which it has fallen.

The next section discusses the relation between the crisis that led to Portugal's bailout by international institutions in 2011 and the structural weaknesses that have hindered the Portuguese economy's performance over recent decades. Section 2 outlines such weaknesses in order to identify the challenges faced by industrial policies in Portugal. Sections 3 and 4 provide an overview and assessment of the industrial policies that have been adopted. Section 5 concludes with a perspective on how industrial policy should change to be up to the challenges the country is now facing.

1. The 'stuck-in-the-middle trap': how the IMF-ECB-EC bailout missed the target

Like most developed countries, the Portuguese economy was severely hit by the international crisis of 2008–2009, with GDP at constant prices dropping 2.9 percent in 2009 and the unemployment rate increasing by 2.1 percentage points (p.p.) in the same year, up to 10.6 percent. As a combined result of the decrease in tax revenues, the rise in social transfers and, to a lesser extent, the countercyclical measures adopted by the government, gross public debt increased by 12 p.p., reaching 84 percent of the GDP in that year.

The performance of the Portuguese economy in the immediate aftermath of the Great Recession, as described above, was not particularly distinctive in the European context. However, the country was soon to be caught in the so-called 'sovereign debt crisis', together with other countries of the EU periphery. From the beginning of 2010, the interest rates demanded by international private investors on Portuguese sovereign debt started to decouple from the rates on German Federal bonds, ultimately reaching unsustainable levels and leading to the need to resort to international financial assistance in May 2011.

The growing reluctance of international investors to buy Portuguese debt has to be understood in light of the structural weaknesses that were already apparent prior to 2008–2009. In fact, between 2000 and 2008, Portugal experienced the second lowest GDP growth rate in the EU (averaging 1 percent per year, in volume), slightly above Italy and half of the EU average. Even more significantly, the country's external indebtedness, measured by its Net International Investment Position, had been growing continuously since the mid-1990s, reaching 87 percent of the GDP in 2007, only comparable to that of Greece (111 percent) and Spain (79 percent), and well above the euro area average (17 percent). In other words, like other countries in the EU periphery, the Portuguese economy was already rather vulnerable when the crisis hit in late 2008, raising doubts among international creditors regarding the capacity to fulfill its future obligations.

The adjustment programme agreed between the Portuguese government and the troika composed of the International Monetary Fund (IMF), the European Central Bank (ECB) and the European Commission (EC), as a condition to access official financial assistance, included measures aimed at curtailing public expenditures and at increasing revenues in the mid-term, producing a strong recessionary impact in the country. Real GDP in 2013 was down to its 2000 level and the unemployment rate (which was 4.5 percent in 2000) reached a historical high of 16.3 percent.

Besides the measures directly targeted at improving public finances in the mid-term, the adjustment programme included a number of so-called "structural reforms" intended to improve the performance of labour and product markets. The programme assumed that inefficiencies in those markets, together with inadequate budgetary practices, were largely responsible for the dismal performance of the Portuguese economy. In particular, excessive regulation in labour relations and weak regulation in some industries (namely, utilities) were considered to have created negative incentives for productive investment. Accordingly, such 'structural reforms' were expected to unleash the forces of growth in the mid-term.

While improvements in the functioning of labour and product markets may play a relevant role, Portugal's competitiveness problems have deeper roots. As we will discuss in the next section, the erosion of the country's external accounts during the past two decades results from the combination of a fragile specialisation profile, societal obstacles to structural change, a macroeconomic framework which proved to be unsuitable with regard to the country's main challenges, and some unfavourable international developments.

Simply put, the Portuguese economy was 'stuck in the middle': while insufficiently developed to compete in more sophisticated markets, the price of its products in international markets proved to be too high to compete with those from the emerging economies. The strategy followed in the context of the adjustment programme, focusing on austerity-induced internal devaluation of prices and wages, privatisation, and liberalisation of labour and product markets, is hardly sufficient—or even the most suitable—to address some of the most pressing structural weakness of the Portuguese economy and to take Portugal out of such a 'stuck in the middle' trap.

The IMF-ECB-EC adjustment programme enforced in 2011 tackled Portugal's competitiveness problems by endorsing internal devaluation and the liberalisation of labour and product markets. By shrinking the size of the domestic market, the programme intends to reduce the share of non-tradable activities, while the reduction in wages and in the costs of non-tradable goods and services is expected to improve the competitiveness of tradable products. However, even if successful in reducing Portugal's external imbalances in the short/medium term,[2] such a strategy can hardly be appropriate in providing a sustainable basis for development of the Portuguese economy in the longer run.

2. The structural challenges of the Portuguese economy

The Portuguese economy and society present two major, interrelated structural weaknesses which, in spite of some improvements in recent decades, have persisted to the present: the low qualification of the working population and the vulnerable profile of economic specialisation.

When Portugal joined the EEC in 1986, the proportion of working age adults who had completed secondary education was below 20 percent, while the European average was close to 60 percent. Investments in education and training have increased in recent decades, contributing to substantial improvements. However, such a significant gap could hardly be reversed in a short period, as growth in the overall educational levels essentially depends on generational renewal. Thus, despite the policy initiatives launched, it has not been possible to eliminate the backlog in education levels in Portugal: in 2012, 39 percent of the working population had completed secondary school, a figure which almost doubles the 1992 value (20 percent), but which is still far from the EU average (71 percent).

The low educational levels have significant negative consequences, in terms of productivity as well as social progress. In particular, the educational gap is both a cause and a consequence of the second domain of structural weaknesses mentioned above—the specialisation profile of the Portuguese economy.

The Portuguese economic fabric is historically characterised by a large proportion of low value added activities, low knowledge intensity, and low technological intensity (what we will call henceforth the 'three lows' specialisation). The country's process of industrialisation had largely been driven since the 1960s by successive waves of foreign direct investment (FDI), which were based on that specialisation profile. In the late 1980s, Portugal's

EEC membership and the prospect of participation in the European Single Market made the prevailing low wage levels even more attractive to international investors, giving rise to a new wave of FDI. However, the rapid pace of globalisation of production—stemming from advances in ICT and trade liberalisation—soon began to put increasing competitive pressure on domestic products based on low labour costs.

Together with these changes, Portugal started to prepare its participation in the European Economic and Monetary Union. 'Nominal convergence' with the EU average—and, in particular, exchange rate stability—became a top priority of macroeconomic policy, putting an end to the prevailing 'crawling-peg' exchange rate regime, which had been recurrently used in the past to compensate for losses in competitiveness. In practice, this translated into a significant real exchange rate appreciation,[3] further hindering the competitiveness of traditional sectors in Portugal.

The increasing difficulty in relying on lower costs to improve competitiveness could have stimulated a shift towards higher value-added activities. However, this path to structural change faced two main obstacles. First, the skills (including managerial skills) required for the rapid development of the most knowledge-intensive sectors and for the upgrading of traditional industries were scarce, thus limiting the expansion of new, more sophisticated activities. Second, the macroeconomic environment that prevailed during most of the 1990s—marked by the deregulation of financial activities, the growth of the domestic market, the privatisation of companies in regulated industries, in addition to the appreciation of the real exchange rate – created incentives for the expansion of non-tradable activities, to the detriment of (traditional or otherwise) tradable sectors.[4] During this period, investment was largely geared towards financial services, transportation, energy distribution, telecoms, construction, and retail trade. Concurrently, the sharp drop in real interest rates and the liberalisation of capital movements within the EU fostered the flows of financial capital from abroad, deepening the indebtedness of firms, households, and the State.

Thus, overspecialisation in the 'three lows' activities remained unchanged until the euro came into force, in 1999. In the subsequent period, the dominant traditional industries would have to face China's entry into the WTO, EU enlargement to the east, and the strong appreciation of the euro against the dollar between 2002 and 2008. The latter development further eroded the price competitiveness of domestic exports, while the first two events increased the vulnerability of Portuguese industry to foreign competition, due to substantial overlap in industry structures (illustrated in Figure 13.1, for the case of China). These developments contributed to Portugal's declining attractiveness for FDI. They also had a disproportionate impact on the traditional sectors of Portuguese industry—notably textiles, clothing, and footwear[5]—whose weight in manufacturing exports fell from 40 percent in 1986, to 28 percent in 1999, and to 16 percent in 2006.

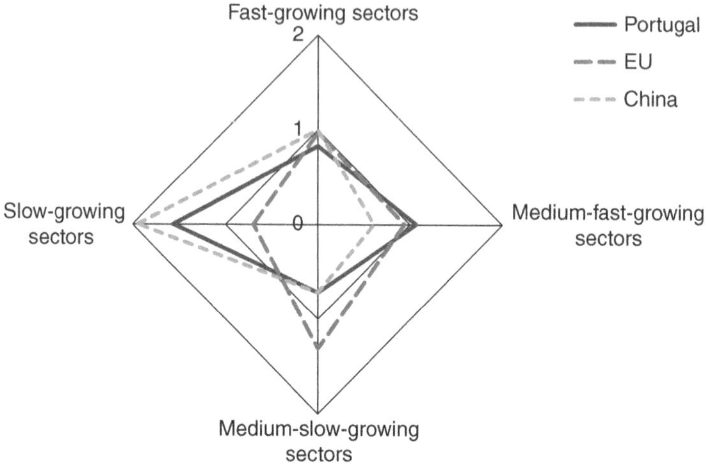

Figure 13.1 Revealed comparative advantages by groups of growth intensity in world exports of goods, 2005–2009.

Source of data: EC (2011).

This decline was partially offset by an increase in the exports of services, as well as of some commodities (which were in high demand from emerging economies in the years that preceded the international crisis). However, this was insufficient to curb the Portuguese trade deficit from its chronic high levels, averaging –8.8 percent of the GDP between 2000 and 2007. Incapable of generating enough revenue through exports to compensate for the repayment of the external debt accumulated since the 1990s, Portugal experienced a fast deterioration of its current account deficit, which rose from an average of 5.6 percent of the GDP in 1986–1999 to 9.5 percent in 2000–2007.

In sum, in the aftermath of the Great Recession, the Portuguese economy was characterised not only by weak public finances, but—more importantly—by high external indebtedness and evident competitiveness problems, on top of its weak economic structure. The discussion above has shown that such structural weaknesses are twofold. On the one hand, the 'three-lows' specialisation, challenged by competitive pressures from emerging economies, has prevented the domestic economy from reverting its chronically high trade deficit. On the other hand, the share of tradable activities in the economy was substantially reduced, further hampering the capacity to generate revenues through international trade. These problems were compounded by the drying up of inward FDI: since the turn of the century, Portugal has been unable to attract a single large, structural change-inducing, foreign investment project.[6]

As Figure 13.2 shows, the substantial drop in the exports of traditional products during the 2000s has not translated into the expansion of more

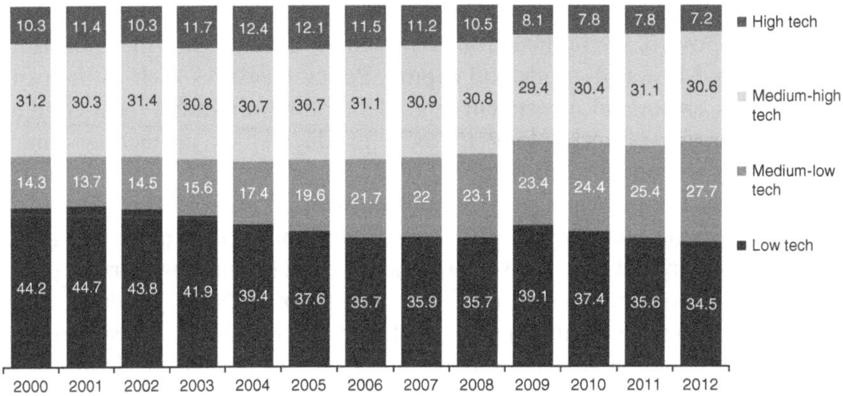

Figure 13.2 Exports of goods by technology intensity group (%).

Source: GEE (2013).

sophisticated products. In the post-2008 period, there was even a small contraction in the share of high-tech and medium–high-tech products in the exports of goods (from 41.3 percent to 37.8 percent), showing that the crisis has hit further the production of more technology-intensive goods. This is all the more worrisome, as this recent evolution has gone in the opposite direction of what has happened in the EU since 2009 (see Eurostat 2013). These trends will ultimately be aggravated by the fact that the adjustment programme is running counter structural change, as it strengthens reliance on cost-based approaches instead of promoting the emergence of more sophisticated, knowledge-intensive activities.

In contrast to this path, Portugal will need to upgrade its productive structure if it is to avoid falling into a debt-trap of prolonged dismal growth and high unemployment. While some ingredients of the adjustment programme in place since 2011 may contribute to such a goal—namely, by increasing the attractiveness of the Portuguese economy for FDI—the policy mix should not dismiss measures that specifically target the structural change of the productive fabric. That is, industrial policy has to be part of the country's development strategy. In fact, to a large extent, this has already been the case in recent decades, as we discuss in the following section.

3. Industrial policies in Portugal in recent decades

It is now widely accepted that public support to the emergence and expansion of the most dynamic economic sectors was a key factor in the success of many of the richest countries (e.g., Chang 2006), as well as of those instances of successful industrialisation in recent decades (e.g., Wade 2003). However, the rules and institutions governing international economic relations today are different than they were in the past, changing the space of possibilities for public action (Rodrik 2007, 2011).

In fact, international institutions such as the WTO and the EU have seen their powers strengthened in fixing and enforcing the rules governing international flows of goods and capital. Policy measures such as imposing constraints on foreign investment (e.g., demanding minimum local contents or the transfer of technology to local producers) or protecting domestic producers from foreign competition are now limited by the WTO. The EU, evoking the principle of 'free and undistorted competition' within the European Single Market, requires even stricter limits on the pursuit of policy instruments targeting specific sectors (such as State-owned enterprises, public procurement, or various forms of State aid to businesses). In short, many of the instruments of public policy deployed when today's richest countries developed are now significantly reduced in scope by international institutions.

Besides these exogenous restrictions, domestic policy options have often pointed in the wrong direction. At times, the economic policy followed in Portugal (as in other members of the euro area) has been a kind of 'reverted industrial policy,' fostering the structural change of the economy towards less, and not more, promising activities. As outlined in Section 3, during the 1990s the Portuguese government gave top priority to fulfilling the conditions for participating in the euro, which was reflected in a real exchange rate appreciation and a substantial drop in real interest rates. Together with the wide-scope privatisation programme and the deregulation of financial activities, this fostered the expansion of the non-tradable goods sector, which absorbed a large share of the investment resources, and attracted most of the (scarce) highly skilled workers in the Portuguese economy. As discussed before, this has contributed to hindering both the development of the tradable goods sector and the attraction of FDI.

Notwithstanding the aforementioned restrictions and the priority attached to 'nominal convergence' with the EU in the 1990s, industrial policies did have a place in the Portuguese policy mix in recent decades. In particular, the availability of the EU's Cohesion Policy funds since the late 1980s has fostered the development of several programmes and support mechanisms which aimed at promoting the upgrading of the productive fabric and improving the productivity of the Portuguese industry. Besides education and training (already mentioned in Section 2), EU structural funds were drawn to the science and technology system, as well as to the business sector's innovation and internationalisation.

The successive Community Support Framework programmes have contributed decisively to the development of 'technology transfer' centres in specific industries, to the promotion of interface organisations and infrastructures in the science and technology system (institutes for new technologies, research infrastructures, science parks, incubators, etc.), and to the expansion of higher education. The emphasis on R&D activities grew further since the late 1990s, with the encouragement of R&D units in business firms (see Box 13.1) and cooperative R&D projects involving different types of institutional players, as well as the further development of the research system.

Box 13.1 The NITEC initiative[7]

The NITEC initiative (NITEC stands for Research and Technological Development Units in Companies) was launched in 2003. Its main objectives were the following: (i) supporting, through grants, the setting up of in-house R&D competencies in Portuguese companies, as well as encouraging companies to enhance such competencies; (2) fostering company efforts aimed at improving design and process capabilities and the assimilation of foreign technological knowledge; and (3) encouraging the development of technologically innovative products and solutions. The main purpose was to enhance companies' absorptive capacity (Cohen and Levinthal 1990) through the creation (or 'formalization') of small R&D groups in firms which had already shown a proclivity to engage in R&D activities or which were already undertaking R&D activities but lacked a formal R&D unit. In the wake of the Barcelona objectives adopted by the EU, it was felt that the low levels of R&D expenditures as well as the weak in-house capabilities inhibited Portuguese firms from providing appropriate responses to the competitive challenges stemming from globalisation. An additional concern was the weakness of the linkages among the various players in the innovation system. Companies' low in-house R&D capabilities constrained the development of co-operation with universities and other scientific and technological organisations. In its initial design, the initiative was in force until 2006.

In 2007, the initiative was revised and re-launched, under the new Competitiveness Factors Operational Programme of the 2007–2013 National Strategic Reference Framework. In the new policy context, the former NITEC initiative gave rise to two sub-programmes: one similar to the 'former' NITEC, addressed to SMEs without specific R&D units; and another (called CITEC: Centres for Research and Technological Development), focused on companies which already carried out 'continuous and [organizationally] structured' R&D activities. Thus, the CITEC sub-programme was envisaged as an instrument for supporting companies to go a step further, assuming some kind of a 'ladder' in the process of developing in-house R&D capabilities. CITECs should have, until the end of the project, a minimum of five full time people assigned to R&D activities, including at least one PhD holder, an R&D to sales ratio above EU average in the industry concerned, and an operational R&D and innovation management system, certified according to the Portuguese standard in that regard.

In recent years, Portugal has put in place virtually all the usual ingredients of an innovation policy mix, including: tax benefits for R&D; grants and soft loans for business R&D investment; support for R&D and innovation infrastructures; R&D and innovation vouchers; incentives for knowledge-based entrepreneurs; support for TTOs in universities; publically financed risk capital funds; public procurement of innovative projects; training and advisory services for SMEs; competitive grants for research and advanced training; and support for clusters and innovation networks.

Formally, most of these policy instruments have a horizontal nature. In practice, however, support is not evenly distributed across industries. For example, Mamede and Feio (2012) analyse the industry distribution of public support granted to firms through tax benefits for large investments, tax benefits for R&D, and direct support to firms (including both soft loans and grants). They conclude that such policy instruments tend to disproportionally favour a limited number of non-traditional industries—namely, IT services, chemicals and pharmaceuticals, automotive industry and components, telecommunications, and electronic products—suggesting the existence of a proactive support of structural change by public authorities, towards more technology-intensive industries.

In many instances, industrial policy instruments were used to foster the presence of foreign direct investments, with the aim of improving the sophistication of the industrial fabric, both directly and indirectly, namely through domestic sourcing efforts. (See Box 13.2 on the automotive sector).

Box 13.2 The development of the Portuguese automotive cluster

The history of the automotive industry in Portugal is the result of an interaction process involving different players (the State, car assemblers, component manufacturers, and car importers) whose roles have changed over time. The most important players in the process have clearly been the first two: the government has adopted specific policies addressed to the industry; and automotive multinational enterprises (MNEs) which have responded to such policies, while contributing to shape them.

Drawing a timeline of the industry in Portugal since the 1960s, five main stages can be identified. The 1960s were marked by the so-called 'assembly law.' This defined the conditions for the import of automotive vehicles, making this conditional on the setting up of manufacturing facilities in Portugal (Guerra 1990). The underlying logic was import substitution (Simões 2003). The second phase stems from the 1972 agreement with the EEC. It was characterised by an 'import offsetting' policy: imports could only be increased to the extent that they were offset by exports of manufactured products. This change led, in 1980, to the first significant and integrated (though not fully) investment in the automotive sector in Portugal: the Renault project. This heralds a third phase, by and large covering the 1980s (Simões 2000). Although there is no agreement about the merits of the Renault project (Schmidt and Almeida 1987; Santos 1996; Féria 1999), there is little doubt that it entailed a key push towards the modernisation of the industry. As a result of the local value added commitments, Renault had to develop Portuguese component manufacturers, while trying to attract foreign ones. As one manager put it, 'they [Renault] supported us in learning and in enhancing our credibility' (Simões 2003: 220).

The fourth stage corresponds to the first two decades of the Auto-Europa (AE) plant. After a long process of negotiation, involving the consideration of

(*Continued*)

Box 13.2 The development of the Portuguese automotive cluster (*Continued*)

alternative locations in Europe, AE was established in Palmela, achieving full speed in 1995, with a capacity of 180,000 vehicles per year, initially focused on the manufacturing of a multi-purpose vehicle (MPV). The setting up of AE marks a new phase, in which three main players have interacted: the State (public authorities played a key role in negotiating the project and promoting alliances between Portuguese and foreign component manufacturers to enhance local value added); MNEs, initially Ford and Volkswagen (VW); and component manufacturers, Portuguese and foreign. AE is *prima facie* a plant: its main function is manufacturing, not research and development (R&D), purchasing, or marketing. This led to significantly different relationship patterns from Renault. Simões (2000, 2003) identified four patterns of relationships between the VW group and its component suppliers: (1) Inter-MNE supply, encompassing two interaction channels, that is, between headquarters and between subsidiaries in Portugal; (2) Direct dialogue from Portugal, in which Portuguese suppliers directly interact with VW's headquarters in R&D and other issues; (3) Wolfsburg dialogue, in which the Portuguese supplier locates product engineering and development units in Germany to facilitate interaction with VW's headquarters, and supply in Portugal; and (4) Intermediation by AE, in which AE plays a facilitating role (Vale 1999), namely through the concept of 'relevant part.' It should be underlined that the extent of the supply by Portuguese firms has been undermined by three main factors: the sheer size of orders (especially in the initial phase); the limited autonomy of AE; and the distrust of VW towards the product engineering and development capabilities of Portuguese suppliers (Veloso et al. 2000). The most successful Portuguese suppliers seem to have been those which followed pattern (3) above: having a presence in Germany was important, since sometimes what matters 'is not so much development [capabilities], but rather being close' to Wolfsburg and 'speaking the German language' (Simões 2003: 223). In spite of several ups and downs, AE keeps running and is still by far the main automotive plant in Portugal and one of the country's largest exporters.

A fifth phase is gradually emerging. It has initially been signalled by the stake on electric mobility, in the context of the demand-led Mobi-e project - see Box 13.3. However, this policy was discontinued. As a result, in 2012 Nissan cancelled an already negotiated project for battery manufacturing. This phase entails significant policy challenges for Portugal, in spite of a recent agreement with Volkswagen for further investment in Portugal.

The selective nature of public policies in the domains of technology and innovation is also clear in the case of public procurement of innovative projects, which has largely benefited companies working in the fields of ICT applications for education and health, renewable energy, or solutions for electrical mobility (see Box 13.3, on the electrical mobility project).[8]

Box 13.3 The initiative to promote electrical mobility[9]

The prospect of replacing vehicles using petroleum products for electric vehicles has huge potential, not only economic, but also political and environmental. An increased use of electric vehicles reduces the need for oil imports and improves a country's energy supply security. In addition, electric vehicles help to make better use of renewable energy by providing a form of storage for the energy produced at off-peak hours. Finally, the large-scale diffusion of electric vehicles would significantly reduce CO2 emissions. Electric vehicles seem thus very appealing for a country like Portugal, which is heavily dependent on imported fossil fuels, with worrying imbalances in the current account and with an ambitious programme of renewable energies.

Accordingly, in the late 2000s, the Portuguese government promoted a national electrical mobility programme. A consortium was formed between three leading national companies operating, respectively, in IT services, electro-mechanics, and electricity supply. The consortium developed the Mobi.E system, consisting of a network of electric charging stations distributed throughout the country, with proper software to manage energy flows and the related financial transactions. This is essentially a non-proprietary solution—it ensures the separation of ownership of charging stations, electricity distribution and energy supply services—together with an innovative business model for the management of energy and financial flows.

The installation of a pilot network of charging stations across the country was indirectly supported by the Portuguese government, through a public fund created as a counterpart for the granting of wind power licenses. But the State's role in the development of the Portuguese Mobi.E has not been limited to such indirect financing. Its action is visible in the regulatory domain (classifying legal entities and the governance of the network, and setting the rules during the trial period), but also through the involvement of various levels of governance in the paradigm of the electric vehicle.

The growing visibility of the Portuguese electric mobility project attracted international interest, opening business opportunities to companies, as well as contributing to the involvement of large multinational companies and major research centres in international projects associated with Mobi.E.

As the sovereign debt crisis developed, austerity measures were implemented, and a new government was elected (expressing doubts regarding the programme), the electrical mobility policy was largely put on hold.[10] Notwithstanding, the Mobi.E consortium became active in attempting to sell abroad (including the US, China, and several other countries) the technological solutions developed in the context of this programme.

In sum, while the macroeconomic context and policy priorities have not been particularly favourable to the upgrading of the industrial fabric towards more advanced, tradable sectors, the policy mix followed in Portugal did include several measures that aimed at promoting the desirable structural change in the economy. In the following section we provide an overall assessment of such measures.

4. Assessing industrial policies in Portugal

As Figure 13.2 illustrates, the Portuguese productive structure did not change significantly since the beginning of the century. While the export share of traditional industries has dropped considerably, this did not translate into a significant increase in the sophistication of domestic tradable production, weakening the prospects for substantial improvements in the competitive performance of the country.

The unsatisfactory pace of structural change in the Portuguese economy, however, does not necessarily imply that the industrial policies in place were essentially misplaced or ineffective. At least three other reasons can account for the relative rigidity in the broad industrial profile. First, as we discussed earlier, the negative incentives deriving from the macroeconomic context (marked by a real exchange rate appreciation, growing indebtedness, and harsh competitive pressures from emerging economies) may have cancelled out the effects of policies aiming to promote the expansion of more sophisticated, tradable industries. Secondly, the low educational levels of the workforce (including both workers and managers) may have hampered the potential for structural change. Finally, it may be the case that there was not enough time for industrial policies to translate into significant changes in the production structure before the advent of the Great Recession—and that the conditions for such changes to occur have deteriorated further in the recessionary context that prevailed thereafter.

In fact, most independent evaluation studies which were conducted in the last decade on the subject provide a generally positive assessment on the adequacy and pertinence of the competitiveness and innovation policies implemented in Portugal during the period (e.g., Augusto Mateus and Associados et al. 2005, 2013; IESE/Quaternaire 2013; Mamede and Fernandes 2013).

In particular, R&D and innovation policies have helped to put in place all the basic elements of a functioning national innovation system: research institutions, education and training organisations, interface organisations, risk capital agents, R&D and innovation performing firms, and so on. Overall, the priorities and criteria that guided the implementation of support mechanisms to those agents have been considered appropriate and broadly aligned with the goal of upgrading the production fabric (e.g., CTC/QREN 2012).

The most immediate results of such policies are, to some extent, evidenced by the performance of Portugal in R&D and innovation indicators. For example, according to the Innovation Union Scoreboard,[11] Portugal has been catching-up with the EU average in innovation performance since 2003, ranking often among the countries with the fastest growth in the innovation index used in this publication. Three types of indicators typically stand out as contributing to such performance: new postgraduate degree holders, scientific outputs (in particular, international co-publications), and R&D expenditures (both public and private). While this reflects, to a large extent, the continuous and substantial investment in the Portuguese science system (both in training and research) since the 1990s, it also encompasses changes in the business sector. In fact, R&D expenditures in the business enterprise sector in percentage of GDP have increased from 0.11 percent in 1995 to 0.78 percent in 2009, accounting for nearly half of the country's total expenditures in R&D (1.64 percent of the GDP, which compares to 0.55 percent in 1995). Largely as a result of the economic crisis, in 2011 total expenditure in R&D in percentage of GDP had dropped to 1.49 percent and business expenditures to 0.69 percent.

Although Portugal still lags behind the EU average[12] in R&D expenditures, it is not clear whether a greater effort should have been put into expanding R&D activities. As Figure 13.3 shows, R&D expenditures as a percentage of the GDP are strongly correlated with the economic structure of each country (measured, in this example, as the weight of knowledge-intensive services and manufacturing industries in the economy). And, even though R&D expenditures in Portugal are below the European average, they are higher than would be expected, given the structure of the Portuguese economy. Without a significant change in the domestic productive structure (which can hardly take place in a short period of time), further policy-induced increases in R&D expenditures bear increasing risks of ineffectiveness and/or undesirable results.

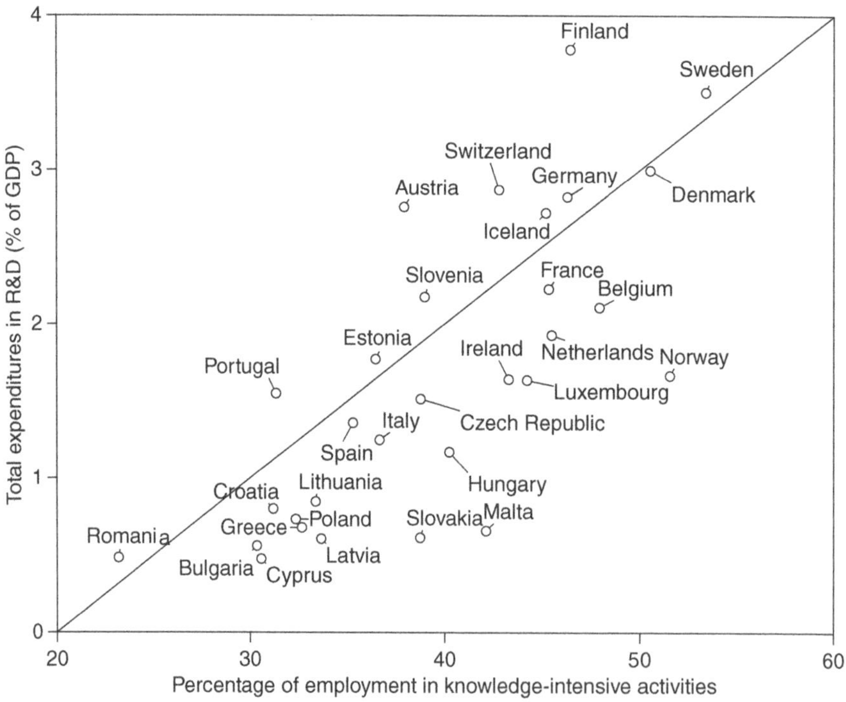

Figure 13.3 Relation between R&D expenditures and economic structure (average 2008–2012).

Source: Based on Eurostat data.

In fact, the impact of R&D investment on innovation and growth is highly contingent on the socioeconomic structure of each economy. For example, Bilbao-Osorio and Rodríguez-Pose (2004) show that the initial level of wealth, the availability of skills, or the presence of high technology sectors play an important role in the capacity of an economy to transform R&D into innovation. In this light, it is not surprising that the growth in R&D expenditures in Portugal—or, for that matter, in scientific training and research—is not overwhelmingly reflected in the evolution of many innovation indicators related to economic outputs, such as international patent applications and revenues, or the export share of knowledge-intensive activities. Simply put, the prevailing economic structure of Portugal does not allow for a substantial increase in the efficiency of R&D in terms of economic results.

Notwithstanding, several indicators suggest that the efforts to strengthen the national innovation and research systems have not been in vain. The number of firms conducting R&D activities on a permanent basis has steadily increased, collaborative R&D projects between companies and research institutions became a common feature in important segments of the economy, and many innovation indicators related to economic output show signs of improvement (FCT 2013).

An interesting development over the last decade has been the increased involvement of Portuguese firms as providers of software, engineering and R&D services in the context of the international outsourcing movement. This has been epitomised in the concept of near-shore in software services, which profits from Portugal's lower costs and short distance to the European market and the east coast of the United States. But it has also extended to R&D services, both intra- and inter-firm. These phenomena have been the main drivers of the improvement in Portugal's balance of technology payments since the mid-2000s.

Although the promotion of research, advanced training, and business R&D in Portugal attracted considerable attention during the 2000s, it is important to keep in mind that SMEs have an overwhelming weight in Portugal's economic fabric, whose main competitive hindrances and innovation barriers are not so much related to the lack of R&D activities, but rather to low human resource skills, all along the company hierarchy, in information-processing and strategy-making capabilities and in cooperative drive. Moreover, the upgrading of traditional industries, which is an essential complement to structural change, is less dependent on R&D as such than on capabilities related with the introduction of manufacturing process improvements, design skills, and the capacity to 'sense' and understand international market trends.

Certainly, the industrial policies followed in Portugal in the last two decades have not been exclusively focused on the most knowledge-intensive segments of the economy. On the contrary, there are important elements of a

DUI (Doing, Using, Interacting) approach (Jensen et al. 2007) to innovation policy, namely in promoting the upgrading of technical, organisational and marketing competences among SMEs, or in fostering interactive learning among firms (calling on science and technology organisation if and when necessary). This is evident in traditional industries (see Box 13.4 on the footwear sector), where the adoption of more sophisticated design, marketing approaches, and organisational practices is gradually spreading (Simões 2008b).

Box 13.4 The case of the footwear sector

In the late 1960s (1967–1969) the low-tech sectors accounted for 76.0 percent of the Portuguese manufacturing exports. As could be expected, the historical trend has been a decline in that share. In the second half of the 1980s (1985–1989), their share was still at 63.1 percent of total exports, but since then and until recently it fell sharply, dropping to 36.8 percent in 2005–2009. In congruence with the historical dominance of low-tech, the three products that topped Portuguese exports by 1990 were knitwear, clothing and footwear, with shares of, respectively, 10.8 percent, 10.6 percent, and 8.0 percent. By 2000 these three products had fallen to third, sixth and fourth in the overall ranking, with shares of, respectively, 7.1 percent, 4.4 percent, and 6.1 percent. In 2012, they declined even further, but with significant changes in their ranking. Now footwear ranks first among them, with a share of 3.6 percent (sixth), knitwear comes behind with 3.5 percent (eighth), and clothing comes last with 1.9 percent (fifteenth).

Regardless of the indicator chosen (employment, number of firms, GVA, export value, trade balance contribution), these three products show a historical decline over the last few decades. However, as can be deduced from the data above, footwear has performed relatively better than the others. Despite footwear employment being now almost half its historical height (59.099 in 1994), the decline in total output, GVA, and exports has not occurred to the same proportion. In fact, in the most recent period, footwear exports seem to be on the rise again, totalling 71 million pairs of shoes in 2012, up from 65 million in 2011, and with the value per pair rising 15.3 percent up to 29.9 USD, putting the country just behind Italy in this respect.

The evolution of the footwear sector provides some interesting lessons with regard to the fate of low-tech sectors in countries like Portugal. Cooperation between the footwear industry association (APPICCAPS), sectoral technology and training centres, the public authorities and, of course, the business companies themselves has been instrumental in a steady upgrading of the products' sophistication and their image abroad. Despite the remaining gap in relation to Italy's export prices, the fact is that the perception of international buyers has been changing and the prices paid have been getting closer to the actual product quality, which experienced an upgrade as a consequence of systematic efforts to improve technology, design, and marketing.

As we have seen in Section 4, a significant share of the funds that have been deployed by the industrial policy programmes has been geared towards attracting foreign investment. FDI can play a key role in structural change, since it provides in a short timeframe a bundle of capabilities that may contribute both directly and indirectly (namely through domestic sourcing effects) to improving the sophistication of the industrial fabric. These investments require however a certain degree of congruency with the domestic fabric in order to generate the expected spill-overs. At the same time, they should be geared towards sectors whose fortunes do not depend on extremely volatile markets. While the case of the automotive sector (see Box 13.2 above) is a good illustration of the role FDI can play in changing the profile of economic specialisation, the fate of FDI projects strongly supported by the Portuguese government have not always been so bright (as illustrated in the case presented in Box 13.5).

Box 13.5 Qimonda: An investment in electronics without the expected pay back

Qimonda was a DRAM producer set up in 2006 as a spin-off of Infineon, a subsidiary of Siemens. The Portuguese authorities, who started to negotiate this investment back in 1995, had envisaged this project as an opportunity to draw the country steadily into the high-tech business. When the investment contract was signed by the company and the Portuguese state, it was the second largest contract of this type to ever be established just behind the one with AutoEuropa (see Box 13.2). By mid-2007, Qimonda Portugal SA had received public funds totalling €102 million. By the end of that year, Qimonda had reached the top position in the ranking of Portuguese exporters with exports of €1.6 billion.

Worldwide, the company had a staff of 13,500 and was number two in the global DRAM business, supplying the PC and server markets. However, international oversupply and a sharp fall in DRAM prices in 2007 and 2008 led Qimonda to file for insolvency in Germany in January 2009.

Its chip packaging complex in Portugal experienced, then, a sharp fall in employment, from more than 1,700 to 235 by the end of 2009. Creditors were forced to take over the activities of the Portuguese plant, establishing Nanium in 2010. This new company has been producing semiconductors under license granted by Infineon. More recently, as the international market for electronic memories warmed up again with the boom in smartphones sales, employment in the plant rose to about 600 by mid-2013.

The activities developed in Portugal have been high in labour content and relatively low in technological intensity, as design capabilities remained abroad. Further, Qimonda did not reach out to domestic companies to the same extent as Renault and Autoeuropa did in the automotive industry. Nanium, the firm that keeps the site operating, may however still play a relevant role in establishing endogenous capabilities in this area in the mid-term.

5. Conclusion: the future challenges for industrial policies in Portugal

As we have shown, Portugal urgently needs to enhance the competitive performance of its economy in order to reduce its external imbalances and improve the prospects for sustained wealth creation. Such a goal can hardly be achieved without upgrading the specialisation profile of the economy, towards more sophisticated, tradable products. While some of the 'structural reforms' implemented under the adjustment programme agreed in 2011 with the troika (IMF-ECB-EC) may play a role in improving the cost-competitiveness of the country, this is insufficient—or even counter-productive—to induce the necessary changes. Clearly put, Portugal should not dismiss the role of policies which specifically aim at enhancing productivity through structural change.

We have shown that a comprehensive set of industrial policies has been put forward in Portugal in recent decades. In spite of shortcomings, such policies have contributed to the development of innovation capacities and, thereby, to the gradual upgrading of traditional industries and the development of some non-traditional ones.

Three main challenges remain, however, for industrial policy in Portugal. These are: setting clear priorities, improving governance, and overcoming the problems related with the crisis and the adjustment programme.

It is widely acknowledged that the country needs to upgrade its economic fabric, both by increasing the value content of traditional products, and by expanding non-traditional activities. To a large extent, this is presently reflected in the design and implementation of several policy programmes and instruments, from tax incentives for innovative business projects to investments in the context conditions for business development (e.g., transport infrastructure).

Notwithstanding, beyond this generic formulation, policy priorities are often ill-defined, whether in terms of support mechanisms, beneficiaries, or expected results. The lack of clear priorities for industrial policy in recent years results from several factors, namely the following: the state of exception resulting from the 2008–2009 international crisis, the sovereign debt crisis starting in 2010, and the adjustment programme in place since 2011 (which have consumed most of the attention of top decision-makers); the political instability resulting from these events, reflected in the early elections and change of government in 2011, as well as in the succession of changes in ministerial positions thereafter; the free-market stance of some decision-makers (who tend to oppose any policy intervention that is seen as 'distortive of the price mechanism'); the fear of making choices that may create enemies among some constituencies; and the dilapidation of institutional capacity in the public sector due to budget cuts.

Although the risks involved in fixing priorities are real, there are at least two good reasons for making selective policy choices. First, the harsh financial constraints associated with the post-2008 economic hurdles increased dramatically the need to allocate public funds in a thoughtful way; even though not all industrial policy actions require significant amounts of public resources, governments cannot escape the need to make choices, preferably in an informed and legitimate manner. Secondly, in a time of crisis and political instability, the attention span of all the relevant agents involved in the policy process—from legislators and implementers to monitoring bodies—is highly constrained, making it advisable to focus their efforts on a short number of key initiatives.

These priorities should focus on improving the most competitive segments of the traditional sectors, pushing them upwards in the respective value-chains, while simultaneously inducing the development of newer, more knowledge-intensive industries. In this regard, these priorities will need to leverage the important development of scientific capacities the country has experienced over the last few decades. At the same time, interaction and cooperation between firms in different industries will need to be bolstered, so that possible related variety effects may be exploited.

Clearer priorities must be accompanied by improvements in the governance of industrial policy. Portugal has made significant progress in the institutional framework for implementing and monitoring industrial policies in several domains. Together with the access to financial resources, improvements in governance (related both with regulatory requirements and institutional capacity building) have been a central result of the EU's Cohesion Policy in Portugal. Mamede and Feio (2012) show how the prevailing governance system for direct support to firms (mainly funded by EU structural funds) has fostered institutional learning while reducing the scope for capture by interest groups, thereby contributing to the efficacy and legitimacy of such policy interventions. The authors also show, however, that the same conditions do not hold in every domain of industrial policy in Portugal, which means that there is still scope for improvement.

Even more important, there is the need to enhance the coordination of policies that are relevant for structural change. For example, research and innovation policies in Portugal have traditionally been carried out, respectively, by the ministries in charge of education and science and in charge of the economy, with very weak links between them (Caraça 1999; Godinho and Simões 2005, 2011; Henriques 2006). In spite of several attempts since the early 2000s to promote coordination between the two ministries, a sustained and integrated approach to research and innovation policies has not been achieved thus far. As a result, research policy was carried out autonomously without having in mind enterprise policy, and vice versa. This lack of coordination often reduces the transformative potential of public interventions, for several reasons: researchers and businessmen are treated as stakeholders of separate policy domains, lacking the incentives to interact with each other; the partial overlapping of responsibilities among ministries in some areas occasionally lead to the duplication of efforts; the success of some policy initiatives that rely on the involvement of more than one ministry may be hampered by lack of political commitment; and so on. The solution to these problems would require decisive choices at the highest level of government regarding coordination and distribution of power between ministries, which are yet to be taken.

One aspect of governance that needs further attention in the future is the capacity to make any chosen priorities sustainable over time. As mentioned previously, some of the strategic choices that have been made in the recent past (e.g., electric mobility) have been notoriously affected by lack of continuity. To remedy this situation, there is the need to seek wide consensus, namely through stakeholder participation in the process of making the relevant policy choices, otherwise those choices will be easily overturned by the next government or even the next minister.

Beyond clarifying priorities and improving governance, the most immediate challenge for industrial policy in Portugal is overcoming the problems related with the financial and economic crisis and the adjustment programme. The highly unfavourable financing conditions faced by SMEs since 2010 are arguably the most urgent obstacle to the development of the Portuguese economy.

The combination of high levels of indebtedness with the synchronised financial deleveraging of all institutional sectors (households, non-financial firms, banks, and the government) has led to high costs of credit, the main source of financing for Portuguese firms. The interest rate on new bank loans (with 1 year maturity) to non-financial companies in Portugal was about 5 percent by the end of 2013—nearly 200 basis points of similar rates in the case of Spain, Ireland and Italy, and more than 300 basis points above the interest rates by German and French firms. As Mazzucato (2013: 864) put it, 'the short-sighted bond (financial) markets that are determining the recipe for the solution to the Eurozone crisis means that the proposed solutions for the weaker EZ countries (…) are not allowing the much needed productive investments to happen: investment in skills, technology, and other determinants of productivity.'

Thus, industrial policy in Portugal faces the immediate challenge of ensuring that the needed financing is available for investment projects that seem *ex-ante* to have high potential to induce structural changes in the desirable direction. However, this may conflict with the need to respond to the prevailing high levels of unemployment, which can often be more effectively achieved by investing in less knowledge-intensive activities (e.g., construction).

Such conflict draws attention to the need to find new ways of dealing with the crisis in the periphery of the euro area. If the goal is to prevent the accumulation of strong macroeconomic imbalances between EU member countries in the future, the adjustment programmes being deployed in countries like Portugal should pay increased attention to the measures needed to foster structural change.

Moreover, our previous discussion has also shown that many policy options that are deemed appropriate at the EU level—regarding international trade agreements, financial regulation, monetary policy, competitiveness policy, and so on—may have harmful effects on the development prospects of some member states. In this sense, fostering structural change and productivity growth in Portugal is, at least, as much a matter of making the right policy options at the national level, as of finding solutions at the EU level that are conducive to a balanced development of each member state and to increased cohesion. A cohesive approach at European level appears to be essential for achieving the very competitiveness of the 'old' Europe in a new competitive landscape, where Asian economies are swiftly gaining ground.

Notes

1 We follow Rodrik (2008) by defining industrial policy as the set of policy instruments that stimulate specific economic activities (including manufacturing, as well as non-traditional agriculture and services) and promote structural change.
2 The current account deficit fell from 10.6 percent of the GDP in 2010 to 1.5 percent in 2012, and is expected to be eliminated by the end of 2013. Note, however, that this adjustment is also explained by the sharp decrease in imports, partly resulting from an unsustainable drop in investment levels. For critical appraisals of the Portuguese adjustment programme and its results, see Abreu et al. (2013) and Mamede (2012).
3 According to IMF data (International Financial Statistics), between 1988 and 1992 the Real Effective Exchange Rate appreciated 28 percent.
4 The share of non-tradable activities in VA rose from 43 percent in 1991 to 49 percent in 2000 and 53 percent in 2007.
5 However, through a process of capability upgrading, the footwear industry has been able to withstand the decline as well as the divestiture by foreign-owned firms from manufacturing activities in Portugal. More on this later.
6 A possible exception may be the recent investments by Embraer, a leading aircraft manufacturer from Brazil.
7 This box is based on Simões (2002, 2008a).
8 This type of initiatives has been discontinued in the context of the adjustment programme in place since 2011, as a result of the international bailout.
9 This case is adapted from Mamede and Feio (2012).
10 This belief was common to most innovation-led public procurement initiatives in the country. Paradoxically, while in the EU increased emphasis was put on demand-led innovation, in Portugal such initiatives have been aborted.
11 Previously known as 'European Innovation Scoreboard,' this publication by the European Commission provides comparative assessments of EU Member States' innovation performance since 2000. See: http://ec.europa.eu/enterprise/policies/innovation/facts-figures-analysis/innovation-scoreboard/.
12 From 2009 to 2011, the last year for which data are available, total expenditure in R&D in percentage of GDP has been close to 2 percent and business expenditures around 1.25 percent.

14 The industrial sector of Spain in search of a new policy

José Molero and Inés Granda

1. Introduction

The intensity of the current crisis has had a remarkable number of repercussions in all sectors of the economy and particularly on the countries of the European periphery. In the Spanish case, the impact of the crisis has been quite severe due to a number of factors, mainly the considerable weight of the construction and related sectors in the economic structure. It impacted directly on employment in the construction and supplier industries and also gave rise to a profound crisis in the financial system. As far as the financial system is concerned, the reason was the huge amount of resources invested in building, particularly by savings banks with a regional base and, therefore, highly dependent on regional political powers. The recovery of those funds deteriorated as the crisis advanced and the solvency of the system thus entered a vicious circle.

Obviously, industry has not escaped the impact of the crisis and has experienced important consequences as well. In this article, particular attention will be paid to this sector, since the way out of the crisis, as many have increasingly acknowledged, has to be based on a more significant role of industry as a guarantee for more robust and sustainable development. A general assessment of the situation requires a twofold perspective: on the one hand, all available quantitative information from the most important statistical sources has to be analysed. On the other, a number of specific features of the industrial sector have to be taken into account, which give industry a relevant position in the economy as a whole. Our focus will thus fall mainly on productivity, technological innovation, the multiplier effect and employment.

In terms of productivity, industrial sectors have a noticeably higher average productivity than the remainder of the productive activities. This is particularly important for the Spanish economy because it has performed badly in this area, with grave consequences for international competitiveness.

Closely linked to this, the capacity of industry with regard to technological innovation has to be considered. Although innovation in services has undoubtedly experienced remarkable development—in particular in production services—it is still possible to state that industry plays a by no means negligible role in the generation, diffusion and implementation of innovation. Furthermore, a significant part of the innovation taking place in service companies is a consequence of the externalisation of those activities by industrial firms.

Thirdly, it should be underlined that industrial sectors have powerful linkages with many other productive activities. This makes industry an essential engine for the economy insofar as its dynamism is transmitted to others more than in the case of other economic sectors.

This leads us to the last argument. Industry is particularly important for new job creation, directly or indirectly. Moreover, these jobs are usually of better quality and offer greater stability because industry demands a more skilled labour force.

2. Industry within the overall economic system

The first contextual data that should be evaluated is the weight of industry in the Spanish economy. As with many other developed countries, the general trend in recent decades has been a reduction in that weight.

As Figure 14.1 shows, until very recently, industry gradually tended to lose ground in the productive system. However, looking at current value added (VA) data, industry has shown a positive evolution from 118,294 million euros in 2000 to 168,601 in 2008, with positive growth rates in all years. 2009 was a dramatic year because industrial VA decreased

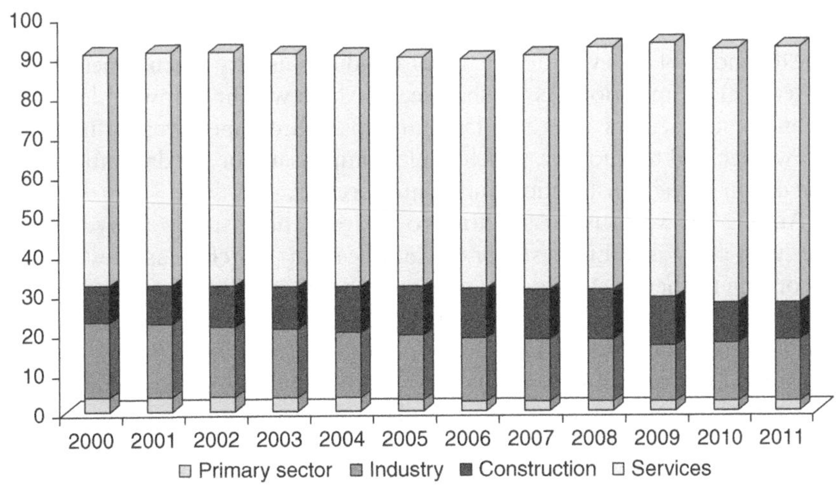

Figure 14.1 Weight (in % of total) of economic sectors in GDP 2000–2011.

Source: Own elaboration with data from National Institute of Statistics (INE), National Accounting for Spain.

11.5 percent to 149,137 million euros. In the last few years, a partial recovery occurred, rising to 165,051 million in 2011. These values are in current euros, meaning that in constant currency, VA production today is clearly below that of 2008.

If we focus on the share of industrial VA in the total, the evolution is characterised by a gradual decrease between 2000 and 2009 (from 18.8 percent to 14.2 percent). This largely resulted from the faster growth of the construction and services sectors. The situation changed after 2009; in particular, the crisis in construction and related activities (including finance) and the relative resistance of industry has led to a recovery of industry VA up to 15.5 percent in 2011. In other words, industry is following a more solid path in the hardest period of the international crisis. The following sections will help us to assess if this opens a window for hope.

A fundamental aspect to consider is the evolution of industrial employment. As Table 14.1 shows, this sector maintained approximately the same number of jobs in the first half of the past decade: the loss was around 3 percent. Since the beginning of the crisis, the situation has worsened and, in the last year, the number of employees was 663,000 lower than that of 2003; the loss has been more than 20 percent of the total. This trend is however better than that of construction, which has lost 1.3 million employees since 2007, more than 48 percent. Services and the primary sector fared comparatively better.

3. Structure of Spanish industry

The diagnosis of the evolution of Spanish industry is very much dependent on its sectoral composition. As we shall see, the high weight of low and medium technological sectors does not facilitate Spanish competitiveness based on knowledge and technology, which could compensate for the dramatic loss of dynamism in the construction and related sectors.

Among the various possibilities to address this issue, we have chosen the well-known OECD sectoral classification which classifies sectors according to their technological content (OECD 1997). The reason for this choice is that it casts light on one of the most prominent factors in explaining international competition and development. In the last few years, a considerable number of authors have underlined the critical importance of technology and innovation to explain the growth of nations and the international division of labour, particularly among industrialised economies (Dosi et al. 1990; Fagerberg and Shrolec 2007). Therefore, the more we can pinpoint the technological composition of industrial sectors, the nearer we shall be to an understanding of the structural competitiveness of a particular economy.

Table 14.1 Employment by economic sector (thousands)

	2000	*2001*	*2002*	*2003*	*2004*	*2005*	*2006*	*2007*	*2008*	*2009*	*2010*	*2011*
Primary sector	942.0	948.2	936.5	925.3	893.5	868.4	821.3	801.2	770.6	738.3	753.0	727.9
Industry	3,024.3	3,017.6	2,980.1	2,978.5	2,955.1	2,931.8	2,870.7	2,809.3	2,768.8	2,421.3	2,337.6	2,315.1
Construction	1,846.6	1,982.4	2,060.2	2,154.3	2,242.7	2,405.0	2,551.2	2,687.1	2,373.6	1,870.6	1,634.4	1,378.6
Services	9,856.6	10,248.9	10,599.9	10,946.8	11,399.1	11,891.4	12,482.9	12,985.8	13,334.5	13,014.3	12,859.8	12,864.6

Source: National Institute of Statistics (INE): National Accounting for Spain.

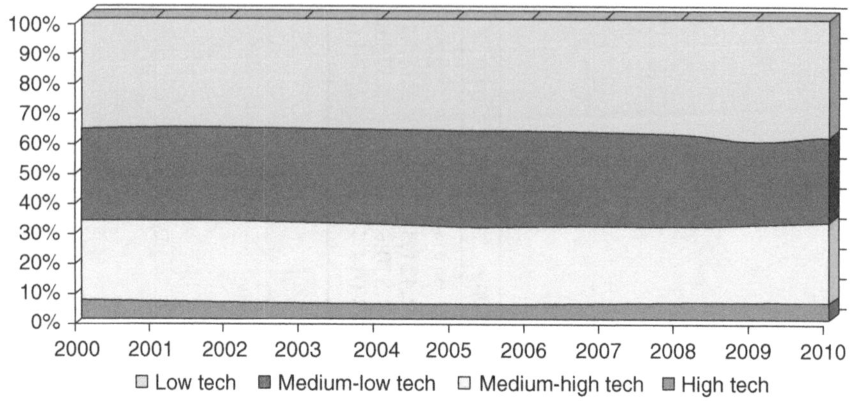

Figure 14.2 Distribution (in %) of industries by technological intensity, Spain.

Source: Own elaboration with Eurostat National Accounts data.

Figure 14.2 has been prepared following OECD taxonomy. Four categories are used: high technology (H-T), medium-high technology (MH-T), medium-low technology (ML-T), and low technology (L-T). Following what we have shown elsewhere (Buesa and Molero 1996; Molero 2012a), the figure confirms a scarce presence of H-T sectors in the VA composition. Furthermore, the permanence of this situation over several decades points to it being one of the dominant features of Spanish industry when compared to other developed economies. Moreover, in recent years, international trade has evolved more rapidly in H-T sectors (OECD 2012a), hence the structural weakness we are referring to has implied a number of difficulties to follow international dynamism. At the same time, the Spanish economy has had more difficulties in generating and using new technological products and processes (Molero 2012a). The extent of this feature is a crucial element in understanding both the greater impact of the crisis and the difficulties in finding a more sustainable path out of the recession.

A comparison with the sectoral composition of other countries is important to obtain a more accurate view of the process. Thus, Figure 14.3 shows the average values for EU-27 countries. The conclusion is easy: the specialissation of Spanish industry has tended towards ML-T and L-T kinds of sectors and constitutes one of the most critical elements conditioning the competitiveness capacity of Spain.

A clearer view of this topic can be achieved through the calculation of a specialissation index, following the formula:

Specialisation index (SI) = (VA type of sector i in spain/
VA total Spanish manufactures)/
(VA type of sector i in EU-27/
VA total manufactures in EU-27)

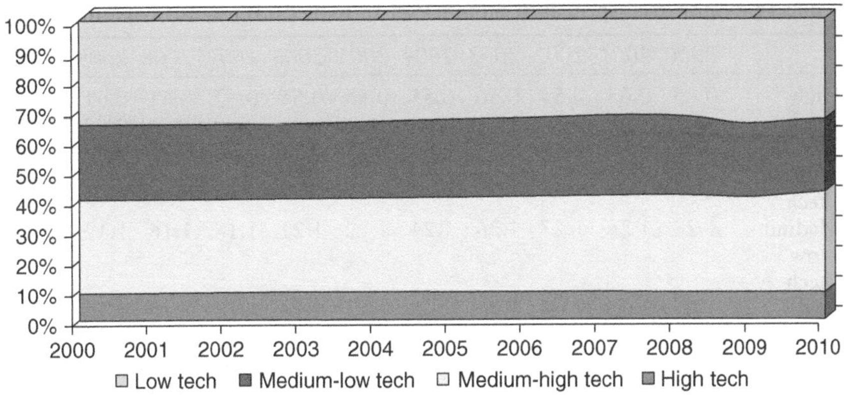

Figure 14.3 Distribution (in %) of industries by technological intensity, EU-27.

Source: Own elaboration with Eurostat National Accounts data.

The interpretation is simple: SI > 1 means Spain is "specialised" in this type of sector, that is, these sectors have more relative importance in Spanish industry than in the EU-27. On the contrary, SI< 1 means these sectors have less relative importance in Spain.

Table 14.2 and Figure 14.4 gather the results of the estimations for the last 11 years, including the crisis period. The first general conclusion we can draw is that Spain has a dual structure characterised by a remarkable specialissation in the L-T and ML-T types of sectors. The other side of the coin is that both the MH-T and H-T categories have a negative specialissation. This dualism goes back for decades (Buesa and Molero 1996) and has persisted in the crisis period.

This persistence notwithstanding, there have been some interesting changes. The most noticeable is the growing specialissation in L-T sectors: from 1.05 to 1.18. This coincides closely with a simultaneously decreasing specialissation in ML-T sectors. In other words, we have witnessed a sort of substitution between these categories of sectors, which may have weakened the overall international position of Spanish industry.

In contrast, in the MH-T and H-T categories, Spain shows an outstanding stability in low scores. It is particularly so in MH-T sectors, whereas H-T sectors have followed a path of two sub-periods: in the first their SI declined, but they recovered the previous values in the second sub-period.

Interestingly, the Spanish configuration is not an exception within the EU. Thus, analyzing the four largest countries (Table 14.3), we find that three—Italy, UK, and France—show specialisation in L-T as well; France has even higher SI values than Spain. Only Germany has a substantially low specialisation in these sectors. Looking at the other extreme—H-T—only the UK has a positive (> 1) index and Germany is close to 1. However, Italy and France record low scores (–0.75 and 0.82 respectively). In other words,

Table 14.2 Industrial specialization index by technological intensity, Spain

	2000	*2001*	*2002*	*2003*	*2004*	*2005*	*2006*	*2007*	*2008*	*2009*	*2010*
High tech	0.65	0.68	0.59	0.56	0.55	0.55	0.55	0.57	0.61	0.61	0.61
Medium-high tech	0.86	0.85	0.87	0.85	0.85	0.81	0.81	0.80	0.79	0.83	0.81
Medium-low tech	1.23	1.26	1.27	1.26	1.24	1.22	1.21	1.18	1.16	1.12	1.15
Low tech	1.05	1.03	1.04	1.06	1.08	1.12	1.14	1.17	1.19	1.16	1.18

Source: Own elaboration with Eurostat National Accounts data.

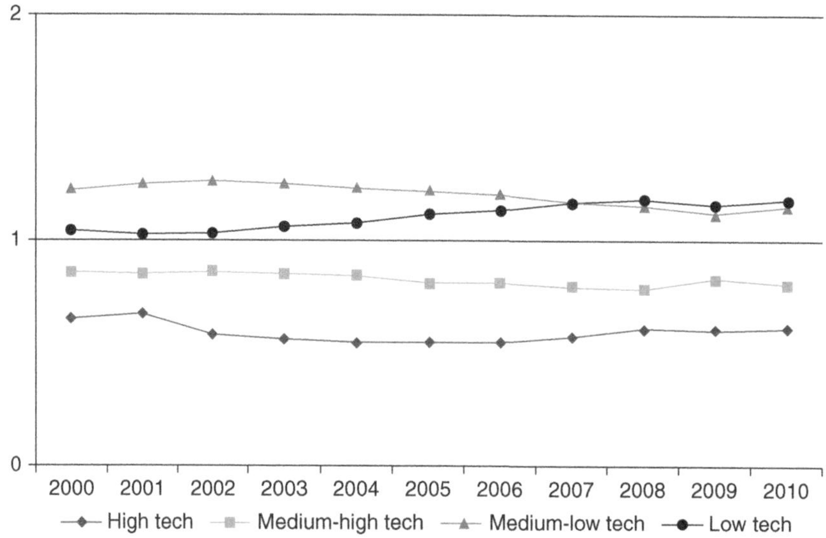

Figure 14.4 Industrial specialization index, EU-27.

Source: Own elaboration with Eurostat National Accounts data.

Table 14.3 Industrial specialization index by tecnological intensity, 2010

Country	*H-T*	*MH-T*	*ML-T*	*L-T*
Spain	0.61	0.81	1.15	1.18
Italy	0.75	0.83	1.12	1.15
UK	1.59	0.88	0.88	1.05
Germany	0.96	1.43	0.90	0.65
France	0.82	0.82	1.28	1.21

Source: Own elaboration with Eurostat National Acoounts data.

the problem of a low presence of H-T sectors is a widespread characteristic of many European economies and is a sensitive part of their capacity to compete with other better adjusted industrial economies, including some important emerging countries.

4. Internationalisation

A basic component of the present situation of Spanish industry is revealed by the trend of its international performance. To tackle this issue, we will address two main components: international trade and foreign direct investment.

As far as international trade is concerned, Table 14.4 shows the main figures for industrial exports and imports in the last few years. In fact, two different periods can be identified: before and after 2009. Before 2009, imports experienced steady growth, due to the demand created by domestic industries and final consumption; between 2005 and 2008, industrial imports grew more than 20 percent in current prices. Similarly, exports grew more than 27 percent, due to the increasing capacity of Spanish companies, including foreign subsidiaries, as is the case of the automotive industry.

The result was a smooth increase in the rate of cover from 72.75 percent in 2005 to 76 percent in 2008. Nevertheless, the deficit continued to be remarkable, because 24 percent was more than 41,000 million in current euros.

The year of 2009 was a turning point as can be derived from the following facts. Regarding imports, a steep fall in that year is the beginning of a new context characterised by domestic depression and a weak demand for foreign industrial products. Hence, in spite of irregular recovery in the following years, the level in 2012 is still 80 percent of that of 2008 at current prices. The case of exports is very different. Since 2009, a significant increase has taken place and the 142,974 million euros in 2012 is 36 percent higher than exports in 2009. The combination of weak domestic demand with a remarkable effort to reduce costs (mainly labour ones) has significantly improved the international competitiveness of a by no means insignificant part of Spanish industry.

Table 14.4 International industrial trade 2005–2012 (million €)

	Exports	*Imports*	*Balance*	*Coverage rate*
2005	103,494	142,256	-38,762	72.8%
2006	114,557	157,652	-23,094	72.7%
2007	124,957	174,641	-49,684	71.6%
2008	131,838	173,464	-41,626	76.0%
2009	105,182	122,295	-17,113	86.0%
2010	121,728	140,845	-19,117	86.4%
2011	143,319	152,093	-8,774	94.2%
2012	142,974	138,778	4,195	103.0%

Source: National Institute of Statistics.

The combination of both processes has led to a rapid reduction in the external deficit to the point that in 2012 there was a surplus of 4,195 million, which is a very singular fact in the recent history of Spanish industry. In other words, the rate of coverage went from 76.0 percent in 2008 to 103.0 percent in 2012. The relevant question is, to what extent will this particular evolution continue once internal demand returns to its historical levels and the margin for competing through labour costs disappears.

Although it is not exactly an answer to this question, an important element for a better understanding of the structural background of the figures presented above has to do with the different levels of foreign trade. Following our argument regarding the low development of H-T sectors, Table 14.5 gathers information on foreign trade in these sectors, summarised in the rate of cover.

The first conclusion we can draw is the different situation of HT sectors with regard to that cover. Figure 14.5 includes the evolution of both rates and it is clear how international competitiveness is significantly smaller in H-T. Thus, in spite of growth over the last few years, it is still below 50 percent. An in-depth analysis by individual sectors shows that the weakness is particularly relevant in Office Machines and Computer Equipment (19.9 percent), Electronic Equipment (28.9 percent), Scientific Instruments (33.8 percent), and Electrical Machinery and Equipment (47.3 percent). The opposite is clear for Mechanical Machinery and Equipment (228.9 percent), Chemical Products (120.8 percent), and Construction of Aeronautical and Space Equipment (123.3 percent).

In short, Spain stands out as one of the OECD countries in which HT industries have a clear negative contribution to the manufacturing trade balance. Figure 14.6 clearly supports this claim.

The second main aspect of internationalisation refers to Foreign Direct Investment (FDI). In what follows, we shall comment on both inward and outward flows.[1] Inward FDI flow into the Spanish economy did not experience a regular and systematic pattern throughout the 2000s, as was also the case for other developed European countries. In fact, in 2000, the gross inward flow was 38,396 million euros, but after two more years with similar figures, in 2003, the figure dropped sharply: 18,730 in 2003, 19,017 in 2004 and 13,952 in 2006. Then, an important increase took place, reaching 38,843 million in 2008 and since then, a kind of fluctuating pattern can be seen, with a maximum of 30,786 in 2009 and a minimum of 19,455 million in 2012.

With regard to outward FDI, the trend has also been irregular, but with higher values. Thus, in 2000 the gross flow was 60,486 million euros and then a continuing decline occurred reaching a minimum of 31,800 in 2003. A combination of growing and decreasing years followed, with a maximum of 112,079 million in 2007 and a minimum of 25,495 million in 2009. After two more years of positive increments, 2012 registered one of the worst years with just 15,034 million.

Table 14.5 Coverage rate of foreign trade: high-tech products (%)

	2000	*2001*	*2002*	*2003*	*2004*	*2005*	*2006*	*2007*	*2008*	*2009*	*2010*	*2011*
1. Manufacture of aircraft and spacecraft	19.79	31.2	55.7	56.7	54.9	49	44	54.7	64.3	129.1	88.5	123.3
2. Office machinery and computers	41.14	37	28.6	26.4	23.4	17.9	15.1	15.6	12.7	17.2	16	19.9
3. Electronic material, radio, television, and communications equipment	38.01	42.4	43.7	48.2	36.2	33.1	25.4	15.1	12.9	27.2	30.8	28.9
4. Pharmaceutical products	62.41	59.4	54.9	45.3	51	52.3	46.9	42.9	43.2	39	50.3	59.6
5. Scientific instruments	32.86	34.8	35.1	35.9	31.5	26.7	23.8	30.7	29.6	28	30.9	33.8
6. Electrical machinery and material	26.83	46.1	48.5	52.1	37.6	56.8	70.6	31.7	22.9	26	29.5	47.3
7. Chemical products	74.1	64.2	69.7	76	67.8	76.6	88.4	69.9	75.3	57.9	67.2	120.8
8. Mechanical machinery and equipment	49.97	69.9	79.5	61.2	67	67.6	73.5	114.7	127.5	173.8	143.2	228.9
9. Weapons and ammunition	93.82	100.4	103.3	52.8	98.1	64.1	74.5	113.9	93.6	112.1	96.4	63
Coverage rate of the foreign trade of high-tech products	38.4	43	45.1	44.7	39.4	36.8	32.4	29.1	27.9	39.1	40.3	49.4
Coverage rate of total foreign trade	77.12	74.9	76	74.6	72.2	66.5	64.9	64.9	66.8	77.6	77.8	81.8

Source: National Institute of Statistics (Spain).

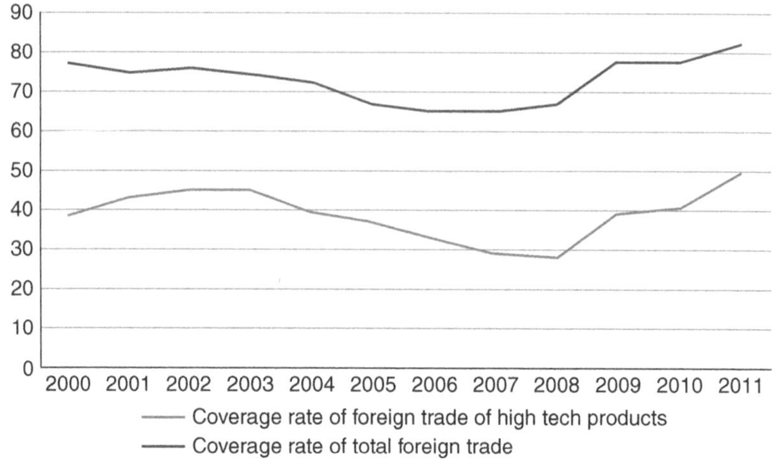

Figure 14.5 Coverage rate of foreign trade (%).

Source: National Institute of Statistics (Spain).

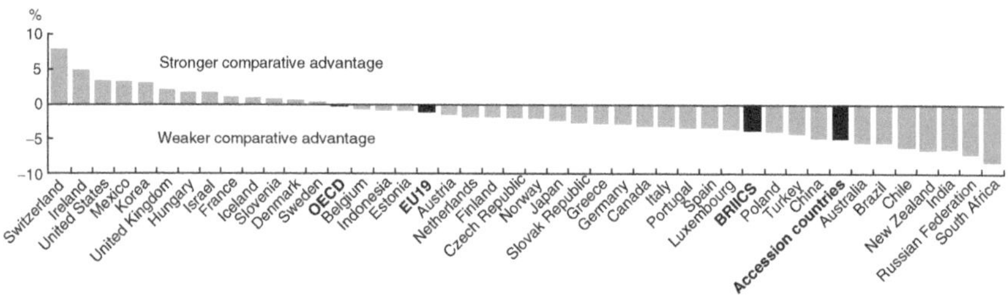

Figure 14.6 Contribution of high-technology industries to the manufacturing trade balance, 2007 (as a percentage of manufacturing trade).

Source: OECD Science, 88 Technology and Industry Scoreboard 2009, p. 89.

In short, in this period, outward FDI was clearly above inward FDI. In both cases, non-systematic behaviour can be found, and for both, 2012 was one of the worst years. Nevertheless, if we consider that in these years global FDI investment also suffered from irregularities and changes (UNCTAD 2013), Spain's performance is not particularly worse than many other developed economies; Figures 14.7 and 14.8 confirm this assertion.

However, we are particularly interested in the FDI flows of industrial firms. Thus, Table 14.6 and Figure 14.9 show the evolutions of three magnitudes. For incoming FDI, only one series of data is employed, using manufacturing sectors as the variable to gather the information. For outward FDI, however, we have used two different sets of data: one is overall Spanish investment in foreign manufacturing sectors, regardless of the sector of origin (in other

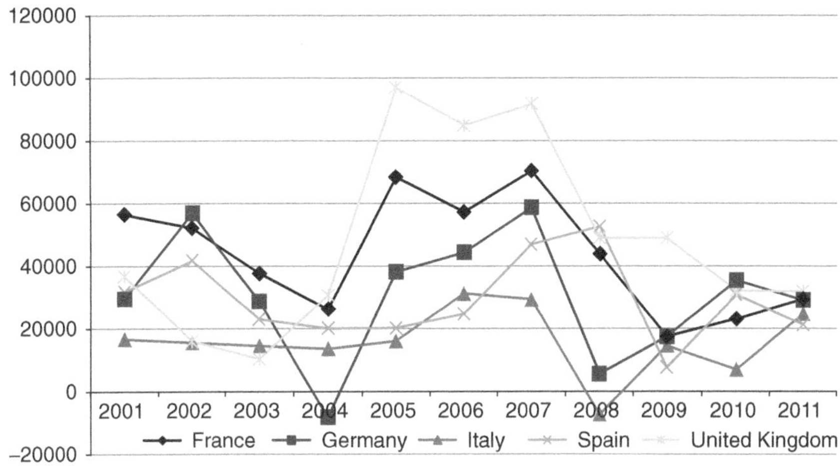

Figure 14.7 Total inward FDI (millions €).

Source: OECD: International Direct Investment Database.

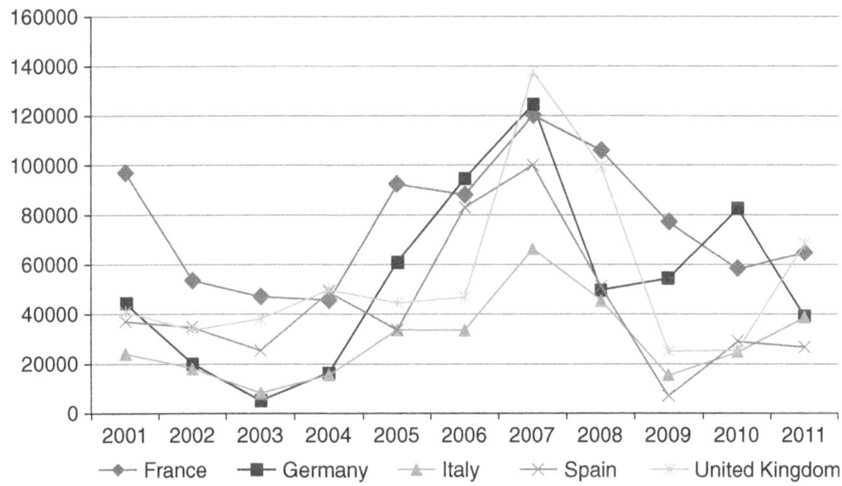

Figure 14.8 Total outward FDI (millions €).

Source: OECD: International Direct Investment Database.

words, the interest of manufacturing activities for Spanish investment). The other is FDI flows to foreign sectors but restricted to those in which the origin is a Spanish manufacturing firm.

As far as inward FDI is concerned, irregularity is also present. It reached a maximum in 2002, with 19,275 million euros. Since then, a continuous decline has been recorded, to a minimum of 3,912 million in 2006. It was

Table 14.6 Foreign direct investment and manufacturing sectors (thousand €)

	2000	*2001*	*2002*	*2003*	*2004*	*2005*	*2006*	*2007*	*2008*	*2009*	*2010*	*2011*	*2012*
Inward FDI	2,553,572	14,001,513	19,275,283	9,581,995	8,324,029	5,108,652	3,912,264	8,221,307	7,940,323	6,535,116	12,254,341	6,445,776	5,625,418
Outward FDI of Spanish manufacturing firms	7,991,718	7,906,184	6,514,236	5,046,799	3,979,701	7,967,094	6,243,729	13,619,832	5,460,538	1,527,991	1,510,539	2,644,832	1,183,436
FDI of Spain on foreign manufacturing sectors	7,322,303	11,571,424	21,442,132	18,371,854	12,418,532	7,934,044	7,814,203	20,578,353	11,749,080	4,195,621	4,440,389	5,475,598	2,904,541

Source: DATAINVEX. Ministry of Industry, Energy and Tourism (Spain).

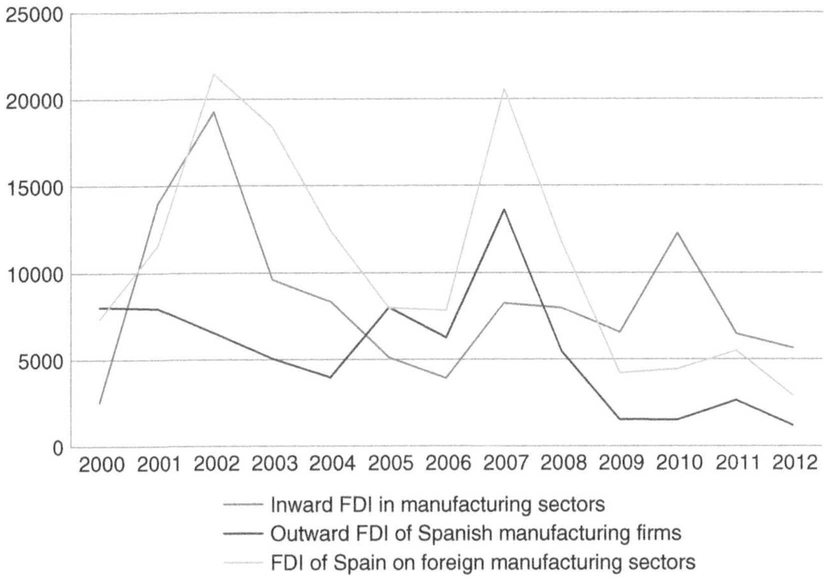

Figure 14.9 Foreign direct investment and manufacturing sectors (million €).

Source: DATAINVEX. Ministry of Industry, Energy and Tourism (Spain).

followed by another period of growth until 2010, when FDI reached 12,254 million. In the last two years, another fall occurred to a new minimum of 5,625 million in 2012. In short, with the exception of 2010, the general trend has been towards lower levels of incoming FDI and hence, a loss of attractiveness in Spanish industry might be the reason.

In the case of outward FDI, the first and perhaps most significant finding is that there are non-manufacturing institutions and firms which have invested outwardly in manufacturing companies. This is probably the case of banks and other financial enterprises. A second general feature is that since 2005, the two FDI series follow a very similar path, although with minor values for FDI coming from Spanish manufacturing firms. Thirdly, after 2007, the process is clearly downward, probably reflecting the domestic difficulties of many sectors, as was explained in Section 2.

Looking at detailed sectoral data, it is interesting to note that a number of sectors are important in inward and outward flows. In fact, 2012 data show that for inward flows, the outstanding sectors are: Manufacturing of Other Non-Metallic Products (1,501 million euros), Metallurgy, Iron and Steel (1,030 million), Vehicles (732 million), Food (585 million), Beverages (257 million), Paper (307 million) and Chemistry (370 million). Outward data show a very similar pattern: in first place we have Metallurgy, Iron and Steel (1,558 million euro), then Other mineral non-Metallic products (307 Million), Vehicles (235 million), Paper (232 million), Food (109 million) and Beverages (80 million). These data suggest that the technological content of our industry is reflected in FDI, both inward and outward. In other words, a large part of the activity is in the hands of L-T or ML-T sectors. The two most remarkable exceptions are Vehicles and Chemicals, both included in the MH-T category. In all these cases, we can speak of a kind of intra-sectoral flow, insofar as they receive and send FDI permanently. Nevertheless, most H-T sectors are not as active, perhaps as a result of their lower development in Spain.

5. Technological innovation

As we have stressed previously, in the current competitive world, knowledge and technology have acquired a prominent role, particularly for developed countries. Historically, the position of Spain with respect to this factor has been a deficient one (Molero 2001). Since the 1980s a number of significant policy measures had been put in place with the aim of reducing such a significant shortfall. More than 20 years after the approval of the Spanish Science and Technology Law (1986) and taking into account the importance of Spain's economic development, the current balance can be established as follows.

First, there has been a notable improvement in the process of technological innovation; just as a rough indicator, R&D expenditures over GDP went from less than 1 percent at the end of the 1990s to 1.35 in the last few years. Although this improvement is more visible in the public sector (i.e., scientific publications, public budgets devoted to R&D), it has also occurred in the private entrepreneurial sector (i.e., an increasing number of innovative firms or increased funds devoted to innovation).

However, a number of weaknesses still persist dominating the process of innovation in Spain. First, Spain has not yet caught up with the most developed, technologically advanced economies. This general fact is based on a number of disadvantages still dominating the innovation system: the reduced number of innovative firms, the insufficient effort they make in devoting resources to innovation, the reduced collaborative activity they perform, or the low development of risk capital are only some of the most prominent factors (Molero 2012a; Laviña and Molero 2012).

What has happened in the last few years of economic crisis? The most general and worrying aspect has to do with the slump in the positive expectations created after a quarter of a century. The starting point has to be the general position of the Spanish economy regarding innovation effort. To this end, the strongest indicator may be the Innovation Scoreboard developed by the European Commission (*EU Innovation Scoreboard, 2013*. DG Enterprise and Industry), which gathers and standardises 25 indicators belonging to eight dimensions and grouped into three main groups: enablers, firm activity, and outputs.

Figure 14.10 shows the results for 2012 and classifies countries into four groups according to their scores with regard to the composite

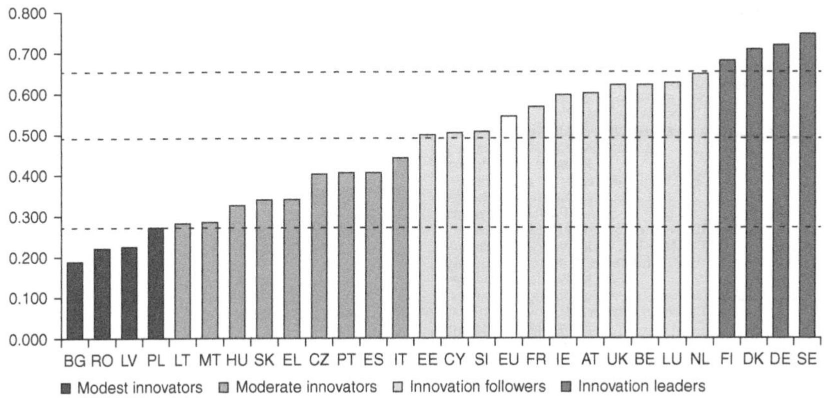

Figure 14.10 EU member states' innovation performance.

Source: Innovation Union Scoreboard 2013 (in http://ec.europa.eu/enterprise/policies/innovation/facts-figures-analysis/innovation-scoreboard/, accessed in November 2013).

Note: Average performance is measured using a composite indicator building on data for 24 indicators going from a lowest possible performance of 0 to a maximum possible performance of 1. Average performance reflects performance in 2010/2011 due to a lag in data availability.

index: Innovation Leaders, Innovation Followers, Moderate Innovators and Modest Innovators. The Spanish position, among Moderate Innovators, clearly shows the distance the Spanish economy has to cover to reach the level of the most dynamic, innovative European countries. Moreover, an in-depth analysis of the dimensions and indicators provided in Figure 14.11 clearly shows the previously expressed indicators, illustrating the imbalance between research and general political indicators, in which Spain performs better, and most firms and economic results related to the indicators, which clearly show a backward situation for Spain. In other words, they relate significantly to the industrial structure we expounded in pervious sections of this chapter.

To a great extent the relative backwardness of the Spanish innovative position is a consequence of its lack of specialisation in H-T sectors, as well as other structural dimensions such as the predominance of micro and small firms, the lack of large companies or the insufficient contribution of MNC subsidiaries to the innovation dynamics of the Spanish economy (Molero and Garcia 2008). From the point of view of the Innovation System, other weaknesses also contribute to an understanding of the general result; among others, we can mention the scarce development of risk capital, the short-term orientation of the bulk of the financial system, the still deficient relations between university, public laboratories and firms or the predominance of minor/adapted innovations among the general innovative activity of firms (Molero 2012b).

In recent years, the crisis has seriously affected the innovation process along two broad lines. First, there have been noticeable cuts in the State budget for R&D&I.

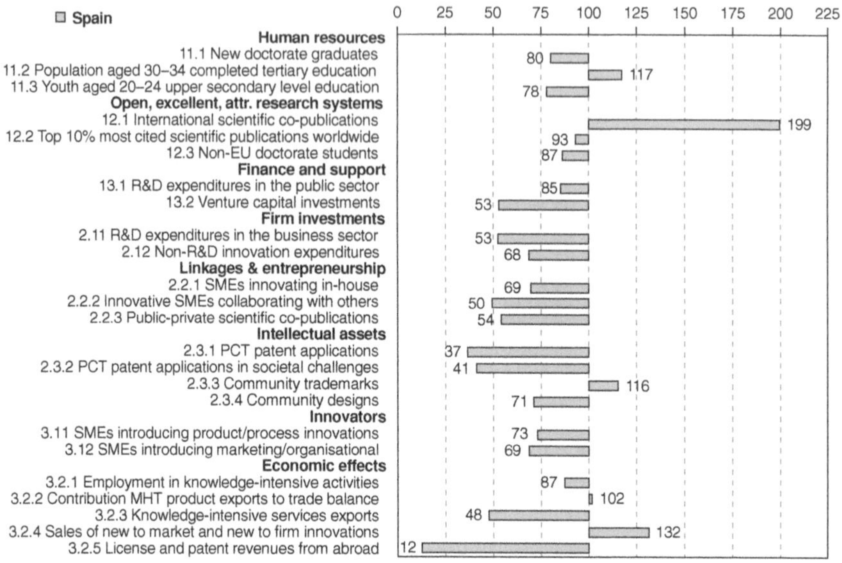

Figure 14.11 Relative indicators values for Spain.

Source: Innovation Union Scoreboard 2013 (in http://ec.europa.eu/enterprise/policies/innovation/facts-figures-analysis/innovation-scoreboard/, accessed in November 2013).

Note: Indicator values relative to the EU27 (EU27=100).

In 2013, this budget is less than 6,000 million euro in current prices, when in 2008 it was more than 9,000. Considering the rate of inflation, we conclude that financial resources in constant euros have dropped to the level of 2004. Moreover, in the same period, there has been an increasing level of non-executed parts of the budget, so the restrictions on the resources placed at the disposal of the innovation system have been dramatic.[2] Second, the latest reports on the innovative activity of enterprises show they also have a reduced volume of R&D and innovation resources (Laviña and Molero 2012). The consequence is that 2011 witnessed the first reduction in the R&D/GDP ratio since statistics have been available in Spain.

6. Policy reactions

The overall balance of the policy measures aimed at overcoming structural deficiencies is a very poor one from the structural point of view. As in many other countries, the economic policy put in place has been a neoclassical, old-fashioned one and can be summarised as follows:

- The bulk of the effort has been concentrated on fiscal adjustment by reducing expenditures, in many cases affecting social policies. Moreover, there has been an increase in important taxes, particularly in value added, which has reinforced the path towards a more intensive decline in economic activity by constraining both private and public consumption.

- When addressing structural adjustments, policy has placed the focus on the labour market. Thus, in the last few years, very significant reforms have been introduced always intended to reduce the cost of firms' adjustment and the elimination of other legal requirements. Until this moment, the effect of these policies has been a dramatic increase in unemployment that, in its turn, has contributed to the fiscal debt, due to the increasing amount of resources devoted to subsidise unemployment.
- A third critical dimension has been the immense effort carried out to save the financial system by giving tens of millions of euros to banks and savings banks. In spite of the positive effect of these measures as far as the financial institution is concerned (today their situation is less severe than two years ago), they caused a critical collateral effect: the severe reduction in credit to firms and households. Therefore, another vicious circle has arisen in the form of more firms foreclosing or reducing their personnel.
- Nevertheless, there has been a notorious absence of other structural policies trying to build the basis of a new economic model, based on innovation and knowledge and to face the significant structural deficiencies shown in this chapter. There have not been industrial measures to change the unfavourable balance of manufacturing sectors; in this regard, confidence in "natural" evolution is the only perspective to deal with this issue.
- Similarly, no other measures has been introduced to address the excessive weight of micro and small firms or to reinforce the international competitiveness of large companies. A clear example of the latter is the absence of incentives to attract foreign R&D investment.
- Two aspects have converged into what we could call a positive industrial policy: energy and innovation. As far as energy is concerned, the positive element was support for renewable energies as a way to reduce a structural dependency on foreign sources and to find a more sustainable model in the future. During the first period, this policy succeeded in changing the balance of different energy sources to the point that renewable ones reached more than 30 percent of the total at the beginning of the 2010s. However, significant public support for new energies was not associated to a positive learning process that allowed the firms involved to continue the international race to technologically lead the sector. Unfortunately, in the last few years, a significant change has taken place, support for these energies has dropped and the sector is currently experiencing a deep crisis.
- In terms of innovation, the already mentioned improvement of the Spanish situation derived to a great extent from constant new measures to foster R&D in the public sector and to encourage private firms to upgrade their situation. Three elements have been crucial in this process. First, the continuous increase in public resources through

the State budget which in 2009 reached around 9,000 million euros.[3] Second, the continuous improvement of policy measures included in the National R&D&I Programme incorporating important policy instruments to stimulate private investment and public-private collaboration; the elaboration of the National Strategy for Innovation in 2011 was the last step in this direction. Third, the constant perspective to obtain greater returns from European programmes.

- The former notwithstanding, in recent years, these policies have mostly stagnated, mainly due to dramatic cuts in public funds, which dropped from 9,000 million in 2009 to around 6,000 million in 2013. Initially, this drop directly affected public institutions such as universities and public research centres, but then it has also affected private companies, insofar as many either depend on public funds or collaborate with public research institutions.

7. Conclusions and policy recommendations

The review we have made of the most significant facts of the recent evolution of Spanish industry leads us to a balance sheet in which it is difficult to separate light and shade. Of course, generally speaking, areas of shade are dominant, because the impact of the crisis is persistent and deep: jobs lost, production declining, stagnation of the domestic market, difficulties to continue previous upward trending paths in technological innovation, and so on. However, there are a few more positive aspects which can help to define some policy actions to improve the situation in the near future.

Our first, most important policy recommendation is clear: a new industrial policy is needed insofar as its absence has led to a dramatic situation with important destruction of production capacity and employment and the lack of prospects for human capital accumulation and technological innovation. This new policy has to fulfil four main criteria (Laviña and Molero 2012):

- First, it must not be focused on direct subsidies and state dirigisme which could reproduce most of the negative consequences many European nations have faced in the last decades; on the contrary, the new policy has to be centred on the creation and diffusion of the competitive factors which today are recognised as the bulk of new development styles, with higher productivity, new products and service creation.
- Second, this policy has to be clear and sustainable over time; we are speaking of medium to long term actions which need time to produce an effect, so sustainability over time is crucial.
- Third, the question of internationalisation, both inward and outward, has to be placed at its very core, because it is the only way to fully take advantage of the fruits of productivity growth.

- Finally, the new policy has to combine elements coming from many different policy areas; if innovation is the core, it also means other policies such as education, labour market, and public sector, have to be guided in the same direction or, as claimed many years ago by Myrdal, new policy has to create a cumulative causation towards a new positive virtuous circle in which all elements interact with similar orientations.

From a more specific point of view, some dimensions of that policy can incorporate the following elements:

- Bolstering the transformation of the sectoral configuration. The so-called "new productive model" has in this point its first element. However, the promotion of more technologically advanced sectors must not be made at the cost of abandoning L-T and ML-T sectors. On the contrary, the same policy has to have another critical dimension in giving strong support to the introduction of new technology in those so-called traditional sectors. While new firms and sectors are created, the bulk of industrial employment is located in these sectors and it is here that we have a clear understanding of markets and requirements. Thus, their upgrading is critical to remove a structural obstacle consisting of a remarkable number of traditionally backward sectors.
- Another structural task consists in increasing the average size of Spanish industry. The absolute dominance of micro and small firms is on many occasions a dead weight to the introduction and diffusion of new technology and organisational methods.
- New industrial policy has to foster a massive incorporation of so-called horizontal technologies such as ICT, biotechnology, or new materials. Their advantage is that they can be applied simultaneously in many different areas and enterprises.
- To improve the profile and level of education and training of most of the entrepreneurs who even today still lack the appropriate level of knowledge to incorporate new technologies and to operate productively in new markets.
- Another critical dimension consists in fostering the internationalisation of the sector. This has to be based on a combination of all levels of internationalisation (trade, investment, and technological collaboration), as well as a mix boosting the capacity to attract more technology intensive investment and to develop domestic capabilities in a broader international scenario.

Last but not least, this new perspective requires a new social contract in which politicians, workers, entrepreneurs and scientists share a new vision of the future of international competitiveness and social welfare.

Notes

1 For the next data we have used the official Spanish statistic DATAINVEX of the Ministry of Economy and Competitiveness: http://datainvex.comercio.es.

2 See: J. Molero and J. De NO: *Informe sobre los Presupuestos Generales del Estado, 2013*. COSCE, 2012.

3 Referring only to the central government budget, so funds from regional governments and from European programmes are not considered.

15 Conclusion

Ricardo Paes Mamede

During the first years of the 2010s, the economies of the Eurozone periphery have experienced great strains. In the aftermath of the international financial crisis of 2008–2009, the interest rates on those countries' sovereign bonds increased substantially, detaching from the rates on German bonds and from the levels that prevailed before the crisis. Ultimately, as the financing costs became unsustainable, the governments of Greece, Ireland, Portugal, Spain and Cyprus had to resort to international financial assistance,[1] while a similar denouement was only avoided in Italy due to decisive action by the ECB. The countries under financial assistance programmes agreed to adopt harsh debt-reducing fiscal measures, which led to a historically protracted period of negative economic growth and rising unemployment, also fuelled by the synchronization of restrictive fiscal policies in the Eurozone and by the financial deleveraging of the private sector in each economy.

The growing reluctance of international investors in buying sovereign debt from the countries in the Eurozone periphery was triggered by the high and/or rapidly increasing public debts since 2008, together with the uncertainty regarding the action to be taken by EU institutions in order to deal with the sovereign debt crisis which started in early 2010. By the end of 2013, the conventional and unconventional measures adopted by the ECB have succeeded in reducing the financial instability in the Eurozone. However, the interest rates on the crisis countries' government bonds have remained significantly higher than on the German ones, reflecting the prevailing doubts among international investors regarding the sustainability of public finances in those countries.

While such doubts partly result from the high levels of public debt in the southern Eurozone countries, they were no less determined by the prevailing perspectives on these countries' future growth. As several chapters of this book have shown, the lack of competitiveness of the economies in the southern periphery of the Eurozone was already apparent before the advent of the 2008–2009 international crisis. In spite of differences in economic performance—e.g., between 2000 and 2008, dismal GDP growth in Italy and Portugal (1% per year, on average) contrasted with economic dynamism in Spain and Greece (where GDP grew at 3.1% and 3.6%, respectively)—all these countries have witnessed a rapid deterioration of their external indebtedness in the decade that preceded the international crisis.

The chapters in Parts I and II of this book suggest that two types of self-reinforcing mechanisms may have been at work in recent decades, fostering such external imbalances.

First, at the Eurozone level, the substantial drop in real interest rates during the 1990s, in anticipation of the European Monetary Union, led to a boost in economic activity, which translated into a significant appreciation of the real exchange rates (especially in those countries where real interest rates were traditionally higher). Being strongly reliant on low value-added industries (and, in many cases, on the lower value-added segments of each industry), and facing growing competition at the global level, the industrial sector of the Eurozone's southern periphery was more affected by the real exchange rate developments, leading to a sharp drop in the weight of tradable sectors in these economies. In contrast, construction, real estate, and other activities that are less exposed to international competition, benefited from the drop in interest rates, the unrestricted availability of finance accruing from the liberalisation of capital flows within the EU, and the resulting growth in domestic markets. The concomitant growth of domestic markets and deterioration of external competitiveness translated into growing current account external deficits in the southern periphery of the EMU. The latter were mirrored by growing external surpluses in other EU countries (such as Germany and the Netherlands), which benefited from the overall growth of the EU market and an industry structure more adapted to global competition. Had the southern countries of the Eurozone held their own currencies, such imbalances would soon have led to an exchange rate depreciation, which would not only help to improve external competitiveness, but also increase the costs of external finance, preventing the continuous growth of public and private indebtedness. On the contrary, entering the EMU has prevented currency devaluation and has virtually abolished the exchange rate premium within the Eurozone, thereby fostering the continuing flow of liquidity from surplus to deficit countries. Thus, until the 2008–2009 international crisis, the external surpluses of some Eurozone countries were being used to finance the deficits of the other member states, reinforcing the imbalances that were accumulating since the 1990s. Adding to such a self-reinforcing mechanism, the further liberalisation of world trade, the EU's Eastern Enlargement, and the appreciation of the euro against the US dollar, which produced asymmetric impacts across the Eurozone—mainly due to differences in industry structures—heightened the competitiveness hurdles of the southern Eurozone economies, prior to 2008.

A second self-reinforcing mechanism, in this case operating at the national level, seemed to have been present in the southern periphery of the Eurozone. All of these countries have been historically characterised by low educational levels, when compared with other advanced economies. Enrolment in education and training has been hampered by an industry structure which is biased towards low-skilled activities—in virtually all industries, regardless of their knowledge intensity, both in manufacturing and in services—and therefore has been able to create plenty of job opportunities for low-skilled workers until recently. Together with the dismal initial levels of enrolment and the prevailing inefficiencies in educational and training systems, the high demand for low-skilled workers helps to explain why educational attainment remained at relatively low levels, in spite of the growing allocation of public funds targeting human capital investment. In turn, the lack of skilled workers has contributed to delay the upgrading of the productive structure, being thus at the root of the aforementioned competitiveness problems of these countries.

As the chapters in this book discuss in great detail, policy action at both the European and the national levels has been insufficient to counteract such self-reinforcing mechanisms.

At the EU level, policy priorities and solutions seem to have neglected the deep structural differences across member countries and their macroeconomic consequences for the EU as a whole. As we have seen above, the EMU's architecture has actually favoured an adverse structural change towards non-tradable industries in the southern economies, thereby reinforcing the external imbalances within the Eurozone. The need to correct those structural differences through the development of tradable, higher value-added industries in the southern periphery, has been largely overlooked. The adjustment programmes that have been put in place in the context of the financial bailouts of Greece, Portugal and Spain (among other countries) have largely overlooked the upgrading of the specialisation profile of the crisis countries. In fact, the excessive focus on fiscal consolidation and internal devaluation may not only have deepened the short-term economic and social hurdles in these countries, but may also have enduring negative effects on growth, through the depreciation of human and physical capital. There are worrying signs that the path of cumulative strengthening of the knowledge base which, albeit modest, had been present in these countries before 2008 has been partly reverted in the context of the crisis.

At the national level, policy action has hardly exhausted the opportunities for promoting structural change in the desirable direction. True, the room for manoeuver of national governments in promoting structural change has been substantially reduced in recent decades, especially in the Eurozone, where control over monetary, exchange rate, and international trade policy instruments has been transferred to the EU level, while EU competition and fiscal rules have strongly restricted the discretionary policy action of member states. Notwithstanding, as the chapters in Part III show, governments in the Eurozone periphery did not always take full advantage of the remaining opportunities to foster the upgrading of their economies' specialisation profile. Although the assessment differs among countries, with some good practices deserving due reference, policies targeting knowledge creation and learning may have been given insufficient attention for too long.

At the present juncture, the deep structural differences across member states that were at the roots of the Eurozone crisis remain a central policy challenge for the EU as whole, and especially for the economies in its southern periphery. Macroeconomic governance at the EU level should be able to complement the present emphasis on fiscal sustainability with policy actions that prevent both the accumulation of external imbalances in the future and the current depreciation of human and physical capital in crisis countries. In the same vein, the dominant focus on internal devaluation must not overlook the risks of trying to promote long-term competitiveness exclusively on the basis of lower costs. In sum, there is a need to improve governance of the EMU and the European common market, taking in greater account the need to promote investments in innovation and learning, as well as the fast upgrading of the industrial specialisation of the Eurozone's southern economies.

National governments at the periphery of the Eurozone, on the other hand, must seize the opportunities to promote the upgrading of their economies on the basis of the already accumulated capabilities. Fostering learning, R&D and innovation, in connection with the export orientation of domestic firms and the attraction of high value-added FDI, should be among the highest priorities for policy makers. The deployment of such polices must be accompanied by improvements in governance and institutional capacity in order to assure the efficacy and legitimacy of State intervention.

The Eurozone and, especially, its southern periphery, have painfully learned the costs of overlooking the challenges posed by structural differences among the economies participating in the EMU. Hopefully, the chapters in this book will contribute to improving policy solutions, both at the EU and the national levels, in order to find a sustainable way out of the crisis.

Notes

1 In the case of Spain, financial support was specifically directed to the banking sector.

References

Abramovitz, M. (1979) 'Rapid growth potential and its realisation: the experience of capitalist economics in the post-war period,' in Malinvaud, E. (ed.), *Economic Growth and Resources: The Major Issues*, London: Macmillan, pp. 1–30.

Abramovitz, M. (1986) 'Catching-up, forging ahead and falling behind,' *Journal of Economic History*, 46(2): 386–406.

Abramovitz, M. and David, P.A. (2001) 'Two centuries of American macroeconomic growth from exploitation of resource abundance to knowledge-driven development,' SIEPR Discussion Paper No. 01–05, Stanford Institute for Economic Policy Research, California.

Abreu, A., Mendes, H., Rodrigues, J., Gusmão, J.G., Serra, N., Teles, N., Alves, P. and, Mamede, R. (2013) *A Crise, a Troika e as Alternativas Urgentes*. Lisbon: Tinta da China.

Acemoglu, D. and Guerrieri, V. (2008) 'Capital deepening and nonbalanced economic growth,' *Journal of Political Economy*, 116(3): 467–498.

Aghion, P., Cohen, E. and Pisani-Ferry, J. (2006) '*Politique économique et croissance en Europe*,' Rapport du Conseil d'Analyse Economique, No 59, Paris: La Documentation Française

Aiginger, K. (2010) 'Post crisis policy: some reflections of a Keynesian economist,' WIFO, WP 371. Vienna, Austria.

Aiginger, K. (2011) 'Why growth performance differed across countries in the recent crisis: the impact of pre-crisis conditions,' *Review of Economics and Finance* 4: 35–52.

Aiginger, K. (2012) 'Reconciling the short and the long run: governance reforms to solve, the crisis and beyond,' E.C., Brussels, European Policy Brief (1). Vienna: Austrian Institute of Economic Research (WIFO).

Amable, B. (2003) *The Diversity of Capitalism*. Oxford: Oxford University Press.

Amable, B., Barre R. and Boyer R. (1997) *Les systèmes d'innovation à l'ère de la globalisation*. Paris: Economica.

Amador, J. and Opromolla, L. (2009). '*Textiles and clothing exporting sectors in Portugal – recent trends*,' Economic Bulletin and Financial Stability Report Articles. Banco de Portugal, Economics and Research Department.

AMECO Database (2013), in http://ec.europa.eu/economy_finance/ameco/user/serie/SelectSerie.cfm (accessed in September 2013).

Ansari, M.L. (1992) 'Growth effects of recent structural changes in the Canadian economy: some empirical evidence,' *Applied Economics*, 24: 1233–1240.

Antzoulatos, A.A. (2011) 'Greece in 2010: a tragedy without catharsis,' *International Advances in Economic Research*, 17: 241–257.

Archibugi, D. and Lundvall, B.–Å. (eds.). (2001) *Europe in the Globalising Learning Economy*. Oxford: Oxford University Press.

Arellano, M. and Bond, S. (1991) 'Some tests of specification for panel data: Monte Carlo evidence and an application to employment equations,' *Review of Economic Studies*, 58: 277–297.

Arghyrou, M. G. and Kontonikas, A. (2011). *The EMU sovereign-debt crisis: fundamentals, expectations and contagion* (No. 436). Directorate General Economic and Monetary Affairs (DG ECFIN), European Commission.

Armstrong, K.A., Begg, I. and Zeitlin, J. (2008) 'JCMS symposium: EU governance after Lisbon,' *Journal of Common Market Studies*, 46: 413–450.

Arrow, K. (1962) 'The economic implications of learning–by–doing,' *Review of Economic Studies*, 29(3): 155–173.

Artus, P. (2011) 'L'ajustement demandé aux pays périphériques de la zone euro est–il réalisable? Une comparaison avec l'ajustement réalisé en Allemagne,' *Flash Economie*, no 268, 11 avril.

Artus, P. (2012a) 'En situation de sous–utilisation des capacités, les entreprises concentrent leurs productions dans les pays où elles sont les plus profitables, d'où l'accélération des pertes d'emplois dans les pays où la profitabilité est faible,' *Flash Economie*, no 515, 25 juillet.

Artus, P. (2012b) 'Liquidité mondiale, taille des flux de capitaux, taille des fluctuations des taux de change: pas d'amélioration en vue,' *Flash Marchés*, no 535, 9 août.

Arundel, A., Lorenz, E, Lundvall, B.–Å. and Valeyre, A. (2007) 'How Europe's economies learn: a comparison of work organization and innovation mode for the EU–15,' *Industrial and Corporate Change*, 16(6): 680–693.

Athreye S. and Cantwell, J. (2007) 'Creating competition? Globalisation and the emergence of new technology producers,' *Research Policy* 36: 209–226.

Augier, P., Cadot, O. and Dovis, M. (2013) 'Imports and TFP at the firm level: the role of absorptive capacity,' *Canadian Journal of Economics/Revue Canadienne d'Économique*, 46(3): 956–981.

Augusto Mateus & Associados, CISEP and PriceWaterhouseCoopers (2005). *Actualização da Avaliação Intercalar do Programa de Incentivos à Modernização da Economia*. Lisboa.

Augusto Mateus e Associados (2013). *Avaliação Intercalar do Programa Operacional Factores de Competitividade – Relatório Final*. Lisboa.

Balassa, B. (1965) 'Trade liberalization and 'revealed' comparative advantage'. *The Manchester School of Economic and Social Studies* 33(2): 99–123.

Baldassarri, M. (1993) 'Introduction,' in Baldassarri, M. (ed.), *Industrial Policy in Italy, 1945–1990*. New York, St. Martin's Press.

Baldwin, J.R. and Gu, W. (2003) 'Export–market participation and productivity performance in Canadian manufacturing' *Canadian Journal of Economics/Revue Canadienne d'Économique*, 36(3): 634–657.

Baldwin, J.R. and Gu, W. (2006) 'Plant turnover and productivity growth in Canadian manufacturing,' *Industrial and Corporate Change*, 15(3): 417–465.

Banco de Portugal (2012) *Boletim Estatístico*, Maio 2012, Banco de Portugal, Lisboa.

Barro, R.J. and Lee, J.W. (2013) 'A new data set of educational attainment in the world, 1950–2010,' *Journal of Development Economics*, 104, September 2013: 184–198.
Barro, R. and Sala–i–Martin, X. (1992) 'Convergence,' *Journal of Political Economy*, 100: 223–251.
Baumol, W.J. (1967) 'Macroeconomics of unbalanced growth: the anatomy of urban crisis,' *American Economic Review*, LVII(3): 415–426.
Begg, I. (2001) 'EMU and employment,' Working Paper, South Bank University, London.
Begg, I. (2003) 'Complementing EMU: rethinking cohesion policy,' *Oxford Review of Economic Policy*, 19(1): 161–179.
Belloc, M. and Di Maio, M. (2012) 'Survey of the literature on successful strategies and practices for export promotion by developing countries,' in Johnson, O.E.G. (ed.), *Economic Challenges and Policy Issues in Early Twenty–First–Century Sierra Leone*, Chapter 7, London: International Growth Center, pp. 226–277.
Bender, G. (2006) 'Peculiarities and relevance of non–research–intensive industries in the knowledge–based economy,' Final report of the PILOT project, Brussels: European Commission, www.pilot-project.org/publications/finalreport.pdf.
Bernard, A.B. and Jensen, J.B. (1995) 'Exporters, jobs, and wages in U.S. manufacturing: 1976–1987,' *Brookings Papers on Economic Activity: Microeconomics* 1995, 67–119.
Bernard, A.B. and Jensen, J.B. (2004) 'Exporting and productivity in the USA,' *Oxford Review of Economic Policy*, 20(3): 343–357.
Bernard, A.B., Eaton, J., Jensen, J.B. and Kortum, S. (2003) 'Plants and productivity in international trade,' *American Economic Review*, 93(4): 1268–1290.
Bernstein, J.I. and Nadiri, M.I. (1991) 'Product demand, cost of production, spillovers, and the social rate of return to R&D,' Working Paper No. 3625 National Bureau of Economic Research. Cambridge, MA.
Bianchi, P. and Labory, S. (2011). and Labory, S. (2011) *Industrial Policy after the Crisis*. UK, USA: Edward Elgar.
Bianchi, P. (1993) 'Industrial policies for small and medium firms and the new direction of European Community policies,' in Baldassarri, M. (ed.), *Industrial Policy in Italy, 1945–1990*, New York, St. Martin's Press.
Bigsten, A., Collier, P., Dercon, S., Fafchamps, M., Gauthier, B., Gunning, J.W., Oduro, A., Oostendorp, R., Pattillo, C., Soderbom, M., Teal, F. and Albert, Z. (2004) 'Do African manufacturing firms learn from exporting?,' *Journal of Development Studies*, 40 (3): 115–141.
Bilbao–Osorio, B. and Rodríguez-Pose, A. (2004) 'From R&D to innovation and economic growth in the EU,' *Growth and Change*, 35(4): 434–455.
Blanchard, O. and Leigh, D. (2013) 'Growth forecast errors and fiscal multipliers,' IMF Working Paper, January 2013. Washington, D.C.
Bonatti, L. and Felice, G. (2008) 'Endogenous growth and changing sectoral composition in advanced economies,' *Structural Change and Economic Dynamics*, 19: 109–131.
Bordo, M.D. and Haubrich, J.G. (2012) 'Deep recessions, fast recoveries, and financial crisis: evidence from the American record,' NBER Working Paper 18194, June 2012. Cambridge, MA.
Bottazzi, G., Secchi, A. and Tamagni, F. (2008) 'Productivity, profitability and financial performance'. *Industrial and Corporate Change*, 147(4): 711–751.

Bouvet, F. (2010) 'EMU and the dynamics of regional per capita income inequality,' Working Paper, Department of Economics, Sonoma State University, CA.
Boyer, R. (2000) 'The unanticipated fallout of European Monetary Union: the political and institutional deficits of the Euro,' in Crouch, C. (ed.), *After the Euro: Shaping Institutions for Governance in the Wake of European Monetary Union*, Oxford: Oxford University Press, pp. 24–88.
Boyer, R. (2006) 'The institutional and policy weakness of the European Union: the evolution of the policy mix,' in Coriat, B., Petit, P., Schméder, G. (eds.), *The Hardship of Nations*, Cheltenham: Edward Elgar, pp. 161–187.
Boyer, R. (2009) 'The Lisbon Strategy: merits, difficulties and possible reforms,' in Rodrigues, M.J. (ed.), *Europe, Globalization and Lisbon Agenda*, Cheltenham UK, Northampton (MA): Edward Elgar, pp. 149–187.
Boyer, R. (2010) 'From the Lisbon agenda to the Lisbon treaty: national research system in the context of European integration and globalization,' in Delanghe, H., Muldur, U. and Soete, L. (eds.), *European Science and Technology Policy*, Cheltenham, UK: Edward Elgar Publishing Limited.
Boyer, R. (2010) 'Integracion productiva y financiera en la Union Europea. De la sinergia al conflicto,' *Puente@Europa, Dinamicas productivas de la integración: comercio, moneda, trabajo e industria*, 8(1): 31–47.
Boyer, R. (2011) *Les financiers détruiront–ils le capitalisme?* Paris: Economica.
Boyer, R. (2012) 'The four fallacies of contemporary austerity policies: the lost Keynesian legacy,' *Cambridge Journal of Economics*, 36: 283–312.
Boyer, R. (sous la présidence) (1999) *Le gouvernement économique de la zone euro*. Paris: La documentation française.
Boyer, R. and Dehove, M. (2001) 'Du «gouvernement économique» au gouvernement tout court. Vers un fédéralisme à l'européenne,' *Critique Internationale*, 11: 179–195.
Boyer, R. and Dehove, M. (2006) 'Political goals, legal norms and public goods: the building blocks of Europe,' *Prismes*, no 8 Center Cournot for Economic Studies, Paris.
Boyer, R., Dehove, M. and Plihon, D. (2004) 'Les crises financières,' Rapport du Conseil d'Analyse Economique, no 50, La Documentation française, Paris.
Boyer, R. and Saillard, Y. (eds.). (1995) *Théorie de la Régulation. L'Etat des Savoirs*. Paris: La Découverte.
BP Stats (2013), Statistics online, in http://www.bportugal.pt/pt–PT/Estatisticas/Paginas/default.aspx (accessed in September 2013).
Brancati, R. and Maresca, A. (2013) Le politiche per le imprese in Italia: flussi e obiettivi. Online. Available HTTP: http://www.industrialpolicy.net/materiali/ (accessed November 2013).
Bruno, B. (1992) *Régimes économiques de l'ordre politique. Esquisse d'une Théorie régulationniste des limites de l'état. Économie en liberté*. Paris: Puf.
Buesa, M. and Molero, J. (1996) *Economía Industrial de España*. Madrid: Civitas.
Buiter, W.H. and Rahbari, E. (2010) 'Greece and the fiscal crisis in the EMU,' Citigroup, September 9, 2010.
Buiter, W.H. and Rahbari, E. (2011) 'The future of the euro area: fiscal union, break–up or blundering towards a 'you break it you own it Europe',' Citigroup Global Markets, Global Economics View, September 9, 2011.
Buiter, W.H. and Rahbari, E. (2012) 'The ECB as Lender of Last Resort for Sovereigns in the Euro Area,' *Journal of Common Market Studies*, Special Issue: The JCMS Annual Review of the European Union in 2011, 50 (2): 6–35.

Chalmers, D. and Lodge, M. (2003) The open method of Co-ordination and the European welfare state, ESRC Working Paper, No. 11, London School of Economics, London, June 2003.

Caraça, J. (1999) 'A prática de políticas de ciência e tecnologia em Portugal,' in Godinho, M.M. and Caraça, J. (eds.), *O Futuro Tecnológico: Perspectivas para a Inovação em Portugal.* Oeiras: Celta.

Caraça, J., Lundvall, B.-Å., and Mendonça, S. (2009) 'The changing role of science in the innovation process: from Queen to Cinderella?,' *Technological Forecasting & Social Change*, 76: 861–867.

Carree, M.A., Verheul, I. and Santarelli, E. (2011) 'Sectoral patterns of firm exit in Italian provinces,' *Journal of Evolutionary Economics*, 21 (3): 499–517.

Carreira, C. and Teixeira, P. (2008) 'Internal and external restructuring over the cycle: a firm-based analysis of gross flows and productivity growth in Portugal,' *Journal of Productivity Analysis*, 29(3): 211–220.

Carreira, C. and Teixeira, P. (2011) 'Entry and exit as a source of aggregate productivity growth in two alternative technological regimes,' *Structural Change and Economic Dynamics*, 22: 135–150.

Cassiman, B., Golovko, E. and Martínez-Ros, E. (2010) 'Innovation, exports and productivity,' *International Journal of Industrial Organization*, 28: 372–376.

Castellani, D. (2002) 'Export behavior and productivity growth: evidence from Italian manufacturing firms,' *Weltwirtschaftliches Archiv/Review of World Economics*, 138(4): 605–628.

Castellani, D. and Zanfei, A. (2007) 'Internationalisation, innovation and productivity: how do firms differ in Italy?,' *World Economy* 30(1): 156–176.

Castells, M. (2000) *The Rise of the Network Society, The Information Age: Economy, Society and Culture I.* Cambridge, MA: Blackwell.

Castells, M. (2002) 'The Construction of European Identity,' in Rodrigues, M.J. (ed.), *The Knowledge Economy in Europe*, Cheltenham: Edward Elgar.

Castro, G., Félix, R.M., Júlio, P. and Maria, J. R. (2013) 'Fiscal multipliers in a small euro area economy: How big can they get in crisis times?,' Working Papers w201311, Lisbon: Banco de Portugal, Economics and Research Department.

Chang, H.J. (2006) *Bad Samaritans: Rich Nations, Poor Policies and the Threat to the Developing World.* London: Random House.

Chesbrough, H. (2003) *Open Innovation: The new imperative for creating and profiting from technology.* Boston, MA: Harvard Business School Publishing.

Ciccone, A. and Papaioannou, E. (2009) 'Human Capital, the Structure of Production, and Growth,' *Review of Economics and Statistics*, 91(1): 66–82.

Claessens, S., Mody, A. and Vallée, S. (2012) 'Paths to Eurobonds,' IMF Working Paper WP/12/172, Research Department, July 2012, Washington, D.C.

Clark, B.H. (2000) 'Managerial perceptions of marketing performance: efficiency, adaptability, effectiveness and satisfaction,' *Journal of Strategic Marketing*, 8: 3–25.

Clark, C. (1940) *The Conditions of Economic Progress.* London: Macmillan and Co., Limited.

Coccia, M. (2005) 'Technometrics: origins, historical evolution and new directions,' *Technological Forecasting and Social Change*, 72(8): 944–979.

Coenen, G., Straub, R. and Trabandt, M. (2012) 'Fiscal policy and the great recession in the Euro Area,' *American Economic Review*, 102(3): 71–76.

Cohen, W.M. and Levinthal, D.A. (1990) 'Absorptive capacity: a new perspective on learning and innovation,' *Administrative Science Quarterly*, 35(1): 128–152.

Cohen, W.M. and Levinthal, D.A. (1989) 'Innovation and learning: the two faces of R&D,' *Economic Journal*, 99(397): 569–596.
Commission Staff Working Document, Lisbon Strategy evaluation document, Brussels 2.2.2010 SEC (2010) 114 final. (http://ec.europa.eu/europe2020/pdf/lisbon_strategy_evaluation_en.pdf) (Evaluation 2010)
Communication from the Commission (2010), 'EUROPE 2020 A strategy for smart, sustainable and inclusive growth' Brussels, 3.3.2010 COM (2010) 2020 (EU2020).
Contorti, F. (1993) 'Phases of Italian industrial development and the relationship between the public and private sectors,' in Baldassarri, M. (ed.), *Industrial Policy in Italy, 1945–1990*, New York, St. Martin's Press.
Colin Crouch, C. (ed.) (2000) *After the Euro: Shaping Institutions for Governance in the Wake of European Monetary Union.* Oxford: Oxford University Press.
CTC/QREN (2012). Relatório Anual do QREN, 2011. Lisbon: Comissão Técnica de Coordenação do QREN 2007–2013.
D'Antonio, M. (1993) 'The tortuous road of industry through the mezzogiorno,' in Baldassarri, M. (ed.), *Industrial Policy in Italy, 1945–1990*, New York, St. Martin's Press.
De Benedictis, L. (2005) 'Three decades of Italian comparative advantages,' *The World Economy*, 28: 1679–1709.
De Grauwe, P. (2011) 'The governance of a fragile Eurozone'. Economic Policy, CEPS Working Documents.
De Grauwe, P. and Ji, Y. (2013a) 'Self–fulfilling crises in the Eurozone: an empirical test'. *Journal of International Money and Finance*, 34: 15–36.
De Grauwe, P. (2012) 'The Eurozone's design failures: can they be corrected?,' LSE European Institute inaugural lecture, November 2012.
De Grauwe, P. and Ji, Y. (2013b) 'Panic–driven austerity in the Eurozone and its implications,' VoxEU.org, February 21, 2013.
De Nardi, S. and Traù, F. (2005) Il modello che non c'era. L'Italia e la divisione internazionale del lavoro industriale, Rubbettino, 2005.
Dehove, M. (1997) 'L'Union Européenne inaugure–t–elle un nouveau grand régime d'organisation des pouvoirs publics et de la société internationale?,' *l'Année de la Régulation*, 1: 11–83.
Delgado, M.A., Farinas, J. C. and Ruano, S. (2002) 'Firm productivity and export markets: a non–parametric approach,' *Journal of International Economics*, 57(2): 397–422.
DeLong, J.B. and Summers, L.H. (1991) 'Equipment investment and economic growth,' *Quarterly Journal of Economics*, 106(2): 445–502.
DeLong, J.B. and Summers, L.H. (1993) 'How strongly do developing economies benefit from equipment investment?,' *Journal of Monetary Economics*, 32: 395–415.
Denison, E.F. (1962) *The Sources of Economic Growth in the United States and the Alternatives Before Us*. New York: Committee for Economic Development.
Desmarchelier, B., Djellal, F., and Gallouj, F. (2013) 'Knowledge intensive business services and long term growth,' *Structural Change and Economic Dynamics*, 25(C): 188–205.
Di Maio, M. (2013) 'Industrial policy,' in Currie-Alder, B., Kanbur, R., Malone D. and Medhora, R. (eds.), *International Development: Ideas, Experience, and Prospects*, Chapter 32. Oxford: Oxford University Press.

Di Maio, M. and Tamagni, F., (2008) 'The evolution of world export sophistication and the Italian trade anomaly,' *Review of Economy Policy*, 98(1): 135–174.

Dietrich, A. (2012) 'Does growth cause structural change, or is it the other way around? A dynamic panel data analysis for seven OECD countries,' *Empirical Economics*, 43(3): 915–944.

Disney, R., Haskel, J. and Heden, Y. (2003) 'Restructuring and productivity growth in UK manufacturing,' *Economic Journal*, 113(489): 666–694.

Doornik, J. A. (1996) 'Testing vector error autocorrelation and heteroscedasticity" Unpublished paper, Nuffield College, Oxford, U.K.

Dosi G., Fagiolo, G. and Roventini, A. (2010) 'Schumpeter meeting Keynes: a policy-friendly model of endogenous growth and business cycles,' *Journal of Economic Dynamics and Control*, 34(9): 1748–1767.

Dosi, G., Gambardella, A., Grazzi, M. and Orsenigo, L. (2013) 'Technological revolutions and the evolution of industrial structures: assessing the impact of new technologies on the size, pattern of growth, and boundaries of firms,' in Dosi, G. and Galambos, L. (eds.), *The Third Industrial Revolution in Global Business*, Cambridge: Cambridge University Press.

Dosi, G., Pavitt, K. and Soete, L. (1990) *The Economics of Technical Change and International Trade*. New York: Harvester Wheatsheaf.

Draghi, M. (2012) 'Introductory statement to the press conference,' 2 August. http://www.ecb.int/press/pressconf/2012/html/is120802.en.html

Drucker, P. (1993) *Post–capitalist society*. New York: Harper Collins.

Dutt, A. K. and Lee, K.Y. (1993) 'The service sector and economic growth: some cross–section evidence,' *International Review of Applied Economics*, 7(3): 311–329.

EC (2011) *The Economic Adjustment Program for Portugal*. Brussels: The European Commission.

EC (2012). Member States Competitiveness Performance and Policies 2011: Reinforcing Competitiveness ECB Statistics, in http://www.ecb.int/stats/html/index.en.html (accessed in September 2013).

Echevarria, C. (1997) 'Changes in sectoral composition associated with economic growth,' *International Economic Review*, 38: 431–452.

Eichengreen, B. (2009) 'The Crisis and the Euro,' Real Instituto Elcano, Working Paper 23/2009, May 14, 2009, Madrid.

Eichengreen, B. and O'Rourke, K. (2012) 'A tale of two depressions,' 6 March 2012, www.voxeu.org.

EIS (2009) European Innovation Scoreboard 2008: Comparative Analysis of Innovation Performance. Directorate–General for Enterprise and Industry of the European Commission (available at http://www.proinno–europe.eu/metrics).

EU (2012) Delivering for Consumers: EU Competition Policy. European Union, Luxemburg.

European Commission (1990). Industrial Policy in an open and competitive environment: Guidelines for a Community approach. COM (90)556.

European Commission (2006) 'Policy and Innovation in Low-Tech. Knowledge Formation, Employment and Growth Contributions of the 'Old Economy' Industries in Europe', Pilot final report, DG Research, Brussels.

European Commission (2011) 'Public finances in EMU–2011,' *European Economy*, 1–212.

European Commission (2012a) 'Reaping the benefits of globalization,' European Competitiveness Report. Luxembourg: Publications Office of the European Union.

European Commission (2012b) 'The Economic Adjustment Programme for Portugal, Sixth Review,' European Economy, Occasional Paper 124, December 2012. Brussels: The European Commission.

Eurostat (2013) High–technology and medium–high technology industries, main drivers of EU–27's industrial growth. Statistics in focus 1/2013. Luxemburg: Eurostat.

Eurostat Database (2013), in http://epp.eurostat.ec.europa.eu/portal/page/portal/statistics/search_database (accessed in September 2013).

Evangelista, R. (2007). 'Rilevanza e impatto delle politiche dell'innovazione in Italia. I risultati delle indagini CIS,' *Economia e politica industriale*, 1: 103–124

Fagan, G. and Gaspar, V. (2008) 'Macroeconomic adjustment to monetary union,' Working Paper Series 0946, European Central Bank, Frankfurt am Main.

Fagerberg, J. (1988) 'International competitiveness,' *Economic Journal*, 98: 355–374.

Fagerberg, J. and Srholec, M. (2008) 'National innovation systems, capabilities and economic development,' *Research Policy* 37: 1417–1435.

Fagerberg, J. and Shrolec, M. (2007) 'The competiveness of nations. Why some countries proper and others fall behind,' *World Development*, 35(10): 1595–1620.

Fagerberg, J. (1987) 'A Technology gap approach to why growth rates differ,' *Research Policy*, 16(2–4): 87–99.

Fagiolo, G. and Luzzi, A. (2006) 'Do liquidity constraints matter in explaining firm size and growth? Some evidence from the Italian manufacturing industry,' *Industrial and Corporate Change*, 15(1): 173–202.

Farinas, J.C. and Martin–Marcos, A. (2007) 'Exporting and economic performance: firm–level evidence for Spanish manufacturing,' *World Economy*, 30(4): 618–646.

FCT (2013) *Diagnóstico do Sistema de Investigação e Inovação – Desafios, Forças e Fraquezas rumo a 2020*. Lisboa: Fundação para a Ciência e Tecnologia.

Feenstra, R.C., Inklaar, R. and Timmer, M.P. (2013) 'The Next Generation of the Penn World Table' available for download at www.ggdc.net/pwt.

Féria, L.P. (1999) A história do sector automóvel em Portugal (1895–1995) GEPE Min. Economia, Lisboa, WP DT 19–99.

Fisher, A. (1939) 'Production: primary, secondary and tertiary,' *Economic Record*, 15(1): 24–38.

Fitoussi, J.–P. and Laurent, E. (2009) 'Europe in 2040: Three scenarios,' OFCE/ANR Working Paper No. 10, Sciences Po, Paris.

Fitoussi, J.–P. and Saraceno, F. (2010) 'Inequality and macroeconomic performance,' OFCE/ANR Working Paper No. 13, Sciences Po, Paris.

Foellmi, R. and Zweimüller, J. (2008) 'Structural change, Engel's consumption cycles and Kaldor's facts of economic growth,' *Journal of Monetary Economics*, 55(7): 1317–1328.

Fontana, R. and Mendonça, S. (2013) 'Telecoms through the lens of trademarks: What can we learn about innovation and competitiveness in dynamic markets?,' mimeo.

Forni, L., Gerali, A. and Pisani, M. (2010) 'The macroeconomics of fiscal consolidations in a monetary union: the case of Italy,' Temi di Discussione, Banca d'Italia, nr. 747.

Fosfuri, A. and Giarratana, M.S. (2009) 'Masters of war: Rivals' product innovation and new advertising in mature product markets,' *Management Science*, 55(2): 181–91.

Foster, L., Haltiwanger, J. and Krizan, C.J. (2001) 'Aggregate productivity growth: lessons from microeconomic evidence,' in Hulten, C.R., Dean, E.D. and Harper,

M.J. (eds.), *New developments in productivity analysis*, Chicago: University of Chicago Press, pp. 303–363.

Freedman, C., Kumhof, M., Laxton, D. and Lee, J. (2009) 'The Case for Global Fiscal Stimulus,' IMF, Research Department, March 6, 2009.

Gaspar, V. and St. Aubyn, M. (2009). 'Política orçamental, ajustamento ao euro e crescimento em Portugal e Espanha,' in Lains, P. (ed.), *Sem Fronteiras – os novos horizontes da economia portuguesa*. Lisboa: Instituto de Ciências Sociais, pp. 67–94.

Gault, F. (ed.) (2003) *Understanding Innovation in Canadian Industry*. Montreal and Kingston: McGill-Queens University Press.

Gerschenkron, A. (1962) *Economic Backwardness in Historical Perspective*, Cambridge, MA: Harvard University Press.

Ghani, E. (ed.) (2010) *The Service Revolution in South Asia*. Oxford: Oxford University Press.

Giannitsis, T. (1988) 'The accession into the E.C. and its impact on Industry and Foreign Trade,' Foundation for Mediterranean Countries, Athens, in Greek language.

Giannitsis, T. (2013) 'Greece in the crisis,' Polis, Athens, in Greek language.

Giannitsis, T. and Kager, M. (2009) 'Technology and specialization: dilemmas, options and risks,' Expert group 'Knowledge for Growth' European Commission, Brussels.

Giannitsis, T., Zografakis, St., Kastelli, I. and Mavri, D. (2009) 'Competitiveness and Technology in Greece,' Papazissis, Athens, in Greek language.

Gleeson, A.M. and Ruane, F. (2009) 'How important is exporting and ownership to productivity growth? Micro Evidence from a Small Open Economy,' *Applied Economics Quarterly*, 55(3): 197–218.

Godin, B. (2004) 'The obsession for competitiveness and its impact on statistics: the construction of high-technology indicators,' *Research Policy*, 33(8): 1217–1229.

Godin, B. (2005) Measurement and Statistics on Science and Technology: 1920 to the Present. London: Routledge.

Godinho, M.M. (2013) *Inovação em Portugal*. Lisboa: Fundação Francisco Manuel dos Santos.

Godinho, M.M. and Simões, V.C. (2005) 'R&D, innovation and entrepreneurship 2007–2013,' Report for the QCA/CSF Observatory, Lisboa: ISEG.

Godinho, M.M. and Simões, V.C. (2011) ERAWATCH Country Report Portugal 2010, JRC/IPTS, Luxemburg: European Commission.

Goedhuys M., Janz, N. and Mohnen, P. (2013) 'Knowledge-based productivity in 'low-tech' industries: evidence from firms in developing countries,' *Industrial and Corporate Change*, first published online February 14, 2013 doi:10.1093/icc/dtt006.

Gotsch, M. and Hipp, C. (2012) 'Measurement of innovation activities in the knowledge-intensive services industry: a trademark approach,' *Service Industries Journal*, 32(13): 2167–2184.

Greenaway D. and Kneller, R. (2007) 'Firm heterogeneity, exporting and foreign direct investment,' *Economic Journal*, 117: 134–161.

Greenhalgh, C. and Rogers, M.B. (2012) 'Trade marks and performance in services and manufacturing firms: evidence of Schumpeterian competition through innovation,' *Australian Economic Review*, 45(1): 50–76.

Griliches, Z. and Regev, H. (1995) 'Firm productivity in Israeli industry: 1979–1988,' *Journal of Econometrics*, 65(1): 175–203.

Griliches, Z. (1987) 'R&D and productivity: measurement issues and econometric results,' *Science*, 237: 31–35.

Griliches, Z. and Mairesse, J. (1998) 'Production functions: the search for identification,' in Strøm, S. (ed.), *Econometrics and economic theory in the 20th century: The Ragnar Frisch centennial symposium*, Cambridge: Cambridge University Press, pp. 169–203.

Griliches, Z. (1990) 'Patent statistics as economic indicators: a survey,' *Journal of Economic Literature*, 28(4): 1661–1707.

Griliches, Z. (1992) 'The search for R&D spillovers,' *Scandinavian Journal of Economics*, 94: 29–47.

Gros–Pietro, G.M. (1993) 'The restructuring of large-sized industrial groups,' in Baldassarri, M. (ed.), *Industrial Policy in Italy, 1945–1990*, New York, St. Martin's Press.

Guellec, D. and van Pottelsberghe de la Potterie, B. (2001) 'R&D and productivity growth: panel data analysis of 16 OECD countries,' *OECD Economic Studies*, 33(3): 103–126.

Guellec, D. and van Pottelsberghe de la Potterie, B. (2003) 'The impact of public R&D expenditure on business R&D,' *Economics of Innovation and New Technology*, 13(3): 225–243

Guerra, A.C. (1990) Formas e determinantes do envolvimento externo das empresas: Internacionalização da indústria automóvel e integração da indústria portuguesa na indústria automóvel mundial. Doctoral dissertation, ISEG, Lisboa.

Halpern, L. and Muraközy, B. (2010) 'Innovation, productivity and exports: the case of Hungary,' *Economics, Innovation and New Technology*, 21(2): 151–173.

Hansson, P. and Lundin, N. (2004) 'Exports as indicator on or a promoter of successful Swedish manufacturing firms in the 1990s,' *Weltwirtschaftliches Archiv/Review of World Economics*, 140: 415–445.

Harris, R. and Li, Q.C. (2008) 'Evaluating the contribution of exporting to UK productivity growth: some microeconomic evidence,' *World Economy*, 31(2): 212–235.

Hartwig, J. (2012) 'Testing the growth effects of structural change,' *Structural Change and Economic Dynamics*, 23(1): 11–24.

Hausmann, R. and Klinger, B. (2007) 'The structure of the product space and the evolution of comparative advantage,' CID Working Paper No. 146, April 2007, Harvard University, Cambridge, MA.

Hausmann, R., Hwang, J. and Rodrik, D. (2007) 'What you export matters,' *Journal of Economic Growth*, 12: 1–25.

Hausmann, R. and Klinger, B. (2006) 'Structural transformation and patterns of comparative advantage in the product space,' CID Working Paper No. 128, August 2006, Harvard University, Cambridge, MA.

Henriques, L. (2006) The dynamics of the national system of innovation and the role of the non-profit space: Portugal as a Research Laboratory, PhD Dissertation, Centre nacionale de Sociologie de l'Innovation, ENSMParis, ISEG Lisboa.

Heston, A., Summers, R. and Aten, B. (2012) Penn World Table Version 7.1, Center for International Comparisons of Production, Income and Prices at the University of Pennsylvania, July 2012.

Hidalgo, C., Klinger, B., Barabasi, A. and Hausmann, R. (2007) 'The Product Space Conditions the Development of Nations,' *Science Magazine*, 317: 482–487.

Hipp, C. and Grupp, H. (2005) 'Innovation in the service sector: the demand for service-specific innovation measurement concepts and typologies,' *Research Policy*, 34: 517–535.

Hirsch, C. and Sulis, G. (2009) 'Schooling, Production Structure and Growth: an Empirical Analysis on Italian Regions,' Working Paper IAREG, WP5/18, Brussels: The European Commission.

Hirsch-Kreinsen, H. and Schwintze, I. (2011) 'Knowledge-intensive entrepreneurship and innovativeness in traditional industries: conceptual framework and empirical findings,' AEGIS project deliverable 1.3.1.

Holinski, N., Kool, C. and Muysken, J. (2012) 'Persistent macroeconomic imbalances in the euro area: causes and consequences,' Federal Reserve Bank of St. Louis Review, January/February 2012.

Holm, J., Lorenz, E., Lundvall, B.-Å. and Valeyre, A. (2010) 'Organisational learning and systems of labour market regulationin Europe,' *Industrial and Corporate Change*, 19(4): 1141–1173.

Höpner, M. and Schäfer, A. (2012) 'Integration among unequals. How the heterogeneity of European varieties of capitalism shape the social and democratic potential of the EU,' Discussion Paper 12/5, Max Planck Institute for the Study of Societies, Kohln.

Hummen, W. (1977) 'Greece and the European Community. Problems and Prospects of the Greek Small and Medium Industry. Results of an Empirical Survey,' Berlin, German Development Institute.

IESE & Quaternaire Portugal (2013) *Avaliação Estratégia do QREN – Lote 3: o contributo do QREN para a inovação e internacionalização das empresas.* Lisboa: Observatório do QREN.

IMF (2012) 'Portugal: Third Review under the Extended Arrangement,' April 2012.

IMF (2013c) 'Portugal: Seventh Review under the Extended Arrangement,' June 2013.

IMF (2013a) 'IMF Country Report No. 13/156, Greece: Ex Post Evaluation of Exceptional Access under the 2010 Stand-By Arrangement,' June.

IMF (2013b) 'Country Report No. 13/160. Portugal: Seventh Review Under the Extended Arrangement and Request for Modification of End-June Performance Criteria—Staff Report,' Press Release on the Executive Board Discussion, and Statement by the Executive Director for Portugal. June.

Inklaar, R., Timmer, M.P. and van Ark, B. (2008) 'Market services productivity across Europe and the US,' *Economic Policy*, 23: 139–194.

ISGEP (2008) 'Understanding cross-country differences in exporter premia: comparable evidence for 14 countries,' *Weltwirtschaftliches Archiv/Review of World Economics*, 144(4): 596–635.

IUS (2012) 'Innovation Union Scoreboard 2011: the Innovation Union's performance scoreboard for Research and Innovation,' in *http://ec.europa.eu/enterprise/policies/innovation/files/ius-2011_en.pdf*. Accessed November 2012.

Jensen, M.B., Johnson, B., Lorenz, E. and Lundvall, B.-A. (2007) 'Forms of knowledge and modes of innovation,' *Research Policy*, 36(5): 680–693.

Jones, C.I. (1995) 'R&D based models of economic growth,' *Journal of Political Economy*, 103(4): 759–784.

Jorgenson, D. and Timmer, M. (2011) 'Structural change in advanced nations: a new set of stylised facts' *Scandinavian Journal of Economics*, 113(1): 1–29.

Kaldor, N. (1966) *Causes of the Slow Rate of Growth in UK*. Cambridge: Cambridge UP.

Kapur, B.K. (2012) 'Progressive services, asymptotically stagnant services, and manufacturing: Growth and structural change,' *Journal of Economic Dynamics & Control*, 36: 1322–1339.

Kastelli, I. and Caloghirou, Y. (2014) 'The impact of knowledge-intensive entrepreneurship on the growth and competitiveness of European traditional sectors,' in Hirsch-Kreinsen, H. and Schwinge, I. (eds.), *Knowledge–Intensive Entrepreneurship in Low–Tech Sectors: The Prospects of Traditional Economic Industries*, Cheltenham, UK: Edward Elgar.

Kok, W. and alii (2004) 'Facing the challenge. The Lisbon strategy for growth and employment,' Report from the High Level Group, Luxemburg, November. Luxembourg: Publications of the European Communities.

Krugman, P. (1991) 'Increasing returns and economic geography,' *The Journal of Political Economy*, 99(3): 483–499

Krugman, P. (1993) *Geography and Trade*. Leuven: Leuven University Press, Cambridge: The MIT Press.

Kuznets, S. (1959) 'On comparative study of economic structure and growth of nations,' in National Bureau of Economic Research, *The Comparative Study of Economic Growth and Structure*, New York: NBER.

Labory, S. (2006). La politica industriale in un'economia aperta e basata sulla conoscenza. L'industria, n.s., a. XXVII, n. 2, aprile-giugno

Lall, S. (2004) 'Reinventing industrial strategy,' UNCTAD G–24, Discussion Paper Series No. 122. United Nations, New York and Geneva, April 2004.

Lambrianidis, L. (2011) 'Investing in going abroad: the outflow of scientists from Greece in the globalisation era,' Kritiki, Athens, in Greek language.

Larsson, A. (1998) 'The European Employment Strategy and the EMU: you must invest to be able to save.' The 1998 Meidner Lecture presented at Swedish IRRA Association and the Working Life Institute, 18 March 1998.

Laviña, J. and Molero, J. (2012) *Innovación. Productividad y competitividad para una nueva economía*. Foro de Empresas Innovadoras, Madrid.

Lebre de Freitas, M. and Mamede, R. (2011) 'Structural transformation of Portuguese exports and the role of foreign-owned firms: a descriptive analysis for the period 1995–2005,' *Notas Económicas*, 33: 20–43.

Lebre de Freitas, M., Salvado, S., Nunes, L.C. and Neves, R.C. (2013) 'Productive experience and specialization opportunities for Portugal: an empirical assessment,' GEE Papers No. 10, Gabinete de Estratégia e Estudos, Lisbon: Ministério da Economia.

Leon, P. (1967) *Structural Change and Growth in Capitalism*. Baltimore: Johns Hopkins.

Levinsohn, J. and Petrin, A. (2003) 'Estimating production functions using inputs to control for unobservables,' *Review of Economic Studies*, 70: 317–42.

Linden, M., and Mahmood, T. (2007) 'Long run relationships between sector shares and economic growth – A panel data analysis of the Schengen region,' Keskustelualoitteita No. 50.

Lorenz, E. and Lundvall, B.-Å. (eds.) (2006) *How Europe's Economies Learn: Coordinating Competing Models*. Oxford: Oxford University Press.

Lorenz, E. and Valeyre, A. (2005) 'Organisational innovation, HRM and labour market structure: a comparison of the EU–15,' *Journal of Industrial Relations*, 47(4): 424–442.

Lucas, R.E. (1983) *Studies in Business Cycle Theory*. Cambridge MA, USA: The MIT Press.

Lundvall, B.-Å. and Tomlinson, M (2002) 'International benchmarking as a policy learning tool,' in Rodrigues, M.J. (ed.), *The New Knowledge Economy in Europe: A Strategy for International Competitiveness and Social Cohesion*. Cheltenham: Edward Elgar.

Lundvall, B.-Å. and Lorenz, E. (2011) 'From the Lisbon Strategy to Europe 2020,' in Morel, N., Palier, B. and Palme, J. (eds.), Towards A Social Investment Welfare State?: Ideas, Policies and Challenges, Policy Press, Bristol. Scholarship Online.

Lundvall, B.-Å, Rasmussen, P. and Lorenz, E. (2008) 'Education in the Learning Economy: a European perspective,' *Policy Futures in Education*, 6(2): 681–700.

Lundvall, B.-Å. (1985) *Product Innovation and User–Producer Interaction*. Aalborg: Aalborg University Press.

Lundvall, B.-Å. (2002) Innovation, growth and social cohesion, the Danish model, London: Edward Elgar.

Lundvall, B.-Å. and Johnson, B. (1994) 'The learning economy,' *Journal of Industry Studies*, 1(2): 23–42.

Lütkepohl, H. (2004) 'Vector Autoregressive and Vector Error Correction Models,' in Lütkepohl, H. and Krätzig, M. (eds.), *Applied Time Series Econometrics*, Cambridge: Cambridge University Press, pp. 86–158.

Maddison, A. (1987) 'Growth and slowdown in advanced capitalist economies: techniques of quantitative assessment,' *Journal of Economic Literature*, 25(2): 649–698.

Makkonen, T. and van der Have, R.P. (2013) 'Benchmarking regional innovative performance: composite measures and direct innovation counts,' *Scientometrics*, 94(1): 247–262.

Mamede, R. (2012) 'Causes, consequences, and ways out of the crisis: a perspective from EU's periphery,' *Green European Journal*, 1: 30–46.

Mamede, R. and Fernandes, T. (2013) 'Análise contrafactual dos impactos dos incentivos do POE/PRIME na sobrevivência e no crescimento das empresas,' e-cadernos 5/2013, Observatório do QREN.

Mamede, R. and Feio, P.A. (2012) 'Institutional conditions for effective and legitimate industrial policies: the case of Portugal,' Dinâmia Working Papers 2012/13. ISCTE-IUL, Lisbon.

Maroto-Sánchez, A. and Cuadrado-Roura, J. (2009) 'Is growth of services an obstacle to productivity growth? A comparative analysis,' *Structural Change and Economic Dynamics*, 20: 254–265.

Martins, P.S. and Yang, Y. (2009) 'The impact of exporting on firm productivity: a meta-analysis of the learning-by-exporting hypothesis,' *Weltwirtschaftliches Archiv/Review of World Economics*, 145: 431–445.

Mas, M., Milana, C. and Serrano, L. (2008) 'Spain and Italy: catching up and falling behind. Two different tales of productivity slowdown,' EU KLEMS Working Paper, 37. http://www.euklems.net/pub/no37(online).pdf.

Mateus, A.M. (2006) 'Portugal's convergence process: lessons for accession countries,' in Balcerowicz, L. and Fischer, S. (eds.), *Living Standards and the Wealth of Nations: Successes and Failures in Real Convergence*, Cambridge, MA: MIT Press, pp. 231–250.

Mazzucato, M. (2013) *The Entrepreneurial State*. London: Anthem Press.

Mazzucato, M. (2013) 'Financing innovation: creative destruction vs. destructive creation,' *Industrial and Corporate Change*, 22(4): 851–867.

McKinsey & Company. (2012) Greece 10 years ahead: defining Greece's new growth model and strategy. Athens: McKinsey & Company.

Melitz, M.J. (2003) 'The impact of trade on intra-industry reallocations and aggregate industry productivity,' *Econometrica*, 71(6): 1695–725.

Mendonça, S., Pereira, T.S. and Godinho, M.M. (2004) 'Trademarks as an indicator of innovation and industrial change,' *Research Policy*, 33: 1385–1404.

Mendonça. S. (2012) 'Trademarks as a telecommunications indicator for industrial analysis and policy,' in Hadjiantonis, A.M. and Stiller, B. (eds.), *Telecommunication Economics – Selected Results of the COST Action ISO605 Econ@Tel, Lecture Notes in Computer Science* 7216: 33–41.

Merito, M., Giannangeli, S. and Bonaccorsi, A. (2010) 'Do incentives to industrial R&D enhance research productivity and firm growth? Evidence from the Italian case,' *International Journal of Technology Management*, 49(1/2/3): 25–48.

Merler, S. and Pisani-Ferry, J. (2012) 'Sudden stops in the Euro Area,' Bruegel Policy Contribution, March 2012.

Millot, V. (2009) 'Trademarks as an indicator of product and marketing innovations,' OECD Science, Technology and Industry Working Papers, 2009/6, Paris: OECD publishing.

Minsky, H. (1986) *Stabilizing an Unstable Economy*. New York: McGraw-Hill.

Mishkin, F. and Erbertsson, T. (2006) *Financial Stability in Iceland*. Reykjavick Iceland: Chamber of Commerce.

Molero, J. (2001) *Innovación y Competitividad en Europa*. Madrid: Síntesis.

Molero, J. (2012a) 'Innovación tecnológica y competitividad en tiempos de crisis en Europa,' in *El impacto de la crisis en el área de seguridad y defensa*, Madrid: CESEDEN, Ministry of Defense.

Molero, J. (2012b) 'La industria en espera de una nueva política,' *Economistas*, 135.

Molero, J. and De No, J. (2012) *Informe sobre los Presupuestos Generales del Estado*. Online. Available HTTP: http://www.cosce.org/informes.htm.madrid.

Molero, J. and Garcia, A. (2008) 'The innovative activity of foreign subsidiaries in the Spanish Innovation System: an evaluation of their impact from a sectoral taxonomy approach,' *Technovation*, 28(11): 739–757.

Morrison, A., Pietrobelli, C. and Rabellotti R. (2008) 'Global value chains and technological capabilities: a framework to study learning and innovation in developing countries,' *Oxford Development Studies*, 36(1): 39–58.

MSTI, Main Science and Technology Indicators, OECD, online database, in *http://www.oecd.org/sti/msti.htm*. Accessed date: July 2013.

Mundell, R.A. (1961) 'A Theory of Optimum Currency Areas,' *American Economic Review*, 51(4): 657–665.

Muûls, M. and Pisu, M. (2009) 'Imports and exports at the level of the firm: evidence from Belgium,' *World Economy*, 32(5): 692–734.

Nadiri, M.J. (1993) 'Innovations and technological spillovers,' Working Paper No. 4423, NBER, Cambridge, MA, USA.

National Science Foundation (2012) *Science and Engineering Indicators 2012*. Arlington, Virginia: National Science Foundation.

Nelson, R. and Phelps, E. (1969) 'Investment in Humans, Technological Diffusion, and Economic Growth,' *American Economic Review*, 61: 69–75.

Nesta, L. and Patel, P. (2004) 'National patterns of technology accumulation: use of patent statistics,' in Moed, H., Glänzel W. and Schmoch, U. (eds.), *Handbook of Quantitative Science and Technology Research: The Use of Publication and Patent Statistics in Studies of S&T Systems*, Berlin: Springer Verlag, pp. 531–551.

Ngai, L.R. and Pissarides, C.A. (2007) 'Structural change in a multisector model of growth,' *American Economic Review*, 97(1): 429–443.

Nunes, L.C., Lebre de Freitas, M., Coelho, A.F. (2014) 'Structural transformation and indexes of product relatedness: Which one better fits the data,' Manuscript, Nova School of Business and Economics.

Nunes, L.C., Neves, R.C. and Lebre de Freitas, M. (2013) 'Specialization patterns and structural transformation: the cases of China and India,' Manuscript. A preliminary version is available in the proceedings of the 9th Iberian International business conference, NIPE Universidade do Minho.

O'Mahony, M. (2013) 'Growth and Productivity in EU Services Sectors,' SERVICEGAP Discussion Paper No. 45. SERVICEGAP project, European Commission, Brussels.

O'Mahony, M. and Timmer, M.P. (2009) 'Output, input and productivity measures at the industry level: the EU KLEMS Database,' *Economic Journal*, 119(538): F374–F403.

Obinger, H., Leibfried, S., Castles, F. (2005) 'Bypasses to a social Europe? Lessons from federal experience,' *Journal of European Public Policy*, 12(3): 545–571.

OECD (1994) The OECD Jobs Study: Facts, Analysis, Strategies, Paris: OECD.

OECD (1997) Révision des classifications des secteurs et des produits de haute technologie. Paris

OECD (2004) *Employment Outlook*. Paris: OECD

OECD (2005) Enhancing the performance of the services sector. Paris: OECD.

OECD (2007) Moving Up the Value Chain: Staying Competitive in the Global Economy, Paris: OECD.

OECD (2009) *OECD Strategic Response to the Financial and Economic Crisis: Contributions to the Global Effort*. OECD: Paris.

OECD (2009) Policy Responses to the Economic Crisis: Investing in Innovation for Long-Term Growth June 2009.

OECD (2009a) *Science, Technology and Industry Scoreboard*. Paris: OECD.

OECD (2009b) *Main Science and Technology Indicators 2009*. Paris: OECD.

OECD (2010) *Measuring Innovation: A New Perspective*. Paris: OECD.

OECD (2012) *Main Science and Technology Indicators*, Volume 2011/2, January 2012. OECD. Paris.

OECD (2012) Science, technology and industry Scoreboard, 2011. Paris: OECD.

Olley, G.S. and Pakes, A. (1996) 'The dynamics of productivity in the telecommunications equipment industry,' *Econometrica*, 64(6): 1263–1297.

Onida, F. (1999) 'Quali prospettive per il modello di specializzazione internazionale dell'Italia?,' *Economia Italiana*, 3: 573–626.

Orlean, A. (2004) 'Efficience, finance comportementale et convention : une synthèse théorique,' in Boyer, R., Dehove, M. and Plihon, D. (dir) *Les crises financières*, rapport du Conseil d'Analyse Economique, no 50, octobre, La Documentation Française, Paris, p. 241–279.

Orlean, A. (2009) *De l'euphorie à la panique: penser la crise financière*. Paris: Editions de la rue d'Ulm.

Orlean, A. (2011) *L'empire de la valeur*. Seuil: Paris.

Owen. G. (2012) 'Industrial policy in Europe since the Second Worlds War: What Has Been Learnt?,' ECIPE Occasional Paper No. 1/2012, Brussels.

Pack, H. (1993) 'Technology gaps between industrial and developing countries: are there dividends for latecomers?, *Proceedings of World Bank Annual Conference on Development Economics 1992*, Washington, DC: World Bank.

Pasinetti, L. (1981) *Structural Change and Economic Growth: a Theoretical essay on the dynamics of the wealth of nations*. Cambridge University Press, Cambridge, UK.

Patel, P. and Pavitt, K. (1995) 'Patterns of technological activity: their measurement and interpretation,' in Stoneman (ed.), *Handbook of the Economics of Innovation and Technical Change*, London: Blackwell, pp. 15–51.

Pavitt, K. (1984) 'Sectoral patterns of technical change: towards a taxonomy and a theory,' *Research Policy*, 13: 343–373.

Peneder, M. (2003) 'Industrial structure and aggregate growth,' *Structural Change and Economic Dynamics*, 14(4): 427–448.

Peneder, M. (2007) 'A sectoral taxonomy of educational intensity,' *Empirica*, 34: 189–212.

Pessoa, A. (1998) 'Catch-up' tecnológico, investimento e convergência real: um exercício de contabilidade do crescimento aplicado à economia Portuguesa,' Investigação / Trabalhos em curso, Faculdade de Economia, Universidade do Porto.

Pessoa, A. (2011) 'The Euro Area sovereign debt crisis: Some implications of its systemic dimension,' MPRA Paper 35328, University Library of Munich, Germany.

Pessoa, A. (2012) 'The Euro Area sovereign debt crisis: is fiscal consolidation compatible with economic growth?,' Paper presented at the *Second NIFIP Conference: the present economic and sovereign debt crisis: evaluation and the way-out*, hold at the School of Economics and Management of the University of Porto, at 6 and 7 December 2012. Porto, Portugal.

Pisani-Ferry, J. and Sapir, A. (2006) 'Last exit to Lisbon,' Bruegel Policy Brief, March.

Portes, R. and Baldursson, F. (2007) *The Internationalisation of Iceland's financial sector*. Reykjavick Iceland: Chamber of Commerce.

Portes, J. and Holland, D. (October 2012) 'Self-defeating austerity?,' *National Institute Economic Review*, 222(1): F4–F10.

Prodi, R. and De Giovanni, D. (1993) 'Forty-five years of industrial policy in Italy: protagonists, objectives, and instruments,' in Baldassarri, M. (ed.), *Industrial Policy in Italy, 1945–1990*, New York, St. Martin's Press.

Pugno, M. (2006) 'The service paradox and endogenous economic growth,' *Structural Change and Economic Dynamics*, 17: 99–115.

Purcell, M. (2002) 'The state, regulation, and global restructuring: reasserting the political in political economy,' *Review of International Political Economy* 9(2): 298–332.

Ramos, M. and Simões, M.C.N. (2011) 'Growth and the services sector: the Portuguese Case,' In Šalej, Š.B., Erić, D., Redžepagić, S. and Stošić, I. (Eds.) *Contemporary Issues in the Integration Processes of Western Balkan Countries in the European Union*, Ljubljana, Slovenia: International Center for Promotion of Enterprises, pp. 271–287.

Raveaud, G. (2007) 'The European employment strategy: towards more and better jobs?,' *JCMS: Journal of Common Market Studies* 45(2): 411–434.

Reinhart, C.M. and Rogoff, K. (2009). *This Time Is Different: Eight Centuries of Financial Folly*. Princeton: Princeton University Press.

Reinhart, C.M. and Rogoff, K. (2010). 'Growth in a time of debt,' *American Economic Review: Papers & Proceedings* 100: 573–578.

Reinstaller, A., Hölzl, W., Kutsam, J. and Schmid, C. (2012) The development of productive structures of EU Member States and their international competitiveness. (Vol. Final Report). Vienna: European Commission, DG Enterprise and Industry.

Rodrigues, M.J. (2004) *European policies for a knowledge economy*. Cheltenham: Edward Elgar Publishing.

Rodrigues, M.J. (ed.) (2002) The new Knowledge Economy in Europe. A strategy for international competitiveness with social cohesion, Adelshot: Edward Elgar.

Rodrik, D. 2004 'Industrial Policy for the Twenty-First Century,' Working Paper Series rwp04–047, Harvard University, John F. Kennedy School of Government.

Rodrik, D. (2007) One Economics, Many Recipes: Globalization, Institutions, and Economic Growth. Princeton: Princeton University Press.

Rodrik, D. (2008) 'Normalizing Industrial Policy,' Commission on Growth and Development Working Paper No.3. The World Bank, Washington.

Rodrik, D. (2011) *The Globalization Paradox: Democracy and the Future of the World Economy*. New York: Norton & Company.

Roodman, D. (2009) 'How to do xtabond2: an introduction to difference and system GMM in Stata,' *Stata Journal*, 9(1): 86–136.

Rota, M. (2013) 'Credit and growth: reconsidering Italian industrial policy during the Golden Age,' *European Review of Economic History* 17(4): 431–451 first published online June 19, 2013 doi:10.1093/ereh/het012.

Saltari, E. and Travaglini, G. (2006) Le radici del declino economico. Occupazione e produttività in Italia nell'ultimo decennio, Torino: UTET.

Santos, R.G. (1996) Os efeitos na economia portuguesa do investimento directo no sector automóvel, Master's dissertation, Lisboa: ISEG.

Sapir, A. (2004) *An agenda for a growing Europe*. Oxford: Oxford University Press.

Schautschick, P. and Greenhalgh, C. (2013) 'Empirical studies of trademarks – the existing economic literature,' University of Oxford, Department of Economics Discussion Paper Series (Ref: 659). Oxford, UK.

Schmidt, A. and Almeida, J.C. (1987) *Fabricação automóvel e produção de componentes*. Lisboa: Banco de Fomento Nacional.

Schmoch, U. (2003) 'Service marks as novel innovation indicator,' *Research Evaluation* 12: 149–56.

Schmoch, U. and Gauch, S. (2009) 'Service marks as indicators for innovation in knowledge–based services,' *Research Evaluation* 18(4): 323–35.

Scott, A. (2006) 'The changing global geography of low-technology. labor-intensive industry: clothing, footwear and furniture,' *World Development* 34(9): 1517–1536.

Shambaugh, J.C. (2012) 'The Euro's Three Crises', *Brookings Papers on Economic Activity*, 44, issue 1 (Spring): 157–231.

Shiller, R.J. (1999, 2006) *Irrational Exuberance*. Princeton: Princeton University Press.

Silva Lopes, T. and Casson, M. (2012) 'Brand protection and the globalization of British business,' *Business History Review*, 86(2): 287–310.

Silva, A., Afonso, O. and Africano, A.P. (2012) 'Which manufacturing firms learn by exporting?' *Journal of International Trade & Economic Development: An International and Comparative Review*, 21(6): 773–805

Silva, A., Afonso, O. and Africano, A.P. (2013) 'Do the most productive firms become exporters? Application of a test for the case of Portugal,' *Investigación Económica*, 72(283): 135–161.

Silva, E.G. (2011) 'Portugal and Spain: catching up and falling behind. A comparative analysis of productivity trends and their causes, 1980–2007,' FEP Working Papers No., 459. Porto: Faculdade de Economia do Porto.

Silva, E.G. and Teixeira, A.A.C. (2011) 'Does structure influence growth? A panel data econometric assessment of 'relatively less developed' countries, 1979–2003,' *Industrial and Corporate Change*, 20(2): 433–455.
Silva, E.G. and Teixeira, A.A.C. (2012) 'In the shadow of the financial crisis: dismal structural change and productivity trends in south-western Europe over the last four decades,' WWWforEurope: Workshop on European Governance and the Problems of Peripheral Countries, July 12th and 13th, 2012. Vienna, Austria.
Silva, F. (2008) 'Economics, Politics and Industrial Policy: the Case of Italy,' Mimeo, Università di Milano-Bicocca
Simões, M. (2009) Levels of Education, Technology and Growth: the OECD evidence from a country and industry–level perspective. Coimbra: Imprensa da Universidade de Coimbra.
Simões, M.C.N. and Duarte, A. (2013) 'Human capital and growth in a services economy: the case of Portugal,' Faculty of Economics, University of Coimbra, Estudos do GEMF No., 21.
Simões, V.C. (2000) *Efeitos do investimento estrangeiro sobre a modernização do tecido produtivo nacional: O caso da indústria automóvel.* Lisboa: Associação Industrial Portuguesa.
Simões, V.C. (2002) Report on Innovation Policy in Portugal. TrendChart on Innovation, Brussels.
Simões, V.C. (2003) 'Networks and learning processes: a case study on the automotive industry in Portugal,' in Cantwell, J. and Molero, J. (eds.), *Multinational Enterprises, Innovative strategies and Systems of Innovation*, Cheltenham: Edward Elgar, pp. 206–233.
Simões, V.C. (2008a) 'Assessment of the NITEC programme,' Paper contributed to the OECD Report on SMEs, Entrepreneurship and Innovation. Paris, France.
Simões, V.C. (2008b) 'Improving innovation scorecards: finding a way forward,' Paper delivered at COTEC Europa meeting, Naples, June.
Smets, F. and Wouters, R. (2002) 'An estimated Stochastic Dynamic General Equilibrium Model of the Euro Area,' Working Paper Series, No. 171, European Central Bank (International Seminar on Macroeconomics) August 2002. Frankfurt.
Smith, K. (2002) 'What is the 'Knowledge Economy'? Knowledge Intensity and Distributed Knowledge Bases,' UNU/INTECH Discussion Paper 2002–06, United Nations Tokyo, Japan. Maastricht, The Netherlands.
Smith, K. (2004) 'Measuring innovation,' in Fagerberg, J., Mowery, D.C. and Nelson, R.R. (eds.), *The Oxford Handbook of Innovation*, Oxford University Press, pp. 148–177, Oxford.
Soete, L. (2002) 'The Challenges and the Potential of the Knowledge–Based Economy in a Globalized World,' in Rodrigues, M.J. (ed.), *The new Knowledge Economy in Europe. A strategy for international competitiveness with social cohesion*, Adelshot: Edward Elgar.
Solow, R. (1957) 'Technical change and the aggregate production function,' *Review of Economics and Statistics*, 39(3): 312–320.
Spadavecchia, A. (2007) 'Regional and national industrial policies in Italy, 1950s–1993. Where did the subsidies flow?,' Henley Business School Discussion Papers 048. University of Reading, U.K.
Spilimbergo, A., Symansky, S., Blanchard, O. and Cottarelli, C. (2008) 'Fiscal Policy for the Crisis,' IMF Staff Position Note(SPN/08/01) December 29, 2008.

Stoneman, P. (2009) 'Soft Innovation: towards a more complete picture of Innovative Change,' London, NESTA Research Report, http://bit.ly/Rxs5K4

Stoneman, P. (2010) Soft Innovation: Economics, Product Aesthetics, and the Creative Industries. Oxford: Oxford University Press.

Teixeira, A.A.C. (2005) 'Measuring Aggregate Human capital in Portugal: 1960–2001,' *Portuguese Journal of Social Science*, 4(2): 101–120.

Tinbergen, J. (1952) *On the Theory of Economic Policy*. Amsterdam: North Holland publishing.

Tsekouras, K.D. and Skuras. D. (2005) 'Productive efficiency and exports: an examination of alternative hypotheses for the Greek cement industry,' *Applied Economics*, 37(3): 279–291.

UNCTAD (2013). World Investment Report, 2012. http://unctad.org.

Vale, M. (1999) Geografia da indústria automóvel num contexto de globalização – Imbricação espacial do sistema AutoEuropa, Doctoral thesis. Lisboa: Universidade de Lisboa

van Biesebroeck, J. (2005) 'Exporting raises productivity in Sub-Saharan African manufacturing plants,' *Journal of International Economics*, 67: 373–91.

van Pottelsberghe B. (2008) 'Europe's R&D: missing the wrong targets?,' Bruegel Policy Brief, 2008/03.

van Zon, A. and Muysken, J. (2005) 'Health as a principal determinant of economic growth,' in López-Casanovas, G., Rivera, B., Currais, L. (ed.), *Health and Economic Growth: Findings and Policy Implications*, Cambridge, Mass: MIT Press, pp. 40–65.

Veloso, F., Henry, C., Roth, R. and Clark, J.P. (2000) Global strategies for the development of the Portuguese auto parts industry. Lisboa: IAPMEI.

Veugelers R. and Mrak M. (2009) 'Catching-up member states and the knowledge economy of the European Union,' Knowledge Economists Policy Brief No 5.

Veugelers, R. (2008) 'Towards a Multipolar Science World,' Working Paper for EC–BEPA, Leuven: University of Leuven.

von Graevenitz, G. (2013) 'Trade mark cluttering–evidence from EU enlargement,' *Oxford Economic Papers* 65(3): 721–745.

Wade, R. (2003) *Governing the Market: Economic Theory and the Role of Government in East Asian Industrialization*. Princeton: Princeton University Press.

Wagner, J. (2007) 'Exports and productivity: a Survey of evidence from firm-level data,' *World Economy*, 30: 60–82.

Wanniski, J. (1978) *The Way the World Works: how Economies Fail—and Succeed*. New York: Basic Books.

WDI, *World Development Indicators*, Electronic database, World Bank. (http://databank.worldbank.org/data/views/variableSelection/selectvariables.aspx?source=world-development-indicators).

Woolcock, M. (1998) 'Social capital and economic development: toward a theoretical synthesis and policy framework,' *Theory and Society*, 27(2): 151–207.

Wooldrige, J.M. (2002) Econometric Analysis of Cross Section and Panel Data, Cambridge, MA: MIT Press.

World Bank (1994) *Adjustment in Africa: Reforms, Results, and the Road Ahead*. Washington, DC: The International Bank for Reconstruction and Development/The World Bank.

Wyplosz, C. (1997) 'EMU: Why and how it might happen,' *Journal of Economic Perspective*, 11(4): 3–21.

Yeaple, S.R. (2005) 'A simple model of firm heterogeneity, international trade, and wages,' *Journal of International Economics*, 65: 1–20.

Zambarloukou, S. (2007) 'Is there a South European pattern of post–industrial employment?,' *South European Society and Politics*, 12(4): 425–442.

Zeitlin, J. (2005) 'Social Europe and experimentalist governance: Towards a new constitutional compromise,' European Governance Paper C05–04.

Zeitlin, J. and Pochet, P. (eds.) (2005) The Open Method of Coordination in Action. The European Employment and Social Inclusion Strategies. Brussels: Peter Lang Publishing Group.

Index